The Reign Of Mary Tudor

by

James Anthony Froude

THE REIGN OF MARY TUDOR
by JAMES ANTHONY FROUDE

ISBN: 978-93-59324-55-5

Published by

DOUBLE 9 BOOKS

2/13-B, Ansari Road, Daryaganj
New Delhi – 110002
info@double9books.com
www.double9books.com
Tel. 011-40042856

ABOUT THE AUTHOR

James Anthony Froude was a prominent English historian, biographer, and essayist, born on April 23, 1818, in Dartington, Devon, England. He is best known for his works on the history of England and his biographies of significant figures from the Tudor period. Froude was educated at Westminster School and Oriel College, Oxford. He developed a keen interest in history and literature, particularly in the period of the English Reformation. His writings often reflect his controversial views on religious and political matters, which garnered both acclaim and criticism. One of Froude's most notable works is "The History of England from the Fall of Wolsey to the Defeat of the Spanish Armada," a monumental historical series spanning six volumes. In this series, Froude provides a vivid and dramatic account of the tumultuous events during the reigns of the Tudor monarchs, including Henry VIII and Elizabeth I. Aside from his historical writings, Froude also penned biographies of notable figures such as Thomas Carlyle. His works often tackled complex themes and explored the intersection of politics, religion, and society. James Anthony Froude's writings continue to be studied and debated by scholars, making him a significant figure in the field of historical literature.

CONTENTS

INTRODUCTION

The memory of no English sovereign has been so execrated as that of Mary Tudor. For generations after her death her name, with its horrid epithet clinging round it like the shirt of Nessus, was a bugbear in thousands of Protestant homes. It is true that nearly 300 persons were burnt at the stake in her short reign. But she herself was more inclined to mercy than almost any of her predecessors on the throne. Stubbs speaks of her father's "holocausts" of victims. The persecution of Papists under Edward was not less rigorous than that of Protestants under Mary. When her record is compared with that of Philip of Spain, with his Council of Blood in the Netherlands, or of Charles IX. in France, she appears as an apostle of toleration. Why, then, has her memory been covered through centuries with scorn and obloquy?

Froude will have it that it was due to a national detestation of the crimes which were committed in the name of religion. Those who take a more detached view of history can find little evidence to support the assumption. The nation as a whole seemed to acquiesce in the persecution. The government was weak, there was no standing army, and Mary, like all the Tudors, rested her authority on popular sanction. Plots against her were few, and they were all easily suppressed. Parliament met regularly. It was not the submissive parliament of Henry VIII. It thwarted some of Mary's dearest projects. For some time it offered opposition to, if it did not actively resist, the Spanish marriage. It was inexorably opposed to the restitution of church property. It refused to alter the succession to the Crown as Mary wished. But it never remonstrated against the persecution of Protestants. It cheerfully revived the old acts for the burning of Lollard heretics. Froude suggests that Englishmen were aghast at the use to which they were afterwards put. But though parliament after parliament was summoned after the Smithfield fires had been lit, there was no sign of disapproval or of condemnation. When Edward died, there was an instantaneous return to Catholicism. When Mary died, Elizabeth had to walk warily in bringing about innovations in religion. Mary was crowned with the ceremonies of the Catholic Church. When Elizabeth was crowned, nearly all the bishops, including the "bloody" Bonner, attended, and the service of the mass was used. Harpsfield, the notorious Archdeacon of Canterbury, the last man to condemn heretics to the stake in England, publicly stated, weeks after the accession of Elizabeth, that there should be no change in religion. Later generations, judging events and characters by their own standard, have pitilessly condemned the Marian persecutions. The Englishmen of those days were not so squeamish or so indifferent.

There can be no doubt that Mary was unpopular among her own contemporaries. Two reasons probably account for it. The first was her marriage with Philip of Spain. There is no nation in Europe which has shown itself more tolerant of alien sovereigns than the English. They submitted to William of Normandy almost without a struggle after Senlac. They adopted the Plantagenet as their national line of kings. The Tudors were Welsh; the Stuarts Scotch; William III. was a Dutchman; the Hanoverian dynasty was German. But though tolerant of foreign dynasties, the English have, since the days of John, been excessively jealous of foreign influences. One of the main causes of Henry III.'s unpopularity was the overweening influence of his foreign favourites. From Edward I. downwards the Plantagenets ruled as English sovereigns. Henry VII., though he was crowned on the field of battle and claimed the throne by right of conquest, was too discreet to maintain his power, as Mary was once tempted to do, by the aid of Welsh guards. The fiercest hostility was evoked by James I., William III., and the first two Georges, because they surrounded themselves with favourites from their own countries. Foreigners might sit on the throne of England, but they had to rule as English sovereigns and rest their power on the support of the English people. This intense national jealousy was unhappily aroused by Mary. The strict limitations which were placed on her husband's powers should have warned her of her danger. Philip was allowed the empty title of king, but from the realities of power he was studiously excluded. Philip was careful to maintain the spirit as well as the letter of his obligations. He made no attempt to encroach upon the sovereignty of Mary. He advised her, as it was his duty to do, but he did not interfere with the government of the country. No Spanish troops were landed in England, even when war had broken out with France, and the coasts of England were unguarded. Yet the morbid suspicions of the people were not allayed. The Dudley plot and the Stafford invasion were justified by their authors, not on the ground of Mary's bloody persecutions, but because it was feared that Philip was planning a *coup d'état*. Mary's popularity began to wane with her marriage; it sunk lower and lower till it almost disappeared when England was dragged into a war with France in the interests of Spain. St. Quintin and Gravelines for a time roused a feeble enthusiasm for the war, but the loss of Calais finally extinguished the Queens popularity. Mary is reported to have said that if her body were opened Calais would be found written on her heart. Froude disbelieves the report. But whether the story be apocryphal or not, there is no doubt that the loss of Calais was accountable, if not for the death of the Queen, for the permanent destruction of her fame.

Calais was called the "brightest jewel in the English crown." It was the last relic of the French possessions of the Plantagenets. It was the Gibraltar of the sixteenth century. It helped to make of the narrow seas an English channel. It was a mart for English goods. It afforded a foothold for Continental enterprises. To some extent it linked England with her traditional allies, the old Burgundian possessions in the Netherlands. By us, looking back over the chequered story of the last three centuries, the loss of Calais is seen to have been a blessing in disguise. England gained by it as she did by the loss of Normandy under John, and of Hanover at the accession of Queen Victoria. But to Mary's subjects it was a corroding humiliation.

"If Spain should rise suddenly into her ancient strength," Froude truly remarks, "and tear Gibraltar from us, our mortification would be faint, compared to the anguish of humiliated pride with which the loss of Calais distracted the subjects of Mary."

It was the galling reflection that Calais was lost to the French in a Spanish quarrel that crowned the poor Queen's obloquy. She had lost it through wanton neglect. Had the warnings of Wentworth and Grey been heeded, Calais might have been saved. Calais need never have been imperilled had the Queen thought more of English interests and less of the needs of her Spanish husband.

The odium in which Mary's memory was held was turned to account by the friends of the new religion. Early in the next reign there appeared one of the most remarkable books ever written—Foxe's *Book of Martyrs*. The authenticity of its narrative has been impugned by Lingard and other Catholic historians; Froude bears testimony to its trustworthiness wherever it can be tested, except when it deals with purely hearsay evidence. When

Foxe's narrative of the horrible Guernsey case was challenged by a Catholic controversialist in the reign of Elizabeth, the matter was inquired into, and the account was found to be absolutely true. No one will be found, however, in these days to assert that a book, written by an avowed partisan, in an uncritical age, recording transactions of which from the very nature of things he could have had no personal knowledge, was not too highly coloured in parts and in others absolutely untrustworthy. Few books, nevertheless, have exercised a more abiding influence on the course of our national life. Its simplicity, its directness, its poignant style, and its dramatic power combined to make it an English classic. If it loaded Bonner and Gardiner with shame and hatred, it fixed for three centuries the popular estimate of Mary Tudor. Froude used it with extraordinary skill. His relation of the death of a young Protestant martyr, an apprentice from Essex, taken as it is almost bodily from Foxe, must thrill even yet the least emotional of his readers. The permanence of Mary's hideous title and her abiding unpopularity are more due to the compelling power of a work of genius than to any outstanding demerits, as judged by contemporary standards, in the Catholic Queen.

Instead of being condemned to eternal infamy, poor Mary Tudor might well have expected a juster as well as a more charitable verdict from posterity. From her girlhood to her grave her story was tragic in its sadness. When she was in the first bloom of maidenhood, she was taken by her father to hold her Court of the Welsh Marches at Ludlow in 1525. The title of Princess of Wales was not conferred upon her, but she was surrounded by all the pomps and emblems of sovereignty. The Court was the Princess's Court, as it had been Prince Henry's Court in her father's youth. Three years later she was degraded from her high estate, and deprived of her Court. Henceforth, throughout her father's reign, she was known as the Lady, not the Princess, Mary. She was old enough to feel all the bitterness of her mother's tragedy. She remembered to her dying day the humiliation of the Boleyn marriage. She never ceased to resent the birth of her sister Elizabeth. Her brother Edward was born in lawful wedlock after Queen Catherine's death, and Mary was always perfectly loyal and obedient to him as she was to her father. But she looked with cold disfavour, mingled with morbid jealousy, on the budding promise of Elizabeth. Her very existence was an insult to Mary's mother and a menace to Mary's religion. If Elizabeth was legitimate, Catherine of Arragon was rightly divorced, and Mary herself had no claim to the throne other than by her father's will. Elizabeth could never be reconciled to Rome without casting an aspersion on Anne Boleyn's honour.

No woman was ever more lonely or loveless than the ill-starred and ill-favoured Queen Mary. She had no near relatives in England except Elizabeth, and Elizabeth, by the irony of fate, was worse than a stranger to her. The awful solitude of a throne excluded her, even more than her own ill-health and brooding temper, from the joys of friendship. Philip of Spain was at once her nearest relation on her mother's side, and the only man she ever confided in except Cardinal Pole. She lavished all the pent-up affection of an unloved existence on her husband. She was repaid by cold neglect, studied indifference, and open and vulgar infidelity. Philip made no pretence to care for his wife. She was older in years, she was ungainly in person, she possessed no charm of manner or grace of speech, her very voice was the deep bass of a man. In the days of her joyous entrance into London, amid the acclamations of the populace, her high spirit, her kind heart, and the excitement of adventure lent a passing glow to her sallow cheeks. But ill-health and disillusion followed. She became morbid and sullen, sometimes remaining for days in a dull stupor, at other times giving way to gusts of hysterical passion. But beneath her forbidding exterior there beat a warm, tender, womanly heart, which yearned for some one to love and to cherish. Her mother had died when she was yet young, her father never encouraged her to display her affection for him, and she was verging on middle age before she saw Philip. He became her hero, her master. Wifely obedience became to her the greatest of virtues; she held herself and England at his service. She longed for a son who would bind her husband more closely to herself and who would save England from the hated Elizabeth, and still more from Elizabeth's hated religion. When old and ill, and on the brink of the grave, she still cherished the vain dream of giving birth to the saviour of England and the champion of the faith.

But Froude dwells with malicious irony on the frustration of the poor woman's hopes. He covers the incident with a ridicule which must jar on all sensitive minds. The fact that Cardinal Pole encouraged her belief adds zest to Froude's satisfaction. No purer soul ever set himself to right the world than Reginald Pole; no one failed more completely in his cherished plans. He and Mary died on the same day; the bells that tolled their knell rang out the order for which they stood. But the utter failure of their hopes roused no emotion save that of bitter contempt in Froude. He saw no merit in the "hysterical dreamer" who had sacrificed his all for his religion; he saw no pathos in the life of that lone woman who was condemned, almost from her cradle, to a loveless existence and a forlorn death. His final epitaph on her is that "she had reigned little more than five years, and she descended into the grave amidst curses deeper than the acclamations which had welcomed her accession." The only excuse he can find for her is that she was suffering from "hysterical derangement" akin to insanity, which placed her absolutely under the domination of Gardiner and Pole. When we remember her magnanimity towards Lady Jane Grey at her accession, when we contrast her conduct towards the formidable Elizabeth with Elizabeth's subsequent conduct towards Mary Queen of Scots, her generosity to the causes she had at heart with Elizabeth's unfailing parsimony, and her open and straightforward dealings both in matters of Church and of State with her sister's mean and tortuous subterfuges, we may well extend not only our pity to the woman, but some tribute of admiration to the Queen. At least we may agree with Froude that "few men or women have lived less capable of doing knowingly a wrong thing."

W. LLEWELYN WILLIAMS.

February 3, 1910.

CHAPTER I-QUEEN JANE AND QUEEN MARY

On the 7th of July the death of Edward VI. was ushered in with signs and wonders, as if heaven and earth were in labour with revolution. The hail lay upon the grass in the London gardens as red as blood. At Middleton Stony in Oxfordshire, anxious lips reported that a child had been born with one body, two heads, four feet and hands. [1] About the time when the letters patent were signed there came a storm such as no living Englishman remembered. The summer evening grew black as night. Cataracts of water flooded the houses in the city and turned the streets into rivers; trees were torn up by the roots and whirled through the air, and a more awful omen — the forked lightning — struck down the steeple of the church where the heretic service had been read for the first time. [2]

The king died a little before nine o'clock on Thursday evening. His death was made a secret; but in the same hour a courier was galloping through the twilight to Hunsdon to bid Mary mount and fly. Her plans had been for some days prepared. She had been directed to remain quiet, but to hold herself ready to be up and away at a moment's warning. The lords who were to close her in would not be at their posts, and for a few hours the roads would be open. The Howards were looking for her in Norfolk; and thither she was to ride at her best speed, proclaiming her accession as she went along, and sending out her letters calling loyal Englishmen to rise in her defence.

So Mary's secret friends had instructed her to act as her one chance. Mary, who, like all the Tudors, was most herself in the moments of greatest danger, followed a counsel boldly which agreed with her own opinion; and when Lord Robert Dudley came in the morning with a company of horse to look for her, she was far away. Relays of horses along the road, and such other precautions as could be taken without exciting suspicion, had doubtless not been overlooked.

Far different advice had been sent to her by the new ambassadors of the emperor. Scheyfne, who understood England and English habits, and who was sanguine of her success, had agreed to a course which had probably been arranged in concert with him; but on the 6th, the day of Edward's death, Renard and M. de Courières arrived from Brussels. To Renard, accustomed to countries where governments were everything and peoples nothing, for a single woman to proclaim herself queen in the face of those who had the armed force of the kingdom in their hands, appeared like madness. Little confidence could be placed in her supposed friends, since they had wanted resolution to refuse their signatures to the instrument of her deposition. The emperor could not move; although he might wish well to her cause, the alliance of England was of vital importance to him, and he would not compromise himself with the faction whose success, notwithstanding Scheyfne's assurance, he looked upon as certain. Renard, therefore, lost not a moment in entreating the princess not to venture upon a course from which he anticipated inevitable ruin. If the nobility or the people desired to have her for queen, they would make her queen. There was no need for her to stir. [3] The remonstrance agreed fully with the opinion of Charles himself, who replied to Renard's account of his conduct with complete approval of it. [4] The emperor's power was no longer equal to an attitude of menace; he had been taught, by the repeated blunders of Reginald Pole, to distrust accounts of popular English sentiment; and he disbelieved entirely in the ability of Mary and her friends to cope with a conspiracy so broadly contrived, and supported by the countenance of France. [5] But Mary was probably gone from Hunsdon before advice arrived, to which she had been lost if she had listened. She had ridden night and day without a halt for a hundred miles to Keninghal, a castle of the Howards on the Waveney river. There, in safe hands, she would try the effect of an appeal to her country. If the nation was mute, she would then escape to the Low Countries. [6]

In London, during Friday and Saturday, the death of Edward was known and unknown. Every one talked of it as certain. Yet the Duke of Northumberland still spoke of him as living, and public business was carried on in his name. On the 8th of July the mayor and aldermen were sent for to Greenwich to sign the letters patent. From them the truth could not be concealed, but they were sworn to secrecy before they were allowed to leave the palace. The conspirators desired to have Mary under safe custody in the Tower before the mystery was published to the world, and another difficulty was not yet got over.

The novelty of a female sovereign, and the supposed constitutional objection to it, were points in favour of the alteration which Northumberland was unwilling to relinquish. The "device" had been changed in favour of Lady Jane; but Lady Jane was not to reign alone: Northumberland intended to hold the reins tight-grasped in his own hands, to keep the power in his own family, and to urge the sex of Mary as among the prominent occasions of her incapacity. [7] England was still to have a king, and that king was to be Guilford Dudley.

Jane Grey, eldest daughter of the Duke of Suffolk, was nearly of the same age with Edward. Edward had been precocious to a disease; the activity of his mind had been a symptom, or a cause, of the weakness of his body. Jane Grey's accomplishments were as extensive as Edward's; she had acquired a degree of learning rare in matured men, which she could use gracefully, and could permit to be seen by others without vanity or consciousness. Her character had developed with their talents. At fifteen she was learning Hebrew and could write Greek; at sixteen she corresponded with Bullinger in Latin at least equal to his own; but the matter of her letters is more striking than the language, and speaks more for her than the most elaborate panegyrics of admiring courtiers. She has left a portrait of herself drawn by her own hand; a portrait of piety, purity, and free, noble innocence, uncoloured, even to a fault, with the emotional weaknesses of humanity. [8] While the effects of the Reformation of England had been chiefly visible in the outward dominion of scoundrels and in the eclipse of the hereditary virtues of the national character, Lady Jane Grey had lived to show that the defect was not in the reformed faith, but in the absence of all faith — that the graces of a St. Elizabeth could be rivalled by the pupil of Cranmer and Ridley. The Catholic saint had no excellence of which Jane Grey was without the promise; the distinction was in the freedom of the Protestant from the hysterical ambition for an unearthly nature, and in the presence, through a more intelligent creed, of a vigorous and practical understanding.

When married to Guilford Dudley, Jane Lady had entreated that, being herself so young, and her husband scarcely older, she might continue to reside with her mother. [9] Lady Northumberland had consented; and the new-made bride remained at home till a rumour went abroad that Edward was on the point of death, when she was told that she must remove to her father-in-law's house, till "God should call the king to his mercy;" her presence would then be required at the Tower, the king having appointed her to be the heir to the crown.

This was the first hint which she had received of the fortune which was in store for her. She believed it to be a jest, and took no notice of the order to change her residence, till the Duchess of Northumberland came herself to fetch her. A violent scene ensued with Lady Suffolk. At last the duchess brought in Guilford Dudley, who commanded Lady Jane, on her allegiance as a wife, to return with him; and, "not choosing to be disobedient to her husband," she consented. The duchess carried her off, and kept her for three or four days a prisoner. Afterwards she was taken to a house of the duke's at Chelsea, where she remained till Sunday, the 9th of July, when a message was brought that she was wanted immediately at Sion House, to receive an order from the king.

She went alone. There was no one at the palace when she arrived; but immediately after Northumberland came, attended by Pembroke, Northampton, Huntingdon, and Arundel. The Earl of Pembroke, as he approached, knelt to kiss her hand. Lady Northumberland and Lady Northampton entered, and the duke, as President of the Council, rose to speak.

"The king," he said, "was no more. A godly life had been followed, as a consolation to their sorrows, by a godly end, and in leaving the world he had not forgotten his duty to his subjects. His majesty had prayed on his death-bed that Almighty God would protect the realm from false opinions, and especially from his unworthy sister; he had reflected that both the Lady Mary and the Lady Elizabeth had been cut off by act of parliament from the succession as illegitimate; [10] the Lady Mary had been disobedient to her father; she had been again disobedient to her brother; she was a capital and principal enemy of God's word; and both she and her sister were bastards born; King Henry did not intend that the crown should be worn by either of them; King Edward, therefore, had, before his death, bequeathed it to his cousin the Lady Jane; and, should the Lady Jane die without children, to her younger sister; and he had entreated the council, for their honours' sake and for the sake of the realm, to see that his will was observed."

Northumberland, as he concluded, dropped on his knees; the four lords knelt with him, and, doing homage to the Lady Jane as queen, they swore that they would keep their faith or lose their lives in her defence.

Lady Jane shook, covered her face with her hands, and fell fainting to the ground. Her first simple grief was for Edward's death; she felt it as the loss of a dearly loved brother. The weight of her own fortune was still more agitating; when she came to herself, she cried that it could not be; the crown was not for her, she could not bear it—she was not fit for it. Then, knowing nothing of the falsehoods which Northumberland had told her, she clasped her hands, and, in a revulsion of feeling, she prayed God that if the great place to which she was called was indeed justly hers, He would give her grace to govern for his service and for the welfare of his people. [11]

So passed Sunday, the 9th of July, at Sion House. In London, the hope of first securing Mary being disappointed, the king's death had been publicly acknowledged; circulars were sent out to the sheriffs, mayors, and magistrates in the usual style, announcing the accession of Queen Jane, and the troops were sworn man by man to the new sovereign. Sir William Petre and Sir John Cheke waited on the emperor's ambassador to express a hope that the alteration in the succession would not affect the good understanding between the courts of England and Flanders. The preachers were set to work to pacify the citizens; and, if Scheyfne is to be believed, a blood cement was designed to strengthen the new throne; and Gardiner, the Duke of Norfolk, and Lord Courtenay [12] were directed to prepare for death in three days. [13] But Northumberland would scarcely have risked an act of gratuitous tyranny. Norfolk, being under attainder, might have been put to death without violation of the *forms* of law, by warrant from the crown; but, Gardiner was uncondemned, and Courtenay had never been accused of crime.

The next day, Monday, the 10th of July, the royal barges came down the Thames from Richmond; and at three o'clock in the afternoon Lady Jane landed at the broad staircase at the Tower, as queen, in undesired splendour. A few scattered groups of spectators stood to watch the arrival; but it appeared, from their silence, that they had been brought together chiefly by curiosity. As the gates closed, the heralds-at-arms, with a company of the archers of the guard, rode into the city, and at the cross in Cheapside, Paul's Cross, and Fleet Street they proclaimed "that the Lady Mary was unlawfully begotten, and that the Lady Jane Grey was queen." The ill-humour of London was no secret, and some demonstration had been looked for in Mary's favour; [14] but here, again, there was only silence. The heralds cried "God save the queen!" The archers waved their caps and cheered, but the crowd looked on impassively. One youth only, Gilbert Potter, whose name for those few days passed into fame's trumpet, ventured to exclaim, "The Lady Mary has the better title." Gilbert's master, one "Ninian Sanders," denounced the boy to the guard, and he was seized. Yet a misfortune, thought to be providential, in a few hours befell Ninian Sanders. Going home to his house down the river, in the July evening, he was overturned and drowned as he was shooting London Bridge in his wherry; the boatmen, who were the instruments of Providence, escaped.

Nor did the party in the Tower rest their first night there with perfect satisfaction. In the evening messengers came in from the eastern counties with news of the Lady Mary, and with letters from herself. She had written to Renard and Scheyfne to tell them that she was in good hands, and for the moment was safe. She had proclaimed herself queen. She had sent addresses to the peers, commanding them on their allegiance to come to her; and she begged the ambassadors to tell her instantly whether she might look for assistance from Flanders; on the active support of the emperor, so far as she could judge, the movements of her friends would depend.

The ambassadors sent a courier to Brussels for instructions; but, pending Charles's judgment to the contrary, they thought they had better leave Mary's appeal unanswered till they could see how events would turn. There was one rumour current indeed that she had from ten to fifteen thousand men with her; but this they could ill believe. For themselves, they expected every hour to hear that she had been taken by Lord Warwick and Lord Robert Dudley, who were gone in pursuit of her, and had been put to death. [15]

The lords who were with the new queen were not so confident. They were in late consultation with the Duchess of Northumberland and the Duchess of Suffolk, when, after nightfall, a letter was brought in to them from Mary. The lords ordered the messenger into arrest. The seal of the packet was broken, and the letter read aloud. It was dated the day before, Sunday, July 9: —

"My lords," wrote Mary, "we greet you well, and have received sure advertisement that our deceased brother the king, our late Sovereign Lord, is departed to God's mercy; which news how they be woeful to our heart He only knoweth to whose will and pleasure we must and do submit us and all our wills. But in this so lamentable a case that is, to wit, now, after his majesty's departure and death, concerning the crown and governance of this realm of England, that which hath been provided by act of parliament and the testament and last will of our dearest father, you know — the realm and the whole world knoweth. The rolls and records appear, by the authority of the king our said father, and the king our said brother, and the subjects of this realm; so that we verily trust there is no true subject that can pretend to be ignorant thereof; and of our part we have ourselves caused, and as God shall aid and strengthen us, shall cause, our right and title in this behalf to be published and proclaimed accordingly.

"And, albeit, in this so weighty a matter, it seemeth strange that the dying of our said brother upon Thursday at night last past, we hitherto had no knowledge from you thereof; yet we consider your wisdom and prudence to be such, that having eftsoons amongst you debated, pondered, and well-weighed the present case, with our estate, with your own estate, the commonwealth, and all our honours, we shall and may conceive great hope and trust, with much assurance in your loyalty and service; and therefore, for the time, we interpret and take things not for the worst; and that ye yet will, like noblemen, work the best. Nevertheless, we are not ignorant of your consultation to undo the provisions made for our preferment, nor of the great banded provisions forcible whereunto ye be assembled and prepared, by whom and to what end God and you know; and nature can fear some evil. But be it that some consideration politic, or whatsoever thing else, hath moved you thereunto; yet doubt ye not, my lords, but we can take all these your doings in gracious part, being also right ready to remit and also pardon the same, with that freely to eschew bloodshed and vengeance against all those that can or will intend the same; trusting also assuredly you will take and accept this grace and virtue in good part as appertaineth, and that we shall not be enforced to use the service of other our true subjects and friends which, in this our just and rightful cause, God, in whom our whole affiance is, shall send us.

"Whereupon, my lords, we require and charge you, and every of you, on your allegiance, which you owe to God and us, and to none other, that for our honour and the surety of our realm, only you will employ yourselves; and forthwith, upon receipt hereof, cause our right and title to the crown and government of this realm to be proclaimed in our city of London, and such other places as to your wisdom shall seem good, and as to this cause appertaineth, not failing hereof, as our very trust is in you; and this our letter, signed with our own hand, shall be your sufficient warrant." [16]

The lords, when the letter was read to the end, looked uneasily in each other's faces. The ladies screamed, sobbed, and were carried off in hysterics. There was yet time to turn back; and had the Reformation been, as he pretended, the true concern of the Duke of Northumberland, he would have brought Mary back himself, bound by conditions which, in her present danger, she would have accepted. But Northumberland cared as little for religion as for any other good thing. He was a great criminal, throwing a stake for a crown; and treason is too conscious of its guilt to believe retreat from the first step to be possible.

Another blow was in store for him that night, before he laid his head upon his pillow. Lady Jane, knowing nothing of the letter from Mary, had retired to her apartment, when the Marquis of Winchester came in to wish her joy. He had brought the crown with him, which she had not sent for; he desired her to put it on, and see if it required alteration. She said it would do very well as it was. He then told her that, before her coronation, another crown was to be made for her husband. Lady Jane started; and it seemed as if for the first time the dreary suspicion crossed her mind that she was, after all, but the puppet of the ambition of the duke to raise his family to the throne. Winchester retired, and she sat indignant [17] till Guilford Dudley appeared, when she told him that, young as she was, she knew that the crown of England was not a thing to be trifled with. There was no Dudley in Edward's will, and, before he could be crowned, the consent of Parliament must be first asked and obtained. The boy-husband went whining to his mother, while Jane sent for Arundel and Pembroke, and told them that it was not for her to appoint kings. She would make her husband a duke if he desired it; that was within her prerogative; but king she would not make him. As she was speaking, the Duchess of Northumberland rushed in with her son, fresh from the agitation of Mary's letter. The mother stormed; Guilford cried like a spoilt child that he would be no duke, he would be a king: and, when Jane stood firm, the duchess bade him come away, and not share the bed of an ungrateful and disobedient wife. [18]

The first experience of royalty had brought small pleasure with it. Dudley's kingship was set aside for the moment, and was soon forgotten in more alarming matters. To please his mother, or to pacify his vanity, he was called "Your Grace." He was allowed to preside in the council, so long as a council remained, and he dined alone [19] — tinsel distinctions, for which the poor wretch had to pay dearly.

The next day (July 11) restored the conspirators to their courage. No authentic accounts came in of disturbances. London was still quiet; so quiet, that it was thought safe to nail Gilbert Potter by the ears in the pillory, and after sufficient suffering, to slice them off with a knife. Lord Warwick and Lord Robert were still absent, and no news had come from them — a proof that they were still in pursuit. The duke made up his mind that Mary was watching only for an opportunity to escape to Flanders; and the ships in the river, with a thousand men-at-arms on board them, were sent to watch the Essex coast, and to seize her, could they find opportunity. Meanwhile he himself penned a reply to her letter. "The Lady Jane," he said, "by the antient laws of the realm," and "by letters patent of the late king," signed by himself, and countersigned by the nobility, was rightful queen of England. The divorce of Catherine of Arragon from Henry VIII. had been prescribed by the laws of God, pronounced by the Church of England, and confirmed by act of parliament; the daughter of Catherine was, therefore, illegitimate, and could not inherit; and the duke warned her to forbear, at her peril, from molesting her lawful sovereign, or turning her people from their allegiance. If she would submit and accept the position of a subject, she should receive every reasonable attention which it was in the power of the queen to show to her.

During the day rumours of all kinds were flying, but Mary's friends in London saw no reasonable grounds for hope. Lord Robert was supposed by Renard [20] to be on his way to the Tower with the princess as his prisoner; and if she was once within the Tower walls, all hope was over. It was not till Wednesday morning (July 12) that the duke became really alarmed. Then at once, from all sides, messengers came in with unwelcome tidings. The Dudleys had come up with Mary the day before, as she was on her way from Keninghal to Framlingham. They had dashed forward upon her escort, but their own men turned sharp round, declared for the princess, and attempted to seize them; they had been saved only by the speed of their horses. [21] In the false calm of the two preceding days, Lord

Bath had stolen across the country into Norfolk. Lord Mordaunt and Lord Wharton had sent their sons; Sir William Drury, Sir John Skelton, Sir Henry Bedingfield, and many more, had gone in the same direction. Lord Sussex had declared also for Mary; and, worse than all, Lord Derby had risen in Cheshire, and was reported to be marching south with twenty thousand men. [22] Scarcely were these news digested, when Sir Edmund Peckham, cofferer of the household, was found to have gone off with the treasure under his charge. Sir Edward Hastings, Lord Huntingdon's brother, had called out the musters of Buckinghamshire in Mary's name, and Peckham had joined him; while Sir Peter Carew, the very hope and stay of the western Protestants, had proclaimed Mary in the towns of Devonshire.

Now, when too late, it was seen how large an error had been committed in permitting the princess's escape. But it was vain to waste time in regrets. Her hasty levies, at best, could be but rudely armed; the duke had trained troops and cannon, and, had he been free to act, with no enemies but those in the field against him, he had still the best of the game. But Suffolk and Northampton, the least able of the council, were, nevertheless, the only members of it on whom he could rely. To whom but to himself could he trust the army which must meet Mary in the field? If he led the army in person, whom could he leave in charge of London, the Tower, and Lady Jane? Winchester and Arundel knew his dilemma, and deliberately took advantage of it. The guard, when first informed that they were to take the field, refused to march. After a communication with the Marquis of Winchester, they withdrew their objections, and professed themselves willing to go. Northumberland, uneasy at their conduct, or requiring a larger force, issued a proclamation offering tenpence a day to volunteers who would go to bring in the Lady Mary. [23] The lists were soon filled, but filled with the retainers and servants of his secret enemies. [24]

The men being thus collected, Suffolk was first thought of to lead them, or else Lord Grey de Wilton; [25] but Suffolk was inefficient, and his daughter could not bring herself to part with him; Grey was a good soldier, but he had been a friend of Somerset, and the duke had tried hard to involve him with Arundel and Paget in Somerset's ruin. [26] Northampton's truth could have been depended upon, but Northampton four years before had been defeated by a mob of Norfolk peasants. Northumberland, the council said, must go himself—"there was no remedy." No man, on all accounts, could be so fit as he; "he had achieved the victory in Norfolk once already, and was so feared, that none durst lift their weapons against him:" [27] Suffolk in his absence should command the Tower. Had the duke dared, he would have delayed; but every moment that he remained inactive added to Mary's strength, and whatever he did he must risk something. He resolved to go, and as the plot was thickening, he sent Sir Henry Dudley to Paris to entreat the king to protect Calais against Charles, should the latter move upon it in his cousin's interest.

Noailles had assured him that this and larger favours would be granted without difficulty; while, as neither Renard nor his companions had as yet acknowledged Lady Jane, and were notoriously in correspondence with Mary, the French ambassador suggested also that he would do wisely to take the initiative himself, to send Renard his passports, and commit the country to war with the emperor. [28] Northumberland would not venture the full length to which Noailles invited him; but he sent Sir John Mason and Lord Cobham to Renard, with an intimation that the English treason laws were not to be trifled with. If he and his companions dared to meddle in matters which did not concern them, their privileges as ambassadors should not protect them from extremity of punishment. [29]

Newmarket was chosen for the rendezvous of the army. The men were to go down in companies, in whatever way they could travel most expeditiously, with the guns and ammunition waggons. The duke himself intended to set out on Friday at dawn. In his calculations of the chances, hope still predominated—his cannon would give him the advantage in the field, and he trusted to the Protestant spirit in London to prevent a revolution in his absence. But he took the precaution of making the council entangle themselves more completely by taking out a commission under the Great Seal, as general of the army, which they were forced to sign; and before he left the Tower, he made a parting appeal to their good faith. If he believed they would betray him, he said, he could still provide for his own safety; but, as they were well aware that Lady Jane was on the throne by no will of her own, but through his influence and theirs, so he trusted her to their honours to keep the oaths which they had sworn. "They were all in the same guilt," one of them answered; "none could excuse themselves." Arundel especially wished the duke God speed upon his way, and regretted only that he was not to accompany him to the field. [30]

This was on Thursday evening. Northumberland slept that night at Whitehall. The following morning he rode out of London, accompanied by his four sons, Northampton, Grey, and about six hundred men. The streets were thronged with spectators, but all observed the same ominous silence with which they had received the heralds' proclamation. "The people press to see us," the duke said, "but not one saith God speed us." [31]

The principal conspirator was now out of the way; his own particular creatures—Sir Thomas and Sir Henry Palmer, and Sir John Gates, who had commanded the Tower guard, had gone with him. Northampton was gone. The young Dudleys were gone all but Guilford. Suffolk alone remained of the faction definitely attached to the duke; and the duke was marching to the destruction which they had prepared for him. But prudence still warned those who were loyal to Mary to wait before they declared themselves; the event was still uncertain; and the disposition of the Earl of Pembroke might not yet, perhaps, have been perfectly ascertained.

Pembroke, in the black volume of appropriations, was the most deeply compromised. Pembroke, in Wilts and Somerset, where his new lands lay, was hated for his oppression of the poor, and had much to fear from a Catholic sovereign, could a Catholic sovereign obtain the reality as well as the name of power; Pembroke, so said Northumberland, had been the first to propose the conspiracy to him, while his eldest son had married Catherine Grey. But, as Northumberland's designs began to ripen, he had endeavoured to steal from the court; he was a distinguished soldier, yet he was never named to command the army which was to go against Mary; Lord Herbert's marriage was outward and nominal merely—a form, which had not yet become a reality, and never did. Although Pembroke was the first of the council to do homage to Jane, Northumberland evidently doubted him. He was acting and would continue to act for his own personal interests only. With his vast estates and vast hereditary influence in South Wales and on the Border, he could bring a larger force into the field than any other single nobleman in England; and he could purchase the secure possession of his acquisitions by a well-timed assistance to Mary as readily as by lending his strength to buttress the throne of her rival.

Of the rest of the council, Winchester and Arundel had signed the letters patent with a deliberate intention of deserting or betraying Northumberland, whenever a chance should present itself, and of carrying on their secret measures in Mary's favour [32] with greater security. The other noblemen in the Tower perhaps imperfectly understood each other. Cranmer had taken part unwillingly with Lady Jane; but he meant to keep his promise, having once given it. Bedford had opposed the duke up to the signature, and might be supposed to adhere to his original opinion; but he was most likely hesitating, while Lord Russell had been trusted with the command of the garrison at Windsor. Sir Thomas Cheyne and Shrewsbury might be counted among Mary's friends; the latter certainly. Of the three secretaries, Cecil's opposition had put his life in jeopardy; Petre was the friend and confidant of Paget, and would act as Paget should advise; Cheke, a feeble enthusiast, was committed to the duke.

The task of bringing the council together was undertaken by Cecil. Cecil and Winchester worked on Bedford; and Bedford made himself responsible for his son, for the troops at Windsor, and generally for the western counties. The first important step was to readmit Paget to the council. Fresh risings were reported in Northamptonshire and Lincolnshire; [33] Sir John Williams was proclaiming Mary round Oxford; and on Friday night or Saturday morning (July 15) news came from the fleet which might be considered decisive as to the duke's prospects. The vessels, so carefully equipped, which left the Thames on the 12th, had been driven into Yarmouth Harbour by stress of weather. Sir Henry Jerningham was in the town raising men for Mary; and knowing that the crews had been pressed, and that there had been desertions among the troops before they were embarked, [34] he ventured boldly among the ships. "Do you want our captains?" some one said to him. "Yea, marry," was the answer. "Then they shall go with you," the men shouted, "or they shall go to the bottom." Officers, sailors, troops, all declared for Queen Mary, and landed with their arms and artillery. The report was borne upon the winds; it was known in a few hours in London; it was known in the duke's army, which was now close to Cambridge, and was the signal for the premeditated mutiny. "The noblemen's tenants refused to serve their lords against Queen Mary." [35] Northumberland sent a courier at full speed to the council for reinforcements. The courier returned "with but a slender answer." [36]

The lords in London, however, were still under the eyes of the Tower garrison, who watched them narrowly. Their first meeting to form their plans was within the Tower walls, and Arundel said "he liked not the air." [37] Pembroke and Cheyne attempted to escape, but failed to evade the guard; Winchester made an excuse to go to his own house, but he was sent for and brought back at midnight. Though Mary might succeed, they might still lose their own lives, which they were inclined to value.

On Sunday, the 16th, the preachers again exerted themselves. Ridley shrieked against Mary at Paul's Cross; [38] John Knox, more wisely, at Amersham, in Buckinghamshire, foretold the approaching retribution from the giddy ways of the past years; Buckinghamshire, Catholic and Protestant, was arming to the teeth; and he was speaking at the peril of his life among the troopers of Sir Edward Hastings.

"Oh England!" cried the saddened Reformer, "now is God's wrath kindled against thee—now hath he begun to punish as he hath threatened by his true prophets and messengers. He hath taken from thee the crown of thy glory, and hath left thee without honour, and this appeareth to be only the beginning of sorrows. The heart, the tongue, the hand of one Englishman is bent against another, and division is in the realm, which is a sign of desolation to come. Oh, England, England! if thy mariners and thy governors shall consume one another, shalt not thou suffer shipwreck? Oh England, alas! these plagues are poured upon thee because thou wouldst not know the time of thy most gentle visitation." [39]

At Cambridge, on the same day, another notable man preached — Edwin Sandys, then Protestant Vice-Chancellor of the University, and afterwards Archbishop of York. Northumberland the preceding evening brought his mutinous troops into the town. He sent for Parker, Lever, Bill, and Sandys to sup with him, and told them he required their prayers, or he and his friends were like to be "made deacons of." [40] Sandys, the vice-chancellor, must address the university the next morning from the pulpit.

Sandys rose at three o'clock in the summer twilight, took his Bible, and prayed with closed eyes that he might open at a fitting text. His eyes, when he lifted them, were resting on the 16th of the 1st of Joshua: "The people answered Joshua, saying, All thou commandest us we will do; and whithersoever thou sendest us we will go; according as we hearkened unto Moses, so will we hearken unto thee, only the Lord thy God be with thee as he was with Moses."

The application was obvious. Edward was Moses, the duke was Joshua; and if a sermon could have saved the cause, Lady Jane would have been secure upon her throne. [41]

But the comparison, if it held at all, held only in its least agreeable features. The deliverers of England from the Egyptian bondage of the Papacy had led the people out into a wilderness where the manna had been stolen by the leaders, and there were no tokens of a promised land. To the universities the Reformation had brought with it desolation. To the people of England it had brought misery and want. The once open hand was closed; the once open heart was hardened; the ancient loyalty of man to man was exchanged for the scuffling of selfishness; the change of faith had brought with it no increase of freedom, and less of charity. The prisons were crowded, as before, with sufferers for opinion, and the creed of a thousand years was made a crime by a doctrine of yesterday; monks and nuns wandered by hedge and highway, as missionaries of discontent, and pointed with bitter effect to the fruits of the new belief, which had been crimsoned in the blood of thousands of English peasants. The English people were not yet so much in love with wretchedness that they would set aside for the sake of it a princess whose injuries pleaded for her, whose title was affirmed by act of parliament. In the tyranny under which the nation was groaning, the moderate men of all creeds looked to the accession of Mary as to the rolling away of some bad black nightmare.

On Monday Northumberland made another effort to move forward. His troops followed him as far as Bury, and then informed him decisively that they would not bear arms against their lawful sovereign. He fell back on Cambridge, and again wrote to London for help. As a last resource, Sir Andrew Dudley, instructed, it is likely, by his brother, gathered up a hundred thousand crowns' worth of plate and jewels from the treasury in the Tower, and started for France to interest Henry — to bribe him, it was said, by a promise of Guisnes and Calais — to send an army into England. [42] The duke foresaw, and dared the indignation of the people; but he had left himself no choice except between treason to the country or now inevitable destruction. [43] When he called in the help of France he must have known well that his ally, with a successful army in England, would prevent indeed the accession of Mary Tudor, but as surely would tear in pieces the paper title of the present queen and snatch the crown for his own Mary, the Queen of Scots, and the bride of the Dauphin.

But the council was too quick for Dudley. A secret messenger followed or attended him to Calais, where he was arrested, the treasure recovered, and his despatches taken from him.

The counter-revolution could now be accomplished without bloodshed and without longer delay. On Wednesday the 19th July word came that the Earl of Oxford had joined Mary. A letter was written to Lord Rich admonishing him not to follow Oxford's example, but to remain true to Queen Jane, which the council were required to sign. Had they refused, they would probably have been massacred. [44] Towards the middle of the day, Winchester, Arundel, Pembroke, Shrewsbury, Bedford, Cheyne, Paget, Mason, and Petre found means of passing the gates, and made their way to Baynard's Castle, [45] where they sent for the mayor, the aldermen, and other great persons of the city. When they were all assembled, Arundel was the first to speak.

The country, he said, was on the brink of civil war, and if they continued to support the pretensions of Lady Jane Grey to the crown, civil war would inevitably break out. In a few more days or weeks the child would be in arms against the father, the brother against the brother; the quarrels of religion would add fury to the struggle; the French would interfere on one side, the Spaniards on the other, and in such a conflict the triumph of either party would be almost equally injurious to the honour, unity, freedom, and happiness of England. The friends of the commonwealth, in the face of so tremendous a danger, would not obstinately persist in encouraging the pretensions of a faction. It was for them where they sate to decide if there should be peace or war, and he implored them, for the sake of the country, to restore the crown to her who was their lawful sovereign.

Pembroke rose next. The words of Lord Arundel, he said, were true and good, and not to be gainsaid. What others thought he knew not; for himself, he was so convinced, that he would fight in the quarrel with any man; and if words are not enough, he cried, flashing his sword out of the scabbard, "this blade shall make Mary Queen, or I will lose my life." [46]

Not a voice was raised for the Twelfth-day Queen, as Lady Jane was termed, in scornful pity, by Noailles. Some few persons thought that, before they took a decisive step, they should send notice to Northumberland, and give him time to secure his pardon. But it was held to be a needless stretch of consideration; Shrewsbury and Mason hastened off to communicate with Renard; [47] while a hundred and fifty men were marched directly to the Tower gates, and the keys were demanded in the queen's name.

It is said that Suffolk was unprepared: but the goodness of his heart and the weakness of his mind alike saved him from attempting a useless resistance: the gates were opened, and the unhappy father rushed to his daughter's room. He clutched at the canopy under which she was sitting, and tore it down; she was no longer queen, he said, and such distinctions were not for one of her station. He then told her briefly of the revolt of the council. She replied that his present words were more welcome to her than those in which he had advised her to accept the crown; [48] her reign being at an end, she asked innocently if she might leave the Tower and go home. [49] But the Tower was a place not easy to leave, save by one route too often travelled.

Meanwhile the lords, with the mayor and the heralds, went to the Cross at Cheapside to proclaim Mary Queen. Pembroke himself stood out to read; and this time there was no reason to complain of a silent audience. He could utter but one sentence before his voice was lost in the shout of joy which thundered into the air. "God save the queen," "God save the queen," rung out from tens of thousands of throats. "God save the queen," cried Pembroke himself, when he had done, and flung up his jewelled cap and tossed his purse among the crowd. The glad news spread like lightning through London, and the pent-up hearts of the citizens poured themselves out in a torrent of exultation. Above the human cries, the long-silent church-bells clashed again into life; first began St. Paul's, where happy chance had saved them from destruction; then, one by one, every peal which had been spared caught up the sound; and through the summer evening and the summer night, and all the next day, the metal tongues from tower and steeple gave voice to England's gladness. The lords, surrounded by the shouting multitude, walked in state to St. Paul's, where the choir again sang a Te Deum, and the unused organ rolled out once more its mighty volume of music. As they came out again, at the close of the service, the apprentices were heaping piles of wood for bonfires at the cross-ways. The citizens were spreading tables in the streets, which their wives were loading with fattest capons and choicest wines; there was free feasting for all comers; and social jealousies, religious hatreds, were forgotten for the moment in the ecstasy of the common delight. Even the retainers of the Dudleys, in fear or joy, tore their badges out of their caps, and trampled on them. [50]

At a night session of the council, a letter was written to Northumberland, which Cranmer, Suffolk, and Sir John Cheke consented to sign, ordering him in the name of Queen Mary to lay down his arms. If he complied, the lords undertook to intercede for his pardon. If he refused, they said that they would hold him as a traitor, and spend their lives in the field against him. [51]

While a pursuivant bore the commands of the council to the duke, Arundel and Paget undertook to carry to Mary at Framlingham their petition for forgiveness, in which they declared that they had been innocent at heart of any share in the conspiracy, [52] and had only delayed coming forward in her favour from a desire to prevent bloodshed.

The two lords immediately mounted and galloped off into the darkness, followed by thirty horse, leaving the lights of illuminated London gleaming behind them.

The duke's position was already desperate: on the 18th, before the proclamation in London, Mary had felt herself strong enough to send orders to the Mayor of Cambridge for his arrest; [53] and, although he had as yet been personally unmolested, he was powerless in the midst of an army which was virtually in Mary's service. The news of the revolution in London first reached him by a private hand. He at once sent for Sandys, and, going with him to the market cross, he declared, after one violent clutch at his beard, that he had acted under orders from the council; the council, he understood, had changed their minds, and he would change his mind also; therefore he cried, "God save Queen Mary," and with a strained effort at a show of satisfaction, he, too, like Pembroke, threw up his cap. The queen, he said to Sandys, was a merciful woman, and there would be a general pardon. "Though the queen grant you a pardon," Sandys answered, "the lords never will; you can hope nothing from those who now rule." [54]

It was true that he could hope nothing—the hatred of the whole nation, which before his late treasons he had brought upon himself, would clamour to the very heavens for judgment against him. An hour after the proclamation of Mary (July 20), Rouge-cross herald arrived with the lords' letter from London. An order at the same time was read to the troops informing them that they were no longer under the duke's command, and an alderman of the town then ventured to execute the queen's warrant for his arrest. Northumberland was given in charge to a guard of his own soldiers; he protested, however, that the council had sent no instructions for his detention; and in some uncertainty, or perhaps in compassion for his fate, the soldiers obeyed him once more, and let him go. It was then night. He intended to fly; but he put it off till the morning, and in the morning his chance was gone. Before he could leave his room he found himself face to face with Arundel, who, after delivering the council's letter to the queen, had hastened to Cambridge to secure him.

Northumberland, who, while innocent of crime, had faced death on land and sea like a soldier and a gentleman, flung himself at the earl's feet. "Be good to me, for the love of God," he cried; "consider I have done nothing but by the consent of you and the council." He knew what kind of consent he had extorted from the council. "My lord," said Arundel, "I am sent thither by the Queen's Majesty; and in her name I do arrest you." — "I obey, my lord," the duke replied; "yet show me mercy, knowing the case as it is." — "My lord," was the cold answer, "you should have sought for mercy sooner; I must do according to my commandment." [55]

At the same moment Sandys was paying the penalty for his sermon. The university, in haste to purge itself of its heretical elements, met soon after sunrise to depose their vice-chancellor. Dr. Sandys, who had gone for an early stroll among the meadows to meditate on his position, hearing the congregation-bell ringing, resolved, like a brave man, to front his fortune; he walked to the senate-house, entered, and took his seat. "A rabble of Papists" instantly surrounded him. He tried to speak, but the masters of arts shouted "Traitor;" rough hands shook or dragged him from his chair: and the impatient theologian, in sudden heat, drew his dagger, and "would have done a mischief with it," had not some of his friends disarmed him. [56] He, too, was handed over to a guard, lashed to the back of a lame horse, and carried to London.

Mary, meanwhile, notwithstanding the revolution in her favour, remained a few more days at Framlingham, either suspicious of treachery or uncertain whether there might not be another change. But she was assured rapidly that the danger was at an end by the haste with which the lords and gentlemen who were compromised sought their pardon at her feet. On the 21st and 22nd Clinton, Grey, Fitzgerald, Ormond, Fitzwarren, Sir Henry Sidney, and Sir James Crofts presented themselves and received forgiveness. Cecil wrote, explaining his secret services, and was taken into favour. Lord Robert and Lord Ambrose Dudley, Northampton and a hundred other gentlemen—Sir Thomas Wyatt among them—who had accompanied the duke to Bury, were not so fortunate. The queen would not see them, and they were left under arrest. Ridley set out for Norfolk, also, to confess his offences; but, before he arrived at the court, he was met by a warrant for his capture, and carried back a prisoner to the Tower.

The conspiracy was crushed, and crushed, happily, without bloodshed. The inquiry into its origin, and the punishment of the guilty, could be carried out at leisure. There was one matter, however, which admitted of no delay. Mary's first anxiety, on feeling her crown secure, was the burial of her dead brother, who, through all these scenes, was still lying in his bed in his room at Greenwich. In her first letter to the Imperial ambassadors, the day after the arrival of Arundel and Paget at the court, she spoke of this as her greatest care; to their infinite alarm, she announced her intention of inaugurating her reign with Requiem and Dirige, and a mass for the repose of his soul.

Their uneasiness requires explanation.

While on matters of religion there was in England almost every variety of opinion, there was a very general consent that the queen should not marry a foreigner. The dread that Mary might form a connection with some continental prince, had formed the strongest element in Northumberland's cause; all the Catholics, except the insignificant faction who desired the restoration of the Papal authority, [57] all the moderate Protestants, wished well to her, but wished to see her married to some English nobleman; and, while her accession was still uncertain, the general opinion had already fixed upon a husband for her in the person of her cousin Edward Courtenay, the imprisoned son of the Marquis of Exeter. The interest of the public in the long confinement of this young nobleman had invested him with all imaginary graces of mind and body. He was the grandchild of a Plantagenet, and a representative of the White Rose. He had suffered from the tyranny, and was supposed to have narrowly escaped murder at the hands of the man whom all England most hated. Nature, birth, circumstances, all seemed to point to him as the king-consort of the realm. [58] The emperor had thought of Mary for his son; and it has been seen that the fear of such an alliance induced the French to support Northumberland. To prevent the injury which the report, if credited in England, would have done to her cause, Mary, on her first flight to Keninghal, empowered Renard to assure the council that she had no thought at all of marrying a stranger. The emperor and the bishop of Arras, in assuring Sir Philip Hoby that the French intended to strike for the Queen of Scots, declared that, for themselves they wished only to see the queen settled in her own realm, as her subjects desired; and especially they would prevent her either from attempting innovations in religion without their consent, or from marrying against their approbation. [59]

But the emperor's disinterestedness was only the result of his despondency. While the crisis lasted, neither Charles nor Henry of France saw their way to a distinct course of action. Charles, on the 20th of July, ignorant of the events in London, had written to Renard, despairing of Mary's success. Jane Grey he would not recognise; the Queen of Scots, he thought, would shortly be on the English throne. Henry, considering, at any rate, that he might catch something in troubled waters, volunteered to Lord William Howard, [60] in professed compliance with the demands of Northumberland, to garrison Guisnes and Calais for him. Howard replied that the French might come to Calais if they desired, but their reception might not be to their taste. [61] The revolution of the 19th altered the aspect of the situation both at the courts of Paris and of Brussels. The accession of Mary would be no injury to France, provided she could be married in England; and Henry at once instructed Noailles to congratulate the council on her accession. Noailles himself indeed considered, that, should she take Courtenay for a husband, the change might, after all, be to their advantage. The emperor, on the other hand, began to think again of his original scheme. Knowing that the English were sincere in their detestation of the Papacy, and imperfectly comprehending the insular distinction between general attachment to Catholic tradition and indifference to Catholic unity, he supposed that the country really was, on the whole, determined in its adherence to the reformed opinions. But the political alliance was still of infinite importance to him; and therefore he was anxious beyond everything that the princess whom he intended to persuade to break her word about her marriage should be discreet and conciliatory about religion. He lost not a moment, after hearing that she was proclaimed queen, in sending her his congratulations; but he sent with them an earnest admonition to be cautious; to be content with the free exercise for herself of her own creed, to take no step whatever without the sanction of parliament, and to listen to no one who would advise her, of her own authority, to set aside the Act of Uniformity. Her first duty was to provide for the quiet of the realm; and she must endeavour, by prudence and moderation, to give reasonable satisfaction to her subjects of all opinions. Above all things, let her remember to be a good Englishwoman (*bonne Anglaise*). [62]

It was, in consequence, with no light anxiety that Renard learnt from Mary her intention of commencing her reign with an act which was so far at variance with the emperor's advice, and which would at once display the colours of a party. To give the late king a public funeral with a ceremonial forbidden by the law, would be a strain of the prerogative which could not fail to create jealousy even among those to whom the difference between a Latin mass and an English service was not absolutely vital; and the judicious latitudinarianism to which the lay statesmen of the better sort were inclining, would make them dread the appearance of a disposition that would encourage the revolutionists. She owed her crown to the Protestants as well as to the Catholics. If she broke the law to please the prejudices of the latter, Renard was warned that her present popularity would not be of long continuance. [63]

Yet, as the ambassador trembled to know, a carelessness of consequences and an obstinate perseverance in a course which she believed to be right were the principal features in Mary's character. He wrote to her while she was still at Framlingham, using every argument which ought, as he considered, to prevail. He reminded her of the long and unavailing struggle of the emperor to bring back Germany out of heresy, where the obstinacy of the Romanists had been as mischievous to him as the fanaticism of the Lutherans. "Her duty to God was of course the first thing to be considered; but at such a time prudence was a part of that duty. The Protestant heresies had taken a hold deep and powerful upon her subjects. In London alone there were fifteen thousand French, Flemish, and German refugees, most of them headstrong and ungovernable enthusiasts. The country dreaded any fresh convulsions, and her majesty should remember that she had instructed him to tell the council that she was suspected unjustly, and had no thought of interfering with the existing settlement of the realm." [64]

With all his efforts, however, Renard could but bring the queen to consent to a few days' delay; and fearing that she would return to her purpose, he sent to the emperor a copy of his letter, which he urged him to follow up. Charles on the 29th replied again, lauding the ambassador's caution, and suggesting an argument more likely to weigh with his cousin than the soundest considerations of public policy. Edward had lived and died in heresy, and the Catholic services were intended only for the faithful sons of the Church. [65] He desired Renard to remind her that those who had been her most valuable friends were known to hold opinions far from orthodox; and he once more implored her to be guided by parliament, and to take care that the parliament was free. She had asked whether she should imitate Northumberland and nominate the members of the House of Commons. He cautioned her against so dangerous an example; he advised her to let the counties and towns send deputies of their own choice; and if the writs were sent into Cornwall and the northern counties, which had remained most constant to the Catholic religion, these places might be expected to return persons who would support her own sentiments. [66]

If the emperor had been equally earnest in urging Mary to consult the wishes of her subjects on her marriage, he would have been a truer friend to her than he proved to be. But prudential arguments produced no effect on the eager queen; Renard had warned her not to resist Northumberland; she had acted on her own judgment, and Northumberland was a prisoner, and she was on the throne. By her own will she was confident that she could equally well restore the mass, and in good time the pope's authority. The religious objection to the funeral was more telling, and on this point she hesitated. Meantime she began to move slowly towards London, and at the end of the month the reached her old house of Newhall in Essex, where she rested till the preparations were complete for her entry into the city.

The first point on which she had now to make up her mind concerned the persons with whom she was to carry on the government. The emperor was again clear in his advice, which here she found herself obliged to follow. She was forced to leave undisturbed in their authorities such of her brother's late ministers as had contributed to the revolution in her favour. Derby, Sussex, Bath, Oxford, who had hurried to her support at Framlingham, were her loyal subjects, whom she could afford to neglect, because she could depend upon their fidelity. Pembroke and Winchester, Arundel and Shrewsbury, Bedford, Cobham, Cheyne, Petre, too powerful to affront, too uncertain to be trusted as subjects, she could only attach to herself by maintaining in their offices and emoluments. She would restore the Duke of Norfolk to the council; Gardiner should hold office again; and she could rely on the good faith of Paget, the ablest, as well as the most honest, of all the professional statesmen. But Norfolk was old, and the latitudinarian Paget and the bigoted Gardiner bore each other no good will; so that, when the queen had leisure to contemplate her position, it did not promise to be an easy one. She would have to govern with the assistance of men who were gorged with the spoils of the church, suspected of heresy, and at best indifferent to religion.

In Mary's absence, the lords in London carried on the government as they could on their own responsibility. On the 21st Courtenay was released from the Tower. Gardiner was offered liberty, but he waited to accept it from the queen's own hand. He rejoined the council, however, and on the first or second day of his return to the board, he agitated their deliberations by requiring the restoration of his house in Southwark, which had been appropriated to the Marquis of Northampton, and by reminding Pembroke that he was in possession of estates which had been stolen from the See of Winchester.

On the 25th Northumberland and Lord Ambrose Dudley were brought in from Cambridge, escorted by Grey and Arundel, with four hundred of the guard. Detachments of troops were posted all along the streets from Bishopsgate, where the duke would enter, to the Tower, to prevent the mob from tearing him in pieces. It was but twelve days since he had ridden out from that gate in the splendour of his power; he was now assailed from all sides with yells and execrations; bareheaded, with cap in hand, he bowed to the crowd as he rode on, as if to win some compassion from them; but so recent a humility could find no favour. His scarlet cloak was plucked from his back; the only sounds which greeted his ears were, "Traitor, traitor, death to the traitor!" He hid his face, sick at heart with shame, and Lord Ambrose, at the gate of the Tower, was seen to burst into tears. [67] Edwin Sandys, Northampton, Ridley, Lord Robert Dudley, the offending judges Cholmley and Montague, with many others, followed in the few next days. Montague had protested to the queen that he had acted only under compulsion, but his excuses were not fully received. Lady Northumberland went to Newhall to beg for mercy for her sons, but Mary refused to admit her. [68]

In general, however, there was no desire to press hard upon the prisoners. Few had been guilty in the first degree; in the second degree so many were guilty, that all could not be punished, and to make exceptions would be unjust and invidious. The emperor recommended a general pardon, from which the principal offenders only should be excluded, and Mary herself was as little inclined to harshness. Her present desire was to forget all that had passed, and take possession of her power for the objects nearest to her heart. Her chief embarrassment for the moment was from the overloyalty of her subjects. The old-fashioned lords and country gentlemen who had attended her with their retainers from Norfolk, remained encamped round Newhall, unable to persuade themselves that they could leave her with safety in the midst of the men who had been the ministers of the usurpation. [69]

Her closest confidence the queen reserved for Renard. On the 28th of July she sent for him at midnight. On the 2nd of August he was again with her, and the chief subject of her thoughts was still the funeral. "She could not have her brother committed to the ground like a dog," she said. While her fortunes were uncertain, she allowed Renard to promise for her that she would make no changes in religion, but "she had now told the lords distinctly that she would not recognise any of the laws which had been passed in the minority, [70] and she intended to act boldly; timidity would only encourage the people to be insolent;" "the lords were all quarrelling among themselves, and accusing one another; she could not learn the truth on any point of the late conspiracy; she did not know who were guilty or who were innocent; and, amidst the distracted advices which were urged upon her, she could not tell whether she could safely venture to London or not; but outward acquiescence in the course which she chose to follow she believed that she could compel, and she would govern as God should direct her. The emperor, she added, had written to her about her marriage, not specifying any particular person, but desiring her to think upon the subject. She had never desired to marry while princess, nor did she desire it now;

but if it were for the interests of the church, she would do whatever he might advise."

On this last point Renard knew more of the emperor's intentions than Mary, and was discreetly silent; on other point he used his influence wisely. He constrained her, with Charles's arguments, to relinquish her burial scheme. "Edward, as a heretic, should have a heretic funeral at Westminster Abbey; she need not be present, and might herself have a mass said for him in the Tower. As to removing to London, in his opinion she had better go thither at once, take possession of her throne, and send Northumberland to trial. Her brother's body ought to be examined also, that it might be ascertained whether he had been poisoned; and if poisoned, by whom and for what purpose." [71]

Mary rarely paused upon a resolution. Making up her mind that, as Renard said, it would be better for her to go to London, she set out thither the following day, Thursday, the 3rd of August. Excitement lent to her hard features an expression almost of beauty, [72] as she rode in the midst of a splendid cavalcade of knights and nobles. Elizabeth, escorted by two thousand horse and a retinue of ladies, was waiting to receive her outside the gates. The first in her congratulations, after the proclamation, yet fearful of giving offence, Elizabeth had written to ask if it was the queen's pleasure that she should appear in mourning; but the queen would have no mourning, nor would have others wear it in her presence. The sombre colours which of late years had clouded the court were to be banished at once and for ever; and with the dark colours, it seemed for a time as if old dislikes and suspicions were at the same time to pass away. The sisters embraced; the queen was warm and affectionate, kissing all the ladies in Elizabeth's train; and side by side the daughters of Henry VIII. rode through Aldgate at seven in the evening, amidst the shouts of the people, the thunder of cannon, and pealing of church bells. [73] At the Tower gates the old Duke of Norfolk, Gardiner, Courtenay, and the Duchess of Somerset were seen kneeling as Mary approached. "These are my prisoners," she said as she alighted from her horse, and stooped and kissed them. Charmed by the enthusiastic reception and by the pleasant disappointment of her anxieties, she could find no room for hard thoughts of any one; so far was she softened, Renard wrote, that she could hardly be brought to consent to the necessary execution of justice. Against Northumberland himself she had no feeling of vindictiveness, and was chiefly anxious that he should be attended by a confessor; Northampton was certainly to be pardoned; Suffolk was already free; Northumberland should be spared, if possible; and, as to Lady Jane, justice forbade, she said, that an innocent girl should suffer for the crimes of others. [74]

The emperor had recommended mercy; but he had not advised a general indemnity, as Renard made haste to urge. The imperialist conception of clemency differed from the queen's; and the same timidity which had first made the ambassadors too prudent, now took the form of measured cruelty. Renard entreated that Lady Jane should not be spared; "conspirators required to be taught that for the principals in treason there was but one punishment; the duke must die, and the rival queen and her husband must die with him." "We set before her"—Renard's own hand is the witness against him—"the examples of Maximus and his son Victor, both executed by the Emperor Theodosius; Maximus, because he had usurped the purple; Victor, because, as the intended heir of his father, he might have been an occasion of danger had he lived." [75]

Looking also, as Renard was already doing, on the scenes which were around him, chiefly or solely as they might affect the interests of his master's son, he had been nervously struck by the entourage which surrounded Elizabeth and the popularity which she, as well as the queen, was evidently enjoying.

Elizabeth, now passing into womanhood, was the person to whom the affections of the liberal party in England most definitely tended. She was the heir-presumptive to the crown; in matters of religion she was opposed to the mass, and opposed as decidedly to factious and dogmatic Protestantism; while from the caution with which she had kept aloof from political entanglements, it was clear that her brilliant intellectual abilities were not her only or her most formidable gifts. Already she shared the favour of the people with the queen. Let Mary offend them (and in the intended marriage offence would unquestionably have to be given), their entire hearts might be transferred to her. The public finger had pointed to Courtenay as the husband which England desired for the queen. When Courtenay should be set aside by Mary, he might be accepted by Elizabeth; and Elizabeth, it was rumoured, looked upon him with an eye of favour. [76] On all accounts, therefore, Elizabeth was dangerous. She was a figure on the stage whom Renard would gladly see removed; and a week or two later he bid Mary look to her, watch her, and catch her tripping if good fortune would so permit: "it was better to prevent than to be prevented." [77]

The queen did not close her ears to these evil whispers; but for the first few days after she came to the Tower her thoughts were chiefly occupied with religion, and her first active step was to release and to restore to their sees the deprived and imprisoned bishops. The first week in August, Ponet, by royal order, was ejected from Winchester, Ridley from London, and Scory from Chichester. The See of Durham was reconstituted. Tunstal, Day, and Heath were set at liberty, and returned to their dioceses. The Bishop of Ely was deposed from the chancellorship, and the seals were given to Gardiner. "On the 5th of August," says the *Grey Friars' Chronicle*, "at seven o'clock at night, Edmond Bonner came home from the Marshalsea like a bishop, and all the people by the wayside bade him welcome home, both man and woman, and as many of the women as might kissed him; and so he came to Paul's, and knelt on the steps, and said his prayers, and the people rang the bells for joy." [78]

While Mary was repairing acts of injustice, Gardiner, with Sir William Petre, was looking into the public accounts. The debts of the late government had been reduced, the currency unconsidered, to £190,000. [79] A doubt had been raised whether, after the attempt to set aside the succession, the queen was bound to take the responsibility of these obligations, but Mary preferred honour to convenience; she promised to pay everything as soon as possible. Further, there remain, partly in Gardiner's hand, a number of hasty notes, written evidently in these same first weeks of Mary's reign, which speak nobly for the intentions with which both Mary and himself were setting generally to work. The expenses of the household were to be reduced to the scale of Henry VII., or the early years of Henry VIII.; the garrisons at Berwick and Calais were to be placed on a more economical footing, the navy reduced, the irregular guard dismissed or diminished. Bribery was to be put an end to in the courts of Westminster, at quarter sessions, and among justices of the peace; "the laws were to be restored to their authority without suffering any matters to be ordered otherwise than as the laws should appoint." [80] These first essentials having been attended to, the famous or infamous book of sales, grants, and exchanges of the crown lands was to be looked into; the impropriation of benefices was to cease, and decency to be restored to the parish churches, where the grooms and gamekeepers should give way to competent ministers; economy, order, justice, and reverence were to heal the canker of profligate profanity which had eaten too long into the moral life of England.

In happier times Mary might have been a worthy queen, and Gardiner an illustrious minister; [81] but the fatal superstition which confounded religion with orthodox opinion was too strong for both of them.

Edward's body was meanwhile examined. The physicians reported that without doubt he had died of poison, and there was a thought of indicting the Duke of Northumberland for his murder: but it was relinquished on further inquiry; the poison, if the physicians were right, must have been administered by negligence or accident. The corpse was then buried (August 6) with the forms of the Church of England at Westminster Abbey; the Archbishop of Canterbury, who had so far been left at liberty, read the service; it was the last and saddest function of his public ministry which he was destined to perform. Simultaneously, as Mary had determined, requiems were chanted in the Tower Chapel; and Gardiner, in the presence of the queen and four hundred persons, sung the mass for the dead with much solemnity. The ceremony was, however, injured by a misfortune; after the gospel the incense was carried round, and the chaplain who bore it was married; Doctor Weston, who was afterwards deprived of the deanery of Windsor for adultery, darted forward and snatched the censer out of the chaplain's hand. "Shamest thou not to do thine office," he said, "having a wife, as thou hast? The queen will not be censed by such as thou." [82] Nor was scandal the worst part of it. Elizabeth had been requested to attend, and had refused; angry murmurs and curses against the Bishop of Winchester were heard among the yeomen of the guard; while the queen made no secret of her desire that the example which she had set should be imitated. Renard trembled for the consequences; Noailles anticipated a civil war; twenty thousand men, the latter said, would lose their lives before England would be cured of heresy; [83] yet Mary had made a beginning, and as she had begun she was resolved that others should continue.

In the Tower she felt her actions under restraint. She was still surrounded by thousands of armed men, the levies of Derby and Hastings, the retainers of Pembroke and Arundel and Bedford; the council were spies upon her actions; the sentinels at the gates were a check upon her visitors. She could receive no one whose business with her was not made public to the lords, and whose reception they were not pleased to sanction; even Renard was for a time excluded from her, and in her anxiety to see him she suggested that he might come to her in disguise. [84] Such a thraldom was irksome and inconvenient. She had broken the promise which Renard had been allowed to make for her about religion; she had been troubled, it is easy to believe, with remonstrances, to which she was not likely to have answered with temper; Pembroke absented himself from the presence; he was required to retire and to reduce the number of his followers; the quarrels which began while the queen was at Newhall broke out with worse violence than ever; Lord Derby complained to Renard that those who had saved her crown were treated with neglect, while men like Arundel, Bedford, and Pembroke, who had been parties to the treasons against her, remained in power; Lord Russell was soon after placed under arrest; Pembroke and Winchester were ordered to keep their houses, and the court was distracted with suspicion, discord, and uncertainty. [85]

From such a scene Mary desired to escape to some place where she could be at least mistress of her own movements; her impatience was quickened by a riot at St. Bartholomew's, where a priest attempted to say mass; and on Saturday, the 12th of August, she removed to Richmond.

Her absence encouraged the insubordination of the people. On Sunday, the 13th, another priest was attacked at the altar; the vestments were torn from his back, and the chalice snatched from his hands. Bourne, whom the queen had appointed her chaplain, preached at Paul's Cross. A crowd of refugees and English fanatics had collected round the pulpit; and when he spoke something in praise of Bonner, and said that he had been unjustly imprisoned, [86] yells rose of "Papist, Papist! Tear him down!" A dagger was hurled at the preacher, swords were drawn, the mayor attempted to interfere, but he could not make his way through the dense mass of the rioters; and Bourne would have paid for his rashness with his life had not Courtenay, who was a popular favourite, with his mother, the Marchioness of Exeter, thrown themselves on the pulpit steps, while Bradford sprung to his side, and kept the people back till he could be carried off.

But the danger did not end there. The Protestant orators sounded the alarm through London. Meetings were held, and inflammatory placards were scattered about the streets. If religion was to be tampered with, men were heard to say, it was better at once to fetch Northumberland from the Tower.

Uncertain on whom she could rely, Mary sent for Renard (August 16), who could only repeat his former cautions, and appeal to what had occurred in justification of them. He undertook to pacify Lord Derby; but in the necessity to which she was so soon reduced of appealing to him, a foreigner, in her emergencies, he made her feel that she could not carry things with so high a hand. She had a rival in the Queen of Scots, beyond her domestic enemies, whom her wisdom ought to fear; she would ruin herself if she flew in the face of her subjects; and he prevailed so far with her that she promised to take no further steps till the meeting of parliament. After a consultation with the mayor, she drew up a hasty proclamation, granting universal toleration till further orders, forbidding her Protestant and Catholic subjects to interrupt each other's services, and prohibiting at the same time all preaching on either side without licence from herself.

Being on the spot, the ambassador took the opportunity of again trying Mary's disposition upon the marriage question. His hopes had waned since her arrival in London; he had spoken to Paget, who agreed that an alliance with the Prince of Spain was the most splendid which the queen could hope for; but the time was inopportune, and the people were intensely hostile. The exigencies of the position, he thought, might oblige the queen to yield to wishes which she could not oppose, and accept Lord Courtenay; or possibly her own inclination might set in the same direction; or, again, she might wish to renew her early engagement with the emperor himself. The same uncertainty had been felt at Brussels; the Bishop of Arras, therefore, had charged Renard to feel his way carefully and make no blunder. If the queen inclined to the emperor, he might speak of Philip as more eligible; if she fancied Courtenay, it would be useless to interfere—she would only resent his opposition. [87] Renard obeyed his instructions, and the result was reassuring. When the ambassador mentioned the word "marriage," the queen began to smile significantly, not once, but many times; she plainly liked the topic: plainly, also, her thoughts were not turning in the direction of any English husband; she spoke of her rank, and of her unwillingness to condescend to a subject; Courtenay, the sole remaining representative of the White Rose except the Poles, was the only Englishman who could in any way be thought suitable for her; but she said that she expected the emperor to provide a consort for her, and that, being a woman, she could not make the first advances. Renard satisfied himself from her manner that, if the Prince of Spain was proposed, the offer would be most entirely welcome. [88]

The trials of the conspirators were now resolved upon. The queen was determined to spare Lady Jane Grey, in spite of all which Renard could urge; but the state of London showed that the punishment of the really guilty could no longer be safely delayed. On this point all parties in the council were agreed. On Friday, the 18th of August, therefore, a court of peers was formed in Westminster Hall, with the aged Duke of Norfolk for High Steward, to try John Dudley Duke of Northumberland, the Earl of Warwick, and the Marquis of Northampton for high treason. Forty-four years before, as the curious remarked, the father of Norfolk had sat on the commission which tried the father of Northumberland for the same crime.

The indictments charged the prisoners with levying war against their lawful sovereign. Northumberland, who was called first to the bar, pleaded guilty of the acts which were laid against him, but he submitted two points to the consideration of the court.

1. Whether, having taken the field with a warrant under the Great Seal, he could be lawfully accused of treason.

2. Whether those peers from whom he had received his commission, and by whose letters he had been directed in what he had done, could sit upon his trial as his judges.

The Great Seal, he was answered briefly, was the seal of a usurper, and could convey no warrant to him. If the lords were as guilty as he said, yet, "so long as no attainder was on record against them, they were persons able in law to pass upon any trial, and not to be challenged but at the prince's pleasure." [89]

The duke bowed and was silent.

Northampton and Warwick came next, and, like Northumberland, confessed to the indictment. Northampton, however, pleaded in his defence, that he had held no public office during the crisis; that he had not been present at the making of Edward's device, and had been amusing himself hunting in the country. [90] Warwick, with proud sadness, said merely, that he had followed his father, and would share his father's fortunes; if his property was confiscated, he hoped that his debts would be paid. [91]

But Northampton had indisputably been in the field with the army, and, as his judges perfectly well knew, had been, with Suffolk, the Duke's uniform supporter in his most extreme measures; the queen had resolved to pardon him; but the court could not recognise his excuse. Norfolk rose, in a few words pronounced the usual sentence, and broke his wand; the cold glimmering edge of the Tower axe was turned towards the prisoners, and the peers rose. Northumberland, before he was led away, fell upon his knees; his children were young, he said, and had acted under orders from himself; to them let the queen show mercy; for himself he had his peace to make with Heaven; he entreated for a few days of life, and the assistance of a confessor; if two of the council would come to confer with him, he had important secrets of state to communicate; and, finally, he begged that he might die by the axe like a nobleman. [92]

On the 19th, Sir John and Sir Henry Gates, Sir Andrew Dudley, and Sir Thomas Palmer were tried before a special commission. Dudley had gone with the treasonable message to France; the three others were the boldest and most unscrupulous of the Duke's partisans, while Palmer was also especially hated for his share in the death of Somerset. These four also pleaded guilty, and were sentenced, Palmer only scornfully telling the commissioners that they were traitors as well as he, and worse than he. [93]

Seven had been condemned; three only, the duke, Sir John Gates, and Palmer, were to suffer.

Crime alone makes death terrible: in the long list of victims whose bloody end, at stake or scaffold, the historian of England in the sixteenth century has to relate, two only showed signs of cowardice, and one of those was a soldier and a nobleman, who, in a moment of extreme peril, four years before, had kissed swords with his comrades, and had sworn to conquer the insurgents at Norwich, or die with honour.

The Duke of Northumberland, who since that time had lived very emphatically without God in the world, had not lived without religion. He had affected religion, talked about religion, played with religion, till fools and flatterers had told him that he was a saint; and now, in his extreme need, he found that he had trifled with forms and words, till they had grown into a hideous hypocrisy. The Infinite of death was opening at his feet, and he had no faith, no hope, no conviction, but only a blank and awful horror, and perhaps he felt that there was nothing left for him but to fling himself back in agony into the open arms of superstition. He had asked to speak with some member of the council; he had asked for a confessor. In Gardiner, Bishop of Winchester, he found both.

After the sentence Gardiner visited him in the Tower, where he poured out his miserable story; he was a Catholic, he said, he always had been a Catholic; he had believed nothing of all the doctrines for which he had pretended to be so zealous under Edward. "Alas!" he cried, "is there no help for me?" "Let me live but a little longer to do penance for my many sins." Gardiner's heart was softened at the humiliating spectacle; he would speak to the queen, he said, and he did speak, not wholly without success; he may have judged rightly, that the living penitence of the Joshua of the Protestants would have been more useful to the church than his death. [94] Already Mary had expressed a wish that, if possible, the wretched man should be spared; and he would have been allowed to live, except for the reiterated protests of Renard in his own name and in the emperor's.

It was decided at last that he should die; and a priest was assigned him to prepare his soul. Doctor Watts or Watson, the same man whom Cranmer long ago had set in the stocks at Canterbury, took charge of Palmer and the rest—to them, as rough soldiers, spiritual consolation from a priest of any decent creed was welcome.

The executions were fixed originally for Monday, the 21st; but the duke's conversion was a triumph to the Catholic cause too important not to be dwelt upon a little longer. Neither Northampton, Warwick, Andrew Dudley, or Sir Henry Gates were aware that they were to be respited, and, as all alike availed themselves of the services of a confessor and the forms of the Catholic faith, their compliance could be made an instrument of a public and edifying lesson. The lives of those who were to suffer were prolonged for twenty-four hours. On Monday morning "certain of the citizens of London" were requested to be in attendance at the Tower chapel, where Northumberland, Northampton, Dudley, Henry Gates, and Palmer were brought in; and, "first kneeling down, every one of them, upon his knees, they heard mass, saying devoutly, with the bishop, [95] every one of them, *Confiteor*."

"After the mass was done, the duke rose up, and looked back upon my lord marquis, and came unto him, asking them all forgiveness, the one after the other, upon their knees, one to another; and the one did heartily forgive the other. And then they came, every one of them, before the altar, every one of them kneeling, and confessing to the bishop that they were the same men in the faith according as they had confessed to him before, and that they all would die in the Catholic faith." When they had all received the sacrament, they rose and turned to the people, and the duke said: —

"Truly, good people, I profess here before you all, that I have received the sacrament according to the true Catholic faith: and the plague that is upon the realm and upon us now is that we have erred from the faith these sixteen years; and this I protest unto you all from the bottom of my heart."

Northampton, with the rest, "did affirm the same with weeping tears." [96]

Among the spectators were observed the sons of the Duke of Somerset.

In exhibiting to the world the humiliation of the professors of the gospel, the Catholic party enjoyed a pardonable triumph. Northumberland, in playing a part in the pageant, was hoping to save his wretched life. When it was over he wrote (August 22) a passionate appeal to Arundel.

"Alas, my lord," he said, "is my crime so heinous as no redemption but my blood can wash away the spots thereof? An old proverb there is, and that most true — A living dog is better than a dead lion; oh that it would please her good grace to give me life, yea, the life of a dog, if I might but live and kiss her feet, and spend both life and all in her honourable service."

But Arundel could not save him — would not have saved him, perhaps, had he been able — and he had only to face the end with such resolution as he could command.

The next morning, at nine o'clock, Warwick and Sir John Gates heard mass in the Tower chapel; the two Seymours were again present with Courtenay: and before Gates received the sacrament, he said a few words of regret to the latter for his long imprisonment, of which he admitted himself in part the cause. [97] On leaving the chapel Warwick was taken back to his room, and learned that he was respited. Gates joined Palmer, who was walking with Watson in the garden, and talking with the groups of gentlemen who were collected there. Immediately after, the duke was brought out. "Sir John," he said to Gates, "God have mercy on us; forgive me as I forgive you, although you and your council have brought us hither." "I forgive you, my lord," Gates answered, "as I would be forgiven; yet it was you and your authority that was the only original cause of all." They bowed each. The duke passed on, and the procession moved forward to Tower Hill.

The last words of a worthless man are in themselves of little moment; but the effect of the dying speech of Northumberland lends to it an artificial importance. Whether to the latest moment he hoped for his life, or whether, divided between atheism and superstition, he thought, if any religion was true, Romanism was true, and it was prudent not to throw away a chance, who can tell? At all events, he mounted the scaffold with Heath, the Bishop of Worcester, at his side; and then deliberately said to the crowd, that his rebellion and his present fall were owing to the false preachers who had led him to err from the Catholic faith of Christ; the fathers and the saints had ever agreed in one doctrine; the present generation were the first that had dared to follow their private opinions; and in England and in Germany, where error had taken deepest root, there had followed war, famine, rebellion, misery, tokens all of them of God's displeasure. Therefore, as they loved their country, as they valued their souls, he implored his hearers to turn, all of them, and turn at once, to the church which they had left; in which church he, from the bottom of his heart, avowed his own steadfast belief. For himself he called them all to witness that he died in the one true Catholic faith; to which, if he had been brought sooner, he would not have been in his present calamity.

He then knelt; "I beseech you all," he said again, "to believe that I die in the Catholic faith." He repeated the *Miserere* psalm, the psalm *De Profundis*, and the *Paternoster*. The executioner, as usual, begged his pardon. "I have deserved a thousand deaths," he muttered. He made the sign of the cross upon the saw-dust, and kissed it, then laid down his head, and perished.

The shame of the apostasy shook down the frail edifice of the Protestant constitution, to be raised again in suffering, as the first foundations of it had been laid, by purer hands and nobler spirits. [98] In his better years Northumberland had been a faithful subject and a fearless soldier, and, with a master's hand over him, he might have lived with integrity, and died with honour. Opportunity tempted his ambition—ambition betrayed him into crime—and, given over to his lower nature, he climbed to the highest round of the political ladder, to fall and perish like a craven. He was one of those many men who can follow worthily, yet cannot lead; and the virtue of the beginning was not less real than the ignominy of the end.

Gates was the second sufferer. He, too, spoke in the same key. He had been a great reader of Scripture, he said, but he had not read it to be edified, but to be seditious—to dispute, to interpret it after his private affection; to him, therefore, the honey had been poison, and he warned all men how they followed his ill example; God's holy mysteries were no safe things to toy or play with. Gates, in dying, had three strokes of an axe;—"Whether," says an eye-witness, [99] "it was by his own request or no was doubtful"—remarkable words: as if the everlasting fate of the soul depended on its latest emotion, and repentance could be intensified by the conscious realisation of death.

Last came Sir Thomas Palmer, in whom, to judge by his method of taking leave of life, there was some kind of nobleness. It was he who led the cavalry forlorn hope, at Haddington, when the supplies were thrown in for the garrison.

He leapt upon the scaffold, red with the blood of his companions. "Good morning to you all, good people," he said, looking round him with a smile; "ye come hither to see me die, and to see what news I have; marry, I will tell you; I have seen more in yonder terrible place [he pointed towards the Tower] than ever I saw before throughout all the realms that ever I wandered in; for there I have seen God, I have seen the world, and I have seen myself; and when I beheld my life, I saw nothing but slime and clay, full of corruption; I saw the world nothing else but vanity, and all the pleasures and treasures thereof nought worth; I saw God omnipotent, his power infinite, his mercy incomprehensible; and when I saw this, I most humbly submitted myself unto him, beseeching him of mercy and pardon, and I trust he hath forgiven me; for he called me once or twice before, but I would not turn to him, but even now by this sharp kind of death he hath called me unto him. I trust the wings of his mercy shall spread over me and save me; and I do here confess, before you all, Christ to be the very Son of God the Father, born of the Virgin Mary, which came into the world to fulfil the law for us, and to bear our offences on his back, and suffered his passion for our redemption, by the which I trust to be saved."

Like his fellow-sufferers, Palmer then said a few prayers, asked the queen's forgiveness, knelt, and died.

Stunned by the apostasy on the scaffold of the man whom they had worshipped as a prophet, the ultra-faction among the Protestants became now powerless. The central multitude, whose belief was undefined, yielded to the apparent sentence of Heaven upon a cause weakened by unsuccessful treason, and disavowed in his death by its champion. Edward had died on the anniversary of the execution of More; God, men said, had visited his people, and "the Virgin Mary" had been set upon the throne for their redemption. [100] Dr. Watson, on the 20th of August, preached at Paul's Cross under a guard of soldiers; on the 24th, two days after the scene on Tower Hill, so little was a guard necessary, that mass was said in St. Paul's Church in Latin, with matins and vespers. The crucifix was replaced in the roodloft, the high altar was re-decorated, the real presence was defended from the pulpit, and, except from the refugees, not a murmur was heard. [101] Catching this favourable opportunity, the queen charmed the country with the announcement that the second portion of the last subsidy granted by Parliament should not be collected; she gave her word that the currency at the earliest moment should be thoroughly restored;

while she gained credit on all sides for the very moderate vengeance with which she appeared to be contenting herself. Ridley only, Renard wrote, on the 9th of September, would now be executed; the other prisoners were to be all pardoned. The enthusiasm was slightly abated, indeed, when it was announced that their forgiveness would not be wholly free. Montague and Bromley, on their release from the Tower, were fined £7000 a-piece; Suffolk, Northampton, and other noblemen and gentlemen, as their estates would bear. But, to relieve the burdens of the people at the expense of those who had reaped the harvest of the late spoliations was, on the whole, a legitimate retribution; the moneyed men were pleased with the recognition of Edward's debts, and provided a loan of 25,000 crowns for the present necessities of the government. London streets rang again with shouts of "God Save the Queen;" and Mary recovered a fresh instalment of popularity to carry her a few steps further. [102]

The refugees were the first difficulty. They were too numerous to imprison; and the most influential among them — men like Peter Martyr — having come to England on the invitation of the late government, it was neither just nor honourable to hand them over to their own sovereigns. But both Mary and her Flemish adviser were anxious to see them leave the country as quickly as possible. The emperor recommended a general intimation to be given out, that criminals of all kinds taking refuge in England would be liable to seizure, offences against religion being neither specially mentioned nor specially excepted. [103] The foreign preachers were ordered to depart by proclamation; and Peter Martyr, who had left Oxford, and was staying with Cranmer at Lambeth, expecting an arrest, received, instead of it, a safe-conduct, of which he instantly availed himself. The movements of others were quickened with indirect menaces; while Gardiner told Renard, with much self-satisfaction, that a few messages desiring some of them to call upon him at his house had given them wings. [104]

Finding her measures no longer opposed, the queen refused next to recognise the legality of the marriage of the clergy. Married priests should either leave their wives or leave their benefices; and on the 29th of August, Gardiner, Bonner, Day, and Tunstal, late prisoners in the Tower, were appointed commissioners to examine into the conditions of their episcopal brethren. Convocation was about to meet, and must undergo a preliminary purification. Unhappy Convocation! So lately the supreme legislative body in the country, it was now patched, clipped, mended, repaired, or altered, as the secular government put on its alternate hues. The Protestant bishops had accepted their offices on Protestant terms — *Quamdiu se bene gesserint,* on their good behaviour; and, with the assistance of so pliant a clause, a swift clearance was effected. Barlow, to avoid expulsion, resigned Bath. Paul Bush retreated from Bristol. Hooper, ejected from Worcester by the restoration of Heath, was deprived of Gloucester for heresy and marriage, and, being a dangerous person, was committed on the 1st of September to the Fleet. Ferrars, of St. David's, left in prison by Northumberland for other pretended offences, was deprived on the same grounds, but remained in confinement. Bird, having a wife, was turned out of Chester; Archbishop Holgate out of York. Coverdale, Ridley, Scory, and Ponet had been already disposed of. The bench was wholesomely swept. [105]

The English Protestant preachers seeing that priests everywhere held themselves licensed *ex officio* to speak as they pleased from the pulpit, began themselves also, in many places, to disobey the queen's proclamation. They were made immediately to feel their mistake, and were brought to London to the Tower, the Marshalsea, or the Fleet, to the cells left vacant by their opponents. Among the rest came one who had borne no share in the late misdoings, but had long foreseen the fate to which those doings would bring him and many more. When Latimer was sent for, he was at Stamford. On the 4th of September six hours' notice was given him of his intended arrest; and so obviously his escape was desired, that the pursuivant who brought the warrant left him to obey it at his leisure; his orders, he said, were not to wait. But Latimer had business in England. While the fanatics who had provoked the catastrophe were slinking across the Channel from its consequences, Latimer determined to stay at home, and help to pay the debts which they had incurred. He went quietly to London, appeared before the council, where his "demeanour" was what they were pleased to term "seditious," [106] and was committed to the Tower. "What, my friend," he said to a warder who was an old acquaintance there, "how do you? I am come to be your neighbour again." Sir Thomas Palmer's rooms in the garden were assigned for his lodging. In the winter he was left without a fire, and, growing infirm, he sent a message to the Lieutenant of the Tower to look better after him, or he should give him the slip yet. [107]

And there was another besides Latimer who would not fly when the chance was left open to him. Archbishop Cranmer had continued at Lambeth unmolested, yet unpardoned; his conduct with respect to the letters patent had been more upright than the conduct of any other member of the council by whom they had been signed; and on this ground, therefore, an exception could not easily be made in his disfavour. But his friends had interceded vainly to obtain the queen's definite forgiveness for him; treason might be forgotten; the divorce of Catherine of Arragon could never be forgotten. So he waited on, watching the reaction gathering strength, and knowing well the point to which it tended. In the country the English service was set aside and the mass restored with but little disturbance. No force had been used or needed; the Catholic majorities among the parishioners had made the change for themselves. The archbishop's friends came to him for advice; he recommended them to go abroad; he was urged to go himself while there was time; he said, "it would be in no ways fitting for him to go away, considering the post in which he was; and to show that he was not afraid to own all the changes that were by his means made in religion in the last reign." [108]

Neither was it fitting for him to sit by in silence. The world, misconstruing his inaction, believed him false like Northumberland; the world reported that he had restored mass at Canterbury; the world professed to have ascertained that he had offered to sing a requiem at Edward's funeral. In the second week of September, therefore, he made a public offer, in the form of a letter to a friend, to defend the communion service, and all the alterations for which he was responsible, against any one who desired to impugn them; he answered the stories against himself with a calm denial; and, though the letter was not printed, copies in manuscript were circulated through London so numerously that the press, said Renard, would not have sent out more. [109]

The challenge was answered by an immediate summons before the council; the archbishop was accused of attempting to excite sedition among the people, and was forthwith committed to the Tower to wait, with Ridley and Latimer, there, till his fate should be decided on. Meantime the eagerness with which the country generally availed itself of the permission to restore the Catholic ritual, proved beyond a doubt that, except in London and a few large towns, the popular feeling was with the queen. The English people had no affection for the Papacy. They did not wish for the re-establishment of the religious orders, or the odious domination of the clergy. But the numerical majority among them did desire a celibate priesthood, the ceremonies which the customs of centuries had sanctified, and the ancient faith of their fathers, as reformed by Henry VIII. The rights of conscience had found no more consideration from the Protestant doctrinalists than from the most bigoted of the persecuting prelates; and the facility with which the professors of the gospel had yielded to moral temptations, had for the time inspired moderate men with much distrust for them and for their opinions.

Could Mary have been contented to pursue her victory no further, she would have preserved the hearts of her subjects; and the reaction, left to complete its own tendencies, would in a few years, perhaps, have accomplished in some measure her larger desires. But few sovereigns have understood less the effects of time and forbearance. She was deceived by the rapidity of her first success; she flattered herself that, difficult though it might be, she could build up again the ruined hierarchy, could compel the holders of church property to open their hands, and could reunite the country to Rome. Before she had been three weeks on the throne, she had received, as will be presently mentioned, a secret messenger from the Vatican; and she had opened a correspondence with the pope, entreating him, as an act of justice to herself and to those who had remained true to their Catholic allegiance, to remove the interdict. [110]

Other actors in the great drama which was approaching were already commencing their parts.

Reginald Pole having attempted in vain to recover a footing in England on the accession of Edward, having seen his passionate expectations from the Council of Trent melt into vapour, and Germany confirmed in heresy by the Peace of Passau, was engaged, in the summer of 1553, at a convent on the Lago di Garda, in re-editing his book against Henry VIII., with an intended dedication to Edward, of whose illness he was ignorant. The first edition, on the failure of his attempt to raise a Catholic crusade against his country, had been withdrawn from circulation; the world had not received it favourably, and there was a mystery about the publication which it is difficult to unravel. In the interval between the first despatch of the book into England as a private letter in the summer of 1536, and the appearance of it in print at Rome in the winter of 1538-9, it was re-written, as I have already stated, enlarged, and divided into parts. In a letter of apology which Pole wrote to Charles V., in the summer or early autumn of 1538, [111] he spoke of that division as having been executed by himself; [112] he said that he had kept his book secret till the church had spoken; but Paul having excommunicated Henry, he could no longer remain silent; he dwelt at length on the history of the work which he was then editing, [113] and he sent a copy at the same time with a letter, or he wrote a letter with the intention of sending a copy, to James V. of Scotland. [114]

But Charles had refused to move; the book injured Henry not at all, and injured fatally those who were dear to Pole; he checked the circulation of the copies, and he declared to the Cardinal of Naples that it had been published only at the command of the pope — that his own anxiety had been for the suppression of it. [115] Thirteen years after this, however, writing to Edward VI., he forgot that he had described himself to Charles as being himself engaged in the publication; and he assured the young king that he had never thought of publishing the book, that he had abhorred the very thought of publishing it; that it was prepared, edited, and printed by his friends at Rome during his own absence; [116] now, at length, he found himself obliged in his own person to give it forth, because an edition was in preparation elsewhere from one of the earlier copies; and he selected the son of Henry as the person to whom he could most becomingly dedicate the libel against his father's memory.

Edward did not live to receive this evidence of Pole's good feeling. He died before the edition was completed; and as soon as Northumberland's failure and Mary's accession were known at Rome, England was looked upon in the Consistory as already recovered to the faith, and Pole was chosen by the unanimous consent of the cardinals as the instrument of the reconciliation. The account of the proclamation of the queen was brought to the Vatican on the 6th of August by a courier from Paris; the pope in tears of joy drew his commission and despatched it on the instant to the Lago di Garda; and on the 9th Pole himself wrote to Mary to say that he had been named legate, and waited her orders to fly to England. He still clung to his conviction that the revolution in all its parts had been the work of a small faction, and that he had but himself to set his foot upon the shore to be received with an ovation; his impulse was therefore to set out without delay; but the recollection, among other things, that he was attainted by act of parliament, forced him to delay unwillingly till he received formal permission to present himself.

Anxious for authentic information as to the state of England and the queen's disposition, Julius had before despatched also a secret agent, Commendone, afterwards a cardinal, with instructions to make his way to London to communicate with Mary, and if possible to learn her intentions from her own lips. Rapid movement was possible in Europe even with the roads of the sixteenth century. Commendone was probably sent from Rome as soon as Edward was known to be dead; he was in London, at all events, on the 8th of August, [117] disguised as an Italian gentleman in search of property which he professed had been bequeathed him by a kinsman. By the favour of Providence, [118] he fell in with an acquaintance, a returned Catholic refugee, who had a place in the household; and from this man he learnt that the queen was virtually a prisoner in the Tower, and that the heretics on the council allowed no one of whose business they disapproved to have access to her. Mary, however, was made acquainted with his arrival; a secret interview was managed, at which she promised to do her very best in the interests of the church; but she had still, she said, to conquer her kingdom, and Pole's coming, much as she desired it, was for the moment out of the question; before she could draw the spiritual sword she must have the temporal sword more firmly in her grasp, and she looked to marriage as the best means of strengthening herself. If she married abroad, she thought at that time of the emperor; if she accepted one of her subjects, she doubted—in her dislike of Courtenay—whether Pole might not return in a less odious capacity than that of Apostolic Legate; as the queen's intended husband the country might receive him; he had not yet been ordained priest, and deacon's orders, on a sufficient occasion, could perhaps be dispensed with. [119] The visit, or visits, were concealed even from Renard. Commendone was forbidden, under the strictest injunctions, to reveal what the queen might say to him, except to the pope or to Pole; and it is the more likely that she was serious in her expressions about the latter, from the care with which she left Renard in ignorance of Commendone's presence.

The papal messenger remained long enough to witness a rapid change in her position; he saw the restoration of the mass; he was in London at the execution, and he learnt the apostasy, of Northumberland; and he carried letters from Mary to the pope with assurances of fidelity, and entreaties for the absolution of the kingdom. But Mary was obliged to say, notwithstanding, that for the present she was in the power of the people, of whom the majority mortally detested the Holy See; that the lords of the council were in possession of vast estates which had been alienated from the church, and they feared their titles might be called in question; [120] and, although she agreed herself in all which Pole had urged (she had received his letter before Commendone left England), yet that, nevertheless, necessity acknowledged no law. Her heretical sister was in every one's mouth, and might at any moment take her place on the throne, and for the present, she said, to her deep regret, she could not, with prudence or safety, allow the legate to come to her.

The queen's letters were confirmed by Commendone himself; he had been permitted to confer in private with more than one good Catholic in the realm; and every one had given him the same assurances, [121] although he had urged upon them the opposite opinion entertained by Pole: [122] he had himself witnessed the disposition with which the people regarded Elizabeth, and he was satisfied that the queen's alarm on this head was not exaggerated. [123]

In opinions so emphatically given, the pope was obliged to acquiesce, and the same view was enforced upon him equally strongly by the emperor. Charles knew England tolerably well; he was acquainted perfectly well with the moral and intellectual unfitness of the intended legate for any office which required discretion; and Julius, therefore, was obliged to communicate to the eager cardinal the necessity of delay, and to express his fear that, by excess of zeal, he might injure the cause and alienate the well-affected queen. [124] Though Pole might not go to England, however, he might go, as he went before, to the immediate neighbourhood; he might repair to Flanders, with a nominal commission to mediate in the peace which was still hoped for. In Flanders, though the pope forbore to tell him so, he would be under the emperor's eyes and under the emperor's control, till the vital question of the queen's marriage had been disposed of, or till England was in a calmer humour.

About the marriage Charles was more anxious than ever; Pole was understood to have declined the honour of being a competitor; [125] Renard had informed the emperor of the present direction of the queen's own inclinations; and treating himself, therefore, as out of the question on the score of age and infirmities, he instructed his minister to propose the Prince of Spain as a person whom the religious and the political interests of the world alike recommended to her as a husband. The alliance of England, Spain, and Flanders would command a European supremacy; their united fleets would sweep the seas, and Scotland, deprived of support from France, must become an English province; while sufficient guarantees could be provided easily for the security of English liberties. These, in themselves, were powerful reasons; Renard was permitted to increase their cogency by promises of pensions, lands, and titles, or by hard money in hand, in whatever direction such liberality could be usefully employed. [126]

The external advantages of the connection were obvious; it recommended itself to the queen from the Spanish sympathies which she had contracted in her blood, and from the assistance which it promised to afford her in the great pursuit of her life. The proposal was first suggested informally. Mary affected to find difficulties; yet, if she raised objections, it was only to prolong the conversation upon a subject which delighted her. She spoke of her age; Philip was twenty-seven, she ten years older; she called him "boy;" she feared she might not be enough for him; she was unsusceptible; she had no experience in love; [127] with such other phrases, which Renard interpreted at their true importance. With the queen there would be no difficulty; with the council it was far otherwise. Lord Paget was the only English statesman who listened with any show of favour.

The complication of parties is not to be easily disentangled. Some attempt, however, may be partially successful.

The council, the peers, the Commons, the entire lay voices of England, liberal and conservative alike, were opposed to Rome; Gardiner was the only statesman in the country who thought a return to Catholic union practicable or desirable; while there was scarcely an influential family, titled or untitled, which was not, by grant or purchase, in possession of confiscated church property.

There was an equal unanimity in the dread that if Mary became the wife of a Spanish sovereign England would, like the Low Countries, sink into a provincial dependency; while, again, there was the utmost unwillingness to be again entangled in the European war; the French ambassador insisted that the emperor only desired the marriage to secure English assistance; and the council believed that, whatever promises might be made, whatever stipulations insisted on, such a marriage, sooner or later, would implicate them. The country was exhausted, the currency ruined, the people in a state of unexampled suffering, and the only remedy was to be looked for in quiet and public economy; there were attractions in the offer of a powerful alliance, but the very greatness of it added to their reluctance; they desired to isolate England from European quarrels, and marry their queen at home. With these opinions Paget alone disagreed, while Gardiner was loudly national.

On the other hand, though Gardiner held the restoration of the papal authority to be tolerable, yet he dreaded the return of Pole, as being likely to supersede him in the direction of the English Church; [128] the party who agreed with the chancellor about the marriage, and about Pole, disagreed with him about the pope; while Paget, who was in favour of the marriage, was with the lords on the supremacy, and, as the Romanising views of the queen became notorious, was inclining, with Arundel and Pembroke, towards the Protestants.

No wonder, therefore, that the whole council were in confusion and at cross purposes. No sooner were Charles's proposals definitely known than the entire machinery of the government was dislocated. Mary represented herself to Renard as without a friend whom she could trust; and the letters, both of Renard and Noailles, contain little else but reports how the lords were either quarrelling, or had, one after the other, withdrawn in disgust to their country houses. Now it was Pembroke that was gone, now Mason, now Paget; then Courtenay was a prisoner in his house; then Lord Winchester was forbidden to appear at court: the ministers were in distrust of each other and of their mistress; the queen was condemned to keep them in their offices because she durst not make them enemies; while the Stanleys, Howards, Talbots, and Nevilles were glooming apart, indignant at the neglect of their own claims.

The queen herself was alternately angry and miserable; by the middle of September Renard congratulated Charles on her growing ill-humour; the five Dudleys and Lady Jane, he hoped, would be now disposed of, and Elizabeth would soon follow.

Elizabeth's danger was great, and proceeded as much from her friend's indiscretion as from the hatred of her enemies. Every one who disliked the queen's measures, used Elizabeth's name. Renard was for ever hissing his suspicions in the queen's ear, and, unfortunately, she was a too willing listener—not, indeed, that Renard hated Elizabeth for her own sake, for he rather admired her—or for religion's sake, for he had a most statesmanlike indifference to religion; but he saw in her the queen's successful rival in the favour of the people, the heir-presumptive to the crown, whose influence would increase the further the queen travelled on the road on which he was leading her, and, therefore, an enemy who, if possible, should be destroyed. An opportunity of creating a collision between the sisters was not long wanting. The lords of the council were now generally present at mass in the royal chapel. Elizabeth, with Anne of Cleves, had as yet refused to appear. Her resistance was held to imply a sinister intention; and on the 2nd and 3rd of September the council were instructed to bring her to compliance. [129] Yet the days passed, the priest sang, and the heir to the crown continued absent. Gardiner, indeed, told Renard that she was not obdurate; he had spoken to her, and she had seemed to say that, if he could convince her, her objections would cease; [130] but they had not ceased so far; she did not attend. In the happiness of her first triumph Mary had treated Elizabeth like a sister, but her manner had relapsed into coldness; and the princess, at length, knowing how her name was made use of, requested a private interview, which, with difficulty, was granted. The sisters, each accompanied by a single lady, met in a gallery with a half-door between them. Elizabeth threw herself on her knees. She said that she perceived her majesty was displeased with her; she could not tell what the cause might be, unless it was religion; and for this, she said, she might be reasonably forgiven; she had been educated, as the queen was aware, in the modern belief, and she understood no other; if her majesty would send her books and teachers, she would read; she would listen; she could say no more.

Mary, at the moment, was delighted. Like a true Catholic, however, she insisted that obedience must precede faith; come to the mass, she said, and belief will be the reward of your submission; make your first trial on the mass of the Nativity of the Blessed Virgin. [131]

Elizabeth consented. She was present, but present reluctantly; pretending, as Renard said, to be ill; the next Sunday she was again absent. The queen, knowing the effect which her conduct would produce, again sent for her, and asked her earnestly what she really believed; the world said that, although she had complied once, her compliance was feigned, and that she had submitted out of fear; she desired to hear the truth. Elizabeth could reply merely that she had done as the queen had required her to do, with no ulterior purpose; if her majesty wished she would make a public declaration to that effect. [132] The queen was obliged to receive her answer; but she told Renard that her sister trembled as she spoke, and well, Renard said, he understood her agitation; she was the hope of the heretics, and the heretics were raising their heads; the Papists, they said, had had their day, but it was waning; if Elizabeth lived, England would again apostatise.

There was no difficulty in keeping the queen's jealousy alive against her sister. Courtenay was another offence in the eye of the ambassador, as the rival to Philip, who found favour with the English council. The queen affected to treat Courtenay as a child; she commanded him to keep to his house; she forbade him to dine abroad without special permission; the title of Earl of Devon was given to him, and he had a dress made for him to take his seat in, of velvet and gold, but the queen would not allow him to wear it: [133] and yet, to her own and the ambassador's mortification, she learnt that he affected the state of a prince; that he spoke of his marriage with her as certain; that certain prelates, Gardiner especially, encouraged his expectation, and one or more of them had knelt in his presence. [134] The danger had been felt from the first that, if she persisted in her fancy for the Prince of Spain, Courtenay might turn his addresses to Elizabeth; the lords would in that case fall off to his support, and the crown would fall from her head as easily as it had settled there.

More afflicting to Mary than these personal grievances was the pertinacity with which the council continued, in their public documents, to describe her as Head of the Church, the execrable title which was the central root of the apostasy. In vain she protested; the hateful form—indispensable till it was taken away by parliament—was thrust under her eyes in every paper which was brought to her for signature, and she was obliged to acknowledge the designation with her own hand and pen.

Amidst these anxieties, September wore away. Parliament was to open on the fifth of October, and either before or after the meeting the queen was to be crowned. The ceremony was an occasion of considerable agitation; Mary herself was alarmed lest the holy oil should have lost its efficacy through the interdict; and she entreated Renard to procure her a fresh supply from Flanders, blessed by the excellent hands of the Bishop of Arras. But the oil was not the gravest difficulty. As the rumour spread of the intended Spanish marriage, libellous handbills were scattered about London; the people said it should not be till they had fought for it. A disturbance at Greenwich, on the 25th of September, extended to Southwark, where Gardiner's house was attacked, [135] and a plot was discovered to murder him: in the day he wore a shirt of mail under his robes, and he slept with a guard of a hundred men. Threatening notices were even found on the floor of the queen's bedroom, left there by unknown hands. Noailles assured the lords that his own government would regard the marriage as little short of a declaration of war, so inevitably would war be the result of it; and Gardiner, who was unjustly suspected of being in the Spanish interest, desired to delay the coronation till parliament should have met; intending that the first act of the assembly should be to tie Mary's hands with a memorial which she could not set aside. She inherited under her father's will, by which her accession was made conditional on her marrying not without the consent of the council; parliament might remind her both of her own obligation to obey her father's injunctions, and of theirs to see that they were obeyed.

With the same object, though not with the same object only, the lords of the council supported the Bishop of Winchester. They proposed to alter the form of the coronation oath, and to bind the queen by an especial clause to maintain the independence of the English Church—a precaution, as it proved, not unnecessary—for the existing form was already inconvenient, and Mary was meditating how, when called on to swear to observe the laws and constitutions of the realm, she could introduce an adjective *sub silentio*; she intended to swear only that she would observe the JUST laws and constitutions. [136] But she looked with the gravest alarm to the introduction of more awkward phrases; if words were added which would be equivalent (as she would understand them) to a denial of Christ and his Church, she had resolved to refuse at all hazards. [137]

But her courage was not put to the test. The true grounds on which the delay of the coronation was desired could not be avowed. The queen was told that her passage through the streets would be unsafe until her accession had been sanctioned by parliament, and the act repealed by which she was illegitimatised. With Paget's help she faced down these objections, and declared that she would be crowned at once; she appointed the 1st of October for the ceremony; on the 28th of September she sent for the council to attempt an appeal to their generosity. She spoke to them at length of her past life and sufferings, of the conspiracy to set her aside, and of the wonderful Providence which had preserved her and raised her to the throne; her only desire, she said, was to do her duty to God and to her subjects; and she hoped, turning as she spoke, pointedly to Gardiner, that they would not forget their loyalty, and would stand by her in her extreme necessity. Observing them hesitate, she cried, "My lords, on my knees I implore you"—and flung herself on the ground at their feet. [138]

The most skilful acting could not have served Mary's purpose better than this outburst of natural emotion; the spectacle of their kneeling sovereign overcame for a time the scheming passions of her ministers; they were affected, burst into tears, and withdrew their opposition to her wishes. [139]

On the 30th, the procession from the Tower to Westminster through the streets was safely accomplished. The retinues of the lords protected the queen from insult, and London put on its usual outward signs of rejoicing; St. Paul's spire was rigged with yards like a ship's mast, an adventurous sailor sitting astride on the weathercock five hundred feet in the air: [140] there was no interruption; and the next day (October 1), Arras having sent the necessary unction, [141] the ceremony was performed at the Abbey without fresh burdens being laid on Mary's conscience.

The banquet in the great hall passed off with equal success; Sir Edward Dymocke, the champion, rode in and flung down his gage, and was listened to with becoming silence: on the whole, Mary's friends were agreeably disappointed; only Renard observed that, between the French ambassador and the Lady Elizabeth there seemed to be some secret understanding; the princess saluted Noailles as he passed her; Renard she would neither address nor look at—and Renard was told that she complained to Noailles of the weight of her coronet, and that Noailles "bade her have patience, and before long she would exchange it for a crown." [142]

The coronation was a step gained; it was one more victory, yet it produced no material alteration. Rome, and the Spanish marriage, remained as before, insoluble elements of difficulty; the queen, to her misfortune, was driven to rely more and more on Renard; and at this time she was so desperate and so ill-advised as to think of surrounding herself with an Irish bodyguard; she went so far as to send a commission to Sir George Stanley for their transport. [143]

The scheme was abandoned, but not because her relations with her own people were improved. Before parliament met, an anonymous pamphlet appeared by some English nobleman on the encroachments of the House of Austria, and on the treatment of other countries which had fallen through marriages into Austrian hands. In Lombardy and Naples every office of trust was described as held by a Spaniard; the Prince of Salerno was banished, the Prince of Benevento was a prisoner in Flanders, the Duke of Calabria a prisoner in Spain. Treating Mary's hopes of children as ridiculous, the writer pictured England, bound hand and foot, at the mercy of the insolent Philip, whose first step, on entering the country, would be to seize the Tower and the fleet, the next, to introduce a Spanish army and suppress the parliament. The free, glorious England of the Plantagenets would then be converted into a prostrate appanage of the dominions of Don Carlos. The pamphlet was but the expression of the universal feeling. Gardiner, indeed, perplexed between his religion and his country, for a few days wavered. Gardiner had a long debt to pay off against the Protestants, and a Spanish force, divided into garrisons for London and other towns, would assist him materially. [144] Partly, however, from attachment to Courtenay, partly from loyalty to his country, he shook off the temptation and continued to support the opposition. [145]

Mary, except for the cautious support of Paget, stood otherwise alone coquetting with her fancy, and played upon by the skilful Renard. The queen and the ambassador were incessantly together, and Philip was the never-tiring subject of conversation between them. She talked of his disposition. She had heard, she said, that he was proud; that he was inferior to his father in point of ability; and then he was young, and she had been told sad stories about him; if he was of warm temperament, he would not suit her at all, she said, considering the age at which she had arrived. [146] Moreover, when she was married, she must obey as God commanded; her husband, perhaps, might wish to place Spaniards in authority in England, and she would have to refuse; and that he would not like. To all of which, being the fluttering of the caught fly, Renard would answer that his highness was more like an angel than a man; his youth was in his favour, for he might live to see his child of age, and England had had too much experience of minorities. Life, he added remarkably, was shorter than it used to be; sixty was now a great age for a king; and as the world was, men were as mature at thirty as in the days of his grandfather they were considered at forty. [147] Then touching the constant sore—"her majesty," he said, "had four enemies, who would never rest till they had destroyed her or were themselves destroyed—the heretics, the friends of the late Duke of Northumberland, the courts of France and Scotland, and, lastly, her sister Elizabeth. Her subjects were restless, turbulent, and changeable as the ocean of which they were so fond; [148] the sovereigns of England had been only able to rule with a hand of iron, and with severities which had earned them the name of tyrants; [149] they had not spared the blood royal in order to secure their thrones, and she too must act as they had acted, leaning for support, meanwhile, on the arm of a powerful prince."

To these dark hints Mary ever listened eagerly—meantime she was harassed painfully from another quarter.

Reginald Pole, as might have been expected from his temperament, could ill endure the delay of his return to England. The hesitation of the queen and the objections of the emperor were grounded upon arguments which he assured himself were fallacious; the English nation, he continued to insist, were devoted to the Holy See; so far from being himself unpopular, the Cornish in the rebellion under Edward had petitioned for his recall, and had even designated him by the forbidden name of cardinal; they loved him and they longed for him; and, regarding himself as the chosen instrument of Providence to repair the iniquities of Henry VIII., he held the obstructions to his return not only to be mistaken, but to be impious. The duty of the returning prodigal was to submit; to lay aside all earthly considerations—to obey God, God's vicegerent the pope, and himself the pope's representative.

Mendoza had been sent by Charles to meet Pole on his way to Flanders, and reason him into moderation. In return the legate wrote himself to Charles's confessor, commanding him to explain to his master the sin which he was committing. "The objection to his going to England," as Pole understood, "was the supposed danger of an outbreak". Were the truth as the emperor feared, the queen's first duty would be, nevertheless, to God, her own soul, and the souls of the millions of her subjects who were perishing in separation from the church; for no worldly policy or carnal respect ought she to defer for a moment to apply a remedy to so monstrous a calamity. [150] But the danger was imaginary—or, rather, such danger as there was, arose from the opposite cause. The right of the queen to the throne did not rest on an act of parliament; it rested on her birth as the lawful child of the lawful marriage between Henry and Catherine of Arragon. Parliament, he was informed, would affirm the marriage legitimate, if nothing was said about the pope; but, unless the pope's authority was first recognised, parliament would only stultify itself; the papal dispensation alone made valid a connection which, if the pope had no power to dispense, was incestuous, and the offspring of it illegitimate. God had made the peaceful settlement of the kingdom dependent on submission to the Holy See, [151] and for parliament to interfere and give an opinion upon the subject would be but a fresh act of schism and disobedience.

The original letter, being in our own State Paper Office, was probably given by the confessor to Charles, and by Charles sent over to England. Most logical it was; so logical that it quite outwitted the intention of the writer. While it added to the queen's distress, it removed, nevertheless, all objections which might have been raised by the anti-papal party against the act to legitimatise her. So long as there was a fear that, by a repeal of the Act of Divorce between her father and mother, the pope's authority might indirectly be admitted, some difficulty was to be anticipated; as a new assertion of English independence, it could be carried with unanimous alacrity.

What parliament would or would not consent to, however, would soon cease to be a mystery. The advice of the emperor on the elections had been, for the most part, followed. It was obvious, indeed, that a sovereign who was unable to control her council was in no position to dictate to constituencies. There were no circulars to the lords-lieutenant of counties, such as Northumberland had issued, or such as Mary herself, a year later, was able to issue; while the unusual number of members returned to the Lower House—four hundred and thirty, it will be seen, voted on one great occasion—shows that the issue of writs had been on the widest scale. On the whole, it was, perhaps, the fairest election which had taken place for many years. In the House of Lords the ejection of the Reforming bishops and the restoration of their opponents—the death, imprisonment, or disgrace of three noblemen on the Reforming side, and the return to public life of the peers who, in the late reign, had habitually absented themselves, had restored a conservative majority. How the representatives of the people would conduct themselves was the anxious and all-agitating question. The queen, however, could console herself with knowing that Protestantism, as a system of belief, had made its way chiefly among the young; the votes were with the middle-aged and the old.

The session opened on the 5th of October with the ancient form, so long omitted, of the mass of the Holy Ghost. Two Protestant bishops, Taylor of Lincoln and Harley of Hereford, who had been left as yet undisturbed in their sees, on the service commencing, rose and went out; they were not allowed to return. Two prebends, Alexander Nowel and Doctor Tregonwell had been returned to the Lower House; Nowel as a member of Convocation was declared ineligible; [152] Tregonwell, being a layman, was on consideration allowed to retain his seat. These were the only ejections which can be specifically traced, and the silence of those who were interested in making the worst of Mary's conduct, may be taken to prove that they did not know of any more. [153] The Houses, purged of these elements, then settled to their work; and, plunging at once into the great question of the time, the Commons came to an instant understanding that the lay owners of church lands should not be disturbed in their tenures under any pretext whatsoever.

Commendone, on returning to Rome, had disregarded his obligations to secrecy, and had related all that the queen had said to him in the open consistory; from the consistory the account travelled back to England, and arrived inopportunely at the opening of parliament. The fatal subject of the lands had been spoken of, and the queen had expressed to Commendone her intention to restore them, if possible, to the church. The council cross-questioned her, and she could neither deny her words nor explain them away; the Commons first, the Lords immediately after, showed her that, whatever might be her own hopes or wishes, their minds on that point were irrevocably fixed. [154]

No less distinct were the opinions expressed in the Lower House on the Papacy. The authority of the pope, as understood in England, was not a question of doctrine, nor was the opposition to it of recent origin. It had been thrown off after a struggle which had lasted for centuries, and a victory [155] so hardly won was not to be lightly parted with. Lord Paget warned the queen that Pole's name must not be so much as mentioned, or some unwelcome resolution about him would be immediately passed; [156] and she was in hourly dread that before they would consent to anything, they would question her whether she would or would not maintain the royal supremacy. [157] On the other hand, if no difficulties were raised about the pope or the church lands, the preliminary discussion, both among Lords and Commons, showed a general disposition to re-establish religion in the condition in which Henry left it—provided, that is to say, no penalties were to attach to nonconformity; and the Houses were ready also to take the step so much deprecated by Pole, and pass a measure legitimatising the queen, provided no mention was to be made of the papal dispensation. Some difference of opinion on the last point had shown itself in the House of Commons, [158] but the legate's ingenuity had removed all serious obstacles.

Again parliament seemed determined that the Act of Succession, and the will of Henry VIII., should not be tampered with, to the disfavour of Elizabeth. It is singular that Renard, and probably, therefore, Mary, were unaware of the position in which Elizabeth was placed towards the crown. They imagined that her only title was as a presumptively legitimate child; that if the Act of Divorce between Catherine of Arragon and Henry was repealed, she must then, as a bastard, be cut off from her expectations. Had Elizabeth's prospects been liable to be affected by the legitimisation of her sister, the queen would have sued as vainly for it as she sued afterwards in favour of her husband. With unmixed mortification Renard learnt that Elizabeth, in the eye of the law, had been as illegitimate as Mary, and that her place in the order of succession rested on her father's will. He flattered himself, at first, that Henry's dispositions could be set aside; [159] but he very soon found that there was no present hope of it.

These general features of the temper of parliament were elicited in conversation in the first few days of the session. The Marchioness of Exeter, during the same days, was released from her attainder, Courtenay was restored in blood, and a law, similar to that with which Somerset commenced his Protectorate, repealed all late treason acts, restricted the definition of treason within the limits of the statute of Edward III., and relieved the clergy of the recent extensions of the Premunire. The queen gave her assent to these three measures on the 21st of October; and there was then an interval of three days, during which the bishops were consulted on the view taken by parliament of the queen's legitimacy. Renard told the Bishop of Norwich, Thirlby, that they must bend to the times, and leave the pope to his fortunes. They acted on the ambassador's advice. An act was passed, in which the marriage from which the queen was sprung, was declared valid, and the pope's name was not mentioned; but the essential point being secured, the framers of the statute were willing to gratify their mistress by the intensity of the bitterness with which the history of the divorce was related. [160] The bishops must have been glad to escape from so mortifying a subject, and to apply themselves to the more congenial subject of religion.

As soon as the disposition of parliament had been generally ascertained, the restoration of the mass was first formally submitted, for the sake of decency, to the clergy of Convocation.

The bench had been purged of dangerous elements. The Lower House contained a small fraction of Protestants just large enough to permit a controversy, and to insure a triumph to their antagonists. The proceedings opened with a sermon from Harpsfeld, then chaplain of the Bishop of London, in which, in a series of ascending antitheses, Northumberland was described as Holofernes, and Mary as Judith; Northumberland was Haman, and Mary was Esther; Northumberland was Sisera, and Mary was the mother in Israel. Mary was the sister who had chosen the better part: religion ceased and slept until Mary arose a virgin in Israel, and with the mother of God Mary might sing, "Behold, from henceforth all generations shall call me blessed." The trumpet having thus sounded, the lists were drawn for the combat; the bishops sat in their robes, the clergy stood bareheaded, and the champions appeared. Hugh Weston, Dean of Windsor, Dean of Westminster afterwards, Dr. Watson, Dr. Moreman, and the preacher Harpsfeld undertook to defend the real presence against Phillips Dean of Rochester, Philpot, Cheny, Aylmer, and Young.

The engagement lasted for a week. The reforming theologians fought for their dangerous cause bravely and temperately; and Weston, who was at once advocate and prolocutor, threw down his truncheon at last, and told Philpot that he was meeter for Bethlehem than for a company of grave and learned men, and that he should come no more into their house. [161] The orthodox thus ruled themselves the victors: but beyond the doors of the Convocation House they did not benefit their cause. The dispute, according to Renard, resolved itself, in the opinion of the laity, into scandalous railing and recrimination; [162] the people were indignant; and the Houses of Parliament, disgusted and dissatisfied, resumed the discussion among themselves, as more competent to conduct it with decency. In eight days the various changes introduced by Edward VI. were argued in the House of Commons, and points were treated of there, said Renard, which a general council could scarcely resolve. At length, by a majority, which exceeded Gardiner's most sanguine hopes, of 350 against 80, the mass was restored, and the clergy were required to return to celibacy. [163]

The precipitation with which Somerset, Cranmer, and Northumberland had attempted to carry out the Reformation, was thus followed by a natural recoil. Protestant theology had erected itself into a system of intolerant dogmatism, and had crowded the gaols with prisoners who were guilty of no crime but Nonconformity; it had now to reap the fruits of its injustice, and was superseded till its teachers had grown wiser. The first parliament of Mary was indeed more Protestant, in the best sense of that word, than the statesmen and divines of Edward. While the House of Commons re-established the Catholic services, they decided, after long consideration, that no punishment should be inflicted on those who declined to attend those services. [164] There was to be no pope, no persecution, no restoration of the abbey lands — resolutions, all of them disagreeable to a reactionary court. On the Spanish marriage both Lords and Commons were equally impracticable. The Catholic noblemen — the Earls of Derby, Shrewsbury, Bath, and Sussex were in the interest of Courtenay. The chancellor had become attached to him in the Tower when they were fellow-prisoners there; and Sir Robert Rochester, Sir Francis Englefield, Sir Edward Waldegrave, the queen's tried and faithful officers of the household, went with the chancellor. Never, on any subject, was there greater unanimity in England than in the disapproval of Philip as a husband for the queen, and, on the 29th of October, the Lower House had a petition in preparation to entreat her to choose from among her subjects.

To Courtenay, indeed, Mary might legitimately object. Since his emancipation from the Tower he had wandered into folly and debauchery; he was vain and inexperienced, and his insolence was kept in check only by the quality so rare in an Englishman of personal timidity. But to refuse

Courtenay was one thing, to fasten her choice on the heir of a foreign kingdom was another. Paget insisted, indeed, that, as the Queen of Scots was contracted to the Dauphin, unless England could strengthen herself with a connection of corresponding strength, the union of the French and Scottish crowns was a menace to her liberties. [165] But the argument, though important in itself, was powerless against the universal dread of the introduction of a foreign sovereign, and it availed only to provide Mary with an answer to the protests and entreaties of her other ministers.

Perhaps, too, it confirmed her in her obstinacy, and allowed her to persuade herself that, in following her own inclination, she was consulting the interests of her subjects. Obstinate, at any rate, she was beyond all reach of persuasion. Once only she wavered, after her resolution was first taken. Some one had told her that, if she married Philip, she would find herself the step-mother of a large family of children who had come into the world irregularly. A moral objection she was always willing to recognise. She sent for Renard, and conjured him to tell her whether the prince was really the good man which he had described him; Renard assured her that he was the very paragon of the world.

She caught the ambassador's hand.

"Oh!" she exclaimed, "do you speak as a subject whose duty is to praise his sovereign, or do you speak as a man?"

"Your majesty may take my life," he answered, "if you find him other than I have told you."

"Oh that I could but see him!" she said.

She dismissed Renard gratefully. A few days after she sent for him again, when she was expecting the petition of the House of Commons. "Lady Clarence," one of the queen's attendants, was the only other person present. The holy wafer was in the room on an altar, which she called her protector, her guide, her adviser. [166] Mary told them that she spent her days and nights in tears and prayers before it, imploring God to direct her; and as she was speaking her emotions overcame her; she flung herself on her knees with Renard and Lady Clarence at her side, and the three together before the altar sang the *Veni Creator*. The invocation was heard in the breasts from which it was uttered. As the chant died into silence, Mary rose from the ground as if inspired, and announced the divine message. The Prince of Spain was the chosen of Heaven for the virgin queen; if miracles were required to give him to her, there was a stronger than man who would work them; the malice of the world should not keep him from her; she would cherish him and love him, and him alone; and never thenceforward, by a wavering thought, would she give him cause for jealousy. [167]

It was true that she had deliberately promised not to do what she was now resolved on doing, but that was no matter.

The Commons' petition was by this time (November) ready, but the agitation of the last scene brought on a palpitation of the heart which for the time enabled the queen to decline to receive it; while Renard assailed the different ministers, and extracted from them their general views on the state of the country, and the measures which should be pursued.

The Bishop of Winchester he found relaxing in his zeal for Rome, and desiring a solid independent English government, the re-enactment of the Six Articles, and an Anglican religious tyranny supported by the lords of the old blood. Nobles and people were against the pope, Gardiner said, and against foreign interference of all sorts; Mary could not marry Philip without a papal dispensation, which must be kept secret; the country would not tolerate it; [168] the French would play into the hands of the heretics, and the Spanish alliance would give them the game; there would be a cry raised that Spanish troops would be introduced to inflict the pope upon the people by force. If the emperor desired the friendship of England, he would succeed best by not pressing the connection too close. Political marriages were dangerous. Cromwell tied Henry VIII. to Anne of Cleves; the marriage lasted a night, and destroyed him and his policy. Let the queen accept the choice of her people, marry Courtenay, send Elizabeth to the Tower, and extirpate heresy with fire and sword.

These were the views of Gardiner, from whom Renard turned next to Paget.

If the queen sent Elizabeth to the Tower, Lord Paget said, her life would not be safe for a day. Paget wished her to be allowed to choose her own husband; but she must first satisfy parliament that she had no intention of tampering with the succession. Should she die without children, the country must not be left exposed to claims from Spain on behalf of Philip, or from France on behalf of the Queen of Scots. His own advice, therefore, was, that Mary should frankly acknowledge her sister as her presumptive successor; Elizabeth might be married to Courtenay, and, in default of heirs of her own body, it might be avowed and understood that those two should be king and queen. Could she make up her mind to this course, could she relinquish her dreams of restoring the authority of the pope, of meddling with the church lands, and interfering with the liberties of her people, she might rely on the loyalty of the country, and her personal inclinations would not be interfered with. [169]

Both the lines of conduct thus sketched were consistent and intelligible, and either might have been successfully followed. But neither the one nor the other satisfied Mary. She would have Philip, she would have the pope, and she would not recognise her sister. If she insisted on choosing a husband for herself, she felt it would be difficult to refuse her; her object was to surprise the council into committing themselves, and she succeeded. On the 8th of November, when they were in session in a room in the palace, Renard presented Mary in the emperor's name with a formal offer of Philip's hand, and requested a distinct answer, Yes or no. The queen said she would consult her ministers, and repaired in agitation to the council-room. [170] Distrusting one another, unprepared for the sudden demand, and unable to consult in her presence, the lords made some answer, which she interpreted into acquiescence: Mary returned radiant with joy, and told the ambassador that his proposal was accepted.

A momentary lull followed, during which Thomas Cranmer, Archbishop of Canterbury, Lady Jane Grey, Lord Guilford, Lord Ambrose, and Lord Henry Dudley were taken from the Tower on foot to the Guildhall, and were there tried, found guilty of high treason, and sentenced to die. Lady Jane the queen still intended to spare; the Dudleys she meant to pause upon. Cranmer, in a grave, mild letter, explained what his conduct had been with respect to his so-called treason; but his story, creditable to him as it was, produced no effect; Cranmer was immediately to be put to death. That was the first intention, though it was found necessary to postpone his fate through a superstitious scruple. The archbishop had received the pallium from Rome, and, until degraded by apostolic authority, he could not, according to Catholic rule, be condemned by a secular tribunal. But there was no intention of sparing him at the time of his trial; in a few days, Renard wrote on the 17th of November, "the archbishop" will be executed; and Mary, triumphant, as she believed herself, on the question nearest to her heart, had told him that the melancholy which had weighed upon her from childhood was rolling away; she had never yet known the meaning of happiness, and she was about to be rewarded at last. [171]

The struggle had told upon her. She was looking aged and worn, [172] and her hopes of children, if she married, were thought extremely small. But she considered that she had won the day, and was now ready to face the Commons; the House had chafed at the delay: they had talked largely of their intentions; if the queen's answer was unsatisfactory, they would dissolve themselves, they said, and return to their counties. On the 16th of November a message was brought that the Speaker would at last be admitted to the presence. The interview which followed, Mary thus herself described to Renard. The council were present; the Speaker was introduced, and the queen received him standing.

In an oration, she said, replete to weariness with fine phrases and historic precedents, the Speaker requested her, in the name of the commonwealth, to marry. The succession was perplexed; the Queen of Scots made pretensions to the crown; and, in the event of her death, a civil war was imminent. Let her majesty take a husband, therefore, and with God's grace the kingdom would not be long without an heir whose title none would dispute. Yet, in taking a husband, the Speaker said, her majesty's faithful Commons trusted she would not choose from abroad. A foreign prince had interests of his own which might not be English interests; he would have command of English armies, fleets, and fortresses, and he might betray his trust; he might involve the country in wars; he might make promises and break them; he might carry her highness away out of the realm; or he might bring up her children in foreign courts and in foreign habits. Let her marry, therefore, one of her own subjects.

The Speaker was so prolix, so tedious, so confused, the queen said—his sentences were so long drawn and so little to the purpose—that she sate down before he had half-finished. When he came to the words "Marry a subject," she could remain silent no longer.

Replies to addresses of the House of Commons were usually read by the chancellor; but, careless of forms, she again started to her feet, and spoke:— [173]

"For your desire to see us married we thank you; your desire to dictate to us the consort whom we shall choose we consider somewhat superfluous; the English parliament has not been wont to use such language to their sovereigns, and where private persons in such cases follow their private tastes, sovereigns may reasonably challenge an equal liberty. If you, our Commons, force upon us a husband whom we dislike, it may occasion the inconvenience of our death; [174] if we marry where we do not love, we shall be in our grave in three months, and the heir of whom you speak will not have been brought into being. We have heard much from you of the incommodities which may attend our marriage; we have not heard from you of the commodities thereof — one of which is of some weight with us, the commodity, namely, of our private inclination. We have not forgotten our coronation oath. We shall marry as God shall direct our choice, to his honour and to our country's good."

She would hear no reply. The Speaker was led out, and as he left the room Arundel whispered to Gardiner that he had lost his office; the queen had usurped it. At the same moment the queen herself turned to the chancellor — "I have to thank you, my lord, for this business," she said.

The chancellor swore in tears that he was innocent; the Commons had drawn their petition themselves; for himself it was true he was well inclined towards Courtenay; he had known him in the Tower.

"And is your having known him in the Tower," she cried, "a reason that you should think him a fitting husband for me? I will never, never marry him — that I promise you — and I am a woman of my word; what I say I do."

"Choose where you will," Gardiner answered, "your majesty's consort shall find in me the most obedient of his subjects."

Mary had now the bit between her teeth, and, resisting all efforts to check or guide her, was making her own way with obstinate resolution.

The next point was the succession, which, notwithstanding the humour of parliament, should be re-arranged, if force or skill could do it. There were four possible claimants after herself, she told Renard, and in her own opinion the best title was that of the Queen of Scots. But the country objected, and the emperor would not have the English crown fall to France. The Greys were out of the question, but their mother, the Duchess of Suffolk, was eligible; and there was Lady Lennox, also, Darnley's mother, who perhaps, after all, would be the best choice that could be made. [175] Elizabeth, she was determined, should never, never succeed. She had spoken to Paget about it, she said, and Paget had remonstrated; Paget had said marry her to Courtenay, recognise her as presumptive heir, and add a stipulation, if necessary, that she become a Catholic; but, Catholic or no Catholic, she said, her sister should never reign in England with consent of hers; she was a heretic, a hypocrite, and a bastard, and her infamous mother had been the cause of all the calamities which had befallen the realm.

Even Renard was alarmed at this burst of passion. He had fed Mary's suspicions till they were beyond either his control or her own; and the attitude of parliament had lately shown him that, if any step were taken against Elizabeth without provocation on her part, it would infinitely increase the difficulty of concluding the marriage. He was beginning to believe, and he ventured to hint to the queen, that Paget's advice might be worth consideration; but on this subject she would listen to nothing.

Elizabeth had hitherto, when at court, taken precedence of all other ladies. The queen now compelled her to walk behind Lady Lennox and the Duchess of Suffolk, as a sign of the meditated change; [176] and the ladies of the court were afraid to be seen speaking to her. But in reply to Mary's derogatory treatment, the young lords, knights, and gentlemen gathered ostentatiously round the princess when she rode abroad, or thronged the levees at her house; old-established statesmen said, in Renard's ear, that, let the queen decide as she would, no foreigner should reign in England; and Lord Arundel believed that Elizabeth's foot was already on the steps of the throne. A large and fast-growing party, which included more than one member of the Privy Council, were now beginning to consider, as the best escape from Philip, that Courtenay had better fly from the court, taking Elizabeth with him—call round him in their joint names all who would strike with him for English independence, and proclaim the queen deposed.

There was uncertainty about Elizabeth herself; both Noailles and Renard believed that she would consent to this dangerous proposal; but she had shown Courtenay, hitherto, no sign of favour; while Courtenay, on his side, complained that he was frightened by her haughty ways. Again there was a serious difficulty in Courtenay's character; he was too cowardly for a dangerous enterprise, too incapable for an intricate one, and his weak humour made men afraid to trust themselves to a person who, to save himself, might at any moment betray them. Noailles, however, said emphatically that, were Courtenay anything but what he was, his success would be certain. [177]

The plot grew steadily into definite form. Devonshire and Cornwall were prepared for insurrection, and thither, as to the stronghold of the Courtenay family, Elizabeth was to be first carried. Meantime the ferment of popular feeling showed in alarming symptoms through the surface. The council were in continual quarrel. Parliament, since the rebuff of the Speaker, had not grown more tractable, and awkward questions began to be asked about a provision for the married clergy. All had been already gained which could be hoped for from the present House of Commons; and, on the 6th of December, the session ended in a dissolution. The same day a dead dog was thrown through the window of the presence chamber with ears cropped, a halter about its neck, and a label saying that all the priests in England should be hanged.

Renard, who, though not admitted, like Noailles, into the confidence of the conspirators, yet knew the drift of public feeling, and knew also Arundel's opinion of the queen's prospects, insisted that Mary should place some restraint upon herself, and treat her sister at least with outward courtesy; Philip was expected at Christmas, should nothing untoward happen in the interval; and the ambassador prevailed on her, at last, to pretend that her suspicions were at an end. His own desire, he said, was as great as Mary's that Elizabeth should be detected in some treasonable correspondence; but harshness only placed her on her guard; she would be less careful, if she believed that she was no longer distrusted. The princess, alarmed perhaps at finding herself the unconsenting object of dangerous schemes, had asked permission to retire to her country house. It was agreed that she should go; persons in her household were bribed to watch her; and the queen, yielding to Renard's entreaties, received her when she came to take leave with an appearance of affection so well counterfeited, that it called out the ambassador's applause. [178] She made her a present of pearls, with a head-dress of sable; and the princess, on her side, implored the queen to give no more credit to slanders against her. They embraced; Elizabeth left the court; and, as she went out of London, five hundred gentlemen formed about her as a voluntary escort. [179] There were not wanting fools, says Renard, who would persuade the queen that her sister's last words were honestly spoken; but she remembers too acutely the injuries which her mother and herself suffered at Anne Boleyn's hands; and she has a fixed conviction that Elizabeth, unless she can be first disposed of, will be a cause of infinite calamities to the realm. [180]

CHAPTER II-THE SPANISH MARRIAGE

The fears of Renard and the hopes of Noailles were occasioned by the unanimity of Catholics and heretics in the opposition to the marriage; yet, so singular was the position of parties, that this very unanimity was the condition which made the marriage possible. The Catholic lords and gentlemen were jealous of English independence, and, had they stood alone, they would have coerced the queen into an abandonment of her intentions: but, if they dreaded a Spanish sovereign, they hated unorthodoxy more, and if they permitted, or assisted in the schemes of the Reformers, they feared that they might lose the control of the situation when the immediate object was obtained. Those who were under the influence of Gardiner desired to restore persecution; and persecution, which was difficult with Mary on the throne, would be impossible under a sovereign brought in by a revolution. They made a favourite of Courtenay, but they desired to marry him to the queen, not to Elizabeth: Gardiner told the young earl that he would sooner see him the husband of the vilest drab who could be picked out of the London kennels. [181]

Thus, from their murmurs, they seemed to be on the edge of rebellion; yet, when the point of action came, they halted, uncertain what to do, unwilling to acquiesce, yet without resolution to resist. From a modern point of view the wisest policy was that recommended by Paget. The claim of the Queen of Scots on the throne unquestionably made it prudent for England to strengthen herself by some powerful foreign alliance; sufficient precautions could be devised for the security of the national independence; and, so far from England being in danger of being drawn into the war on the continent, Lord Paget said that, if England would accept Philip heartily, the war would be at an end. Elizabeth of France might marry Don Carlos, taking with her the French pretensions to Naples and Milan as a dowry. Another French princess might be given to the expatriated Philibert, and Savoy and Piedmont restored with her. "You," Paget said to Noailles, "by your Dauphin's marriage forced us to be friends with the Scots; we, by our queen's marriage, will force you to be friends with the emperor." [182]

Paget, however, was detested as an upstart, and detested still more as a latitudinarian; he could form no party, and the queen made use of him only to support her in her choice of the Prince of Spain, as in turn she would use Gardiner to destroy the Protestants; and thus the two great factions in the state neutralised each other's action in a matter in which both were equally anxious; and Mary, although with no remarkable capacity, without friends and ruined, if at any moment she lost courage, was able to go her own way in spite of her subjects.

The uncertainty was, how long so anomalous a state of things would continue. The marriage, being once decided on, Mary could think of nothing else, and even religion sank into the second place. Reginald Pole, chafing the imperial bridle between his lips, vexed her, so Renard said, from day to day, with his untimely importunities; [183] the restoration of the mass gave him no pleasure so long as the papal legate was an exile; and in vain the queen laboured to draw from him some kind of approval. He saw her only preferring carnal pleasures to her duty to Heaven; and, indifferent himself to all interests save those of the See of Rome, he was irritated with the emperor, irritated with the worldly schemes to which he believed that his mission had been sacrificed. He talked angrily of the marriage. The queen heard, through Wotton the ambassador at Paris, that he had said openly, it should never take place; [184] while Peto, the Greenwich friar, who was in his train, wrote to her, reflecting impolitely on her age, and adding Scripture commendations of celibacy as the more perfect state. [185] It was even feared that the impatient legate had advised the pope to withhold the dispensations.

Mary, beyond measure afflicted, wrote to Pole at last, asking what in his opinion she ought to do. He sent his answer through a priest, by whom it could be conveyed with the greatest emphasis. First, he said, she must pray to God for a spirit of counsel and fortitude: next, she must, at all hazards, relinquish the name of Head of the Church; and, since she could trust neither peer nor prelate, she must recall parliament, go in person to the House of Commons, and demand permission with her own mouth for himself to return to England. The holy see was represented in his person, and was freshly insulted in the refusal to receive him; the pope's vast clemency had volunteered unasked to pardon the crimes of England; if the gracious offer was not accepted, the legacy would be cancelled, the national guilt would be infinitely enhanced. The emperor talked of prudence; in the service of God prudence was madness; and, so long as the schism continued, her attempts at reform were vanity, and her seat upon the throne was usurpation. Let her tell the truth to the House of Commons, and the House of Commons would hear. [186]

"Your majesty will see," wrote Renard, enclosing to Charles a copy of these advices, "the extent of the cardinal's discretion, and how necessary it is that for the present he be kept at a distance." The pope was not likely to reject the submission of England at any moment, late or early, when England might be pleased to offer it, and could well afford to wait. Julius was wiser than his legate. Pole was not recalled, but exhorted to patience, and a letter or message from Rome cooled Mary's anxieties. Meanwhile the marriage was to be expedited with as much speed as possible; the longer the agitation continued, the greater the danger; while the winter was unfavourable to revolutionary movements, and armed resistance to the prince's landing would be unlikely so long as the season prevented large bodies of men from keeping the field. [187]

The emperor, therefore, in the beginning of December, sent over the draft of a marriage treaty; and if the security that the articles would be observed had equalled the form in which they were conceived, the English might have afforded to lay aside their alarms. Charles seemed to have anticipated almost every point on which the insular jealousy would be sensitive. The Prince of Spain should bear the title of King of England so long, but so long only as the queen should be alive; and the queen should retain the disposal of all affairs in the realm, and the administration of the revenues. The queen, in return, should share Philip's titles, present and prospective, with the large settlement of £60,000 a year upon her for her life. Don Carlos, the prince's child by his first wife, would, if he lived, inherit Spain, Sicily, the Italian provinces, and the Indies. But Burgundy and the Low Countries should be settled on the offspring of the English marriage, and be annexed to the English crown; and this prospect, splendid in itself, was made more magnificent by the possibility that Don Carlos might die. Under all contingencies, the laws and liberties of the several countries should be held inviolate and inviolable.

In such a treaty the emperor conferred everything, and in return received nothing; and yet, to gain the alliance, a negotiation already commenced for the hand of the Infanta of Portugal was relinquished. The liberality of the proposals was suspicious, but they were submitted to the council, who, unable to refuse to consider them, were obliged to admit that they were reasonable. Five additional clauses were added, however, to which it was insisted that Philip should swear before the contract should be completed—

1. That no foreigner, under any circumstances, should be admitted to any office in the royal household, in the army, the forts, or the fleet.

2. That the queen should not be taken abroad without her own consent; and that the children – should children be born – should not be carried out of England without consent of parliament, even though among them might be the heir of the Spanish empire.

3. Should the queen die childless, the prince's connection with the realm should be at an end.

4. The jewel-house and treasury should be wholly under English control, and the ships of war should not be removed into a foreign port.

5. The prince should maintain the existing treaties between England and France; and England should not be involved, directly or indirectly, in the war between France and the empire. [188]

These demands were transmitted to Brussels, where they were accepted without difficulty, and further objection could not be ventured unless constraint was laid upon the queen. The sketch of the treaty, with the conditions attached to it, was submitted to such of the Lords and Commons as remained in London after the dissolution of parliament, and the result was a sullen acquiescence.

An embassy was immediately announced as to be sent from Flanders. Count Egmont, M. de Courières, the Count de Lalaing, and M. de Nigry, Chancellor of the Golden Fleece, were coming over as plenipotentiaries of the emperor. Secret messengers went off to Rome to hasten the dispensations – a dispensation for Mary to marry her cousin, and a dispensation which also was found necessary permitting the ceremony to be performed by a bishop in a state of schism. The marriage could be solemnised at once on their arrival, the ambassadors standing as Philip's representatives, while Sir Philip Hoby, Bonner, Bedford, and Lord Derby would go to Spain to receive the prince's oaths, and escort him to England. Again and again the queen pressed haste. Ash-Wednesday fell on the 6th of February, and in Lent she might not marry. Renard assured her that the prince should be in her arms before Septuagesima, and all her trials would be over. The worst danger which he now anticipated was from some unpleasant collision which might arise after the prince's landing; and he had advised the emperor to have the Spaniards who would form the retinue selected for their meekness. They would meet with insolence from the English, which they would not endure, if they had the spirit to resent it; their dispositions, therefore, must be mild and forgiving. [189]

And yet Renard could not hide from himself, and the lords did not hide from Mary, that their consent was passive only; that their reluctance was vehement as ever. Bedford said, if he went to Spain, he must go without attendance, for no one would accompany him. Lord Derby refused to be one of the ambassadors, and with Sir Edward Waldegrave and Sir Edward Hastings told the queen that he would leave her service if she persisted. The seditious pamphlets which were scattered everywhere created a vague terror in the court, and the court ladies wept and lamented in the queen's presence. The council in a body again urged her to abandon her intention. The peers met again to consider the marriage articles. Gardiner read them aloud, and Lord Windsor, a dull Brutus, who till then had never been known to utter a reasonable word, exclaimed, amidst general applause, "You have told us fine things of the queen, and the prince, and the emperor; what security have we that words are more than words?" Corsairs from Brest and Rochelle hovered in the mouth of the Channel to catch the couriers going to and fro between Spain and London and Brussels, and to terrify Philip with the danger of the passage. The Duke of Suffolk's brother and the Marquis of Winchester had been heard to swear that they would set upon him when he landed; and Renard began to doubt whether the alliance, after all, was worth the risk attending it. [190] Mary, however, brave in the midst of her perplexities, vowed that she would relinquish her hopes of Philip only with her life. An army of spies watched Elizabeth day and night, and the emperor, undeterred by Renard's hesitation, encouraged the queen's resolution. There could be no conspiracy as yet, Charles said, which could not be checked with judicious firmness; and dangerous persons could be arrested and made secure. A strong hand could do much in England, as was proved by the success for a time of the late Duke of Northumberland. [191]

The advice fell in with Mary's own temperament; she had already been acting in the spirit of it. A party of Protestants met in St. Matthew's Church on the publication of the acts of the late session, to determine how far they would obey them. Ten or twelve were seized on the spot, and two were hanged out of hand. [192] The queen told Hastings and Waldegrave that she would endure no opposition; they should obey her or they should leave the council. She would raise a few thousand men, she said, to keep her subjects in order, and she would have a thousand Flemish horse among them. There was a difficulty about ways and means; as fast as money came into the treasury she had paid debts with it, and, as far as her means extended, she had replaced chalices and roods in the parish churches. But, if she was poor, five millions of gold had just arrived in Spain from the New World; and, as the emperor suggested, her credit was good at Antwerp from her honesty. Lazarus Tucker came again to the rescue. In November,

Lazarus provided £50,000 for her at fourteen per cent. In January she required £100,000 more, and she ordered Gresham to find it for her at low interest or high. [193] Fortunately for Mary the project of a standing army could not be carried out by herself alone, and the passive resistance of the council saved her from commencing the attempt. Neither Irish mercenaries, nor Flemish, nor Welsh, as, two months after she was proposing to herself, were permitted to irritate England into madness.

While Mary was thus buffeting with the waves, on the 23rd, Count Egmont and his three companions arrived at Calais. The French had threatened to intercept the passage, and four English ships-of-war had been ordered to be in waiting as their escort: these ships, however, had not left the Thames, being detained either by weather, as the admiral pretended, or by the ill-humour of the crews, who swore they would give the French cruisers small trouble, should they present themselves. [194] On Christmas-day ill-looking vessels were hanging in mid-channel, off Calais harbour, but the ambassadors were resolved to cross at all risks. They stole over in the darkness on the night of the 26th, and were at Dover by nine in the morning. Their retinue, a very large one, was sent on at once to London; snow was on the ground, and the boys in the streets saluted the first comers with showers of balls. The ambassadors followed the next day, and were received in silence, but without active insult. The emperor's choice of persons for his purpose had been judicious. The English ministers intended to be offensive, but they were disarmed by the courtesy of Egmont, who charmed every one. In ten days the business connected with the treaty was concluded. The treaty itself was sent to Brussels to be ratified, and the dispensations from Rome, and the necessary powers from the Prince of Spain, were alone waited for that the marriage might be concluded in public or in private, whichever way would be most expeditious. The queen cared only for the completion of the irrevocable ceremony, which would bring her husband to her side before Lent. [195]

The interval of delay was consumed in hunting-parties [196] and dinners at the palace, where the courtiers played off before the guests the passions of their eager mistress. [197] The enemies of the marriage, French and English, had no time to lose, if they intended to prevent the completion of it.

When the queen's design was first publicly announced, the King of France directed Noailles to tell her frankly the alarm with which it was regarded at Paris. Henry and Montmorency said the same repeatedly, and at great length, to Dr. Wotton. The queen might have the best intentions of remaining at peace, but events might be too strong for her; and they suggested, at last, that she might give a proof of the good-will which she professed by making a fresh treaty with them. [198] That a country should be at peace while its titular king was at war, was a situation without a precedent. Intricate questions were certain to arise; for instance, if a mixed fleet of English and Spanish ships should escort the prince, or convoy his transports or treasure, or if the English ships having Spaniards on board, should enter French harbours. A thousand difficulties such as these might occur, and it would be wise to provide for them beforehand.

The uneasiness of the court of Paris was not allayed when the queen met this most reasonable proposal with a refusal. [199] A clause, she replied, was added to the marriage articles for the maintenance of the existing treaties with France, and with that and with her own promises the French government ought to be content. In vain Noailles pointed out that the existing treaties would not meet the new conditions; she was obstinate, and both Noailles and the King of France placed the worst interpretation upon her attitude. Philip, after his arrival, would unquestionably drag or lead her into his quarrels; and they determined, therefore, to employ all means, secret and open, to prevent his coming, and to co-operate with the English opposition.

The time to act had arrived. Rumours were industriously circulated that the Prince of Spain was already on the seas, bringing with him ten thousand Spaniards, who were to be landed at the Tower, and that eight thousand Germans were to follow from the Low Countries. Noailles and M. d'Oysel, then on his way through London to Scotland, had an interview with a number of lords and gentlemen, who undertook to place themselves at the head of an insurrection, and to depose the queen. The whole country was crying out against her, and the French ministers believed that the opposition had but to declare itself in arms to meet with universal sympathy. They regarded the persons with whom they were dealing as the representatives of the national discontent; but on this last point they were fatally mistaken.

Noailles spoke generally of lords and gentlemen; but those with whom d'Oysel and himself had communicated were a party of ten or twelve of the pardoned friends of the Duke of Northumberland, or of men otherwise notorious among the ultra-Protestants; the Duke of Suffolk and his three brothers, Lord Thomas, Lord John, and Lord Leonard Grey; the Marquis of Northampton; Sir Thomas Wyatt, son of the poet; Sir Nicholas Throgmorton; Sir Peter Carew; Sir Edmund Warner; Lord Cobham's brother-in-law; and Sir James Crofts, the late deputy of Ireland. [200] Courtenay, who had affected orthodoxy as long as he had hopes of the queen, was admitted into the confederacy. Cornwall and Devonshire were to be the first counties to rise, where Courtenay would be all-powerful by his name. Wyatt undertook to raise Kent, Sir James Crofts the Severn border, Suffolk and his brothers the midland counties. Forces from these four points were to converge on London, which would then stir for itself. The French Admiral Villegaignon promised to keep a fleet on the seas, and to move from place to place among the western English harbours, wherever his presence would be most useful. Plymouth had been tampered with, and the mayor and aldermen, either really, or as a ruse to gain information, affected a desire to receive a French garrison. [201] For the sake of their cause the Protestant party were prepared to give to France an influence in England as objectionable in itself, and as offensive to the majority of the people, as the influence of Spain; and the management of the opposition to the queen was snatched from the hands of those who might have brought it to some tolerable issue, by a set of men to whom the Spanish marriage was but the stalking-horse for the reimposition of their late tyranny. If the Duke of Northumberland, instead of setting up a rival to Mary, had loyally admitted her to the throne which was her right, he might have tied her hands, and secured the progress of moderate reform. Had the great patriotic anti-papal party been now able to combine, with no disintegrating element, they could have prevented the marriage or made it harmless. But the ultra-party plunged again into treason, in which they would succeed only to restore the dominion of a narrow and blighting sectarianism. [202]

The conspirators remained in London till the second week in January. Wyatt went into Kent, Peter Carew ran down the Channel to Exmouth in a vessel of his own, and sent relays of horses as far as Andover for Courtenay, Sir Nicholas Throgmorton undertaking to see the latter thus far upon his way. The disaffection was already simmering in Devonshire. There was a violent scene among the magistrates at the Christmas quarter-sessions at Exeter. A countryman came in and reported that he had been waylaid and searched by a party of strange horsemen in steel saddles, "under the gallows at the hill top," at Fair-mile, near Sir Peter Carew's house. His person had been mistaken, it seemed, but questions were asked, inquiries made, and ugly language had been used about the queen. On Carew's arrival the ferment increased. One of his lacqueys, mistaking intention for fact, whispered in Exeter that "my Lord of Devonshire was at Mohun's Ottery." [203] Six horses heavily loaded passed in, at midnight, through the city gates. The panniers were filled with harness and hand-guns from Sir Peter's castle at Dartmouth. [204] Sir John Chichester, Sir Arthur Champernowne, Peter and Gawen Carew, and Gybbes of Silverton, had met in private, rumour said for no good purpose; and the Exeter Catholics were anxious and agitated. They had been all disarmed after the insurrection of 1549, the castle was in ruins, the city walls were falling down. Should Courtenay come, the worst consequences were anticipated. But Courtenay did not come. After Carew had left London, he became nervous; when the horses were reported to be ready, he lingered about the court; he flattered himself that the queen had changed her mind in his favour; and two nights before the completion of the treaty he sate up, affecting to expect to be sent for to marry her on the spot. [205] Finding the message did not arrive, he gave an order to his tailor to prepare a splendid court costume, adding perhaps some boasting words, which were carried to Gardiner. The chancellor's regard for him was sincere, and went beyond a desire to make him politically useful. He sent for him, cross-questioned him, and by the influence of a strong mind over a weak one, drew out as much as Courtenay knew of the secrets of the plot. [206]

The intention was to delay, if possible, an open declaration of rebellion a few weeks longer — till the Prince of Spain's arrival should raise the ferment to boiling point. Gardiner, who was determined, at all events, to prevent the Protestants from making head, informed the queen, without mentioning Courtenay's name, that he had cause to suspect Sir Peter Carew. A summons was despatched to Devonshire to require Sir Peter and his brother to return to London; and thus either to compel them to rise prematurely, without Courtenay's assistance, or, if they complied, to enable the court to secure their persons. The desired effect was produced; Carew had waded too deep in treason to trust himself in Gardiner's hands. He wrote an excuse, yet protesting his loyalty; and he invited the inhabitants of Exeter to join in a petition to the crown against the marriage, as a first step towards a rising.

But the Carews were notorious and unpopular; the justices of the peace at the sessions had been just occupied with a Protestant outrage committed by one of their nearest friends, [207] and their true object was suspected. The barns of Crediton were not forgotten, nor the massacre of the prisoners at Clyst, and without Courtenay they were powerless. Their invitation met with no response; and Chichester and Champernowne, seeing how the tide was setting, washed their hands of the connection. Sir Thomas Dennys, a Catholic gentleman of the county, took command of Exeter, sent express for the sheriff, Sir Richard Edgecumbe, of Cotteyll, to come to his help, and as well as he could he put the city in a state of defence. [208] Carew retired to Mohun's Ottery, when an order came to Dennys from the court for his arrest.

Dennys, who desired Carew's escape more than his capture, replied that for the moment he could not execute the order. Mohun's Ottery could not be taken without cannon, and wet weather had made the roads impassable. Meantime he gave Sir Peter notice of his danger; and Sir Peter, disposing in haste of his farm stock to raise a supply of money, crossed the country to Weymouth, embarked in a vessel which "Mr. Walter Raleigh" had brought round to meet him, and sailed for France. [209]

One arm of the conspiracy was thus lopped off at the first blow. But, although Courtenay's treachery was known, some days elapsed before the ill success of Carew was heard of in London. Courtenay had been trusted only so far as his intended share in the action had made it necessary to trust him, and the confederates were chiefly anxious that, having broken down, he should be incapacitated from doing further mischief by being restored to the Tower. Courtenay, wrote Noailles, has thrown away his chance of greatness, and will now probably die miserably. Lord Thomas Grey was heard to say that, as Courtenay had proved treacherous he would take his place, and run his chance for the crown or the scaffold. [210]

They would, perhaps, have still delayed till they had received authentic accounts from Devonshire; but the arrest of Sir Edmund Warner, and one or two others, assured them that too much of their projects had transpired; and on the 22nd of January Sir Thomas Wyatt called a meeting of his friends at Allingham Castle, on the Medway. The commons of Kent were the same brave, violent, and inflammable people whom John Cade, a century before, had led to London; the country gentlemen were generally under Wyatt's influence. Sir R. Southwell, the sheriff for the year, had been among the loudest objectors in parliament to the marriage; and if Southwell joined in the rising he would bring with him Lord Abergavenny. [211] Lord Cobham, Wyatt's uncle, was known to wish him well. Sir Thomas Cheyne, the only other person of weight in the county, would be loyal to the queen, but Wyatt had tampered with his tenants; Cheyne could bring a thousand men into the field, but they would desert when led out, and there was nothing to fear from them. Whether Southwell and Cobham would act openly on Wyatt's side was the chief uncertainty; it was feared that Southwell might desire to keep within the limits of loyal opposition; Cobham offered to send his sons, but "the sending of sons," some member of the meeting said, "was the casting away of the Duke of Northumberland; their lives were as dear to them as my Lord Cobham's was to him; let him come himself and set his foot by them." [212] The result of the conference was a determination to make the venture. Thursday the 25th was the day agreed on for the rising, and the gentlemen present went in their several directions to prepare the people.

Meantime Gardiner was following the track which Courtenay had opened. He knew generally the leaders of the conspiracy, yet uncertain, in the universal perplexity, how any one would act, he knew not whom to trust. To send Courtenay out of the way, he allowed a project to be set on foot for despatching him on an embassy to Brussels (January 23); and anxious, perhaps, not to alarm Mary too much, he simply told her what she and Renard knew already, that treasonable designs were on foot to make Elizabeth queen. In a conversation about Elizabeth the chancellor agreed with Renard that it would be well to arrest her without delay. "Were but the emperor in England," Gardiner said, "she would be disposed of with little difficulty." [213] Unfortunately, the spies had as yet detected no cause for suspicion on which the government could act legitimately.

Mary, ignorant that she was in immediate danger, and only vaguely uneasy, looked to Philip's coming as the cure of her discomforts. "Let the prince come," she said to Renard, "and all will be well." She said she would raise eight thousand men and keep them in London as his guard and hers; she would send a fleet into the Channel and sweep the French into their harbours; only let him come before Lent, which was now but a fortnight distant: "give him my affectionate love," she added; "tell him that I will be all to him that a wife ought to be; and tell him, too [delightful message to an already hesitating bridegroom], tell him to bring his own cook with him" for fear he should be poisoned, [214] The ceremony, could it have been accomplished, would have been a support to her; but the forms from Rome were long in coming. On the 24th of January the emperor was at last able to send a brief, which, in the absence of the bulls, he trusted might be enough to satisfy the queen's scruples. Cuthbert Tunstal, who had been consecrated before the schism, might officiate, and the pope would remove all irregularities afterwards. [215] But when the letter and the brief arrived Mary was at no leisure to be married.

Wyatt, having arranged the day for the rising, sent notice to the Duke of Suffolk, who was still in London. On the morning of the 25th an officer of the court appeared at the duke's house, with an intimation that he was to repair to the queen's presence. Suffolk was in a riding dress—"Marry!" he said, "I was coming to her grace; ye may see I am booted and spurred; I will but break my fast and go." [216] The officer retired. The duke collected as much money as he could lay hands on—sent a servant to warn his brothers, and, though in bad health, mounted his horse and rode without stopping to Lutterworth, where, on the Sunday following, Lord John and Lord Thomas Grey joined him.

The same morning of the 25th an alarm was rung on the church bells in the towns and villages in all parts of Kent; and copies of a proclamation were scattered abroad, signifying that the Spaniards were coming to conquer the realm, and calling on loyal Englishmen to rise and resist them. Wyatt's standard was raised at Rochester, the point at which the insurgent forces were to unite; his friends had done their work well, and in all directions the yeomen and the peasants rose in arms. Cheyne threw himself into Dover Castle: Southwell and Abergavenny held to the queen as had been feared; Abergavenny raised two thousand men, and attacked and dispersed a party of insurgents under Sir Henry Isly on Wrotham Heath; but Abergavenny's followers deserted him immediately afterwards, and marched to Rochester to Wyatt; Southwell could do nothing; he believed that the rebellion would spread to London, and that Mary would be lost. [217]

On the 26th, Wyatt, being master of Rochester and the Medway, seized the queen's ships that were in the river, took possession of their guns and ammunition, proclaimed Abergavenny, Southwell, and another gentleman traitors to the commonwealth, [218] and set himself to organise the force which continued to pour in upon him. Messengers, one after another, hurried to London with worse and worse news; Northampton was arrested and sent to the Tower, but Suffolk and his brothers were gone; and, after all which had been said of raising troops, when the need came for them there were none beyond the ordinary guard. The queen had to rely only on the musters of the city and the personal retainers of the council and the other peers; both of which resources she had but too much reason to distrust. In fact, the council, dreading the use to which the queen might apply a body of regular troops, had resisted all her endeavours to raise such a body; Paget had laboured loyally for a fortnight, and at the end he assured the queen on his knees that he had not been allowed to enlist a man. [219] Divided on all other points, the motley group of ministers agreed to keep Mary powerless; with the exception of Gardiner and Paget, they were all, perhaps, unwilling to check too soon a demonstration which, kept within bounds, might prove the justice of their own objections.

The queen, however, applied to the corporation of the city (January 27), and obtained a promise of five hundred men; she gave the command to the Duke of Norfolk, on whose integrity she knew that she could rely; and, sending a herald to Rochester with a pardon, if the rebels would disperse, she despatched Norfolk, Sir Henry Jerningham, and the young Lord Ormond, to Gravesend, without waiting for an answer. The city bands were to follow them immediately. Afraid that Elizabeth would fly before she could be secured, the queen wrote a letter to her studiously gracious, in which she told her that, in the disturbed state of the country, she was uneasy for her safety, and recommended her to take shelter with herself in the palace. [220] Had Elizabeth obeyed, she would have been instantly arrested; but she was ill, and wrote that she was unable to move. The next day evidence came into Gardiner's hands which he trusted would consign her at last to the scaffold.

The King of France had sent a message to the confederates that he had eighty vessels in readiness, with eighteen companies of infantry, and that he waited to learn on what part of the coast they should effect a landing. [221] The dangerous communication had been made known to the court. The French ambassador had been narrowly watched, and one of his couriers who left London on the 26th with despatches for Paris was followed to Rochester, where he saw, or attempted to see, Wyatt. The courier, after leaving the town, was waylaid by a party of Lord Cobham's servants in the disguise of insurgents; his despatches were taken from him and sent to the chancellor, who found in the packet a letter of Noailles to the king in cypher, and a copy of Elizabeth's answer to the queen. Although in the latter there was no treason, yet it indicated a suspicious correspondence. The cypher, could it be read, might be expected to contain decisive evidence against her. [222]

Meantime the herald had not been admitted into Rochester. He had read the queen's message on the bridge (January 27), and, being answered by Wyatt's followers that they required no pardon, for they had done no wrong, he retired. Sir George Harper, who was joint commander with Wyatt, stole away the same evening to Gravesend, and presented himself to

Norfolk. The rebels, he said, were discontented and irresolute; for himself he desired to accept the queen's pardon, which he was ready to earn by doing service against them; if the duke would advance without delay, he would find no resistance, and Wyatt would fall into his hands.

The London bands arrived the following afternoon (January 28), and Norfolk determined to take Harper's advice. The weather was "very terrible." On Monday morning it blew so hard that no boat could live; Wyatt, therefore, would be unable to escape by the river, and an immediate advance was resolved upon. Sir Thomas Cheyne was coming up from Dover; Lord William Howard was looked for hourly, and Abergavenny was again exerting himself: Lord Cobham had urged the duke to wait a few days, and had told him that he had certain knowledge from Wyatt himself that "the Londoners would not fight:" [223] but Norfolk was confident; the men had assured him of their loyalty; and at four o'clock on Monday afternoon he was on the sloping ground facing towards Rochester, within cannon-shot of the bridge. The duke was himself in front, with Ormond, Jerningham, and eight "field-pieces," which he had brought with him. A group of insurgents were in sight across the water, a gun was placed in position to bear upon them; and the gunner was blowing his match, when Sir Edward Bray galloped up, crying out that the "white coats," as the London men were called, were changing sides. The duke had fallen into a trap which Harper had laid for him. Turning round, he saw Brett, the London captain, with all his men, and with Harper at his side, advancing and shouting, "A Wyatt! a Wyatt! we are all Englishmen!" The first impulse was to turn the gun upon them; the second, and more prudent, was to spring on his horse, and gallop with half a dozen others for his life. His whole force had deserted, and guns, money, baggage, and five hundred of the best troops in London fell into the insurgents' hands, and swelled their ranks.

No sooner was the duke gone, than Wyatt in person came out over the bridge. "As many as will tarry with us," he cried, "shall be welcome; as many as will depart, let them go," Very few accepted the latter offer. Three parts, even of Norfolk's private attendants, took service with the rebel leader.

The prestige of success decided all who were wavering in the county. Abergavenny was wholly forsaken; Southwell escaped to the court; Cheyne wrote to the council that he was no longer sure of any one; "the abominable treason of those that came with the Duke of Norfolk had infected the whole population." [224] Cobham continued to hold off, but his sons came into

Rochester the evening of the duke's flight; and Wyatt sent a message to the father expressing his sorrow that he had been hitherto backward; promising to forgive him, however, and requiring him to be in the camp the next day, when the army would march on London. Cobham still hesitating, two thousand men were at the gates of his house [225] by daybreak the next morning (January 30). He refused to lower the drawbridge, but the chains were cut with a cannon-shot, the gates were blown open, and the rebels were storming in when his servants forced him to surrender. The house was pillaged; an oath was thrust on Cobham that he would join, which he took with the intention of breaking it; and the rebels, perhaps seeing cause to distrust him, carried him off to Wyatt as a prisoner. [226] That night the insurgents rested at Gravesend. The next day (January 31) they reached Dartford. Their actual numbers were insignificant, but their strength was the disaffection of London, where the citizens were too likely to follow the example which had been set at Rochester.

Mary's situation was now really alarming: she was without money, notwithstanding the Jews; she had no troops; of all her ministers Paget alone was sincerely anxious to do her service; for Gardiner, on the subject of the marriage, was as unwilling as ever. It was rumoured that the King of Denmark intended to unite with the French in support of the revolutionists, and Renard began calmly to calculate that, should this report prove true, the queen could not be saved. Pembroke and Clinton offered to raise another force in the city and fight Wyatt; but, so far as Mary could tell, they would be as likely to turn against her as to fight in her defence; and she declined their services. Renard offered Gardiner assistance from the Low Countries—Gardiner replied with extreme coldness that he had no desire to see Flemish soldiers in England—and the council generally were "so strange" in their manner, and so languid in their action, that the ambassador could not assure himself that they were not Wyatt's real instigators. Not a man had been raised to protect the queen, and part of her own guard had been among the deserters at Rochester. She appealed to the honour of the lords to take measure for her personal safety; but they did nothing, and, it seemed, would do nothing; if London rose, they said merely, she must retire to Windsor.

The aspect of affairs was so threatening, that Renard believed that the marriage at least would have to be relinquished. It seemed as if it could be accomplished only with the help of an invading army; and although

Mary would agree to any measure which would secure Philip, the presence of foreign troops, as the emperor himself was aware, could only increase the exasperation. [227] The queen's resolution, however, grew with her difficulties. If she could not fight she would not yield; and, taking matters into her own hands, she sent Sir Thomas Cornwallis and Sir Edward Hastings to Dartford, with directions to speak with Wyatt, if possible, alone; to tell him that she "marvelled at his demeanour," "rising as a subject to impeach her marriage;" she was ready to believe, however, that he thought himself acting in the interests of the commonwealth; she would appoint persons to talk over the subject with him, and if it should appear that the marriage would not, as she supposed, be beneficial to the realm, she would sacrifice her wishes. [228]

The message was not strictly honest, for the queen had no real intention of sacrificing anything. She desired merely to gain time; and, should Wyatt refuse, as she expected, she wished to place herself in a better position to appeal to her subjects for help. [229] But the move under this aspect was skilful and successful; when Cornwallis and Hastings discharged their commission, Wyatt replied that he would rather be trusted than trust; he would argue the marriage with pleasure, but he required first the custody of the Tower, and of the queen's person, and four of the council must place themselves in his hands as hostages. [230]

Had Wyatt, said Noailles, been able to reach London simultaneously with this answer, he would have found the gates open and the whole population eager to give him welcome. To his misfortune he lingered on the way, and the queen had time to use his words against him. The two gentlemen returned indignant at his insolence. The next morning (February 1), Count Egmont waited on Mary to say that he and his companions were at her service, and would stand by her to their death. Perplexed as she was, Egmont said he found her "marvellously firm." The marriage, she felt, must, at all events, be postponed for the present; the prince could not come till the insurrection was at an end; and, while she was grateful for the offer, she not only thought it best to decline the ambassadors' kindness, but she recommended them, if possible, to leave London and the country without delay. Their party was large enough to irritate the people, and too small to be of use. She bade Egmont, therefore, tell the emperor that from the first she had put her trust in God, and that she trusted in Him still; and for themselves, she told them to go at once, taking her best wishes with them. They obeyed. Six Antwerp merchant sloops were in the river below the bridge, waiting to sail. They stole on board, dropped down the tide, and were gone.

The afternoon of the same day the queen herself, with a studied air of dejection, [231] rode through the streets to the Guildhall, attended by Gardiner and the remnant of the guard. In St. Paul's Churchyard she met Pembroke, and slightly bowed as she passed him. Gardiner was observed to stoop to his saddle. The hall was crowded with citizens: some brought there by hatred, some by respect, many by pity, but more by curiosity. When the queen entered she stood forward on the steps, above the throng, and, in her deep man's voice, she spoke to them. [232]

Her subjects had risen in rebellion against her, she said; she had been told that the cause was her intended marriage with the Prince of Spain; and, believing that it was the real cause, she had offered to hear and to respect their objections. Their leader had betrayed in his answer his true motives; he had demanded possession of the Tower of London and of her own person. She stood there, she said, as lawful Queen of England, and she appealed to the loyalty of her great city to save her from a presumptuous rebel, who, under specious pretences, intended to "subdue the laws to his will, and to give scope to rascals and forlorn persons to make general havoc and spoil." As to her marriage, she had supposed that so magnificent an alliance could not have failed to be agreeable to her people. To herself, and, she was not afraid to say, to her council, it seemed to promise high advantage to the commonwealth. Marriage, in itself, was indifferent to her; she had been invited to think of it by the desire of the country that she should have an heir; but she could continue happy in the virgin state in which she had hitherto passed her life. She would call a parliament and the subject should be considered in all its bearings; if, on mature consideration, the Lords and Commons of England should refuse to approve of the Prince of Spain as a fitting husband for her, she promised, on the word of a queen, that she would think of him no more.

The spectacle of her distress won the sympathy of her audience; the boldness of her bearing commanded their respect; the promise of a parliament satisfied, or seemed to satisfy, all reasonable demands: and among the wealthy citizens there was no desire to see London in possession of an armed mob, in whom the Anabaptist leaven was deeply interfused. The speech, therefore, had remarkable success. The queen returned to Westminster, leaving the corporation converted to the prudence of supporting her. Twenty-five thousand men were enrolled the next day for the protection of the crown and the capital; Lord William Howard was associated with the mayor in the command; and Wyatt, who had reached Greenwich on Thursday, and had wasted two days there, uncertain whether he should not cross the river in boats to Blackwall, arrived on Saturday morning at Southwark, to find the gates closed on London Bridge, and the drawbridge flung down into the water.

Noailles, for the first time, believed now that the insurrection would fail. Success or failure, in fact, would turn on the reception which the midland counties had given to the Duke of Suffolk; and of Suffolk authentic news had been brought to London that morning.

On the flight of the duke being known at the court, it was supposed immediately that he intended to proclaim his daughter and Guilford Dudley. Rumour, indeed, turned the supposition into fact, [233] and declared that he had called on the country to rise in arms for Queen Jane. But Suffolk's plan was identical with Wyatt's; he had carried with him a duplicate of Wyatt's proclamation, and, accompanied by his brother, he presented himself in the market-place at Leicester on the morning of Monday the 29th. Lord Huntingdon had followed close upon his track from London; but he assured the Mayor of Leicester that the Earl of Huntingdon was coming, not to oppose, but to join with him. No harm was intended to the queen; he was ready to die in her defence; his object was only to save England from the dominion of foreigners.

In consequence of these protestations, he was allowed to read his proclamation; the people were indifferent; but he called about him a few scores of his tenants and retainers from his own estates in the country; and, on Tuesday morning, while the insurgents in Kent were attacking Cowling Castle, Suffolk rode out of Leicester, in full armour, at the head of his troops, intending first to move on Coventry, then to take Kenilworth and Warwick, and so to advance on London. The garrison at Warwick had been tampered with, and was reported to be ready to rise. The gates of Coventry he expected to find open. He had sent his proclamation thither the day before, by a servant, and he had friends within the walls who had undertaken to place the town at his disposal.

The state of Coventry was probably the state of most other towns in England. The inhabitants were divided. The mayor and aldermen, the fathers of families, and the men of property, were conservatives, loyal to the queen, to the mass, and to "the cause of order." The young and enthusiastic, supported by others who had good reasons for being in opposition to established authorities, were those who had placed themselves in correspondence with the Duke of Suffolk.

Suffolk's servant (his name was Thomas Rampton), on reaching the town, on Monday evening, made a mistake in the first person to whom he addressed himself, and received a cold answer. Two others of the townsmen, however, immediately welcomed him, and told him that "the whole place was at his lord's commandment, except certain of the town council, who feared that, if good fellows had the upper hand, their extremities heretofore should be remembered." [234] They took Rampton into a house, where, presently, another man entered of the same way of thinking, and, in his own eyes, a man of importance. "My lord's quarrel is right well known," this person said, "it is God's quarrel, let him come; let him come, and make no stay, for this town is his own. I say to you assuredly this town is his own. I am it."

It was now night; no time was to be lost, the townsmen said. They urged Rampton to return at once to Suffolk, and hasten his movements. They would themselves read the proclamation at the market-cross forthwith, and raise the people. Rampton, who had ridden far, and was weary, wished to wait till the morning; if they were so confident of success, a few hours could make no difference: but it appeared shortly that the "good fellows" in Coventry were not exclusively under the influence of piety and patriotism. If a rising commenced in the darkness, it was admitted that "undoubted spoil and peradventure destruction of many rich men would ensue," and with transactions of this kind the duke's servant was unwilling to connect himself.

Thus the hours wore away, and no resolution was arrived at; and, in the meantime, the town council had received a warning to be on their guard. Before daybreak the constables were on the alert, the decent citizens took possession of the gates, and the conspirators had lost their opportunity. In the afternoon Suffolk arrived with a hundred horse under the walls, but there was no admission for him. Whilst he was hesitating what course to pursue, a messenger came in to say that the Earl of Huntingdon was at Warwick. The plot for the revolt of the garrison had been detected, and the whole country was on the alert. The people had no desire to see the Spaniards in England; but sober, quiet farmers and burgesses would not rise at the call of the friend of Northumberland, and assist in bringing back the evil days of anarchy.

The Greys had now only to provide for their personal safety.

Suffolk had an estate a few miles distant, called Astley Park, to which the party retreated from Coventry. There the duke shared such money as he had with him among his men, and bade them shift for themselves. Lord Thomas Grey changed coats with a servant, and rode off to Wales to join Sir James Crofts. Suffolk himself, who was ill, took refuge with his brother, Lord John, in the cottage of one of his gamekeepers, where they hoped to remain hidden till the hue and cry should be over, and they could escape abroad.

The cottage was considered insecure. Two bowshots south of Astley Church there stood in the park an old decaying tree, in the hollow of which the father of Lady Jane Grey concealed himself; and there, for two winter days and a night, he was left without food. A proclamation had been put out by Huntingdon for Suffolk's apprehension (January 30), and the keeper, either tempted by the reward, or frightened by the menace against all who should give him shelter, broke his trust—a rare example of disloyalty—and going to Warwick Castle, undertook to betray his master's hiding-place. A party of troopers were despatched, with the keeper for a guide; and, on arriving at Astley, they found that the duke, unable to endure the cold and hunger longer, had crawled out of the tree, and was warming himself by the cottage fire. Lord John was discovered buried under some bundles of hay. [235] They were carried off at once to the Tower, whither Lord Thomas Grey and Sir James Crofts, who had failed as signally in Wales, soon after followed them. [236]

The account of his confederates' failure saluted Wyatt on his arrival in Southwark, on the 3rd of February. The intelligence was being published, at the moment, in the streets of London; Wyatt himself, at the same time, was proclaimed traitor, and a reward of a hundred pounds was offered for his capture, dead or alive. The peril, however, was far from over; Wyatt replied to the proclamation by wearing his name, in large letters, upon his cap; the success of the queen's speech in the city irritated the council, who did not choose to sit still under the imputation of having approved of the Spanish marriage. They declared everywhere, loudly and angrily, that they had not approved of it, and did not approve; in the city itself public feeling again wavered, and fresh parties of the train-bands crossed the water and deserted. The behaviour of Wyatt's followers gave the lie to the queen's charges against them: the prisons in Southwark were not opened; property was respected scrupulously; the only attempt at injury was at Winchester House, and there it was instantly repressed; the inhabitants of the Borough entertained them with warm hospitality; and the queen, notwithstanding her efforts, found herself as it were besieged, in her principal city, by a handful of commoners, whom no one ventured, or no one could be trusted, to attack. So matters continued through Saturday, Sunday, Monday, and Tuesday. The lawyers at Westminster Hall pleaded in harness, the judges wore harness under their robes; Doctor Weston sang mass in harness before the queen; tradesmen attended in harness behind their counters. The metropolis, on both sides of the water, was in an attitude of armed expectation, yet there was no movement, no demonstration on either side of popular feeling. The ominous strangeness of the situation appalled even Mary herself. [237]

By this time (February 5) the intercepted letter of Noailles had been deciphered. It proved, if more proof was wanted, the correspondence between the ambassador and the conspirators; it explained the object of the rising—the queen was to be dethroned in favour of her sister; and it was found, also, though names were not mentioned, that the plot had spread far upwards among the noblemen by whom Mary was surrounded. Evidence of Elizabeth's complicity it did not contain; while, to Gardiner's mortification, it showed that Courtenay, in his confessions to himself, had betrayed the guilt of others, but had concealed part of his own. In an anxiety to shield him the chancellor pronounced the cypher of Courtenay's name to be unintelligible. The queen placed the letter in the hands of Renard, by whom it was instantly read, and the chancellor's humour was not improved; Mary had the mortification of feeling that she was herself the last object of anxiety either to him or to any of her council; though Wyatt was at the gates of London, the council could only spend the time in passionate recriminations; Paget blamed Gardiner for his religious intolerance; Gardiner blamed Paget for having advised the marriage; some exclaimed against Courtenay, some against Elizabeth; but, of acting, all alike seemed incapable. If the queen was in danger, the council said, she might fly to Windsor, or to Calais, or she might go to the Tower. "Whatever happens," she exclaimed to Renard, "I am the wife of the Prince of Spain; crown, rank, life, all shall go before I will take any other husband." [238]

The position, however, could not be of long continuance. Could Wyatt once enter London, he assured himself of success; but the gates on the bridge continued closed. Cheyne and Southwell had collected a body of men on whom they could rely, and were coming up behind from Rochester. Wyatt desired to return and fight them, and then cross the water at Greenwich, as had been before proposed; but his followers feared that he meant to escape;

a backward movement would not be permitted, and his next effort was to ascertain whether the passage over the bridge could be forced.

London Bridge was then a long, narrow street. The gate was at the Southwark extremity; the drawbridge was near the middle. On Sunday or Monday night Wyatt scaled the leads of the gatehouse, climbed into a window, and descended the stairs into the lodge. The porter and his wife were nodding over the fire. The rebel leader bade them, on their lives, be still, and stole along in the darkness to the chasm from which the drawbridge had been cut away. There, looking across the black gulf where the river was rolling below, he saw the dusky mouths of four gaping cannon, and beyond them, in the torch-light, Lord Howard himself, keeping watch with the guard: neither force nor skill could make a way into the city by London Bridge.

The course which he should follow was determined for him. The lieutenant of the Tower, Sir John Brydges, a soldier and a Catholic, had looked over the water with angry eyes at the insurgents collected within reach of his guns, and had asked the queen for permission to fire upon them. The queen, afraid of provoking the people, had hitherto refused; on the Monday, however, a Tower boat, passing the Southwark side of the water, was hailed by Wyatt's sentries; the watermen refused to stop, the sentries fired, and one of the men in the boat was killed. The next morning (February 6) (whether permission had been given at last, or not, was never known), the guns on the White Tower, the Devil's Tower, and all the bastions, were loaded and aimed, and notice was sent over that the fire was about to open. The inhabitants addressed themselves, in agitation, to Wyatt; and Wyatt, with a sudden resolution, half felt to be desperate, resolved to march for Kingston Bridge, cross the Thames, and come back on London. His friends in the city promised to receive him, could he reach Ludgate by daybreak on Wednesday.

On Tuesday morning, therefore, Shrove Tuesday, which the queen had hoped to spend more happily than in facing an army of insurgents, Wyatt, accompanied by not more than fifteen hundred men, pushed out of Southwark. He had cannon with him, which delayed his march, but at four in the afternoon he reached Kingston. Thirty feet of the bridge were broken away, and a guard of three hundred men were on the other side; but the guard fled after a few rounds from the guns, and Wyatt, leaving his men to refresh themselves in the town, went to work to repair the passage. A row of barges lay on the opposite bank; three sailors swam across, attached ropes to them, and towed them over; and, the barges being moored where the bridge was broken, beams and planks were laid across them, and a road was made of sufficient strength to bear the cannon and the waggons.

By eleven o'clock at night the river was crossed, and the march was resumed. The weather was still wild, the roads miry and heavy, and through the winter night the motley party plunged along. The Rochester men had, most of them, gone home, and those who remained were the London deserters, gentlemen who had compromised themselves too deeply to hope for pardon, or fanatics, who believed they were fighting the Lord's battle, and some of the Protestant clergy. Ponet, the late Bishop of Winchester, was with them; William Thomas, the late clerk of the council; Sir George Harper, Anthony Knyvet, Lord Cobham's sons, Pelham, who had been a spy of Northumberland's on the continent, [239] and others more or less conspicuous in the worst period of the late reign.

From the day that Wyatt came to Southwark the whole guard had been under arms at Whitehall, and a number of them, to the agitation of the court ladies, were stationed in the queen's ante-chamber. But the guard was composed of dangerous elements. Sir Humfrey Radcliff, the lieutenant, was a "favourer of the gospel;" [240] and the "Hot Gospeller" himself, on his recovery from his fever, had returned to his duties. [241] No additional precautions had been taken, nor does it seem that, on Wyatt's departure, his movements were watched. Kingston Bridge having been broken, his immediate approach was certainly unlooked for; nor was it till past midnight that information came to the palace that the passage had been forced, and that the insurgents were coming directly back upon London. Between two and three in the morning the queen was called from her bed. Gardiner, who had been, with others of the council, arguing with her in favour of Courtenay the preceding day, was in waiting; he told her that her barge was at the stairs to carry her up the river, and she must take shelter instantly at Windsor.

Without disturbing herself, the queen sent for Renard. Shall I go or stay? she asked.

Unless your majesty desire to throw away your crown, Renard answered, you will remain here till the last extremity; your flight will be known, the city will rise, seize the Tower, and release the prisoners; the heretics will massacre the priests, and Elizabeth will be proclaimed queen.

The lords were divided. Gardiner insisted again that she must and should go. The others were uncertain, or inclined to the opinion of Renard. At last Mary said that she would be guided by Pembroke and Clinton. If those two would undertake to stand by her, she would remain and see out the struggle. [242]

They were not present, and were sent for on the spot. Pembroke for weeks past had certainly wavered; Lord Thomas Grey believed at one time that he had gained him over, and to the last felt assured of his neutrality. Happily for Mary, happily, it must be said, for England — for the Reformation was not a cause to be won by such enterprises as that of Sir Thomas Wyatt — he decided on supporting the queen, and promised to defend her with his life. At four o'clock in the morning drums went round the city, calling the train-bands to an instant muster at Charing Cross. Pembroke's conduct determined the young lords and gentlemen about the court, who with their servants were swiftly mounted and under arms; and by eight, more than ten thousand men were stationed along the ground, then an open field, which slopes from Piccadilly to Pall Mall. The road or causeway on which Wyatt was expected to advance ran nearly on the site of Piccadilly itself. An old cross stood near the head of St. James's Street, where guns were placed; and that no awkward accident like that at Rochester might happen on the first collision, the gentlemen, who formed four squadrons of horse, were pushed forwards towards Hyde Park Corner.

Wyatt, who ought to have been at the gate of the city two hours before, had been delayed in the meantime by the breaking down of a gun in the heavy road at Brentford. Brett, the captain of the city deserters, Ponet, Harper, and others, urged Wyatt to leave the gun where it lay and keep his appointment. Wyatt, however, insisted on waiting till the carriage could be repaired, although in the eyes of every one but himself the delay was obvious ruin. Harper, seeing him obstinate, stole away a second time to gain favour for himself by carrying news to the court. Ponet, unambitious of martyrdom, told him he would pray God for his success, and, advising Brett to shift for himself, made away with others towards the sea and Germany. [243] It was nine o'clock before Wyatt brought the draggled remnant of his force, wet, hungry, and faint with their night march, up the hill from Knightsbridge. Near Hyde Park Corner a lane turned off; and here Pembroke had placed a troop of cavalry. The insurgents straggled on without order. When half of them had passed, the horse dashed out, and cut them in two, and all who were behind were dispersed or captured. Wyatt, caring now only to press forward, kept his immediate followers together, and went straight on. The queen's guns opened, and killed three of his men; but, lowering his head, he dashed at them and over them; then, turning to the right, to avoid the train-bands, he struck down towards St. James's, where his party again separated. Knyvet and the young Cobhams, leaving St. James's to their left, crossed the park to Westminster. Wyatt went right along the present Pall Mall, past the line of the citizens. They had but to move a few steps to intercept his passage, close in, and take him; but not a man advanced, not a hand was lifted; where the way was narrow they drew aside to let him pass. At Charing Cross Sir John Gage was stationed, with part of the guard, some horse, and among them, Courtenay, who in the morning had been heard to say he would not obey orders; he was as good a man as Pembroke. As Wyatt came up Courtenay turned his horse towards Whitehall, and began to move off, followed by Lord Worcester. "Fie! my lord," Sir Thomas Cornwallis cried to him, "is this the action of a gentleman?" [244] But deaf, or heedless, or treacherous, he galloped off, calling Lost, lost! all is lost! and carried panic to the court. The guard had broken at his flight, and came hurrying behind him. Some cried that Pembroke had played false. Shouts of treason rung through the palace. The queen, who had been watching from the palace gallery, alone retained her presence of mind. If others durst not stand the trial against the traitors, she said, she herself would go out into the field and try the quarrel, and die with those that would serve her. [245]

At this moment Knyvet and the Cobhams, who had gone round by the old palace, came by the gates as the fugitive guard were struggling in. Infinite confusion followed. Gage was rolled in the dirt, and three of the judges with him. The guard shrunk away into the offices and kitchens to hide themselves. But Knyvet's men made no attempt to enter. They contented themselves with shooting a few arrows, and then hurried on to Charing Cross to rejoin Wyatt. At Charing Cross, however, their way was now closed by a company of archers, who had been sent back by Pembroke to protect the court. Sharp fighting followed, and the cries rose so loud as to be heard on the leads of the White Tower. At last the leaders forced their way up the Strand; the rest of the party were cut up, dispersed, or taken. [246]

Wyatt himself, meanwhile, followed by three hundred men, had hurried on through lines of men who still opened to give him passage. He passed Temple Bar, along Fleet Street, and reached Ludgate. The gate was open as he approached, when some one seeing a number of men coming up, exclaimed, "These be Wyatt's antients." Muttered curses were heard among the bystanders; but Lord Howard was on the spot; the gates, notwithstanding the murmurs, were instantly closed; and, when Wyatt knocked, Howard's voice answered, "Avaunt! traitor; thou shalt not come in here." "I have kept touch," Wyatt exclaimed; but his enterprise was hopeless now. He sat down upon a bench outside the Belle Sauvage Yard. His followers scattered from him among the by-lanes and streets; and, of the three hundred, twenty-four alone remained, among whom were now Knyvet and one of the young Cobhams. With these few he turned at last, in the forlorn hope that the train-bands would again open to let him pass. Some of Pembroke's horse were coming up. He fought his way through them to Temple Bar, where a herald cried, "Sir, ye were best to yield; the day is gone against you; perchance ye may find the queen merciful." Sir Maurice Berkeley was standing near him on horseback, to whom, feeling that further resistance was useless, he surrendered his sword; and Berkeley, to save him from being cut down in the tumult, took him up upon his horse. Others in the same way took up Knyvet and Cobham, Brett and two more. The six prisoners were carried through the Strand back to Westminster, the passage through the city being thought dangerous; and from Whitehall Stairs, Mary herself looking on from a window of the palace, they were borne off in a barge to the Tower.

The queen had triumphed, triumphed through her own resolution, and would now enjoy the fruits of victory.

Had Wyatt succeeded, Mary would have lost her husband and her crown; and had the question been no more than a personal one, England could have well dispensed both with her and Philip. But Elizabeth would have ascended a throne under the shadow of treason. The Protestants would have come back to power in the thoughtless vindictiveness of exasperated and successful revolutionists; and the problem of the Reformation would have been more hard than ever of a reasonable solution. The fanatics had made their effort, and they had failed; they had shaken the throne, but they had not overthrown it; the queen's turn was come, and, as the danger had been great, so was the resentment. She had Renard at one ear protesting that, while these turbulent spirits were uncrushed, the precious person of the prince could not be trusted to her. She had Gardiner, who, always pitiless towards heretics, was savage at the frustration of his own schemes. Renard in the closet, Gardiner in the pulpit, alike told her that she must show no more mercy. [247] On Ash Wednesday evening, after Wyatt's surrender, a proclamation forbade all persons to shelter the fugitive insurgents under pain of death. The "poor caitiffs" were brought out of the houses where they had hidden themselves, and were given up by hundreds. Huntingdon came in on Saturday with Suffolk and his brothers. Sir James Crofts, Sir Henry Isly, and Sir Gawen Carew followed. The common prisons overflowed into the churches, where crowds of wretches were huddled together till the gibbets were ready for their hanging; the Tower wards were so full that Cranmer, Ridley, and Latimer were packed into a single cell; and all the living representatives of the families of Grey and Dudley, except two young girls, were now within the Tower walls, sentenced, or soon to be sentenced, to death.

The queen's blood is up at last, Renard wrote exultingly to the emperor on the 8th of February; [248] "the Duke of Suffolk, Lord Thomas Grey, and Sir James Crofts have written to ask for mercy, but they will find none; their heads will fall, and so will Courtenay's and Elizabeth's. I have told the queen that she must be especially prompt with these two. We have nothing now to hope for except that France will break the peace, and then all will be well." On the 12th of February the ambassador was still better satisfied. Elizabeth had been sent for, and was on her way to London. A rupture with France seemed inevitable, and as to clemency, there was no danger of it. "The queen," he said, "had told him that Anne of Cleves was implicated;" but for himself he was sure that the two centres of all past and all possible conspiracies were Elizabeth and Courtenay, and that when their heads, and the heads of the Greys, were once off their shoulders, she would have nothing more to fear. The prisoners were heretics to a man; she had a fair plea to despatch them, and she would then settle the country as she pleased; [249] "The house of Suffolk would soon be extinct."

The house of Suffolk would be extinct: that too, or almost that, had been decided on. Jane Grey was guiltless of this last commotion; her name had not been so much as mentioned among the insurgents; but she was guilty of having been once called queen, and Mary, who before had been generously deaf to the emperor's advice, and to Renard's arguments, yielded in her present humour. Philip was beckoning in the distance; and while Jane Grey lived, Philip, she was again and again assured, must remain for ever separated from her arms.

Jane Grey, therefore, was to die—her execution was resolved upon the day after the victory; and the first intention was to put her to death on the Friday immediately approaching. In killing her body, however, Mary desired to have mercy on her soul; and she sent the message of death (February 9) by the excellent Feckenham, afterwards Abbot of Westminster, who was to bring her, if possible, to obedience to the Catholic faith.

Feckenham, a man full of gentle and tender humanity, felt to the bottom of his soul the errand on which he was despatched. He felt as a Catholic priest—but he felt also as a man.

On admission to Lady Jane's room he told her that she was to die the next morning, and he told her, also, for what reason the queen had selected him to communicate the sentence.

She listened calmly. The time was short, she said; too short to be spent in theological discussion; which, if Feckenham would permit, she would decline.

Believing, or imagining that he ought to believe, that, if she died unreconciled, she was lost, Feckenham hurried back to the queen to beg for delay; and the queen, moved with his entreaties, respited the execution till Monday, giving him three more days to pursue his labour. But Lady Jane, when he returned to her, scarcely appreciated the favour; she had not expected her words to be repeated, she said; she had given up all thoughts of the world, and she would take her death patiently whenever her majesty desired. [250]

Feckenham, however, still pressed his services, and courtesy to a kind and anxious old man forbade her to refuse them. He remained with her to the end; and certain arguments followed on faith and justification, and the nature of sacraments; a record of which may be read by the curious in Foxe. [251] Lady Jane was wearied without being convinced. The tedium of the discussion was relieved, perhaps, by the now more interesting account which she gave to her unsuccessful confessor of the misfortune which was bringing her to her death. [252] The night before she suffered she wrote a few sentences of advice to her sister on the blank leaf of a New Testament. To her father, knowing his weakness, and knowing, too, how he would be worked upon to imitate the recantation of Northumberland, she sent a letter of exquisite beauty, in which the exhortations of a dying saint are tempered with the reverence of a daughter for her father. [253]

The iron-hearted Lieutenant of the Tower, Sir John Brydges, had been softened by the charms of his prisoner, and begged for some memorial of her in writing. She wrote in a manual of English prayers the following words: —

"Forasmuch as you have desired so simple a woman to write in so worthy a book, good Master Lieutenant, therefore I shall, as a friend, desire you, and as a Christian, require you, to call upon God to incline your heart to his laws, to quicken you in his way, and not to take the word of truth utterly out of your mouth. Live still to die, that by death you may purchase eternal life, and remember how Methuselah, who, as we read in the Scriptures, was the longest liver that was of a man, died at the last; for, as the Preacher saith, there is a time to be born and a time to die; and the day of death is better than the day of our birth. Yours, as the Lord knoweth, as a friend, Jane Dudley." [254]

Her husband was also to die, and to die before her. The morning on which they were to suffer he begged for a last interview and a last embrace. It was left to herself to consent or refuse. If, she replied, the meeting would benefit either of their souls, she would see him with pleasure; but, in her own opinion, it would only increase their trial. They would meet soon enough in the other world.

He died, therefore, without seeing her again. She saw him once alive as he was led to the scaffold, and again as he returned a mutilated corpse in the death-cart. It was not wilful cruelty. The officer in command had forgotten that the ordinary road led past her window. But the delicate girl of seventeen was as masculine in her heart as in her intellect. When her own turn arrived, Sir John Brydges led her down to the green; her attendants were in an agony of tears, but her own eyes were dry. She prayed quietly till she reached the foot of the scaffold, when she turned to Feckenham, who still clung to her side. "Go now," she said; "God grant you all your desires, and accept my own warm thanks for your attentions to me; although, indeed, those attentions have tried me more than death can now terrify me." [255] She sprung up the steps, and said briefly that she had broken the law in accepting the crown; but as to any guilt of intention, she wrung her hands, and said she washed them clean of it in innocency before God and man. She entreated her hearers to bear her witness that she died a true Christian woman; that she looked to be saved only by the mercy of God and the merits of his Son: and she begged for their prayers as long as she was alive. Feckenham had still followed her, notwithstanding his dismissal. "Shall I say the *Miserere* psalm?" she said to him. [256] When it was done, she let down her hair with her attendants' help, and uncovered her neck. The rest may be told in the words of the chronicler: —

"The hangman kneeled down and asked her forgiveness, whom she forgave most willingly. Then he willed her to stand upon the straw, which doing, she saw the block. Then she said, I pray you despatch me quickly. Then she kneeled down, saying, Will you take it off before I lay me down? and the hangman answered No, Madam. She tied a kerchief about her eyes; then, feeling for the block, she said, What shall I do; where is it? One of the bystanders guiding her thereunto, she laid her head down upon the block, and stretched forth her body, and said, Lord, into thy hands I commend my spirit. And so ended." [257]

The same day Courtenay was sent to the Tower, and a general slaughter commenced of the common prisoners. To spread the impression, gibbets were erected all over London, and by Thursday evening eighty or a hundred bodies [258] were dangling in St. Paul's Churchyard, on London Bridge, in Fleet Street, and at Charing Cross, in Southwark and Westminster. At all cross-ways and in all thoroughfares, says Noailles, "the eye was met with the hideous spectacle of hanging men;" while Brett and a fresh batch of unfortunates were sent to suffer at Rochester and Maidstone. Day after day, week after week, commissioners sat at Westminster or at the Guildhall trying prisoners, who passed with a short shrift to the gallows. The Duke of Suffolk was sentenced on the 17th; on the 23rd he followed his daughter, penitent for his rebellion, but constant, as she had implored him to be, in his faith. His two brothers and Lord Cobham's sons were condemned. William Thomas, to escape torture, stabbed himself, but recovered to die at Tyburn. Lord Cobham himself, who was arrested notwithstanding his defence of his house, Wyatt, Sir James Crofts, Sir William St. Lowe, Sir Nicholas Arnold, Sir Nicholas Throgmorton, and, as the council expressed it, "a world more," were in various prisons waiting their trials. Those who were suspected of being in Elizabeth's confidence were kept with their fate impending over them—to be tempted either with hopes of pardon, or by the rack, to betray their secrets. [259]

But, sooner or later, the queen was determined that every one who could be convicted should die, [260] and beyond, and above them all, Elizabeth. Elizabeth's illness, which had been supposed to have been assumed, was real, and as the feeling of the people towards her compelled the observance of the forms of justice and decency, physicians were sent from the court to attend upon her. On the 18th of February they reported that she could be moved with safety; and, escorted by Lord William Howard, Sir Edward Hastings, and Sir Thomas Cornwallis, she was brought by slow stages, of six or seven miles a day, to London. [261] Renard had described her to the emperor as probably *enceinte* through some vile intrigue, and crushed with remorse and disappointment. [262]

To give the lie to all such slanders, when she entered the city, the princess had the covering of her litter thrown back; she was dressed in white, her face was pale from her illness, but the expression was lofty, scornful, and magnificent. [263] Crowds followed her along the streets to Westminster. The queen, when she arrived at Whitehall, refused to see her; a suite of rooms was assigned for her confinement in a corner of the palace, from which there was no egress except by passing the guard, and there, with short attendance, she waited the result of Gardiner's investigations. Wyatt, by vague admissions, had already partially compromised her, and, on the strength of his words, and the discovery of the copy of her letter in the packet of Noailles, she would have gone direct to the Tower, had the lords permitted. The emperor urged instant and summary justice both on her and on Courtenay; the irritation, should irritation arise, could be allayed afterwards by an amnesty. [264] The lords, however, insisted obstinately on the forms of law, the necessity of witnesses, and of a trial; and Renard watched their unreasonable humours with angry misgivings. It was enough, he said, that the conspiracy was undertaken in Elizabeth's interests; if she escaped now, the queen would never be secure. [265] In fact, while Elizabeth lived, the prince could not venture among the wild English spirits, and Charles was determined that the marriage should not escape him.

As soon as the rebellion was crushed, Egmont, attended by Count Horn, returned to complete his work. He brought with him the dispensations in regular form. He brought also a fresh and pressing entreaty that Elizabeth should be sacrificed. An opportunity had been placed in the queen's hand, which her duty to the church required that she should not neglect; and Egmont was directed to tell her that the emperor, in trusting his son in a country where his own power could not protect him, relied upon her honour not to neglect any step essential to his security. [266] Egmont gave his message. The unhappy queen required no urging; she protested to Renard, that she could neither rest nor sleep, so ardent was her desire for the prince's safe arrival. [267] Courtenay, if necessary, she could kill; against him the proofs were complete; as to Elizabeth, she knew her guilt; the evidence was growing; and she would insist to the council that justice should be done.

About the marriage itself, the lords had by this time agreed to yield. Courtenay's pretensions could no longer be decently advanced, and Gardiner, abandoning a hopeless cause, and turning his attention to the restoration of the church, would consent to anything, if, on his side, he might emancipate the clergy from the control of the civil power, and re-establish persecution. Two factions, distinctly marked, were now growing in the council — the party of the statesmen, composed of Paget, Sussex, Arundel, Pembroke, Lord William Howard, the Marquis of Winchester, Sir Edward Hastings, and Cornwallis: the party of the church, composed of Gardiner, Petre, Rochester, Gage, Jerningham, and Bourne. Divided on all other questions, the rival parties agreed only no longer to oppose the coming of Philip. The wavering few had been decided by the presents and promises which Egmont brought with him from Charles. Pensions of two thousand crowns had been offered to, and were probably accepted by the Earls of Pembroke, Arundel, Derby, and Shrewsbury; pensions of a thousand crowns were given to Sussex, Darcy, Winchester, Rochester, Petre, and Cheyne; pensions of five hundred crowns to Southwell, Waldegrave, Inglefield, Wentworth, and Grey; [268] ten thousand crowns were distributed among the officers and gentlemen who had distinguished themselves against Wyatt. The pensions were large, but, as Renard observed, when Charles seemed to hesitate, several of the recipients were old, and would soon die; and, as to the rest, things in England were changing from day to day, and means of some kind would easily be found to put an early end to the payments. [269]

Unanimity having been thus secured, on the day of Egmont's arrival Renard demanded an audience of the lords, and in the queen's presence requested their opinion whether the condition of England allowed the completion of the contract. The life of the prince of Spain was of great importance to Europe; should they believe in their hearts that he would be in danger, there was still time to close the negotiation. The rebellion having broken out and having failed, the lords replied that there was no longer any likelihood of open violence. Arundel hinted, again, that the prince must bring his own cook and butler with him; [270] but he had nothing else to fear, if he could escape the French cruisers.

These assurances, combined with the queen's secret promises about Elizabeth, were held sufficient; and on the 6th of March, at three o'clock in the afternoon, the ambassadors were conducted by Pembroke into the presence chamber. The queen, kneeling before the sacrament, called it to witness that, in consenting to the alliance with the Prince of Spain, she was moved by no carnal concupiscence, but only by her zeal for the welfare of her realm and subjects; and then, rising up, with the bystanders all in tears, she gave her hand to Egmont as Philip's representative. The blessing was pronounced by Gardiner, and the proxy marriage was completed. [271] The prince was to be sent for without delay, and Southampton was chosen as the port at which he should disembark, "being in the country of the Bishop of Winchester," where the people were, for the most part, good Catholics.

Parliament was expected to give its sanction without further difficulty; the opposition of the country having been neutralised by the same causes which had influenced the council. The queen, indeed, in going through the ceremony before consulting parliament, though she had broken the promise which she made in the Guildhall, had placed it beyond their power to raise difficulties; but other questions were likely to rise which would not be settled so easily. She herself was longing to show her gratitude to Providence by restoring the authority of the pope; and the pope intended, if possible, to recover his first-fruits and Peter's pence, and to maintain the law of the church which forbade the alienation of church property. [272] The English laity were resolute on their side to keep hold of what they had got; and to set the subject at rest, and to prevent unpleasant discussions on points of theology, Paget, with his friends, desired that the session should last but a few days, and that two measures only should be brought forward; the first for the confirmation of the treaty of marriage, the second to reassert the validity of the titles under which the church estates were held by their present owners. If the queen consented to the last, her title of Head of the Church might be dropped informally, and allowed to fall into abeyance. [273]

Gardiner, however, saw in the failure of the insurrection an opportunity of emancipating the church, and of extinguishing heresy with fire and sword. [274] He was preparing a bill to restore the ancient rigorous tyranny of the ecclesiastical courts; and by his own authority he directed that, in the writs for the parliament, the summons should be to meet at Oxford, [275] where the conservatism of the country would be released from the dread of the London citizens. The spirit which, thirteen years before, had passed the Six Articles Bill by acclamation, continued to smoulder in the slow minds of the country gentlemen, and was blazing freely among the lately persecuted priests. The Bishop of Winchester had arranged in his imagination a splendid melodrama. The session was to begin on the 2nd of April; and the ecclesiastical bill was to be the first to be passed. On the 8th of March, Cranmer, Ridley, and Latimer were sent down to the University to be tried before a committee of Convocation which had already decided on its verdict; and the Fathers of the Reformation were either to recant or to suffer the flaming penalties of heresy in the presence of the legislature, as the first-fruits of a renovated church discipline.

Vainly Renard protested. In the fiery obstinacy of his determination, Gardiner was the incarnate expression of the fury of the ecclesiastical faction, smarting, as they were, under their long degradation, and under the irritating consciousness of those false oaths of submission which they had sworn to a power which they loathed. Once before, in the first reaction against Protestant excesses, the Bishop of Winchester had seen the Six Articles Bill carried—but his prey had then been snatched from his grasp. Now, embittered by fresh oppression, he saw his party once more in a position to revenge their wrongs when there was no Henry any longer to stand between them and their enemies. He would take the tide at the flood, forge a weapon keener than the last, and establish the Inquisition. [276] Paget swore it should not be. [277] Charles V. himself, dreading a fresh interruption to the marriage, insisted that this extravagant fervour should be checked; [278] and the Bishop of Arras, the scourge of the Netherlands, interceded for moderation in England. But Gardiner and the clergy were not to be turned from the hope of their hearts by the private alarms of the Imperialists; and in the heart of the queen religious orthodoxy was Philip's solitary rival. Renard urged her to be prudent in religion and cruel to the political prisoners. Gardiner, though eager as Renard to kill Elizabeth, would buy the privilege of working his will upon the Protestants by sparing

Courtenay and Courtenay's friends. Mary listened to the worst counsels of each, and her distempered humour settled into a confused ferocity. So unwholesome appeared the aspect of things in the middle of March that, notwithstanding the formal contract, Renard almost advised the emperor to relinquish the thought of committing his son among so wild a people. [279]

As opposition to extreme measures was anticipated in the House of Lords, as well as among the Commons, it was important to strengthen the bench of bishops. The pope had granted permission without difficulty to fill the vacant sees; and on the 1st of April six new prelates were consecrated at St. Mary Overies, while Sir John Brydges and Sir John Williams of Thame were raised to the peerage.

The Protestants, it must be admitted, had exerted themselves to make Gardiner's work easy to him. On the 14th of March the wall of a house in Aldgate became suddenly vocal, and seventeen thousand persons were collected to hear a message from Heaven pronounced by an angel. When the people said "God save Queen Mary," the wall was silent; when they said "God save Queen Elizabeth," the wall said "Amen!" When they asked, "What is the mass?" the wall said, "It is idolatry." As the nation was holding its peace, the stones, it seemed, were crying out against the reaction. But the angel, on examination, turned out to be a girl concealed behind the plaster. Shortly after, the inhabitants of Cheapside, on opening their shop windows in the morning, beheld on a gallows, among the bodies of the hanged insurgents, a cat in priestly robes, with crown shaven, the fore-paws tied over her head, and a piece of paper clipped round between them, representing the wafer.

More serious were the doings of a part of the late conspirators who had escaped to France. Peter Carew, when he left Weymouth, promised soon to return, and he was received at Paris with a cordiality that answered his warmest hopes. Determined, if possible, to prevent Philip from reaching England, the French had equipped every vessel which they possessed available for sea, and Carew was sent again to the coast of the Channel to tempt across into the French service all those who, like himself, were compromised in the conspiracy, or whose blood was hotter than their fathers'. Every day the queen was chafed with the news of desertions to their dangerous rendezvous. Young men of honourable families, Pickerings, Strangways's, Killegrews, Staffords, Stauntons, Tremaynes, Courtenays, slipped over the water, carrying with them hardy sailors from the western harbours. The French supplied them with arms, ships, and money; and fast-sailing, heavily-armed privateers, officered by these young adventurers in the cause of freedom, were cruising on their own account, plundering

Flemish and Spanish ships, and swearing that the Prince of Spain should set no foot on English shores. [280]

The queen indignantly demanded explanations of Noailles, and, through her ambassador at Paris, she required the French government to seize "her traitors," and deliver them to her. Noailles, alarmed, perhaps, for his own security, suggested that it might be well to conceal Carew, and to affect to make an attempt to arrest him. But Henry, at once more sagacious and more bold, replied to the ambassador that "he was not the queen's hangman:" "these men that you require," he said, "deny that they have conspired anything against the queen; marry, they say they will not be oppressed by mine enemy, and that is no just cause why I should owe them ill-will." [281] He desired Noailles, with quiet irony, to tell her majesty "that there was nothing in the existing treaties to forbid his accepting the services of English volunteers in the war with the emperor: her majesty might remember that he had invited her to make a new treaty, and that she had refused:" "he would act by the just letter of his obligations." [282]

Would her subjects have permitted, the queen would have replied by a declaration of war. As it was, she could only relieve herself with indignant words. [283] But Carew and his friends might depend on support so long as they would make themselves useful to France. Possessed of ships and arms, they were a constant menace to the Channel, and a constant temptation to the disaffected; and, growing bitter at last, and believing that Elizabeth's life was on the point of being sacrificed, they were prepared to support Henry in a second attempt to seize the Isle of Wight, and to accept the French competitor for the English crown in the person of the Queen of Scots. [284] Thus fatally the friends of the Reformation played into the hands of its enemies. By the solid mass of Englishmen the armed interference of France was more dreaded than even a Spanish sovereign; and the heresy became doubly odious which was tampering with the hereditary enemies of the realm. In London only the revolutionary spirit continued vigorous, and broke out perpetually in unexpected forms. At the beginning of March three hundred schoolboys met in a meadow outside the city walls: half were for Wyatt and for France, half for the Prince of Spain; and, not all in play (for evidently they chose their sides by their sympathies), they joined battle, and fought with the fierceness of grown men. The combat ended in the capture of the representative of Philip, who was dragged to a gallows, and would have been hanged upon it, had not the spectators interfered. [285] The boys were laid hands upon. The youngest were whipped, the elder imprisoned. It was said that the queen thought of gibbeting one of these innocents in real fact, for an example; or, as Noailles put it, as an expiation for the sins of the people. [286]

Over Elizabeth, in the meantime, the fatal net appeared to be closing; Lord Russell had received a letter for her from Wyatt, which, though the princess declared that it had never been in her hands, he said that he had forwarded; and Wyatt himself was flattered with hopes of life if he would extend his confession. Renard carried his ingenuity farther; he called in the assistance of Lady Wyatt, and promised her that her husband should be spared; he even urged the queen to gain over, by judicious leniency, a man whose apostasy would be a fresh disgrace to his cause, and who might be as useful as a servant as he had been dangerous as a foe. [287] Wyatt, being a man without solidity of heart, showed signs of yielding to what was required of him; but his revelations came out slowly, and to quicken his confession he was brought to his trial on the 15th of March. He pleaded guilty to the indictment, and he then said that Courtenay had been the instigator of the conspiracy; he had written to Elizabeth, he said, to advise her to remove as far as possible from London, and Elizabeth had returned him a verbal message of thanks. This being not enough, he was sentenced to death; but he was made to feel that he might still earn his pardon if he would implicate Elizabeth more deeply; and though he said nothing definite, he allowed himself to drop vague hints that he could tell more if he pleased. [288]

At all events, however, sufficient evidence had been obtained in the opinion of the court for the committal of the princess to the Tower. On the day of Wyatt's trial, the council met, but separated without a resolution; on Friday, the 16th, Elizabeth was examined before them in person; and when she withdrew, Gardiner required that she should be sent to the Tower instantly. Paget, supported by Sussex, Hastings, and Cornwallis, said that there was no evidence to justify so violent a measure. [289] Which of you, then, said Gardiner, with dexterous ingenuity, will be responsible for the safe keeping of her person?

The guardian of Elizabeth would be exposed to a hundred dangers and a thousand suspicions; the lords answered that Gardiner was conspiring their destruction. No one could be found courageous enough to undertake the charge, and they gave their reluctant consent to his demand. The same night Elizabeth's attendants were removed, a hundred soldiers were picketed in the garden below her window, and on Saturday morning (March 17) the Marquis of Winchester and Lord Sussex waited on her to communicate her destination, and to attend her to a barge.

The terrible name of the Tower was like a death-knell; the princess entreated a short delay till she could write a few words to the queen; the queen could not know the truth, she said, or else she was played upon by Gardiner. Alas! she did not know the queen: Winchester hesitated; Lord

Sussex, more generous, accepted the risk, and promised, on his knees, to place her letter in the queen's hands.

The very lines traced by Elizabeth in that bitter moment may still be read in the State Paper Office, [290] and her hand was more than usually firm.

"If ever any one," she wrote, "did try this old saying that a king's word was more than another man's oath, I most humbly beseech your majesty to verify it in me, and to remember your last promise, and my last demand, that I be not condemned without answer and due proof, which it seems that I now am: for that without cause proved I am by your council from you commanded to go unto the Tower, a place more wonted for a false traitor than a true subject: which, though I know I deserve it not, yet in the face of all this realm appears that it is proved; which I pray God that I may die the shamefullest death that any died, afore I may mean any such thing: and to this present hour I protest, afore God who shall judge my truth, whatsoever malice shall devise, that I never practised, counselled, nor consented to anything that might be prejudicial to your person any way, or dangerous to the state by any means. And I therefore humbly beseech your majesty to let me answer afore yourself, and not suffer me to trust to your councillors; yea, and that afore I go to the Tower, if it is possible; if not, afore I be further condemned. Howbeit, I trust assuredly your highness will give me leave to do it afore I go, for that thus shamefully I may not be cried out on, as now I shall be, yea, and without cause. Let conscience move your highness to take some better way with me, than to make me be condemned in all men's sight, afore my desert known. Also, I most humbly beseech your highness to pardon this my boldness, which innocency procures me to do, together with hope of your natural kindness, which I trust will not see me cast away without desert: which what it is I would desire no more of God than that you truly knew; which thing, I think and believe, you shall never by report know, unless by yourself you hear. I have heard in my time of many cast away for want of coming to the presence of their prince; and in late days I heard my Lord of Somerset say that, if his brother had been suffered to speak with him, he had never suffered; but the persuasions were made to him so great, that he was brought in belief that he could not live safely if the admiral lived, and that made him give his consent to his death. Though these persons are not to be compared to your majesty, yet I pray God as evil persuasions persuade not one sister against the other, and all for that they have heard false reports, and not hearken to the truth known; therefore, once again kneeling with all humbleness of my heart, because I am not suffered to bow the knees of my body, I humbly crave to speak with your highness, which I would not be so bold to desire if I knew not myself most clear, as I know myself most true. And as for the traitor Wyatt, he might peradventure write me a letter, but on my faith I never received any from him; and for the copy of my letter sent to the French king, I pray God confound me eternally if ever I sent him word, message, token, or letter by any means: [291] and to this my truth I will stand to my death your highness's most faithful subject that hath been from the beginning, and will be to the end." Elizabeth.

"I humbly crave but one word of answer from yourself."

Had Elizabeth known the history of those words of the queen to her, to which she appealed, she would have spared herself the trouble of writing this letter. Sussex fulfilled his promise, and during the delay the tide turned, and the barge could not pass London Bridge till the following day. The queen could not venture to send the princess through the streets; and in dread lest, at the last moment, her prey should be snatched from her, she answered the appeal only by storming at the bearer, and at his friends in the council. "They were going no good way," she said, "for their lives they durst not have acted so in her father's time; she wished that he was alive and among them but for a single month." [292]

At nine o'clock the next morning—it was Palm Sunday (March 18)— the two lords returned to Elizabeth to tell her that her letter had failed. As she crossed the garden to the water she threw up her eyes to the queen's window, but there was no sign of recognition. What do the lords mean, she said, that they suffer me thus to be led into captivity? The barge was too deep to approach sufficiently near to the landing-place at the Tower to enable her to step upon the causeway without wetting her feet; it was raining too, and the petty inconveniences, fretting against the dreadful associations of the Traitors' Gate, shook her self-command. She refused to land; then sharply rejecting an offer of assistance, she sprang out upon the mud. "Are all those harnessed men there for me?" she said to Sir John Gage, who was waiting with the Tower guard. "No, madam," Gage answered. "Yes," she said, "I know it is so; it needed not for me, being but a weak woman. I never thought to have come in here a prisoner," she went on, turning to the soldiers; "I pray you all good fellows and friends, bear me witness that I come in no traitor, but as true a woman to the queen's majesty as any is now living, and thereon will I take my death." She threw herself down upon a wet stone; Lord Chandos begged her to come under shelter out of the rain: "better sitting here than in a worse place," she cried; "I know not whither you will bring me."

But it was not in Elizabeth's nature to protract a vain resistance; she rose, and passed on, and as she approached the room intended for her, the heavy doors along the corridor were locked and barred behind her. At the grating of the iron bolts the heart of Lord Sussex sank in him: Sussex knew the queen's true feelings, and the efforts which were made to lash her into cruelty; "What mean ye, my lords," he said to Chandos and Gage, "what will you do?" "she was a king's daughter, and is the queen's sister; go no further than your commission, which I know what it is." [293]

The chief danger was of murder—of some swift desperate act which could not be undone; the lords who had so reluctantly permitted Elizabeth to be imprisoned would not allow her to be openly sacrificed, or indeed permit the queen to continue in the career of vengeance on which she had entered. The executions on account of the rebellion had not ceased even yet. In Kent, London, and in the midland counties, day after day, one, two, or more persons had been put to death; six gentlemen were, at that very moment, on their way to Maidstone and Rochester to suffer. The lords, on the day of Elizabeth's committal, held a meeting while Gardiner was engaged elsewhere; they determined to remonstrate, and, if necessary, to insist on a change of course, and Paget undertook to be the bearer of the message. He found Mary in her oratory after vespers; he told her that the season might remind a sovereign of other duties besides revenge; already too much blood had been shed; the noble house of Suffolk was all but destroyed; and he said distinctly that if she attempted any more executions, he and his friends would interfere; the hideous scenes had lasted too long, and, as an earnest of a return to mercy, he demanded the pardon of the six gentlemen.

Mary, as she lamented afterwards to Renard, was unprepared; she was pressed in terms which showed that those who made the request did not intend to be refused—and she consented. [294] The six gentlemen escaped; and, following up this beginning, the council, in the course of the week, extorted from her the release of Northampton, Cobham, and one of his sons, with five others. In a report to the emperor, Renard admitted that, if the queen attempted to continue her course of justice, there would be resistance; and the party of the chancellor, being the weakest, would in that case be overwhelmed. It was the more necessary, therefore, that, by one means or another, Elizabeth should be disposed of. The queen had condescended to apologise to him for her second act of clemency, which she excused as being an Easter custom. It was not for him to find fault, he said that he had replied, if her majesty was pleased to show mercy at the holy season; but it was his duty to remind her that he doubted whether the prince could be trusted with her.

This argument never failed to drive Mary to madness; and, on the other side, Renard applied to Gardiner to urge despatch in bringing Elizabeth to trial: as long as she lived, there was no security for the queen, for the prince, or for religion. Gardiner echoed the same opinion. If others, he said, would go to work as roundly as himself, all would be well. [295]

In this condition of the political atmosphere parliament assembled on the 2nd of April. The Oxford scheme had been relinquished as impracticable. The Lord Mayor informed the queen that he would not answer for the peace of the city in the absence of the court; the Tower might be surprised and the prisoners released; and to lose the Tower would be to lose the crown. The queen said that she would not leave London while her sister's fate was undetermined. [296] The Houses met, therefore, as usual, as Westminster, and the speech from the throne was read in Mary's presence by the chancellor.

Since the last parliament, Gardiner said, the people of England had given proofs of unruly humour. The queen was their undoubted sovereign, and a measure would be submitted to the Lords and Commons to declare, in some emphatic manner, her claim to her subjects' obedience.

Her majesty desiring, further, in compliance with her subjects' wishes, to take a husband, she had fixed her choice on the Prince of Spain, as a person agreeable to herself and likely to be a valuable friend to the realm: the people, however, had insolently and ignorantly presumed to mutiny against her intentions, and, in her affection for the commonwealth, her majesty had consented to submit the articles of the marriage to the approval of parliament.

Again, her majesty would desire them to take into their consideration the possible failure of the blood royal, and adopt necessary precautions to secure an undisturbed succession to the crown. It would be for the parliament to decide whether the privilege which had been granted to Henry VIII. of bequeathing the crown by will might not be, with propriety, extended to her present majesty. [297]

Finally, and at great length, the chancellor spoke of religion. The late rebellion, he said, was properly a religious rebellion: it was the work of men who despised the sacraments, and were the enemies of truth, order, and godliness. A measure would be laid before the legislature for the better restraint of irregular licence of opinion.

The marriage was to pass quietly. Those of the Lords and Commons who persevered in their disapproval were a small minority, and did not intend to appear. [298] The bill, therefore, passed both Houses by the 12th of April. [299] The marriage articles were those originally offered by the emperor, with the English clauses attached, and some explanatory paragraphs, that no room might be left for laxity of interpretation. [300] Lord Bedford and Lord Fitzwalter had already gone to Plymouth, where a ship was in readiness to carry them to Spain. They waited only till the parliamentary forms were completed, and immediately sailed. Lord William Howard would go to sea with the fleet, at his earliest convenience, to protect the passage, and the prince might be expected in England by the end of May. The bill for the queen's authority was carried also without objection. The forms of English law running only in the name of a king, it had been pretended that a queen could not be a lawful sovereign. A declaratory statute explained that the kingly prerogative was the same, whether vested in male or female. [301] Here, however, unanimity was at an end. The paragraph about the succession in the queen's speech being obviously aimed at Elizabeth, produced such an irritation in the council, as well as in parliament, that Renard expected it would end in actual armed conflict. [302]

From the day of Elizabeth's imprisonment Gardiner had laboured to extort evidence against her by fair means or foul. [303] She had been followed to the Tower by her servants. Sir John Gage desired that her food should be dressed by people of his own. The servants refused to allow themselves to be displaced, [304] and, to the distress of Renard, angry words had been addressed to Gage by Lord Howard, so that they could not be removed by force. [305]

The temptation of life having failed, after all, to induce Wyatt to enlarge his confession beyond his first acknowledgments, it was determined to execute him. On the 11th of April he was brought out of his cell, and on his way to the scaffold he was confronted with Courtenay, to whom he said something, but how much or what it is impossible to ascertain. [306] Finding that his death was inevitable, he determined to make the only reparation which was any longer in his power to Elizabeth. When placed on the platform, after desiring the people to pray for him, lamenting his crime, and expressing a hope that he might be the last person to suffer for the rebellion, he concluded thus:

"Whereas it is said abroad that I should accuse my Lady Elizabeth's Grace and my Lord Courtenay; it is not so, good people, for I assure you neither they nor any other now yonder in hold or durance was privy of my rising or commotion before I began." [307]

The words, or the substance of them, were heard by every one. Weston, who attended as confessor, shouted, "Believe him not, good people! he confessed otherwise before the council." "That which I said then I said," answered Wyatt, "but that which I say now is true." The executioner did his office, and Wyatt's work, for good or evil, was ended.

All that the court had gained by his previous confessions was now more than lost. London rang with the story that Wyatt, in dying, had cleared Courtenay and Elizabeth. [308] Gardiner still thundered in the Star Chamber on the certainty of their guilt, and pilloried two decent citizens who had repeated Wyatt's words; but his efforts were vain, and the hope of a legal conviction was at an end. The judges declared that against Elizabeth there was now no evidence; [309] and, even if there had been evidence, Renard wrote to his master, that the court could not dare to proceed further against her, from fear of Lord William Howard, who had the whole naval force of England at his disposal, and, in indignation at Elizabeth's treatment, might join the French and the exiles. [310] Perplexed to know how to dispose of her, the ambassador and the chancellor thought of sending her off to Pomfret Castle; doubtless, if once within Pomfret walls, to find the fate of the second Richard there: but again the spectre of Lord Howard terrified them.

The threatened escape of her sister, too, was but the beginning of the queen's sorrows. On the 17th of April Sir Nicholas Throgmorton was tried at the Guildhall for having been a party to the conspiracy. The confessions of many of the prisoners had more or less implicated Throgmorton. Cuthbert Vaughan, who was out with Wyatt, swore in the court that Throgmorton had discussed the plan of the insurrection with him; and Throgmorton himself admitted that he had talked to Sir Peter Carew and Wyatt about the probability of a rebellion. He it was, too, who was to have conducted Courtenay to Andover on his flight into Devonshire; and the evidence [311] leaves very little doubt that he was concerned as deeply as any one who did not actually take up arms. Sir Nicholas, however, defended himself with resolute pertinacity; he fought through all the charges against him, and dissected the depositions with the skill of a practised pleader; and in the end, the jury returned the bold verdict of "Not guilty." Sir Thomas Bromley urged them to remember themselves. The foreman answered they had found the verdict according to their consciences.

Their consciences probably found less difficulty in the facts charged against Throgmorton than in the guilt to be attached to them. The verdict was intended as a rebuke to the cruelty with which the rebellion had been punished, and it was received as an insult to the crown. The crowd, as Throgmorton left the court, threw up their caps and shouted. The queen was ill for three days with mortification, [312] and insisted that the jurors should be punished. They were arrested, and kept as prisoners till the following winter, when they were released on payment of the ruinous fine of £2000. Throgmorton himself was seized again on some other pretext, and sent again to the Tower. The council, or Paget's party there, remonstrated against the arrest; they yielded, however, perhaps that they might make the firmer stand on more important matters.

Since Elizabeth could not be executed, the court were the more anxious to carry the Succession Bill. Gardiner's first desire was that Elizabeth should be excluded by name; but Paget said that this was impossible. [313] As little could a measure be passed empowering the queen to leave the crown by will, for that would be but the same thing under another form. Following up his purpose, notwithstanding, Gardiner brought out in the House of Lords a pedigree, tracing Philip's descent from John of Gaunt; and he introduced a bill to make offences against his person high treason. But at the second reading the important words were introduced, "during the queen's lifetime;" [314] the bill was read a third time, and then disappeared; and Paget had been the loudest of its opponents. [315]

Beaten on the succession, the chancellor, in spite of Renard's remonstrances, brought forward next his Religious Persecution Bills. The House of Commons went with him to some extent; and, to secure success in some form or other, he introduced three separate measures, either of which would answer his purpose— a bill for the restoration of the Six Articles, a bill to re-enact the Lollard Statute of Henry IV., *De Hæretico Comburendo*, and a bill to restore (in more than its original vigour) the Episcopal Jurisdiction. The Six Articles had so bad a name that the first bill was read once only, and was dropped; the two others passed the Commons, [316] and, on the 26th of April, the Bishops' Authority Bill came before the Lords. Lord Paget was so far in advance of his time that he could not hope to appeal with a chance of success to his own principles of judicious latitudinarianism; but he determined, if possible, to prevent Gardiner's intended cruelties from taking effect, and he spread an alarm that, if the bishops were restored to their unrestricted powers, under one form or other the holders of the abbey lands would be at their mercy. To allay the suspicion, another bill was carried through the Commons, providing expressly for the safety of the holders of those lands; but the tyranny of the episcopal courts was so recent, and the ecclesiastics had shown themselves uniformly so little capable of distinguishing between right and wrong when the interests of religion were at stake, that the jealousy, once aroused, could not be checked. The irritation became so hot and so general as to threaten again the most dangerous consequences; and Paget, pretending to be alarmed at the excitement which he had raised, urged Renard to use his influence with the queen to dissolve parliament. [317]

Renard, who was only anxious that the marriage should go off quietly, agreed in the desirableness of a dissolution. He told the queen that the reform of religion must be left to a better opportunity; and the prince could not, and should not, set his foot in a country where parties were for ever on the edge of cutting each other's throats. It was no time for her to be indulging Gardiner in humours which were driving men mad, and shutting her ears to the advice of those who could ruin her if they pleased; she must think first of her husband. The queen protested that Gardiner was acting by no advice of hers; Gardiner, she said, was obstinate, and would listen to no one; she herself was helpless and miserable. But Renard was not to be moved by misery. At all events, he said, the prince should not come till late in the summer, perhaps not till autumn, not, in fact, till it could be seen what form these wild humours would assume; summer was the dangerous time in England, when the people's blood was apt to boil. [318]

Gardiner, however, was probably not acting without Mary's secret approbation. Both the queen and the minister especially desired, at that moment, the passing of the Heresy Bill, and Renard was obliged to content himself with a promise that the dissolution should be as early as possible. Though parliament could not meet at Oxford, a committee of Convocation had been sitting there, with Dr. Weston, the adulterous Dean of Windsor, for a president. Cranmer, Ridley, and Latimer had been called upon to defend their opinions, which had been pronounced false and damnable. They had been required to recant, and, having refused, they were sentenced (April 20), so far as the power of the court extended, to the punishment of heretics.

Cranmer appealed from the judgment to God Almighty, in whose presence he would soon stand.

Ridley said the sentence would but send them the sooner to the place where else they hoped to go.

Latimer said, "I thank God that my life has been prolonged that I may glorify God by this kind of death."

Hooper, Ferrars, Coverdale, Taylor, Philpot, and Sandars, who were in the London prisons, were to have been simultaneously tried and sentenced at Cambridge. These six, however, drew and signed a joint refusal to discuss their faith in a court before which they were to be brought as prisoners; and for some reason the proceedings against them were suspended; but whether they refused or consented was of little moment to the Bishop of Winchester; they were in his hands—he could try them when he pleased. A holocaust of heresiarchs was waiting to be offered up, and before a faggot could be lighted, the necessary powers had to be obtained from parliament.

The bishop, therefore, was determined, if possible, to obtain those powers. He had the entire bench of prelates on his side; and Lord Howard, the Earl of Bedford, and others of the lay lords who would have been on the side of humanity, were absent. The opposition had to be conducted under the greatest difficulties. Paget, however, fought the battle, and fought it on broad grounds: the bishops' bill was read twice; on the third reading, on the 1st of May, he succeeded in throwing it out: the Lollards' bill came on the day after, and here his difficulty was far greater; for toleration was imperfectly understood by Catholic or Protestant, and many among the peers, who hated the bishops, equally hated heresy. Paget, however, spoke out his convictions, and protested against the iniquity of putting men to death for their opinions. [319] The bill was read a first time on the day on which it was introduced; on the 4th of May it was read again, [320] but it went no further. The next day parliament was dissolved. The peers assured the queen that they had no desire to throw a shield over heresy; the common law existed independent of statute, and the common law prescribed punishments which could still be inflicted. [321] But, so long as heresy was undefined, Anabaptists, Socinians, or professors of the more advanced forms of opinion, could alone fall within the scope of punishments merely traditional.

The tempers of men were never worse than at that moment, Renard wrote. In the heat of the debate, on the 28th of April, Lord Thomas Grey was executed as a defiance to the liberal party. Gardiner persuaded the queen, perhaps not without reason, that he was himself in danger of being arrested by Paget and Pembroke; [322] and an order was sent to the Lieutenant of the Tower that if the chancellor was brought thither under warrant of the council only, he was not to be received. [323]

On the other hand, twelve noblemen and gentlemen undertook to stand by Mary if she would arrest Paget and Pembroke. The chancellor, Sir Robert Rochester, and the Marquis of Winchester discussed the feasibility of seizing them; but Lord Howard and the Channel fleet were thought to present too formidable an obstacle. With the queen's sanction, however, they armed in secret. It was agreed that, on one pretence or another, Derby, Shrewsbury, Sussex, and Huntingdon should be sent out of London to their counties. Elizabeth, if it could be managed, should be sent to Pomfret, as Gardiner had before proposed; Lord Howard should be kept at sea; and, if opportunity offered, Arundel and Paget might, at least, be secured. [324]

But Pomfret was impossible, and vexation thickened on vexation. Lord Howard was becoming a bugbear at the court. Report now said that two of the Staffords, whom he had named to command in the fleet, had joined the exiles in France; and for Lord Howard himself the queen could feel no security, if he was provoked too far. She was haunted by a misgiving that, while the prince was under his convoy, he might declare against her, and carry him prisoner to France; or if Howard could himself be trusted, his fleet could not. On the eve of sailing for the coast of Spain, a mutiny broke out at Plymouth. The sailors swore that if they were forced on a service which they detested, both the admiral and the prince should rue it. Lord Howard, in reporting to the queen the men's misconduct, said that his own life was at her majesty's disposal, but he advised her to reconsider the prudence of placing the prince in their power. Howard's own conduct, too, was far from reassuring. A few small vessels had been sent from Antwerp to join the English fleet, under the Flemish admiral Chappelle. Chappelle complained that Howard treated him with indifference, and insulted his ships by "calling them cockle-shells." If the crews of the two fleets were on land anywhere together, the English lost no opportunity of making a quarrel, "hustling and pushing" the Flemish sailors; [325] and, as if finally to complete the queen's vexation, Lord Bedford wrote that the prince declined the protection of her subjects on his voyage, and that his departure was postponed for a few weeks longer.

The fleet had to remain in the Channel; it could not be trusted elsewhere; and the necessity of releasing Elizabeth from the Tower was another annoyance to the queen. A confinement at Woodstock was the furthest stretch of severity that the country would, for the present, permit. On the 19th of May, Elizabeth was taken up the river. The princess believed herself that she was being carried off *tanquam ovis*, as she said—as a sheep for the slaughter. But the world thought that she was set at liberty, and as her barge passed under the bridge Mary heard, with indignation, from the palace windows, three salvoes of artillery fired from the Steelyard, as a sign of the joy of the people. [326] A letter from Philip would have been a consolation to her in the midst of the troubles which she had encountered for his sake; but the languid lover had never written a line to her; or, if he had written, not a line had reached her hand; only a ship which contained despatches from him for Renard had been taken, in the beginning of May, by a French cruiser, and the thought that precious words of affection had, perhaps, been on their way to her and were lost, was hard to bear.

In vain she attempted to cheer her spirits with the revived ceremonials of Whitsuntide. She marched day after day, in procession, with canopies and banners, and bishops in gilt slippers, round St. James's, round St. Martin's, round Westminster. [327] Sermons and masses alternated now with religious feasts, now with *Diriges* for her father's soul. But all was to no purpose; she could not cast off her anxieties, or escape from the shadow of her subjects' hatred, which clung to her steps. Insolent pamphlets were dropped in her path and in the offices of Whitehall; she trod upon them in the passages of the palace; they were placed by mysterious hands in the sanctuary of her bedroom. At length, chafed with a thousand irritations, and craving for a husband who showed so small anxiety to come to her, she fled from London, at the beginning of June, to Richmond.

The trials of the last six months had begun to tell upon Mary's understanding: she was ill with hysterical longings; ill with the passions which Gardiner had kindled and Paget disappointed. A lady who slept in her room told Noailles that she could speak to no one without impatience, and that she believed the whole world was in league to keep her husband from her. She found fault with every one — even with the prince himself. Why had he not written? she asked again and again. Why had she never received one courteous word from him? If she heard of merchants or sailors arriving from Spain, she would send for them and question them; and some would tell her that the prince was said to have little heart for his business in England; others terrified her with tales of fearful fights upon the seas; and others brought her news of the French squadrons that were on the watch in the Channel. [328] She would start out of her sleep at night, picturing a thousand terrors, and among them one to which all else were insignificant, that her prince, who had taken such wild possession of her imagination, had no answering feeling for herself — that, with her growing years and wasted figure, she could never win him to love her. [329]

"The unfortunate queen," wrote Henry of France, "will learn the truth at last. She will wake too late, in misery and remorse, to know that she has filled the realm with blood for an object which, when she has gained it, will bring nothing but affliction to herself or to her people." [330]

But the darkest season has its days of sunshine, and Mary's trials were for the present over. If the statesmen were disloyal, the clergy and the Universities appreciated her services to the church, and, in the midst of her trouble, Oxford congratulated her on having been raised up for the restoration of life and light to England. [331] More pleasant than this pleasant flattery was the arrival, on the 19th of June, of the Marquis delas Navas from Spain, with the news that by that time the prince was on his way.

It was even so. Philip had submitted to his unwelcome destiny, and six thousand troops being required pressingly by the emperor in the Low Countries, they attended him for his escort. A paper of advices was drawn for the prince's use by Renard, directing him how to accommodate himself to his barbarous fortune. Neither soldiers nor mariners would be allowed to land. The noblemen, therefore, who formed his retinue, were advised to bring Spanish musketeers, disguised in liveries, in the place of pages and lacqueys; their arms could be concealed amidst the baggage. The war would be an excuse for the noblemen being armed themselves, and the prince, on landing, should have a shirt of mail under his doublet. As to manner, he must endeavour to be affable: he would have to hunt with the young lords, and to make presents to them; and, with whatever difficulty, he must learn a few words of English, to exchange the ordinary salutations. As a friend, Renard recommended Paget to him; he would find Paget "a man of sense." [332]

Philip, who was never remarkable for personal courage, may be pardoned for having come reluctantly to a country where he had to bring men-at-arms for servants, and his own cook for fear of being poisoned. The sea, too, was hateful to him, for he suffered miserably from sickness. Nevertheless, he was coming, and with him such a retinue of gallant gentlemen as the world has rarely seen together. The Marquis de los Valles, Gonzaga, d'Aguilar, Medina Celi, Antonio de Toledo, Diego de Mendoza, the Count de Feria, the Duke of Alva, Count Egmont, and Count Horn—men whose stories are written in the annals of two worlds: some in letters of glorious light, some in letters of blood which shall never be washed out while the history of mankind survives. Whether for evil or good, they were not the meek innocents for whom Renard had at one time asked so anxiously.

In company with these noblemen was Sir Thomas Gresham, charged with half a million of money in bullion, out of the late arrivals from the New World; which the emperor, after taking security from the London merchants, had lent the queen, perhaps to enable her to make her marriage palatable by the restoration of the currency. [333]

Thus preciously freighted, the Spanish fleet, a hundred and fifty ships, large and small, sailed from Corunna at the beginning of July. The voyage was weary and wretched. The sea-sickness prostrated both the prince and the troops, and to the sea-sickness was added the terror of the French—a terror, as it happened, needless, for the English exiles, by whom the prince was to have been intercepted, had, in the last few weeks, melted away from the French service, with the exception of a few who were at Scilly. Sir Peter Carew, for some unknown reason, had written to ask for his pardon, and had gone to Italy; [334] but the change was recent and unknown, and the ships stole along in silence, the orders of the prince being that not a salute should be fired to catch the ear of an enemy. [335] At last, on the 19th of July, the white cliffs of Freshwater were sighted; Lord Howard lay at the Needles with the English fleet; and on Friday, the 20th, at three o'clock in the afternoon, the flotilla was safely anchored in Southampton Water.

The queen was on her way to Winchester, where she arrived the next morning, and either in attendance upon her, or waiting at Southampton, was almost the entire peerage of England. Having made up their minds to endure the marriage, the lords resolved to give Philip the welcome which was due to the husband of their sovereign, and in the uncertain temper of the people, their presence might be necessary to protect his person from insult or from injury.

It was an age of glitter, pomp, and pageantry; the anchors were no sooner down, than a barge was in readiness, with twenty rowers in the queen's colours of green and white; and Arundel, Pembroke, Shrewsbury, Derby, and other lords went off to the vessel which carried the royal standard of Castile. Philip's natural manner was cold and stiff, but he had been schooled into graciousness. Exhausted by his voyage, he accepted delightedly the instant invitation to go on shore, and he entered the barge accompanied by the Duke of Alva. A crowd of gentlemen was waiting to receive him at the landing-place. As he stepped out—not perhaps without some natural nervousness and sharp glances round him—the whole assemblage knelt. A salute was fired from the batteries, and Lord Shrewsbury presented him with the order of the Garter. [336] An enthusiastic eye-witness thus describes Philip's appearance:—

"Of visage he is well favoured, with a broad forehead and grey eyes, straight-nosed and manly countenance. From the forehead to the point of his chin his face groweth small. His pace is princely, and gait so straight and upright as he loseth no inch of his height; with a yellow head and a yellow beard; and thus to conclude, he is so well proportioned of body, arm, leg, and every other limb to the same, as nature cannot work a more perfect pattern, and, as I have learned, of the age of 28 years. His majesty I judge to be of a stout stomach, pregnant-witted, and of most gentle nature." [337]

Sir Anthony Brown approached, leading a horse with a saddlecloth of crimson velvet, embroidered with gold and pearls. He presented the steed, with a Latin speech, signifying that he was his highness's Master of the Horse; and Philip, mounting, went direct to Southampton church, the English and Spanish noblemen attending bareheaded, to offer thanks for his safe arrival. From the church he was conducted to a house which had been furnished from the royal stores for his reception. Everything was, of course, magnificent. Only there had been one single oversight. Wrought upon the damask hangings, in conspicuous letters, were observed the ominous words, "Henry, by the Grace of God, King of England, France, and Ireland, and Supreme Head of the Church of England." [338]

Here the prince was to remain till Monday to recover from his voyage; perhaps to ascertain, before he left the neighbourhood of his own fleet, the humour of the barbarians among whom he had arrived. In Latin (he was unable to speak French) he addressed the lords on the causes which had brought him to England, the chief among those causes being the manifest will of God, to which he felt himself bound to submit. It was noticed that he never lifted his cap in speaking to any one, [339] but he evidently endeavoured to be courteous. With a stomach unrecovered from the sea, and disdaining precautions, he sate down on the night of his arrival to a public English supper; he even drained a tankard of ale, as an example, he said, to his Spanish companions. [340] The first evening passed off well, and he retired to seek such rest as the strange land and strange people, the altered diet, and the firing of guns, which never ceased through the summer night, would allow him.

Another feature of his new country awaited Philip in the morning (July 21); he had come from the sunny plains of Castile; from his window at Southampton he looked out upon a steady downfall of July rain. Through the cruel torrent [341] he made his way to the church again to mass, and afterwards Gardiner came to him from the queen. In the afternoon the sky cleared, and the Duchess of Alva, who had accompanied her husband, was taken out in a barge upon Southampton Water. Both English and Spaniards exerted themselves to be mutually pleasing; but the situation was not of a kind which it was desirable to protract. Six thousand Spanish troops were cooped in the close uneasy transports, forbidden to land lest they should provoke the jealousy of the people; and when, on Sunday (July 22), his highness had to undergo a public dinner, in which English servants only were allowed to attend upon him, the Castilian lords, many of whom believed that they had come to England on a bootless errand, broke out into murmurs. [342]

Monday came at last; the rain fell again, and the wind howled. The baggage was sent forward in the morning in the midst of the tempest. Philip lingered in hopes of a change; but no change came, and after an early dinner the trumpet sounded to horse. Lords, knights, and gentlemen had thronged into the town, from curiosity or interest, out of all the counties round. Before the prince mounted it was reckoned, with uneasiness, that as many as four thousand cavaliers, under no command, were collected to join the procession.

A grey gelding was led up for Philip; he wrapped himself in a scarlet cloak, and started to meet his bride—to complete a sacrifice the least congenial, perhaps, which ever policy of state extracted from a prince.

The train could move but slowly. Two miles beyond the gates a drenched rider, spattered with chalk mud, was seen galloping towards them; on reaching the prince he presented him with a ring from the queen, and begged his highness, in her majesty's name, to come no further. The messenger could not explain the cause, being unable to speak any language which Philip could understand, and visions of commotion instantly presented themselves, mixed, it may be, with a hope that the bitter duty might yet be escaped. Alva was immediately at his master's side; they reined up, and were asking each other anxiously what should next be done, when an English lord exclaimed in French, with courteous irony, "Our queen, sire, loves your highness so tenderly that she would not have you come to her in such wretched weather." [343] The hope, if hope there had been, died in its birth; before sunset, with drenched garments and draggled plume, the object of so many anxieties arrived within the walls of Winchester.

To the cathedral he went first, wet as he was. Whatever Philip of Spain was entering upon, whether it was a marriage or a massacre, a state intrigue or a midnight murder, his opening step was ever to seek a blessing from the holy wafer. He entered, kissed the crucifix, and knelt and prayed before the altar; then taking his seat in the choir, he remained while the choristers sang a *Te Deum laudamus*, till the long aisles grew dim in the summer twilight, and he was conducted by torch-light to the Deanery.

The queen was at the bishop's palace, but a few hundred yards distant. Philip, doubtless, could have endured the postponement of an interview till morning; but Mary could not wait, and the same night he was conducted into the presence of his haggard bride, who now, after a life of misery, believed herself at the open gate of Paradise. Let the curtain fall over the meeting, let it close also over the wedding solemnities which followed with due splendour two days later. There are scenes in life which we regard with pity too deep for words. The unhappy queen, unloved, unlovable, yet with her parched heart thirsting for affection, was flinging herself upon a breast to which an iceberg was warm; upon a man to whom love was an unmeaning word, except as the most brutal of passions. For a few months she created for herself an atmosphere of unreality. She saw in Philip the ideal of her imagination, and in Philip's feelings the reflex of her own; but the dream passed away — her love for her husband remained; but remained only to be a torture to her. With a broken spirit and bewildered understanding, she turned to Heaven for comfort, and, instead of heaven, she saw only the false roof of her creed painted to imitate and shut out the sky.

The scene will change for a few pages to the Low Countries. Charles V. more than any other person was responsible for this marriage. He had desired it not for Mary's sake, not for Philip's sake, not for religion's sake; but that he might be able to assert a decisive preponderance over France; and, to gain his end, he had already led the queen into a course which had forfeited the regard of her subjects. She had murdered Lady Jane Grey at the instigation of his ambassador, and under the same influence she had done her best to destroy her sister. Yet Charles, notwithstanding, was one of nature's gentlemen. If he was unscrupulous in the sacrifice of others to his purposes, he never spared himself; and in the days of his successes he showed to less advantage than now, when, amidst failing fortunes and ruined health, his stormy career was closing.

In the spring he had been again supposed to be dying. His military reputation had come out tarnished from his failure at Metz, and while he was labouring with imperfect success to collect troops for a summer's campaign, Henry of France, unable to prevent the English marriage, was preparing to strike a blow so heavy, as should enable him to dictate peace on his own terms before England was drawn into the quarrel.

In June two French armies took the field. Pietro Strozzi advanced from Piedmont into Tuscany. Henry himself, with Guise, Montmorency, and half the peerage of France, entered the Low Countries, sweeping all opposition before him. First Marienbourg fell, then Dinant fell, stormed with especial gallantry. The young French nobles were taught that they must conquer or die: a party of them flinched in the breach at Dinant, and the next morning Henry sat in judgment upon them sceptre in hand; some were hanged, the rest degraded from their rank: "and whereas one privilege of the gentlemen of France was to be exempt from taylles payable to the crown, they were made tayllable as any other villains." [344]

From Dinant the French advanced to Namur. When Namur should have fallen, Brussels was the next aim; and there was nothing, as it seemed, which could stop them. The imperial army under the Prince of Savoy could but hover, far outnumbered, on their skirts. The reinforcements from Spain had not arrived, and a battle lost was the loss of Belgium.

In the critical temper of England, a decisive superiority obtained by France would be doubly dangerous; and Charles, seeing Philibert perplexed into uncertain movements which threatened misfortune, disregarding the remonstrances of his physicians, his ministers, and his generals, started from his sick bed, flew to the head of his troops, and brought them to Namur, in the path of the advancing French. Men said that he was rushing upon destruction. The headstrong humour which had already worked him so heavy injury was again dragging him into ruin. [345] But fortune had been disarmed by the greatness with which Charles had borne up against calamity, or else his supposed rashness was the highest military wisdom. Before Henry came up he had seized a position at an angle of the Meuse, where he could defend Namur, and could not be himself attacked, except at a disadvantage. The French approached only to retire, and, feeling themselves unable to force the imperial lines, fell back towards the Boullonnois. Charles followed cautiously. An attack on Renty brought on an action in which the French claimed the victory; but the emperor held his ground, and the town could not be taken; and Henry's army, from which such splendid results had been promised, fell back on the frontier and dispersed. The voices which had exclaimed against the emperor's rashness were now as loud in his praise, and the disasters which he was accused of provoking, it was now found that he only had averted. [346] Neither the French nor the Imperialists, in their long desperate struggle, can claim either approval or sympathy; the sufferings which they inflicted upon mankind were not the less real, the selfishness of their rivalry none the less reprehensible, because the disunion of the Catholic powers permitted the Reformation to establish itself. Yet, in this perplexed world the deeds of men may be without excuse, while, nevertheless, in the men themselves there may be something to love, and something more to admire.

CHAPTER III-RECONCILIATION
WITH ROME

Mary had restored Catholic orthodoxy, and her passion for Philip had been gratified. To complete her work and her happiness, it remained to bring back her subjects to the bosom of the Catholic Church. Reginald Pole had by this time awoke from some part of his delusions. He had persuaded himself that he had but to appear with a pardon in his hand to be welcomed to his country with acclamation: he had ascertained that the English people were very indifferent to the pardon, and that his own past treasons had created especial objections to himself. Even the queen herself had grown impatient with him. He had fretted her with his importunities; his presence in Flanders had chafed the parliament, and made her marriage more difficult; while he was supposed to share with the English nobles their jealousy of a foreign sovereign. So general was this last impression about him, that his nephew, Lord Stafford's son, who was one of the refugees, went to seek him in the expectation of countenance and sympathy: and, farther, he had been in correspondence with Gardiner, and was believed to be at the bottom of the chancellor's religious indiscretions. [347] Thus his anxiety to be in England found nowhere any answering desire; and Renard, who dreaded his want of wisdom, never missed an opportunity of throwing difficulties in the way. In the spring of 1554 Pole had gone to Paris, where, in an atmosphere of so violent opposition to the marriage, he had not thought it necessary to speak in favour of it. The words which Dr. Wotton heard that he had used were reported to the emperor; and, at last, Renard went so far as to suggest that the scheme of sending him to England had been set on foot at Rome by the French party in the Consistory, with a view of provoking insurrection and thwarting the Imperial policy. [348]

The emperor, taught by his old experiences of Pole, acquiesced in the views of his ambassador. If England was to be brought back to its allegiance, the negotiation would require a delicacy of handling for which the present legate was wholly unfit; and Charles wrote at last to the pope to suggest that the commission should be transferred to a more competent person.

Impatient language had been heard of late from the legate's lips, contrasting the vexations of the world with the charms of devotional retirement. To soften the harshness of the blow, the emperor said that he understood Pole was himself weary of his office, and wished to escape into privacy.

The respect of Julius for the legate's understanding was not much larger than the emperor's; but he would not pronounce the recall without giving him an opportunity of explaining himself. Cardinal Morone wrote to him to inquire whether it was true that he had thought of retirement; he informed him of the emperor's complaints; and, to place his resignation in the easiest light (while pointing, perhaps, to the propriety of his offering it), he hinted at Pole's personal unpopularity, and at the danger to which he would be exposed by going to England.

But the legate could not relinquish the passionate desire of his life; while, as to the marriage, he was, after all, unjustly suspected. He requested Morone, in reply, to assure the pope that, much as he loved retirement, he loved duty more. He appealed to the devotion of his life to the church as an evidence of his zeal and sincerity; and, although he knew, he said, that God could direct events at his will and dispense with the service of men, yet, so long as he had strength to be of use, he would spend it in his Master's cause. In going to England he was venturing upon a stormy sea; he knew it well; [349] but, whatever befell him, his life was in God's hands.

A fortnight after (May 25), he wrote again, replying more elaborately to the emperor's charges. It was true, he admitted, that in his letters to the queen he had dwelt more upon her religious duties than upon her marriage: it was true that he had been backward in his demonstrations of pleasure, because he was a person of few words. But, so far from disapproving of that marriage, he looked upon it as the distinct work of God; and when his nephew had come with complaints to him, he had forbidden him his presence. He had spoken of the rule of a stranger in England as likely to be a lesson to the people; but he had meant only that, as their disasters had befallen them through their own king Henry, their deliverance would be wrought for them by one who was not their own. When the late parliament had broken up without consenting to the restoration of union, he had consoled the queen with assuring her that he saw in it the hand of Providence; the breach of a marriage between an English king and a Spanish princess had caused the wound which a renewed marriage of a Spanish king and an English queen was to heal. [350]

The defence was elaborate, and, on the whole, may have been tolerably true. The pope would not take the trouble to read it, or even to hear it read; [351] but the substance, as related to him by Morone, convinced him that the emperor's accusations were exaggerated: to recall a legate at the instance of a secular sovereign was an undesirable precedent; [352] and the commission was allowed to stand. Julius wrote to Charles, assuring him that he was mistaken in the legate's feelings, leaving the emperor at the same time, however, full power to keep him in Flanders or to send him to England at his own discretion.

Pole was to continue the instrument of the reconciliation; the conditions under which the reconciliation could take place were less easy to settle. The popes, whose powers are unlimited where the exercise of them is convenient for the interests of the Holy See, have uniformly fallen back upon their inability where they have been called on to make sacrifices. The canons of the church forbade, under any pretext, the alienation of ecclesiastical property; and until Julius could relinquish *ex animo* all intention of disturbing the lay holders of the English abbey lands, there was not a chance that the question of his supremacy would be so much as entertained by either Lords or Commons.

The vague powers originally granted to the legate were not satisfactory; and Pole himself, who was too sincere a believer in the Roman doctrines to endure that worldly objections should stand in the way of the salvation of souls, wrote himself to the Holy See, entreating that his commission might be enlarged. The pope in appearance consented. In a second brief, dated June 28th, he extended the legate's dispensing powers to real property as well as personal, and granted him general permission to determine any unforeseen difficulties which might arise. [353] Ormaneto, a confidential agent, carried the despatch to Flanders, and on Ormaneto's arrival, the legate, believing that his embarrassments were at last at an end, sent him on to the Bishop of Arras, to entreat that the perishing souls of the English people might now be remembered. The pope had given way; the queen was happily married, and the reasons for his detention were at an end. [354]

Both Arras and the emperor, however, thought more of Philip's security than of perishing souls. Arras, who understood the ways of the Vatican better than the legate, desired that, before any steps were taken, he might be favoured with a copy of these enlarged powers. He wished to know whether the question of the property was fairly relinquished to the secular powers in England, and whether the church had finally washed its hands of it; [355] at all events, he must examine the brief. On inspection, the new commission was found to contain an enabling clause indeed, as extensive as words could make it; but the See of Rome reserved to itself the right of sanctioning the settlement after it had been made; [356] and the reservation had been purposely made, in order to leave the pope free to act as he might please at a future time. Morone, writing to Pole a fortnight after the date of the brief, told him that his holiness was still unable to come to a resolution; [357] while Ormaneto said openly to Arras, that, although the pope would be as moderate as possible, yet his moderation must not be carried so far as to encourage the rest of Christendom in an evil example. Catholics must not be allowed to believe that they could appropriate church property without offence, nor must the Holy See appear to be purchasing by concessions the submission of its rebellious subjects. [358]

This language was not even ambiguous; Pole was desired to wait till an answer could be received from England; and the emperor wrote to Renard (August 3), desiring him to lay the circumstances before the queen and his son. He could believe, he said, that the legate himself meant well, but he had not the same confidence in those who were urging him forward, and the pope had given no authority for haste or precipitate movements. [359]

The emperor's letter was laid before a council of state at Windsor, on the 6th of August; and the council agreed with Charles that the legate's anxieties could not for the present be gratified. He was himself attainted, and parliament had shown no anxiety that the attainder should be removed. The reimposition of the pope's authority was a far more ticklish matter than the restoration of orthodoxy, [360] and the temper of the people was uncertain. The cardinal had, perhaps, intelligence with persons in England of a suspicious and dangerous kind, and the execution of his commission must depend on the pleasure of the next parliament. He was not to suppose that he might introduce changes in the constitution of the country by the authority of a papal commission, or try experiments which might put in peril the sacred person of the prince. [361]

Once more the cup of hope was dashed to the ground, and Reginald Pole was sent back to his monastery at Dhilinghen like a child unfit to be trusted with a dangerous plaything. In times of trial his pen was his refuge, and in an appeal to Philip he poured out his characteristic protest.

"For a whole year," he wrote, "I have been now knocking at the door of that kingdom, and no person will answer, no person will ask, Who is there? It is one who has endured twenty years of exile that the partner of your throne should not be excluded from her rights, and I come in the name of the vicar of the King of kings, the Shepherd of mankind. Peter knocks at your door; Peter himself. The door is open to all besides. Why is it closed to Peter? Why does not that nation make haste now to do Peter reverence? Why does it leave him escaped from Herod's prison, knocking?

"Strange, too, that this is the house of Mary. Can it be Mary that is so slow to open? True, indeed, it is, that when Mary's damsel heard the voice she opened not the door for joy; she ran and told Mary. But Mary came with those that were with her in the house; and though at first she doubted, yet, when Peter continued knocking, she opened the door; she took him in, she regarded not the danger, although Herod was yet alive and was king.

"Is it joy which now withholds Mary, or is it fear? She rejoices, that I know, but she also fears. Yet why should Mary fear now when Herod is dead? The providence of God permitted her to fear for awhile, because God desired that you, sire, who are Peter's beloved child, should share the great work with her. Do you, therefore, teach her now to cast her fears away. It is not I only who stand here—it is not only Peter—Christ is here—Christ waits with me till you will open and take him in. You who are King of England, are defender of Christ's faith; yet, while you have the ambassadors of all other princes at your court, you will not have Christ's ambassador; you have rejected your Christ.

"Go on upon your way. Build on the foundation of worldly policy, and I tell you, in Christ's words, that the rain will fall, the floods will rise, the winds will blow, and beat upon that house, and it will fall, and great will be the fall thereof." [362]

The pleading was powerful, yet it could bear no fruits—the door could not open till the pope pronounced the magic words which held it closed. Neither Philip nor Mary was in a position to use violence or force the bars.

After the ceremony at Winchester, the king and queen had gone first to Windsor, and thence the second week in August they went to Richmond. The entry into London was fixed for the 18th; after which, should it pass off without disturbance, the Spanish fleet might sail from Southampton Water. The prince himself had as yet met with no discourtesy; but disputes had broken out early between the English and Spanish retinues, and petty taunts and insolences had passed among them. [363] The prince's luggage was plundered, and the property stolen could not be recovered nor the thieves detected. The servants of Alva and the other lords, who preceded their masters to London, were insulted in the streets, and women and children called after them that they need not have brought so many things, they would be soon gone again. The citizens refused to give them lodgings in their houses, and the friars who had accompanied Philip were advised to disguise themselves, so intense was the hatred against the religious orders. [364] The council soon provided for their ordinary comforts, but increase of acquaintance produced no improvement of feeling.

The entry passed off tolerably. Gog and Magog stood as warders on London Bridge, and there were the usual pageants in the city. Renard conceived that the impression produced by Philip had been rather favourable than otherwise; for the people had been taught to expect some monster but partially human, and they saw instead a well-dressed cavalier, who had learnt by this time to carry his hand to his bonnet. Yet, although there were no open signs of ill-feeling, the day did not end without a disagreeable incident. The conduit in Gracechurch Street had been newly decorated: "the nine Worthies" had been painted round the winding turret, and among them were Henry VIII. and Edward. The first seven carried maces, swords, or pole-axes. Henry held in one hand a sceptre, in the other he was presenting a book to his son, on which was written *Verbum Dei*. As the train went by, the unwelcome figure caught the eye of Gardiner. The painter was summoned, called "knave, traitor, heretic," an enemy to the queen's Catholic proceedings. The offensive Bible was washed out, and a pair of gloves inserted in its place. [365]

Nor did the irritation of the people abate. The Spaniards, being without special occupation, were seen much in the streets; and a vague fear so magnified their numbers that four of them, it was thought, were to be met in London for one Englishman. [366] The halls of the city companies were given up for their use; a fresh provocation to people who desired to be provoked. A Spanish friar was lodged at Lambeth, and it was said at once he was to be Archbishop of Canterbury; at the beginning of September twelve thousand Spanish troops were reported to be coming to "fetch the crown." Rumour and reality inflated each other. The peers, who had collected for the marriage, dispersed to their counties; and on the 10th of September, Pembroke, Shrewsbury, and Westmoreland were believed to have raised a standard of revolt at York. Frays were continually breaking out in the streets, and there was a scandalous brawl in the cloisters at Westminster. Brief entries in diaries and council books tell continually of Englishmen killed, and Spaniards hanged, hanged at Tyburn, or hanged more conspicuously at Charing Cross; and on the 12th, Noailles reported that the feeling in all classes, high and low, was as bad as possible.

There was dread, too, that Philip was bent on drawing England into the war. The French ambassador had been invited to be present at the entry into London; but the invitation had been sent informally by a common messenger not more than half an hour before the royal party were to appear. The brief notice was intended as an affront, and only after some days Noailles appeared at court to offer his congratulations. When he came at last, he expressed his master's hope to Philip that the neutrality of England would continue to be observed. Philip answered with cold significance, that he would keep his promise and maintain the treaties, as long as by doing so he should consult the interest of the realm. [367]

Other menacing symptoms were also showing themselves: the claim for the pensions was spoken of as likely to be revived; the English ships in the Channel were making the neutrality one-sided, and protecting the Spanish and Flemish traders; and Philip, already weary of his bride, was urging on Renard the propriety of his hastening, like an obedient son, to the assistance of his father. Under pretence of escort he could take with him a few thousand English cavalry and men-at-arms, who could be used as a menace to France, and whose presence would show the attitude which England was about to assume. Sick, in these brief weeks, of maintaining the show of an affection which he did not feel, and sick of a country where his friends were insulted if he was treated respectfully himself, he was already panting for freedom, and eager to utilise the instruments which he had bought so dearly. [368]

Happily for the queen's peace of mind, Renard was not a man to encourage impatience. The factions in the council were again showing themselves; Elizabeth lay undisposed of at Woodstock. Pomfret, Belgium, even Hungary, had been thought of as a destination for her, and had been laid aside one after the other, in dread of the people. If she was released, she would again be dangerous, and it was uncertain how long Lord Howard would endure her detention. A plan suggested by Lord Paget seemed, after all, to promise the best—to marry her to Philibert of Savoy, and thus make use of her as a second link to connect England with the House of Austria. But here the difficulty would be with the queen, who in that case would have to recognise her sister's rank and expectations.

The question should be settled before Philip left England, and he must have faced parliament too, and, if possible, have been crowned. If he went now, he would never come back; let him court the people advised the keen Renard; let him play off the people against the lords; there was ill blood between the rich and poor, let him use the opportunity.

The state of public feeling did not improve when, at the end of September, Bonner commenced an inquisition into the conduct and opinions of the clergy of his diocese. In every parish he appointed a person or persons to examine whether the minister was or ever had been married; whether, if married and separated from his wife, he continued in secret to visit her; whether his sermons were orthodox; whether he was a "brawler, scolder, hawker, hunter, fornicator, adulterer, drunkard, or blasphemer;" whether he duly exhorted his parishioners to come to mass and confession; whether he associated with heretics, or had been suspected of associating with them; his mind, his habits, his society, even the dress that he wore, were to be made matter of close scrutiny.

The points of inquiry were published in a series of articles which created an instantaneous ferment. Among the merchants they were attributed to the king, queen, and Gardiner, and were held to be the first step of a conspiracy against their liberties. A report was spread at the same time that the king meditated a seizure of the Tower; barriers were forthwith erected in the great thoroughfares leading into the city, and no one was allowed to pass unchallenged. [369]

The Bishop of London was called to account for having ventured so rash a step without permission of crown or council. He replied that he was but doing his duty; the council, had he communicated with them, would have interfered with him, and in the execution of his office he must be governed by his own conscience. [370] But the attitude of the city was too decided even for the stubborn Bonner, he gave way sullenly, and suspended the execution of his order.

Worse clouds than these nevertheless had many times gathered over the court and dispersed again. It was easy to be discontented; but when the discontent would pass into action, there was nothing definite to be done; and between the leading statesmen there were such large differences of opinion, that they could not co-operate. [371] The court, as Renard saw, could accomplish everything which they desired with caution and prudence. The humours of the people might flame out on a sudden if too hastily irritated, but the opposite tendencies of parties effectually balanced each other; and even the papal difficulty might be managed, and Pole might in time be brought over, if only there was no precipitation, and the pope was compelled to be reasonable.

But prudence was the first and last essential; the legate must be content to wait, and also Philip must wait. The winter was coming on, and the court, Renard said, was giving balls; the English and Spanish noblemen were learning to talk with one another, and were beginning to dance with each other's wives and daughters. The ill-feeling was gradually abating; and, in fact, it was not to be believed that God Almighty would have brought about so considerable a marriage without intending that good should come of it. [372] The queen believed herself *enceinte*, and if her hopes were well founded, a thousand causes of restlessness would be disposed of; but Philip must not be permitted to harass her with his impatience to be gone. She had gathered something of his intentions, and was already pretending more uncertainty than in her heart she felt, lest he should make the assurance of her prospects an excuse for leaving her. In a remarkable passage, Renard urged the emperor on no account to encourage him in a step so eminently injudicious, from a problematic hope of embroiling England and France. "Let parliament meet," he said, "and pass off quietly, and in February his highness may safely go. Irreparable injury may and will follow, however, should he leave England before. Religion will be overthrown, the queen's person will be in danger, and parliament will not meet. A door will be opened for the practices of France; the country may throw itself in self-protection on the French alliance, and an undying hatred will be engendered between England and Spain. As things now are, prudence and moderation are more than ever necessary; and we must allow neither the king nor the queen to be led astray by unwise impatient advisers, who, for the advancement of their private opinions, or because they cannot have all the liberty which they desire, are ready to compromise the commonwealth." [373]

So matters stood at the beginning of October, when parliament was about to be summoned, and the great experiment to be tried whether

England would consent to be re-united to Catholic Christendom. The writs went out on the 6th, and circulars accompanied them, addressed to those who would have the conduct of the elections, stating that, whatever false reports might have been spread, no "alteration was intended of any man's possessions." At the same time the queen required the mayors of towns, the sheriffs, and other influential persons to admonish the voters to choose from among themselves "such as, being eligible by order of the laws, were of a wise, grave, and Catholic sort; such as indeed meant the true honour of God and the prosperity of the commonwealth." [374] These general directions were copied from a form which had been in use under Henry VII., and the citizens of London set the example of obedience in electing four members who were in every way satisfactory to the court. [375] In the country the decisive failure of Carew, Suffolk, and Crofts showed that the weight of public feeling was still in favour of the queen notwithstanding the Spanish marriage; and the reaction against the excesses of the Reformation had not yet reached its limits. On the accession of Mary, the restoration of the mass had appeared impossible, but it had been effected safely and completely almost by the spontaneous will of the people. In the spring the pope's name could not be mentioned in parliament; now, since the queen was bent upon it, and as she gave her word that property was not to be meddled with, even the pope seemed no longer absolutely intolerable.

The reports of the elections were everywhere favourable. In the Upper House, except on very critical points, which would unite the small body of the lay peers, the court was certain of a majority, being supported of course by the bishops—and the question of Pole's coming over, therefore, was once more seriously considered. The pope had been given to understand that, however inconsistent with his dignity he might consider it to appear to purchase English submission by setting aside the canons of the church, he must consent to the English terms, or there was no hope whatever that his supremacy would be recognised. If in accepting these terms he would agree to a humiliating reconciliation, only those who objected on doctrinal grounds to the papal religion were inclined to persist in refusing a return of his friendship. The dream of an independent orthodox Anglicanism which had once found favour with Gardiner was fading away. The indifferent and the orthodox alike desired to put an end to spiritual anarchy; and the excommunication, though lying lightly on the people, and despised even by the Catholic powers, had furnished, and might furnish, a pretext for inconvenient combinations. Singularity of position, where there was no especial cause for it, was always to be avoided.

These influences would have been insufficient to have brought the English of themselves to seek for a reunion. They were enough to induce them to accept it with indifference when offered them on their own conditions, or to affect for a time an outward appearance of acquiescence.

Philip, therefore, consulted Renard, and Charles invited Pole to Brussels. Renard, to whom politics were all-important, and religion useful in its place, but inconvenient when pushed into prominence, adhered to his old opinion. He advised the "king to write privately to the pope, telling him that he had already so many embarrassments on his hands that he could not afford to increase them;" "the changes already made were insincere, and the legatine authority was odious, not only in England, but throughout Europe;" "the queen, on her accession, had promised a general toleration, [376] and it was useless to provoke irritation, when not absolutely necessary." Yet even Renard spoke less positively than before. "If the pope would make no more reservations on the land question — if he would volunteer a general absolution, and submit to conditions, while he exacted none — if he would sanction every ecclesiastical act which had been done during the schism, the marriages and baptisms, the ordinations of the clergy, and the new creations of episcopal sees — above all, if he would make no demand for money under any pretence, the venture might, perhaps, be made." But, continued Renard, "his holiness, even then, must be cautious in his words; he must dwell as lightly as possible on his authority, as lightly as possible on his claims to be obeyed: in offering absolution, he must talk merely of piety and love, of the open arms of the church, of the example of the Saviour, and such other generalities." [377] Finally, Renard still thought the legate had better remain abroad. The reconciliation, if it could be effected at all, could be managed better without his irritating presence.

Pole himself had found the emperor more gracious. Charles professed the greatest anxiety that the papal authority should be restored. He doubted only if the difficulties could be surmounted. Pole replied that the obstacles were chiefly two — one respecting doctrine, on which no concession could be made at all; the other respecting the lands, on which his holiness would make every concession. He would ask for nothing, he would exact nothing; he would abandon every shadow of a claim.

If this was the case, the emperor said, all would go well. Nevertheless, there was the reservation in the brief, and the pope, however generous he might wish to be, was uncertain of his power. The doctrine was of no consequence. People in England believed one doctrine as little as another; [378] but they hated Rome, they hated the religious orders, they hated cardinals; and, as to the lands, *could* the church relinquish them? [379] Pole might believe that she could; but the world would be more suspicious, or less easy to convince. At all events, the dispensing powers must be clogged with no reservations; nor could he come to any decision till he heard again from England.

The legate was almost hopeless; yet his time of triumph—such triumph as it was—had nearly arrived. The queen's supposed pregnancy had increased her influence; and, constant herself in the midst of general indecision, she was able to carry her point. She would not mortify the legate, who had suffered for his constancy to the cause of her mother, with listening to Renard's personal objections; and when the character of the approaching House of Commons had been ascertained, she gained the consent of the council, a week before the beginning of the session, to send commissioners to Brussels to see Pole and inspect his faculties. With a conclusive understanding on the central question, they might tell him that the hope of his life might be realised, and that he might return to his country. But the conditions were explicit. He must bring adequate powers with him, or his coming would be worse than fruitless. If those which he already possessed were insufficient, he must send them to Rome to be enlarged; [380] and although the court would receive him as legate *de latere*, he had better enter the country only as a cardinal and ambassador, till he could judge of the state of things for himself. [381] On these terms the commissioners might conduct him to the queen's presence.

The bearers of this communication were Lord Paget and Sir Edward Hastings, accompanied, it is curious to observe, by Sir William Cecil. [382]

They presented themselves to the emperor, who, after the report which they brought with them, made no more difficulty. The enlarged powers had been sent for three weeks before; but there was no occasion to wait for their arrival. They might be expected in ten days or a fortnight, and could follow the legate to England. [383]

The effect on Pole of the commissioners' arrival "there needed not," as they said themselves, "many words to declare." [384] His eager temperament, for ever excited either with wild hopes or equally wild despondency, was now about to be fooled to the top of its bent. On the pope's behalf, he promised everything; for himself, he would come as ambassador, he would come as a private person, come in any fashion that might do good, so only that he might come.

Little time was lost in preparation. Parliament met on the 12th of November. The opening speech was read, as usual, by Gardiner, and was well received, although it announced that further measures would be taken for the establishment of religion, and the meaning of these words was known to every one. The first measure brought forward was the repeal of Pole's attainder. It passed easily without a dissentient voice, and no obstacle of any kind remained to delay his appearance. Only the cautious Renard suggested that Courtenay should be sent out of the country as soon as possible, for fear the legate should take a fancy to him; and the Prince of Savoy had been invited over to see whether anything could be done towards arranging the marriage with Elizabeth. Elizabeth, indeed, had protested that she had no intention of marrying; nevertheless, Renard said, she would be disposed of, as the emperor had advised, [385] could the queen be induced to consent.

England was ready therefore, and the happy legate set out from Brussels like a lover flying to his mistress. His emotions are reflected in the journal of an Italian friend who attended him. The journey commenced on Tuesday, the 13th; the retinues of Paget and Hastings, with the cardinal's household, making in all a hundred and twenty horse. The route was by Ghent, Bruges, and Dunkirk. On the 19th the party reached Gravelines, where, on the stream which formed the boundary of the Pale, they were received in state by Lord Wentworth, the Governor of Calais. In the eyes of his enthusiastic admirers the apostle of the church moved in an atmosphere of marvel. The Calais bells, which rang as they entered the town, were of preternatural sweetness. The salutes fired by the ships in the harbour were "wonderful." The cardinal's lodging was a palace, and as an august omen, the watchword of the garrison for the night was "God long lost is found." [386] The morning brought a miracle. A westerly gale had blown for many days. All night long it had howled through the narrow streets; the waves had lashed against the piers, and the fishermen foretold a week of storms. At daybreak the wind went down, the clouds broke, a light air from the eastward levelled the sea, and filled the sails of the vessel which was to bear them to England. At noon the party went on board, and their passage was a fresh surprise. They crossed in three hours and a half, and the distance, as it pictured itself to imagination, was forty miles. [387] At Dover the legate slept. The next day Lord Montague came with the Bishop of Ely, bringing letters of congratulation from the queen and Philip, and an intimation that he was anxiously looked for. He was again on horseback after breakfast; and as the news of his arrival spread, respect or curiosity rapidly swelled his train. The Earl of Huntingdon, who had married his sister, sent his son Lord Hastings, with his tenants and servants, as an escort. But there was no danger. Whatever might be the feelings of the people towards the papal legate, they gave to Reginald Pole the welcome due to an English nobleman.

The November evening had closed in when the cavalcade entered Canterbury. The streets were thronged, and the legate made his way through the crowd, amidst the cries of "God save your grace." At the door of the house—probably the archbishop's palace—where he was to pass the night, Harpsfeld, the archdeacon, was standing to receive him, with a number of the clergy; and with the glare of torches lighting up the scene, Harpsfeld commenced an oration as the legate alighted, so beautiful, so affecting, says Pole's Italian friend, that all the hearers were moved to tears. The archdeacon spoke of the mercies of God, and the marvellous workings of his providence. He dwelt upon the history of the cardinal, whom God had preserved through a thousand dangers for the salvation of his country; and, firing up at last in a blaze of enthusiasm, he exclaimed, "Thou art Pole, and thou art our Polar star, to light us to the kingdom of the heavens. Sky, rivers, earth, these disfigured walls—all things—long for thee. While thou wert absent from us all things were sad, all things were in the power of the adversary. At thy coming all things are smiling, all glad, all tranquil." [388] The legate listened so far, and then checked the flood of the adoring eloquence. "I heard you with pleasure," he said, "while you were praising God. My own praises I do not desire to hear. Give the glory to Him."

From Canterbury, Richard Pate, who, as titular Bishop of Worcester, had sat at the council of Trent, was sent forward to the queen with an answer to her letter, and a request for further directions. The legate himself went on leisurely to Rochester, where he was entertained by Lord Cobham, at Cowling Castle. So far he had observed the instructions brought to him by Paget, and had travelled as an ordinary ecclesiastic, without distinctive splendour. On the night of the 23rd, however, Pate returned from the court with a message that the legatine insignia might be displayed. A fleet of barges was in waiting at Gravesend, where Pole appeared early on the 24th; and, as a further augury of good fortune, he found there Lord Shrewsbury, with his early friend the Bishop of Durham, who had come to meet him with the repeal of his attainder, to which the queen had given her assent in parliament the day before.

To the fluttered hearts of the priestly company the coincidence of the repeal, the informality of an act of parliament receiving the royal assent before the close of a session, were further causes of admiration. They embarked; and the Italians, who had never seen a tidal river, discovered, miracle of miracles, that they were ascending from the sea, and yet the stream was with them. The distance to London was soon accomplished. They passed under the bridge at one o'clock on the top of the tide, the legate's barge distinguished splendidly by the silver cross upon the bow. In a few minutes more they were at the palace-stairs at Whitehall, where a pier was built on arches out into the river, and on the pier stood the Bishop of Winchester, with the lords of the council.

The king and queen were at dinner, the arrival not being expected till the afternoon. Philip rose instantly from the table, hurried out, and caught the legate in his arms. The queen followed to the head of the grand staircase; and when Pole reached her, she threw herself on his breast, and kissed him, crying that his coming gave her as much joy as the possession of her kingdom. The cardinal, in corresponding ecstasy, exclaimed, in the words of the angel to the Virgin, "Ave Maria gratia plena, Dominus tecum, benedicta tu in mulieribus." [389] The first rapturous moments over, the king, queen, and legate proceeded along the gallery, Philip and Pole supporting Mary on either side, and the legate expatiating on the mysteries of Providence.

"High thanks, indeed," he exclaimed, "your majesty owes to the favour of the Almighty, seeing that, while he permits you to bring your godly desires to perfection, he has united at this moment in your favour the two mightiest powers upon earth—the majesty of the emperor represented in the king your husband, and the pope's holiness represented in myself." The queen, as she walked, replied "in words of sweet humility," pouring out gentle excuses for past delays. The legate, still speaking with ecstatic metaphor, answered that it was the will of God; God waited till the time was mature, till he could say to her highness, "Blessed be the fruit of thy womb." [390]

In the saloon they remained standing together for another quarter of an hour. When the cardinal took his leave for the day, the king; in spite of remonstrance, re-attended him to the gate. Alva and the Bishop of

Winchester were in waiting to conduct him to Lambeth Palace, which had been assigned him for a residence. The See of Canterbury was to follow as soon as Cranmer could be despatched.

Arrived at Lambeth, he was left to repose after his fatigues and excitements. He had scarcely retired to his apartments when he was disturbed again by a message from the queen. Lord Montague had hurried over with the news that the angelic salutation had been already answered. "The babe had leapt in her womb." [391] Not a moment was lost in communicating the miracle to the world. Letters of council were drawn out for *Te Deums* to be sung in every church in London. The next day being Sunday, every pulpit was made to ring with the testimony of heaven to the truth.

On Monday the 26th the cardinal went to the palace for an audience, and again there was more matter for congratulation. As he was approaching the king's cabinet, Philip met him with a packet of despatches. The last courier sent to Rome had returned with unheard-of expedition, and the briefs and commissions in which the pope relinquished formally his last reservations, had arrived. Never, exclaimed the Catholic enthusiast, in a fervour of devout astonishment—never since the days of the apostles had so many tokens of divine approbation been showered upon a human enterprise. The moment of its consummation had arrived. [392] Since the thing was to be, no one wished for delay. Three days sufficed for the few necessary preparations, and the two Houses of Parliament were invited to be present unofficially at Whitehall on the afternoon of Wednesday the 28th. In the morning there was a procession in the city and a *Te Deum* at St. Paul's. After dinner, the Great Chamber was thrown open, and the Lords and Commons crowded in as they could find room. Philip and Mary entered, and took their seats under the cloth of state; while Pole had a chair assigned him on their right hand, beyond the edge of the canopy. The queen was splendidly dressed, and it was observed that she threw out her person to make her supposed condition as conspicuous as possible. [393] When all were in their places, the chancellor rose.

"My Lords of the Upper House," he said, "and you my masters of the Nether House, here is present the Right Reverend Father in God the Lord Cardinal Pole, come from the Apostolic See of Rome as ambassador to the king's and queen's majesties, upon one of the weightiest causes that ever happened in this realm, and which pertaineth to the glory of God and your universal benefit; the which embassy it is their majesties' pleasure that it be signified unto you all by his own mouth, trusting that you will accept it in as benevolent and thankful wise as their highnesses have done, and that you will give an attent and inclinable ear to him."

The legate then left his chair and came forward. He was now fifty-four years old, and he had passed but little of his life in England; yet his features had not wholly lost their English character. He had the arched eye-brow, and the delicately-cut cheek, and prominent eye of the beautiful Plantagenet face; a long, brown, curling beard flowed down upon his chest, which it almost covered; the mouth was weak and slightly open, the lips were full and pouting, the expression difficult to read. In a low voice, audible only to those who were near him, he spoke as follows:— "My Lords all, and you that are the Commons of this present parliament assembled, as the cause of my repair hither hath been wisely and gravely declared by my Lord Chancellor, so, before I enter into the particulars of my commission, I have to say somewhat touching myself, and to give most humble and hearty thanks to the king's and queen's majesties, and after them to you all — which of a man exiled and banished from this commonwealth, have restored me to be a member of the same, and of a man having no place either here or elsewhere within this realm, have admitted me to a place where to speak and where to be heard. This I protest unto you all, that though I was exiled my native country, without just cause, as God knoweth, yet the ingratitude could not pull from me the affection and desire that I had to your profit and to do you good.

"But, leaving the rehearsal hereof, and coming more near to the matter of my commission, I signify unto you all, that my principal travail is for the restitution of this noble realm to the antient nobility, and to declare unto you that the See Apostolic, from whence I come, hath a special respect to this realm above all others; and not without cause, seeing that God himself, as it were, by providence hath given to this realm prerogative of nobility above others, which, to make plain unto you, it is to be considered that this island first of all islands received the light of Christ's religion."

Going into history for a proof of this singular proposition, the legate said that the Britons had been converted by the See Apostolic, "not one by one, as in other countries, as clocks increase the hours by distinction of times," "but altogether, at once, as it were, in a moment." The Saxons had brought back heathenism, but had again been soon converted; and the popes had continued to heap benefit upon benefit on the favoured people, even making them a present of Ireland, "which pertained to the See of Rome." The country had prospered, and the people had been happy down to the time of the late schism; from that unhappy day they had been overwhelmed with calamities.

The legate dwelt in some detail on the misfortunes of the preceding years. He then went on: "But, when all light of true religion seemed extinct, the churches defaced, the altars overthrown, the ministers corrupted, even

like as in a lamp, the light being covered yet it is not quenched—even so in a few remained the confession of Christ's faith, namely, in the breast of the queen's excellency, of whom to speak without adulation, the saying of the prophet may be verified, *ecce quasi derelicta*: and see how miraculously God of his goodness preserved her highness contrary to the expectations of men, that when numbers conspired against her, and policies were devised to disinherit her, and armed power prepared to destroy her, yet she, being a virgin, helpless, naked, and unarmed, prevailed, and had the victory of tyrants. For all these practices and devices, here you see her grace established in her estate, your lawful queen and governess, born among you, whom God hath appointed to govern you for the restitution of true religion and the extirpation of all errors and sects. And to confirm her grace more strongly in this enterprise, lo how the providence of God hath joined her in marriage with a prince of like religion, who, being a king of great might, armour, and force, yet useth towards you neither armour nor force, but seeketh you by way of love and amity; and as it was a singular favour of God to conjoin them in marriage, so it is not to be doubted but he shall send them issue for the comfort and surety of this commonwealth.

"Of all princes in Europe the emperor hath travailed most in the cause of religion, yet, haply by some secret judgment of God, he hath not obtained the end. I can well compare him to David, which, though he were a man elect of God, yet for that he was contaminate with blood and wars, he could not build the temple of Jerusalem, but left the finishing thereof to Solomon, who was *Rex pacificus*. So it may be thought that the appeasing of controversies of religion in Christendom is not appointed to this emperor, but rather to his son; who shall perform the building that his father had begun, which church cannot be builded unless universally in all realms we adhere to one head, and do acknowledge him to be the vicar of God, and to have power from above—for all power is of God, according to the saying, *non est potestas nisi in Deo*.

"All power being of God, he hath derived that power into two parts here on earth, which is into the powers imperial and ecclesiastical; and these two powers, as they be several and distinct, so have they two several effects and operations. Secular princes be ministers of God to execute vengeance upon transgressors and evil livers, and to preserve the well-doers and innocents from injury and violence; and this power is represented in these two most excellent persons the king's and queen's majesties here present. The other power is of ministration, which is the power of keys and orders in the ecclesiastical state; which is by the authority of God's word and example of the apostles, and of all holy fathers from Christ hitherto attributed and given to the Apostolic See of Rome by special prerogative: from which See I

am here deputed legate and ambassador, having full and ample commission from thence, and have the keys committed to my hands. I confess to you that I have the keys—not as mine own keys, but as the keys of Him that sent me; and yet cannot I open, not for want of power in me to give, but for certain impediments in you to receive, which must be taken away before my commission can take effect. This I protest before you, my commission is not of prejudice to any person. I am come not to destroy, but to build; I come to reconcile, not to condemn; I am not come to compel, but to call again; I am not come to call anything in question already done; but my commission is of grace and clemency to such as will receive it—for, touching all matters that be past, they shall be as things cast into the sea of forgetfulness.

"But the mean whereby you shall receive this benefit is to revoke and repeal those laws and statutes which be impediments, blocks, and bars to the execution of my commission. For, like as I myself had neither place nor voice to speak here amongst you, but was in all respects a banished man, till such time as ye had repealed those laws that lay in my way, even so cannot you receive the benefit and grace offered from the Apostolic See until the abrogation of such laws whereby you had disjoined and dissevered yourselves from the unity of Christ's Church.

"It remaineth, therefore, that you, like true Christians and provident men, for the weal of your souls and bodies, ponder what is to be done in this so weighty a cause, and so to frame your acts and proceedings as they may first tend to the glory of God, and, next, to the conservation of your commonwealth, surety, and quietness."

The speech was listened to by such as could hear it with profound attention, and several persons were observed to clasp their hands again and again, and raise them convulsively before their faces. When the legate sat down, Gardiner gave him the thanks of parliament, and suggested that the two Houses should be left to themselves to consider what they would do. Pole withdrew with the king and queen, and Gardiner exclaimed: A prophet has "the Lord raised up among us from among our brethren, and he shall save us." For the benefit of those who had been at the further end of the hall, he then recapitulated the substance of what had been said. He added a few words of exhortation, and the meeting adjourned.

The next day, Thursday, Lords and Commons sat as usual at Westminster. The repeal of all the acts which directly, or by implication, were aimed at the papacy, would occupy, it was found, a considerable time; but the impatient legate was ready to accept a promise as a pledge of performance, and the general question was therefore put severally in both Houses whether the country should return to obedience to the Apostolic See. Among the Peers no difficulty was made at all. Among the Commons,

in a house of 360, there were two dissentients—one, whose name is not mentioned, gave a silent negative vote; the other, Sir Ralph Bagenall, stood up alone to protest. Twenty years, he said, "that great and worthy prince, King Henry," laboured to expel the pope from England. He for one had "sworn to King Henry's laws," and, "he would keep his oath." [394]

But Bagenall was listened to with smiles. The resolution passed, the very ease and unanimity betraying the hollow ground on which it rested; and, again, devout Catholics beheld the evident work of supernatural agency. Lords and Commons had received separately the same proposition; they had discussed it, voted on it, and come to a conclusion, each with closed doors, and the messengers of the two Houses encountered each other on their way to communicate their several decisions. [395] The chancellor arranged with Pole the forms which should be observed, and it was agreed that the Houses should present a joint petition to the king and queen, acknowledging their past misconduct, engaging to undo the anti-papal legislation, and entreating their majesties, as undefiled with the offences which tainted the body of the nation, to intercede for the removal of the interdict. A committee of Lords and Commons sate to consider the words in which the supplication should be expressed, and all preparations were completed by the evening.

And now St. Andrew's Day was come; a day, as was then hoped, which would be remembered with awe and gratitude through all ages of English history. Being the festival of the institution of the Order of the Golden Fleece, high mass was sung in the morning in Westminster Abbey; Philip, Alva, and Ruy Gomez attended in their robes, with six hundred Spanish cavaliers. The Knights of the Garter were present in gorgeous costume, and nave and transept were thronged with the blended chivalry of England and Castile. It was two o'clock before the service was concluded. Philip returned to the palace to dinner, and the brief November afternoon was drawing in when the parliament reassembled at the palace. At the upper end of the great hall a square platform had now been raised several steps above the floor, on which three chairs were placed as before; two under a canopy of cloth of gold, for the king and queen; a third on the right, removed a little distance from them, for the legate. Below the platform, benches were placed longitudinally towards either wall. The bishops sat on the side of the legate, the lay peers opposite them on the left. The Commons sat on rows of cross benches in front, and beyond them were the miscellaneous crowd of spectators, sitting or standing as they could find room. The cardinal, who had passed the morning at Lambeth, was conducted across the water in a state barge by Lord Arundel and six other peers. The king received him at the gate, and, leaving his suite in the care of the Duke of Alva, who

was instructed to find them places, he accompanied Philip into the room adjoining the hall, where Mary, whose situation was supposed to prevent her from unnecessary exertion, was waiting for them. The royal procession was formed. Arundel and the Lords passed in to their places. The king and queen, with Pole in his legate's robes, ascended the steps of the platform, and took their seats.

When the stir which had been caused by their entrance was over, Gardiner mounted a tribune; and in the now fast-waning light he bowed to the king and queen, and declared the resolution at which the Houses had arrived. Then turning to the Lords and Commons, he asked if they continued in the same mind. Four hundred voices answered, "We do." "Will you then," he said, "that I proceed in your names to supplicate for our absolution, that we may be received again into the body of the Holy Catholic Church, under the pope, the supreme head thereof?" Again the voices assented. The chancellor drew a scroll from under his robe, ascended the platform, and presented it unfolded on his knee to the queen. The queen looked through it, gave it to Philip, who looked through it also, and returned it. The chancellor then rose and read aloud as follows:—

"We, the Lords Spiritual and Temporal, and the Commons of the present parliament assembled, representing the whole body of the realm of England, and dominions of the same, in our own names particularly, and also of the said body universally, in this our supplication directed to your majesties—with most humble suit that it may by your gracious intercession and means be exhibited to the Most Reverend Father in God the Lord Cardinal Pole, Legate, sent specially hither from our Most Holy Father Pope Julius the Third and the See Apostolic of Rome—do declare ourselves very sorry and repentant for the schism and disobedience committed in this realm and dominions of the same, against the said See Apostolic, either by making, agreeing, or executing any laws, ordinances, or commandments against the supremacy of the said See, or otherwise doing or speaking what might impugn the same; offering ourselves, and promising by this our supplication that, for a token and knowledge of our said repentance, we be, and shall be always, ready, under and with the authority of your majesties, to do that which shall be in us for the abrogation and repealing of the said laws and ordinances in this present parliament, as well for ourselves as for the whole body whom we represent. Whereupon we most humbly beseech your majesties, as persons undefiled in the offences of this body towards the Holy See—which nevertheless God by his providence hath made subject to your majesties—so to set forth this, our most humble suit, that we may obtain from the See Apostolic, by the said Most Reverend Father, as well particularly as universally, absolution, release, and discharge from all danger of such censures and sentences as by the laws of the church we be fallen in; and that we may, as children repentant, be received into the bosom and unity of Christ's Church; so as this noble realm, with all the members thereof, may, in unity and perfect obedience to the See Apostolic and pope for the time being, serve God and your majesties, to the furtherance and advancement of his honour and glory." [396]

Having completed the reading, the chancellor again presented the petition. The king and queen went through the forms of intercession, and a secretary read aloud, first, the legate's original commission, and, next, the all-important extended form of it.

Pole's share of the ceremony was now to begin.

He first spoke a few words from his seat: "Much indeed," he said, "the English nation had to thank the Almighty for recalling them to his fold. Once again God had given a token of his special favour to the realm; for as this nation, in the time of the Primitive Church, was the first to be called out of the darkness of heathenism, so now they were the first to whom God had given grace to repent of their schism; and if their repentance was sincere, how would the angels, who rejoice at the conversion of a single sinner, triumph at the recovery of a great and noble people."

He moved to rise; Mary and Philip, seeing that the crisis was approaching, fell on their knees, and the assembly dropped at their example; while, in dead silence, across the dimly-lighted hall, came the low, awful words of the absolution.

"Our Lord Jesus Christ, which with his most precious blood hath redeemed and washed us from all our sins and iniquities, that he might purchase unto himself a glorious spouse without spot or wrinkle, whom the Father hath appointed head over all his Church—he by his mercy absolves you, and we, by apostolic authority given unto us by the Most Holy Lord Pope Julius the Third, his vicegerent on earth, do absolve and deliver you, and every of you, with this whole realm and the dominions thereof, from all heresy and schism, and from all and every judgment, censure, and pain for that cause incurred; and we do restore you again into the unity of our Mother the Holy Church, in the name of the Father, of the Son, and of the Holy Ghost."

Amidst the hushed breathing every tone was audible, and at the pauses were heard the smothered sobs of the queen. "Amen, amen," rose in answer from many voices. Some were really affected; some were caught for the moment with a contagion which it was hard to resist; some threw themselves weeping in each other's arms. King, queen, and parliament, rising from their knees, went immediately — the legate leading — into the chapel of the palace, where the choir, with the rolling organ, sang *Te Deum*; and Pole closed the scene with a benediction from the altar.

"Blessed day for England," cries the Italian describer, in a rapture of devotion. "The people exclaim in ecstasies, we are reconciled to God, we are brought back to God: the king beholds his realm, so lately torn by divisions, at the mercy of the first enemy who would seize upon it, secured on a foundation which never can be shaken: and who can express the joy — who can tell the exultation of the queen? She has shown herself the handmaid of the Lord, and all generations shall call her blessed: she has given her kingdom to God as a thank-offering for those great mercies which He has bestowed upon her." [397]

And the legate; but the legate has described his emotions in his own inimitable manner. Pole went back to Lambeth, not to rest, but to pour out his soul to the Holy Father.

In his last letter he said "he had told his holiness that he had hoped that England would be recovered to the fold at last; yet he had then some fears remaining, so far estranged were the minds of the people from the Holy See, lest at the last moment some compromise might ruin all."

But the godly forwardness of the king and queen had overcome every difficulty; and on that evening, the day of St. Andrew — of Andrew who first brought his brother Peter to Christ — the realm of England had been brought back to its obedience to Peter's See, and through Peter to Christ. The great act had been accomplished, accomplished by the virtue and the labour of the inestimable sovereigns with whom God had blessed the world.

"And oh," he said, "how many things, how great things, may the church our mother, the bride of Christ, promise herself from these her children? Oh piety! oh antient faith! Whoever looks on them will repeat the words of the prophet of the church's early offspring; 'This is the seed which the Lord hath blessed.' How earnestly, how lovingly, did your holiness favour their marriage; a marriage formed after the very pattern of that of our Most High King, who, being Heir of the world, was sent down by his Father from his royal throne, to be at once the Spouse and the Son of the Virgin Mary, and be made the Comforter and the Saviour of mankind: and, in like manner, the greatest of all the princes upon earth, the heir of his father's kingdom, departed from his own broad and happy realms, that he might come hither into this land of trouble, he, too, to be spouse and son of this virgin; for, indeed, though spouse he be, he so bears himself towards her as if he were her son, to aid in the reconciliation of this people to Christ and the church. [398]

"When your holiness first chose me as your legate, the queen was rising up as a rod of incense out of trees of myrrh, and as frankincense out of the desert. And how does she now shine out in loveliness? What a savour does she give forth unto her people. Yea, even as the prophet saith of the mother of Christ, "before she was in labour she brought forth, before she was delivered she hath borne a man-child." Who ever yet hath seen it, who has heard of the similitude of it? Shall the earth bring forth in a day, or shall a nation of men be born together? but Mary has brought forth the nation of England before the time of that delivery for which we all are hoping!"

Unable to exhaust itself in words, the Catholic enthusiasm flowed over in processions, in sermons, masses, and *Te Deums*. Gardiner at Paul's Cross, on the Sunday succeeding, confessed his sins in having borne a part in bringing about the schism. Pole rode through the city between the king and queen, with his legate's cross before him, blessing the people. When the news reached Rome Julius first embraced the messenger, then flung himself on his knees, and said a Paternoster. The guns at St. Angelo roared in triumph. There were jubilees and masses of the Holy Ghost, and bonfires, and illuminations, and pardons, and indulgences. In the exuberance of his hopes, the pope sent a nuncio to urge that, in the presence of this great mercy, peace should be made with France, where the king was devoted to the church; the Catholic powers would then have the command of Europe, and the heretics could be destroyed. [399] One thing only seemed forgotten, that the transaction was a bargain. The papal pardon had been thrust upon criminals, whose hearts were so culpably indifferent that it was necessary to bribe them to accept it; and the conditions of the compromise, even yet, were far from concluded.

The sanction given to the secularisation of church property was a cruel disappointment to the clergy, who cared little for Rome, but cared much for wealth and power. Supported by a party in the House of Commons who had not shared in the plunder, and who envied those who had been more fortunate, [400] the ecclesiastical faction began to agitate for a reconsideration of the question. Their friends in parliament said that the dispensation was unnecessary. Every man's conscience ought to be his guide whether to keep his lands or surrender them. The queen was known to hold the same opinion, and eager preachers began to sound the note of restitution. [401] Growing bolder, the Lower House of Convocation presented the bishops immediately after with a series of remarkable requests. The pope, in the terms on which he was reinstated, was but an ornamental unreality; and the practical English clergy desired substantial restorations which their eyes could see and their hands could handle.

They demanded, therefore, first, that if a statute was brought into parliament for the assurance of the church estates to the present possessors, nothing should be allowed to pass prejudicial to their claims "on lands, tenements, pensions, or tythe rents, which had appertained to bishops, or other ecclesiastical persons."

They demanded, secondly, the repeal of the Statute of Mortmain, and afterwards the abolition of lay impropriations, the punishment of heretics, the destruction of all the English Prayer-books and Bibles, the revival of the act *De Hæretico Comburendo*, the re-establishment of the episcopal courts, the restoration of the legislative functions of Convocation, and the exemption of the clergy from the authority of secular magistrates.

Finally, they required that the church should be restored absolutely to its ancient rights, immunities, and privileges; that no Premunire should issue against a bishop until he had first received notice and warning; that the judges should define "a special doctrine of Premunire," and that the Statutes of Provisors should not be wrested from their meaning. [402]

The petition expressed the views of Gardiner, and was probably drawn under his direction. Had the alienated property been no more than the estates of the suppressed abbeys, the secular clergy would have acquiesced without difficulty in the existing disposition of it. But the benefices impropriated to the abbeys which had been sold or granted with the lands, they looked on as their own; the cathedral chapters and the bishops' sees, which had suffered from the second locust flight under Edward, formed part of the local Anglican Church: and Gardiner and his brother prelates declared that, if the pope chose to set aside the canons, and permit the robbing of the religious orders, he might do as he pleased; but that he had neither right nor powers to sanction the spoliation of the working bishops and clergy. Thus the feast of reconciliation having been duly celebrated, both Houses of Parliament became again the theatre of fierce and fiery conflict.

There were wide varieties of opinion. The lawyers went beyond the clergy in limiting the powers of the pope; the lawyers also said the pope had no rights over the temporalities of bishops or abbots, deans, or rectors; but they did not any more admit the rights of the clergy. The English clergy, regular and secular, they said, had held their estates from immemorial time under the English crown, and it was not for any spiritual authority, domestic or foreign, to decide whether an English king and an English parliament might interfere to alter the disposition of those estates.

On other questions the clerical party were in the ascendant; They had a decided majority in the House of Commons; in the Upper House there was a compact body of twenty bishops; and Gardiner held the proxies of Lord Rich, Lord Oxford, Lord Westmoreland, and Lord Abergavenny. The queen had created four new peers; three of whom, Lord North, Lord Chandos, and Lord Williams, were bigoted Catholics; the fourth, Lord Howard, was absent with the fleet, and was unrepresented. Lord North held the proxy of Lord Worcester; and the Marquis of Winchester, Lord Montague, and Lord Stourton acted generally with the chancellor. Lord Russell was keeping out of the way, being suspected of heresy; Wentworth was at Calais; Grey was at Guisnes; and the proxies of the two last noblemen, which in the late parliament were held by Arundel and Paget, were, for some unknown reason, now held by no one. Thus, in a house of seventy-three members only, reduced to sixty-nine by the absence of Howard, Russell, Wentworth, and Grey, Gardiner had thirty-one votes whom he might count upon as certain; he knew his power, and at once made fatal use of it.

For two parliaments the liberal party had prevented him from recovering the power of persecution. He did not attempt to pass the Inquisitorial Act on which he was defeated in the last session. But the act to revive the Lollard Statutes was carried through the House of Commons in the second week in December; on the 15th it was brought up to the Lords; and although those who had before fought the battle of humanity, struggled again bravely in the same cause, this time their numbers were too small; they failed, and the lives of the Protestants were in their enemies' hands. [403] Simultaneously Gardiner obtained for the bishops' courts their long-coveted privilege of arbitrary arrest and discretionary punishment, and the clergy obtained, as they desired, the restoration of their legislative powers. The property question alone disintegrated the phalanx of orthodoxy, and left an opening for the principles of liberty to assert themselves. The faithful and the faithless among the laity were alike participators in church plunder, and were alike nervously sensitive when the current of the reaction ran in the direction of a demand for restitution.

Here, therefore, Paget and his friends chose their ground to maintain the fight.

It has been seen that Pole especially dreaded the appearance of any sort of composition between the country and the papacy. The submission had, in fact, been purchased, but the purchase ought to be disguised. As soon, therefore, as the parliament set themselves to the fulfilment of their promise to undo the acts by which England had separated itself from Rome, the legate required a simple statute of repeal. The pope had granted a dispensation; it was enough, and it should be accepted gratefully: the penitence of sinners ought not to be mixed with questions of worldly interest; the returning prodigal, when asking pardon at his father's feet, had made no conditions; the English nation must not disfigure their obedience by alluding, in the terms of it, to the pope's benevolence to them.

The holders of the property, on the other hand, thinking more of the reality than the form, were determined that the Act of Repeal should contain, as nearly as possible, a true statement of their case. They *had* made conditions, and those conditions had been reluctantly complied with; and, to prevent future errors, the nature of the compact ought to be explained with the utmost distinctness. They had replaced the bishops in authority, and the bishops might be made use of at some future time, indirectly or directly, to disturb the settlement. A fresh pontiff might refuse to recognise the concessions of his predecessors. The papal supremacy, the secularisation of the church property, and the authority of the episcopal courts should, therefore, be interwoven inextricably to stand or fall together; and as the lawyers denied the authority of the Holy See to pronounce upon the matter at all, the legal opinion might be embodied also as a further security.

After a week of violent discussion, the lay interest in the House of Lords found itself the strongest. Pole exclaimed that, if the submission and the dispensation were tied together, it was a simoniacal compact; the pope's holiness was bought and sold for a price, he said, and he would sooner go back to Rome, and leave his work unfinished, than consent to an act so derogatory to the Holy See. But the protest was vain; if the legate was so anxious, his anxiety was an additional reason why the opposition should persevere; if he chose to go, his departure could be endured. [404]

So keen was the debate that there was not so much as a Christmas recess. Christmas Day was kept as a holyday. On the 26th the struggle began again, and, fortunately, clouds had risen between the House of Commons and the court. Finding more difficulty than he expected in embroiling England with France, Philip, to feel the temper of the people, induced one of the peers to carry a note to the Lower House to request an opinion whether it was not the duty of a son to assist his father. An answer was instantly returned that the question had been already disposed of by the late parliament in the marriage treaty, and the further discussion of it was unnecessary. [405] Secretary Bourne, at the instigation of Gardiner, proposed to revive the claims on the pensions; but he met with no better reception. And the court made a further blunder. Mary had become so accustomed to success, that she assured herself she could obtain all that she desired. The object of the court was to secure the regency for Philip, with full sovereign powers, should she die leaving a child; should she die childless, to make him her successor. The first step would be Philip's coronation, which had been long talked of, and which the House of Commons was now desired to sanction. The House of Commons returned a unanimous refusal. [406]

The effects of these cross influences on the papal statute, though they cannot be traced in detail, must have been not inconsiderable. At length, on the 4th of January, after passing backwards and forwards for a fortnight between the two Houses, the Great Bill, as it was called, emerged, finished, in the form of a petition to the crown: —

"Whereas," so runs the preamble, [407] "since the 20th year of King Henry VIII., of famous memory, much false and erroneous doctrine hath been taught, preached, and written, partly by divers natural-born subjects of this realm, and partly being brought in hither from sundry foreign countries, hath been sown and spread abroad within the same—by reason whereof as well the spiritualty as the temporalty of your highness's realm and dominions have swerved from the obedience of the See Apostolic, and declined from the unity of Christ's Church, and so have continued until such time as—your majesty being first raised up by God, and set in the seat royal over us, and then by his divine and gracious Providence knit in marriage with the most noble and virtuous prince the king our sovereign lord your husband—the pope's holiness and the See Apostolic sent hither unto your majesties, as unto persons undefiled, and by God's goodness preserved from the common infection aforesaid, and to the whole realm, the Most Reverend Father in God the Lord Cardinal Pole, Legate *de Latere*, to call us again into the right way, from which we have all this long while wandered and strayed; and we, after sundry and long plagues and calamities, seeing, by the goodness of God, our own errours, have knowledged the same unto the said Most Reverend Father, and by him have been and are (the rather at the contemplation of your majesties) received and embraced into the unity of Christ's Church, upon our humble submission, and promise made for a declaration of our repentance to repeal and abrogate such acts and statutes as had been made in parliament since the said 20th year of the said King Henry VIII., against the supremacy of the See Apostolic, as in our submission exhibited to the said most Reverend Father in God, by your majesties appeareth—it may like your majesty, for the accomplishment of our promise, that all such laws be repealed. That is to say:—

"The Act against obtaining Dispensations from Rome for Pluralities and non-Residence. [408]

"The Act that no person shall be cited out of the Diocese where he or she dwelleth. [409]

"The Act against Appeals to the See of Rome. [410]

"The Act against the Payment of Annates and First-fruits to the See of Rome. [411]

"The Act for the Submission of the Clergy. [412]

"The Act for the Election and Consecration of Bishops. [413]

"The Act against Exactions from the See of Rome. [414]

"The Act of the Royal Supremacy. [415]

"The Act for the Consecration of Suffragan Bishops. [416]

"The Act for the Reform of the Canon Law. [417]

"The Act against the Authority of the Pope. [418]

"The Act for the Release of those who had obtained Dispensations from Rome. [419]

"The Act authorising the King to appoint Bishops by Letters Patent. [420]

The Act of Precontracts and Degrees of Consanguinity. [421]

The Act for the King's Style. [422]

The Act permitting the Marriage of Doctors of Civil Law." [423]

In the repeal of these statutes the entire ecclesiastical legislation of Henry VIII. was swept away; and, so far as a majority in a single parliament could affect them, the work was done absolutely and with clean completeness.

But there remained two other acts collaterally and accidentally affecting the See of Rome; for the repeal of which the court was no less anxious than for the repeal of the Act of Supremacy, where the parliament were not so complaisant.

Throughout the whole reaction under Mary there was one point on which the laity never wavered. Attempts such as that which has been just mentioned were made incessantly, directly or indirectly, to alter the succession and cut off Elizabeth. They were like the fretful and profitless chafings of waves upon a rock. The two acts on which Elizabeth's claims were rested [424] touched, in one or other of their clauses, the papal prerogative, and were included in the list to be condemned. But, of these acts, "so much only" as affected the See of Rome was repealed. The rest was studiously declared to continue in force.

Yet, with this reservation, the parliament had gone far in their concessions, and it remained for them to secure their equivalent.

They reinstated the bishops, but, in giving back a power which had been so much abused, they took care to protect — not, alas! the innocent lives which were about to be sacrificed — but their own interests. The bishops and clergy of the Province of Canterbury having been made to state their case and their claims, in a petition to the crown, they were then compelled formally to relinquish those claims; and the petition and the relinquishment were embodied in the act as the condition of the restoration of the authority of the church courts. [425] In continuation, the Lords and Commons desired that, for the removal "of all occasion of contention, suspicion, and trouble, both outwardly and inwardly, in men's conscience," the pope's holiness, as represented by the legate, "by dispensation, toleration, or permission, as the case required," would recognise all such foundations of colleges, hospitals, cathedrals, churches, schools, or bishoprics as had been established during the schism, would confirm the validity of all ecclesiastical acts which had been performed during the same period; and, finally, would consent that all property, of whatever kind, taken from the church, should remain to its present possessors—"so as all persons having sufficient conveyance of the said lands, goods, and chattels by the common laws, or acts, or statutes of the realm, might, without scruple of conscience, enjoy them without impeachment or trouble, by pretence of any general council, canon, or ecclesiastical law, and clear from all dangers of the censures of the church." The petitions, both of clergy and parliament, the act went on to say, had been considered by the cardinal; and the cardinal had acquiesced. He had undertaken, in the pope's name, that the possessors of either lands or goods should never be molested either then or in time to come, in virtue of any papal decree, or canon, or council; that if any attempt should be made by any bishop or other ecclesiastic to employ the spiritual weapons of the church to extort restitution, such act or acts were declared vain and of none effect. The dispensation was pronounced, nor could the legate's protests avail to prevent it from appearing in the act. He was permitted, only in consideration of the sacrifice, to interweave amidst the legal technicalities some portion of his own feeling. The impious detainers of holy things, while permitted to maintain their iniquity, were reminded of the fate of Belshazzar, and were urged to restore the patines, chalices, and ornaments of the altars. The impropriators of benefices were implored, in the mercy of Christ, to remember the souls of the people, and provide for the decent performance of the services of the churches. [426]

Here the act might have been expected to end. The nature of the transaction between the parliament and the pope had been made sufficiently clear. Yet, had nothing more been said, the surrender of their claims by the clergy would have implied that they had parted with something which they might have legitimately required. Under the inspiration of the lawyers, therefore, a series of clauses were superadded, explaining that, notwithstanding the dispensation, "The title of all lands, possessions, and hereditaments in their majesties' realms and dominions was grounded in the laws, statutes, and customs of the same, and by their high jurisdiction, authority royal, and crown imperial, *and in their courts only*, might be impleaded, ordered, tried, and judged, and none otherwise:" and, therefore, "whosoever, by any process obtained out of any ecclesiastical court within the realm or without, or by pretence of any spiritual jurisdiction or otherwise, contrary to the laws of the realm, should inquiet or molest any person or persons, or body politic, for any of the said lands or things above specified, should incur the danger of Premunire, and should suffer and incur the forfeitures and pains contained in the same." [427]

Vainly the clergy had entreated for a limitation or removal of Premunire. That spectre remained unexorcised in all its shadowy terror; and while it survived, the penitence of England went no deeper than the lips, however fine the words and eloquent the phrases in which it was expressed. As some compensation, the Mortmain Act was suspended for twenty years. Yet, as if it were in reply to Pole's appeal, a mischievous provision closed the act, that, notwithstanding anything contained in it, laymen entitled to tithes might recover them with the same readiness as before the first day of the present parliament. [428]

Such was the great statute of reconciliation with Rome, with which, in the inability to obtain a better, the legate was compelled to be satisfied, and to reconsider his threat of going back to Italy.

This first conflict was no sooner ended than another commenced. The Commons would not consent that Philip should be crowned; but, as the queen said she was *enceinte*, provision had to be made for a regency, and a bill was introduced into the Upper House which has not survived, but which, in spirit, was unfavourable to the king. [429] Gardiner, in the course of the debate, attempted to put in a clause affecting Elizabeth, [430] but the success was no better than usual. The act went down to the Commons, where, however, it was immediately cancelled. Though the Commons would give Philip no rights as king, they were better disposed towards him than the Lords; and they drew another bill of their own, in which they declared the father to be the natural and fitting guardian of the child. The experience of protectorates, they said, had been uniformly unfortunate, and should the queen die leaving an heir, Philip should be regent of the realm during the minority; if obliged to be absent on the Continent, he might himself nominate his deputy; [431] and so long as it should be his pleasure to remain in England, his person should be under the protection of the laws of high treason.

Taking courage from the apparent disposition of the House, the friends of the court proposed that, should the queen die childless, the crown should devolve absolutely upon him for his life. [432] But in this they were going too far. The suggestion was listened to coldly; and Philip, who had really calculated on obtaining from parliament, in some form or other, a security for his succession, despatched Ruy Gomez to Brussels, to consult the emperor on the course which should be pursued. [433] On the whole, however, could the bill of the House of Commons be carried, Renard was disposed to be contented; the queen was confident in her hopes of an heir, and it might not be worth while to irritate the people unnecessarily about Elizabeth. [434] The clause empowering Philip to govern by deputy in his absence was especially satisfactory. [435]

But the peers, whom the Commons had refused to consult on the new form of the measure, would not part so easily with their own opinions; they adopted the phraseology of the Lower House, but this particular and precious feature in it they pared away. The bill, as it eventually passed, declared Philip regent till his child should be of age, and so long as he continued in the realm; but, at the same time, fatally for the objects at which he was aiming, it bound him again to observe all the articles of the marriage treaty, "which, during the time that he should hold the government, should remain and continue in as full force and strength, as if they were newly inserted and rehearsed in the present act." [436]

The disposition of the House of Lords was the more dangerous, because the bishops, of course, voted with the government, and the strength of the opposition, therefore, implied something like unanimity in the lay peers. The persecuting act had been carried with difficulty, and in the reconciliation with Rome the legate had been studiously mortified. On the succession and the coronation the court had been wholly baffled; and in the Regency Bill they had obtained but half of what they had desired. At the least Mary had hoped to secure for the king the free disposal of the army and the finances, and she had not been able so much as to ask for it. Compelled to rest contented with such advantages as had been secured, the court would not risk the results of further controversy by prolonging the session; and on the 16th of January, at four o'clock in the afternoon, the king and queen came to the House of Lords almost unattended, and with an evident expression of dissatisfaction dissolved the parliament. [437]

I have been particular in relating the proceedings of this parliament, because it marks the point where the flood tide of reaction ceased to ascend, and the ebb recommenced. From the beginning of the Reformation in 1529, two distinct movements had gone on side by side—the alteration of doctrines, and the emancipation of the laity from papal and ecclesiastical domination.

With the first, the contemporaries of Henry VIII., the country gentlemen and the peers, who were the heads of families at the period of Mary's accession, had never sympathised; and the tyranny of the Protestants while they were in power had converted a disapproval which time would have overcome, into active and determined indignation. The papacy was a mixed question; the Pilgrims of Grace in 1536, and the Cornish rebels in 1549, had demanded the restoration of the spiritual primacy to the See of St. Peter, and Henry himself, until Pole and Paul III. called on Europe to unite in a crusade against him, had not determined wholly against some degree of concession. In the pope, as a sovereign who claimed reverence and tribute, who interfered with the laws of the land, and maintained at Rome a supreme court of appeal—who pretended a right to depose kings and absolve subjects from their allegiance—who held a weapon in excommunication as terrible to the laity as Premunire was terrible to ecclesiastics—in the pope under this aspect, only a few insignificant fanatics entertained any kind of interest.

But experience had proved that to a nation cut off from the centre of Catholic union, the maintenance of orthodoxy was impossible: the supremacy of the pope, therefore, came back as a tolerated feature in the return to the Catholic faith, and the ecclesiastical courts were reinstated in authority to check unlicensed extravagance of opinion. Their restored power, however, was over opinion only; wherever the pretensions of the church would come in collision with the political constitution, wherever they menaced the independence of the temporal magistrate or the tenure of property, there the progress of restoration was checked by the rock, and could eat no further into the soil. The pope and the clergy recovered their titular rank, and in one direction unhappily they recovered the reality of power. But the temporal spoils of the struggle remained with the laity, and if the clergy lifted a hand to retake them, their weapons would be instantly wrenched from their grasp.

If the genuine friends of human freedom had acquiesced without resistance in this conclusion, if the nobility had contented themselves with securing their worldly and political interests, and had made no effort to restrain or modify the exercise of the authority which they were giving back, they might be accused of having accepted a dishonourable compromise. But they did what they could. They worked with such legal means as were in their power, and for two parliaments they succeeded in keeping persecution at bay; they failed in the third, but failed only after a struggle. The Protestants themselves had created, by their own misconduct, the difficulty of defending them; and armed unconstitutional resistance was an expedient to be resorted to, only when it had been seen how the clergy would conduct themselves. English statesmen may be pardoned if they did not anticipate the passions to which the guardians of orthodoxy were about to abandon themselves. Parliament had maintained the independence of the English courts of law. It had maintained the Premunire. It had forbidden the succession to be tampered with. If this was not everything, it was something — something which in the end would be the undoing of all the rest.

The court and the bishops, however, were for the present absolute in their own province. The persecuting acts were once more upon the Statute Book; and when the realities of the debates in parliament had disappeared, the cardinal and the queen could again give the rein to their imagination. They had called up a phantom out of its grave, and they persuaded themselves that they were witnessing the resurrection of the spirit of truth, that heresy was about to vanish from off the English soil, like an exhalation of the morning, at the brightness of the papal return. The chancellor and the clergy were springing at the leash like hounds with the game in view, fanaticism and revenge lashing them forward. If the temporal schemes of the court were thwarted, it was, perhaps, because Heaven desired that exclusive attention should be given first to the salvation of souls.

For all past political offences, therefore, there was now an amnesty, and such prisoners as remained unexecuted for Wyatt's conspiracy were released from the Tower on the 18th of January. On the 25th a hundred and sixty priests walked in procession through the London streets, chanting litanies, with eight bishops walking after them, and Bonner carrying the host. On the 28th the cardinal issued his first general instructions. The bishops were directed to call together their clergy in every diocese in England, and to inform them of the benevolent love of the Holy Father, and of the arrival of the legate with powers to absolve them from their guilt. They were to relate the acts of the late parliament, with the reconciliation and absolution of the Lords and Commons; and they were to give general notice that authority had been restored to the ecclesiastical courts, to proceed against the enemies of the faith, and punish them according to law.

A day was then to be fixed on which the clergy should appear with their confessions, and be received into the church. In the assignment of their several penances, a distinction was to be made between those who had taught heresy and those who had merely lapsed into it.

When the clergy had been reconciled, they were again in turn to exhort the laity in all churches and cathedrals, to accept the grace which was offered to them; and that they might understand that they were not at liberty to refuse the invitation, a time was assigned to them within which their submissions must be all completed. A book was to be kept in every diocese, where the names of those who were received were to be entered. A visitation was to be held throughout the country at the end of the spring, and all who had not complied before Easter day, or who, after compliance, "had returned to their vomit", would be proceeded against with the utmost severity of the law. [438]

The introduction of the Register was the Inquisition under another name. There was no limit, except in the humanity or the prudence of the bishops, to the tyranny which they would be enabled to exercise. The cardinal professed to desire that, before heretics were punished with death, mild means should first be tried with them; [439] the meaning which he attached to the words was illustrated in an instant example.

The instructions were the signal for the bishops to commence business. On the day of their appearance, Gardiner, Bonner, Tunstal, and three other prelates, formed a court in St. Mary Overy's Church, in Southwark; and Hooper, and Rogers, a canon of St. Paul's, were brought up before them.

Rogers had been distinguished in the first bright days of Protestantism. He had been a fellow-labourer with Tyndal and Coverdale, at Antwerp, in the translation of the Bible. Afterwards, taking a German wife, he lived for a time at Wittenberg, not unknown, we may be sure, to Martin Luther. On the accession of Edward, he returned to England, and worked among the London clergy till the end of the reign; and on Mary's accession he was one of the preachers at Paul's Cross who had dared to speak against the reaction. He had been rebuked by the council, and his friends had urged him to fly; but, like Cranmer, he thought that duty required him to stay at his post, and, in due time, without, however, having given fresh provocation, he was shut up in Newgate by Bonner.

Hooper, when the unfortunate garment controversy was brought to an end, had shown by his conduct in his diocese that in one instance at least doctrinal fanaticism was compatible with the loftiest excellence. While the great world was scrambling for the church property, Hooper was found petitioning the council for leave to augment impoverished livings out of his own income. [440] In the hall of his palace at Gloucester a profuse hospitality was offered daily to those who were most in need of it. The poor of the city were invited by relays to solid meat dinners, and the bishop with the courtesy of a gentleman dined with them, and treated them with the same respect as if they had been the highest in the land. He was one of the first persons arrested after Mary's accession, and the cross of persecution at once happily made his peace with Ridley. In an affectionate interchange of letters, the two confessors exhorted each other to constancy in the end which both foresaw, determining "if they could not overthrow, at least, to shake those high altitudes" of spiritual tyranny. [441] The Fleet prison had now been Hooper's house for eighteen months. At first, on payment of heavy fees to the warden, he had lived in some degree of comfort; but as soon as his deprivation was declared, Gardiner ordered that he should be confined in one of the common prisoners' wards; where "with a wicked man and a wicked woman" for his companions, with a bed of straw and a rotten counterpane, the prison sink on one side of his cell and Fleet ditch on the other, he waited till it would please parliament to permit the dignitaries of the Church to murder him. [442]

These were the two persons with whom the Marian persecution opened. On their appearance in the court, they were required briefly to make their submission. They attempted to argue; but they were told that when parliament had determined a thing, private men were not to call it in question, and they were allowed twenty-four hours to make up their minds. As they were leaving the church Hooper was heard to say, "Come, brother Rogers, must we two take this matter first in hand and fry these faggots?" "Yea, sir, with God's grace," Rogers answered. "Doubt not," Hooper said, "but God will give us strength."

They were remanded to prison. The next morning they were brought again before the court. "The queen's mercy" was offered them, if they would recant; they refused, and they were sentenced to die. Rogers asked to be allowed to take leave of his wife and children. Gardiner, with a savage taunt, rejected the request. The day of execution was left uncertain. They were sent to Newgate to wait the queen's pleasure. On the 30th, Taylor of Hadley, Laurence Sandars, rector of All Hallows, and the illustrious Bradford, were passed through the same forms with the same results. Another, a notorious preacher, called Cardmaker, flinched, and made his submission.

Rogers was to "break the ice," as Bradford described it. [443] On the morning of the 4th of February the wife of the keeper of Newgate came to his bedside. He was sleeping soundly, and she woke him with difficulty to let him know that he was wanted. The Bishop of London was waiting, she said, to degrade him from the priesthood, and he was then to go out and die. Rubbing his eyes, and collecting himself, he hurried on his clothes. "If it be thus." he said, "I need not tie my points." Hooper had been sent for also for the ceremony of degradation. The vestments used in the mass were thrown over them, and were then one by one removed. They were pronounced deposed from the priestly office, incapable of offering further sacrifice — except, indeed, the only acceptable sacrifice which man can ever offer, the sacrifice of himself. Again Rogers entreated permission to see his wife, and again he was refused.

The two friends were then parted. Hooper was to suffer at Gloucester, and returned to his cell; Rogers was committed to the sheriff, and led out to Smithfield. The Catholics had affected to sneer at the faith of their rivals. There was a general conviction among them, which was shared probably by Pole and Gardiner, that the Protestants would all flinch at the last; that they had no "doctrine that would abide the fire." When Rogers appeared, therefore, the exultation of the people in his constancy overpowered the horror of his fate, and he was received with rounds of cheers. His family, whom he was forbidden to part with in private, were waiting on the way to see him — his wife with nine little ones at her side and a tenth upon her breast — and they, too, welcomed him with hysterical cries of joy, as if he were on his way to a festival. [444] Sir Robert Rochester was in attendance at the stake to report his behaviour. At the last moment he was offered pardon if he would give way, but in vain. The fire was lighted. The suffering seemed to be nothing. He bathed his hands in the flame as "if it was cold water," raised his eyes to heaven, and died.

The same night a party of the royal guard took charge of Hooper, the order of whose execution was arranged by a mandate from the crown. As "an obstinate, false, and detestable heretic," he was to be burned in the city "which he had infected with his pernicious doctrines;" and "forasmuch as being a vainglorious person, and delighting in his tongue," he "might persuade the people into agreement with him, had he liberty to use it," care was to be taken that he should not speak either at the stake or on his way to it. [445] He was carried down on horseback by easy stages; and on the forenoon of Thursday, the 7th, he dined at Cirencester, "at a woman's house who had always hated the truth, and spoken all evil she could of him." This woman had shared in the opinion that Protestants had no serious convictions, and had often expressed her belief that Hooper, particularly, would fail if brought to the trial. She found that both in him and in his creed there was more than she had supposed; and "perceiving the cause of his coming, she lamented his case with tears, and showed him all the friendship she could."

At five in the evening he arrived at Gloucester. The road, for a mile outside the town, was lined with people, and the mayor was in attendance, with an escort, to prevent a rescue. But the feeling was rather of awe and expectation, and those who loved Hooper best knew that the highest service which he could render to his faith was to die for it.

A day's interval of preparation was allowed him, with a private room. He was in the custody of the sheriff; "and there was this difference observed between the keepers of the bishops' prisons and the keepers of the crown prisons, that the bishops' keepers were ever cruel; the keepers of the crown prisons showed, for the most part, such favour as they might." [446] After a sound night's rest, Hooper rose early, and passed the morning in solitary prayer. In the course of the day, young Sir Anthony Kingston, one of the commissioners appointed to superintend the execution, expressed a wish to see him. Kingston was an old acquaintance, Hooper having been the means of bringing him out of evil ways. He entered the room unannounced. Hooper was on his knees, and, looking round at the intruder, did not at first know him. Kingston told him his name, and then, bursting into tears, said: —

"Oh, consider; life is sweet and death is bitter; therefore, seeing life may be had, desire to live, for life hereafter may do good."

Hooper answered: —

"I thank you for your counsel, yet it is not so friendly as I could have wished it to be. True it is, alas! Master Kingston, that death is bitter and life is sweet; therefore I have settled myself, through the strength of God's Holy

Spirit, patiently to pass through the fire prepared for me, desiring you and others to commend me to God's mercy in your prayers."

"Well, my Lord," said Kingston, "then there is no remedy, and I will take my leave. I thank God that ever I knew you, for God appointed you to call me, being a lost child. I was both an adulterer and a fornicator, and God, by your good instruction, brought me to the forsaking of the same."

They parted, the tears on both their faces. Other friends were admitted afterwards. The queen's orders were little thought of, for Hooper had won the hearts of the guard on his way from London. In the evening the mayor and aldermen came, with the sheriffs, to shake hands with him. "It was a sign of their good will," he said, "and a proof that they had not forgotten the lessons which he used to teach them." He begged the sheriffs that there might be "a quick fire, to make an end shortly;" and for himself he would be as obedient as they could wish.

"If you think I do amiss in anything," he said, "hold up your fingers, and I have done; for I am not come hither as one enforced or compelled to die; I might have had my life, as is well known, with worldly gain, if I would have accounted my doctrine falsehood and heresy."

In the evening, at his own request, he was left alone. He slept undisturbed the early part of the night. From the time that he awoke till the guard entered, he was on his knees.

The morning was windy and wet. The scene of the execution was an open space opposite the college, near a large elm tree, where Hooper had been accustomed to preach. Several thousand people were collected to see him suffer; some had climbed the tree, and were seated in the storm and rain among the leafless branches. A company of priests were in a room over the college gates, looking out with pity or satisfaction, as God or the devil was in their hearts.

"Alas!" said Hooper, when he was brought out, "why be all these people assembled here, and speech is prohibited me?" He had suffered in prison from sciatica, and was lame, but he limped cheerfully along with a stick, and smiled when he saw the stake. At the foot of it he knelt; and as he began to pray, a box was brought, and placed on a stool before his eyes, which he was told contained his pardon if he would recant.

"Away with it;" Hooper only cried; "away with it!"

"Despatch him, then," Lord Chandos said, "seeing there is no remedy."

He was undressed to his shirt, in the cold; a pound of gunpowder was tied between his legs, and as much more under either arm; he was fastened with an iron hoop to the stake, and he assisted with his own hands to arrange the faggots round him.

The fire was then brought, but the wood was green; the dry straw only kindled, and burning for a few moments was blown away by the wind. A violent flame paralysed the nerves at once, a slow one was torture. More faggots were thrown in, and again lighted, and this time the martyr's face was singed and scorched; but again the flames sank, and the hot damp sticks smouldered round his legs. He wiped his eyes with his hands, and cried, "For God's love, good people, let me have more fire!" A third supply of dry fuel was laid about him, and this time the powder exploded, but it had been ill placed, or was not enough. "Lord Jesu, have mercy on me!" he exclaimed; "Lord Jesu, receive my spirit!" These were his last articulate words; but his lips were long seen to move, and he continued to beat his breast with his hands. It was not till after three-quarters of an hour of torment that he at last expired.

The same day, at the same hour, Rowland Taylor was burnt on Aldham Common, in Suffolk. Laurance Sandars had been destroyed the day before at Coventry, kissing the stake, and crying, "Welcome the cross of Christ! welcome everlasting life!" The first-fruits of the Whitehall pageant were gathered. By the side of the rhetoric of the hysterical dreamer who presided in that vain melodrama, let me place a few words addressed by the murdered Bishop of Gloucester to his friends, a week before his sentence.

"The grace of God be with you, amen. I did write unto you of late, and told you what extremity the parliament had concluded upon concerning religion, suppressing the truth, and setting forth the untruth; intending to cause all men, by extremity, to forswear themselves; and to take again for the head of the church him that is neither head nor member of it, but a very enemy, as the word of God and all ancient writers do record. And for lack of law and authority they will use force and extremity, which have been the arguments to defend the pope and popery since their authority first began in the world. But now is the time of trial, to see whether we fear more God or man. It was an easy thing to hold with Christ whilst the prince and the world held with him; but now the world hateth him, it is the true trial who be his.

"Wherefore in the name, and in the virtue, strength, and power of his Holy Spirit, prepare yourselves in any case to adversity and constancy. Let us not run away when it is most time to fight. Remember, none shall be crowned but such as fight manfully; and he that endureth to the end shall be saved. Ye must now turn your cogitations from the perils you see, and mark the felicity that followeth the peril—either victory in this world of your enemies, or else a surrender of this life to inherit the everlasting kingdom. Beware of beholding too much the felicity or misery of this world; for the consideration and too earnest love or fear of either of them draweth from God. Wherefore think with yourselves as touching the felicity of the world, it is good; but none otherwise than it standeth with the favour of God; it is to be kept, but yet so far forth as by keeping it we lose not God. It is good abiding and tarrying still among our friends here, but yet so that we tarry not therewithal in God's displeasure, and hereafter dwell with the devils in fire everlasting. There is nothing under God but may be kept, so that God, being above all things we have, be not lost. Of adversity judge the same. Imprisonment is painful, but yet liberty upon evil conditions is more painful. The prisons stink; but yet not so much as sweet houses, where the fear and true honour of God lack. I must be alone and solitary; it is better so to be, and have God with me, than to be in company with the wicked. Loss of goods is great, but loss of God's grace and favour is greater. I am a poor simple creature, and cannot tell how to answer before such a great sort of noble, learned, and wise men. It is better to make answer before the pomp and pride of wicked men, than to stand naked, in the sight of all heaven and earth, before the just God at the latter day. I shall die by the hands of the cruel men; but he is blessed that loseth this life full of miseries, and findeth the life of eternal joys. It is pain and grief to depart from goods and friends; but yet not so much as to depart from grace and heaven itself. Wherefore there is neither felicity nor adversity of this world that can appear to be great, if it be weighed with the joys or pains in the world to come." [447]

Of five who had been sentenced, four were thus despatched. Bradford, the fifth, was respited, in the hope that the example might tell upon him. Six more were waiting their condemnation in Bonner's prisons. The enemies of the church were to submit or die. So said Gardiner, in the name of the English priesthood, with the passion of a fierce revenge. So said the legate and the queen, in the delirious belief that they were chosen instruments of Providence.

So, however, did not say the English lay statesmen. The first and unexpected effect was to produce a difference of opinion in the court itself. Philip, to whom Renard had insisted on the necessity of more moderate measures, found it necessary to clear himself of responsibility; and the day after Hooper suffered, Alphonso a Castro, the king's chaplain, preached a sermon in the royal presence, in which he denounced the execution, and inveighed against the tyranny of the bishops. The Lords of the Council "talked strangely;" and so deep was the indignation, that the Flemish ambassador again expected Gardiner's destruction. Paget refused to act with him in the council any more, and Philip himself talked more and more of going abroad. Renard, from the tone of his correspondence, believed evidently at this moment that the game of the church was played out and lost. He wrote to the emperor to entreat that when the king went he might not himself be left behind; he was held responsible by the people for the queen's misdoings; and a party of the young nobility had sworn to kill him. [448]

Among the people the constancy of the martyrs had called out a burst of admiration. It was rumoured that bystanders had endeavoured to throw themselves into the fire to die at their side. [449] A prisoner, on examination before Bonner, was asked if he thought he could bear the flame. You may try me, if you will, he said. A candle was brought, and he held his hand, without flinching, in the blaze. [450] With such a humour abroad, it seemed to Renard that the Lords had only to give the signal, and the queen and the bishops would be overwhelmed.

He expected the movement in the spring. It is singular that, precisely as in the preceding winter, the deliberate intentions of moderate and competent persons were anticipated and defeated by a partial and premature conspiracy. At the end of February a confederate revealed a project for an insurrection, partly religious and partly agrarian. Placards were to be issued simultaneously in all parts of the country, declaring that the queen's pregnancy was a delusion, and that she intended to pass upon the nation a supposititious child; the people were, therefore, invited to rise in arms, drive out the Spaniards, revolutionise religion, tear down the enclosures of the commons, and proclaim Courtenay king under the title of Edward VII. [451] In such a scheme the lords and country gentlemen could bear no part. They could not risk a repetition of the popular rebellions of the late reign, and they resolved to wait the issue of the queen's pregnancy, while they watched over the safety of Elizabeth. The project of the court was now to send her to Flanders, where she was to remain under charge of the emperor; if possible, she was to be persuaded to go thither of her own accord; if she could not be persuaded, she would be otherwise removed. Lord William Howard, her constant guardian, requested permission to see and speak with her, and learn her own feelings. He was refused; but he went to her notwithstanding, and had a long private interview with her; and the court could only talk bitterly of his treason among themselves, make propositions to send him to the Tower which they durst not execute, and devise some other method of dealing with their difficulty. [452]

Meantime, Philip, who had pined for freedom after six weeks' experience of his bride, was becoming unmanageably impatient. A paper of advice and exhortation survives, which was addressed on this occasion by the ambassador to his master, with reflections on the condition of England, and on the conduct which the king should pursue.

"Your majesty must remember," said Renard, "the purpose for which you came to England. The French had secured the Queen of Scotland for the Dauphin. They had afterwards made an alliance with the late king, and spared no pains to secure the support of England. To counteract their schemes, and to obtain a counter advantage in the war, the emperor, on the accession of the queen, resolved that your highness should marry her. Your highness, it is true, might wish that she was more agreeable; [453] but, on the other hand, she is infinitely virtuous, and, things being as they are, your highness, like a magnanimous prince, must remember her condition, and exert yourself, so far as you conveniently may, to assist her in the management of the kingdom.

"Your highness must consider that your departure will be misrepresented, your enemies will speak of it as a flight rather than as a necessary absence. The French will be busy with their intrigues, and the queen will not be pleased to lose you. The administration is in confusion, the divisions in the council are more violent than ever. Religion is unsettled; the heretics take advantage of these late barbarous punishments to say, that they are to be converted by fire, because their enemies are unable to convince them by reason or example. The orthodox clergy are still unreformed, and their scandalous conduct accords ill with the offices to which they are called. [454]

"Further, your highness will do well to weigh the uncertainty of the succession. Should the queen's pregnancy prove a mistake, the heretics will place their hopes in Elizabeth: and here you are in a difficulty whatever be done; for if Elizabeth be set aside, the crown will go to the Queen of Scots; if she succeed, she will restore heresy, and naturally attach herself to France. Some step must be taken about this before you leave the country; and you must satisfy the queen that you will assist her in her general difficulties, as a good lord and husband ought to do. [455]

"The council must be reformed, if possible, and the number diminished; those who remain must be invited to renew their oaths to your majesty. Regard must be had to the navy, and especially to the admiral Lord William Howard; and above all there must be no more of this barbarous precipitancy in putting heretics to death. The people must be won from their errors by gentleness and by better instruction. Except in cases of especial scandal, the bishops must not be permitted to irritate them by cruelty, and the legate must see that a better example is set by the clergy themselves. [456] The debts of the crown must be attended to; and your majesty should endeavour to do something which will give you popularity with the masses. Before all things, attend to the succession.

"You cannot set aside the dispositions of King Henry in favour of Elizabeth without danger of rebellion. To recognise her as heir-presumptive without providing her with a husband, who can control her, will be perilous to the queen. The mean course between the extremes, will be therefore, for your highness to bring about her marriage with the Prince of Savoy. It will please the English, provided that her rights of inheritance are not interfered with; and although they will not go to war for our quarrel, they will not in that case be unwilling to assist in expelling the French from Piedmont.

"If your majesty approve, the thing can be done without delay. At all events, before you leave the country, you should see the princess yourself; give her your advice to be faithful to her sister, and, on your part, promise that you will be her friend, and assist her where you can find opportunity."

CHAPTER IV-THE MARTYRS

The protests of Renard against the persecution received no attention.

The inquisition established by the legate was not to commence till Easter; but the prisons were already abundantly supplied with persons who had been arrested on various pretexts, and the material was ready in hand to occupy the interval. The four persons who had first suffered had been conspicuous among the leaders of the Reformation; but the bishops were for the most part prudent in their selection of victims, and chose them principally from among the poor and unfriended.

On the 9th of February, a weaver named Tomkins (the man who had held his hand in the candle), Pigot, a butcher, Knight, a barber, Hunter, an apprentice boy of 19, Lawrence, a priest, and Hawkes, a gentleman, were brought before Bonner in the Consistory at St. Paul's, where they were charged with denying transubstantiation, and were condemned to die. The indignation which had been excited by the first executions caused a delay in carrying the sentence into effect; but as the menace of insurrection died away the wolves came back to their prey. On the 9th of March, two more were condemned also, Thomas Causton and Thomas Higbed, men of some small property in Essex. To disperse the effect, these eight were scattered about the diocese. Tomkins died at Smithfield on the 16th of March; Causton and Higbed, Pigot and Knight, in different parts of Essex; Hawkes suffered later; Lawrence was burnt at Colchester. The legs of the latter had been crushed by irons in one of Bonner's prisons; he was unable to stand, and was placed at the stake in a chair. "At his burning, he sitting in the fire, the young children came about and cried, as well as young children could speak, Lord strengthen thy servant, and keep thy promise—Lord, strengthen thy servant, and keep thy promise." [457]

Hunter's case deserves more particular mention. The London apprentices had been affected deeply by the Reforming preachers. It was to them that the servant of Anne Askew "made her moan," and gathered subscriptions for her mistress. William Hunter, who was one of them, had been ordered to attend mass by a priest when it was re-established; he had refused, and his master, fearing that he might be brought into trouble, had sent him home to his family at Brentwood, in Essex. [458] Another priest, going one day into Brentwood Church, found Hunter reading the Bible there.

Could he expound Scripture, that he read it thus to himself? the priest asked. He was reading for his comfort, Hunter replied; he did not take on himself to expound. The Bible taught him how to live, and how to distinguish between right and wrong.

It was never merry world, the priest said, since the Bible came forth in English. He saw what Hunter was—he was one of those who disliked the queen's laws, and he and other heretics would broil for it before all was over.

The boy's friends thought it prudent that he should fly to some place where he was not known; but, as soon as he was gone, a Catholic magistrate in the neighbourhood required his father to produce him, on peril of being arrested in his place; and, after a struggle of affection, in which the father offered to shield his son at his own hazard, young Hunter returned and surrendered.

The magistrate sent him to the Bishop of London, who kept him in prison three quarters of a year. When the persecution commenced, he was called up for examination.

Bonner, though a bigot and a ruffian, had, at times, a coarse good-nature in him, and often, in moments of pity, thrust an easy recantation upon a hesitating prisoner. He tried with emphatic anxiety to save this young apprentice. "If thou wilt recant," he said to him, "I will make thee a freeman in the city, and give thee forty pounds in money to set up thy occupation withal; or I will make thee steward of mine house, and set thee in office, for I like thee well."

Hunter thanked him for his kindness; but it could not be, he said; he must stand to the truth: he could not lie, or pretend to believe what he did not believe. Bonner said, and probably with sincere conviction, that if he persisted he would be damned for ever. Hunter said, that God judged more righteously, and justified those whom man unjustly condemned.

He was therefore to die with the rest; and on Saturday, the 23rd of March, he was sent to suffer at his native village. Monday being the feast of the Annunciation, the execution was postponed till Tuesday. The intervening time he was allowed to spend with his friends "in the parlour of the Swan Inn." His father prayed that he might continue to the end in the way that he had begun. His mother said, she was happy to bear a child who could find in his heart to lose his life for Christ's sake. "Mother," he answered, "for my little pain which I shall suffer, which is but a short braid, Christ hath promised me a crown of joy. May you not be glad of that, mother?"

Amidst such words the days passed. Tuesday morning the sheriff's son came and embraced him, "bade him not be afraid," and "could speak no more for weeping." When the sheriff came himself for him, he took his brother's arm and walked calmly to the place of execution, "at the town's end, where the butts stood."

His father was at the roadside as he passed. "God be with thee, son William!" the old man said. "God be with thee, good father," the son answered, "and be of good comfort!"

When he was come to the stake, he took one of the faggots, knelt upon it, and prayed for a few moments. The sheriff read the pardon with the conditions. "I shall not recant," he said, and walked to the post, to which he was chained.

"Pray for me, good people, while you see me alive," he said to the crowd.

"Pray for thee!" said the magistrate who had committed him, "I will no more pray for thee than I will pray for a dog."

"Son of God," Hunter exclaimed, "shine on me!" The sun broke out from behind a cloud and blazed in glory on his face.

The faggots were set on fire.

"Look," shrieked a priest, "how thou burnest here, so shalt thou burn in hell!"

The martyr had a Prayer-book in his hands, which he cast through the flames to his brother.

"William," said the brother, "think on the holy passion of Christ, and be not afraid of death."

"I am not afraid," were his last words. "Lord, Lord, Lord, receive my spirit!"

Ten days later another victim was sacrificed at Carmarthen, whose fate was peculiarly unprovoked and cruel.

Robert Ferrars, who twenty-seven years before carried a faggot with Anthony Dalaber in High Street at Oxford, had been appointed by Somerset Bishop of St. David's. He was a man of large humanity, justice, and uprightness—neither conspicuous as a theologian nor prominent as a preacher, but remarkable chiefly for good sense and a kindly imaginative tenderness. He had found his diocese infected with the general disorders of the times. The Chapter were indulging themselves to the utmost in questionable pleasures. The church patronage was made the prey of a nest of Cathedral lawyers, and, in an evil hour for himself, the bishop endeavoured to make crooked things straight.

After three years of struggle, his unruly canons were unable to endure him longer, and forwarded to the Duke of Northumberland an elaborate series of complaints against him. He was charged with neglecting his books and his preaching, and spending his time in surveying the lands of the see, and opening mines. He kept no manner of hospitality, it was said, but dined at the same table with his servants; and his talk was "not of godliness," "but of worldly matters, as baking, brewing, enclosing, ploughing, mining, millstones, discharging of tenants, and such like."

"To declare his folly in riding (these are the literal words of the accusation), he useth a bridle with white studs and snaffle, white Scottish stirrups, white spurs; a Scottish pad, with a little staff of three quarters [of a yard] long.

"He said he would go to parliament on foot; and to his friends that dissuaded him, alleging that it was not meet for a man in his place, he answered, I care not for that; it is no sin.

"Having a son, he went before the midwife to the church, presenting the child to the priest; and giving the name Samuel with a solemn interpretation of the name, [459] appointed two godfathers and two godmothers contrary to the ordinance, making his son a monster and himself a laughing-stock.

"He daily useth whistling of his child, and saith that he understood his whistle when he was but three years old; and being advertised of his friends that men laughed at his folly, he answered, They whistle their horses and dogs: they might also be contented that I whistle my child; and so whistleth him daily, friendly admonition neglected.

"In his visitation, among other his surveys, he surveyed Milford Haven, where he espied a seal-fish tumbling, and he crept down to the rocks by the water-side, and continued there whistling by the space of an hour, persuading the company that laughed fast at him, he made the fish to tarry there.

"Speaking of the scarcity of herrings, he laid the fault to the covetousness of fishers, who in time of plenty took so many that they destroyed the breeders.

"Speaking of the alteration of the coin, he wished that what metal soever it was made of, the penny should be in weight worth a penny of the same metal."

Such were the charges against Ferrars, which, notwithstanding, were considered serious enough to require an answer; and the bishop consented to reply.

He dined with his servants, he said, because the hall of the palace was in ruins, and for their comfort he allowed them to eat in his own room. For his hospitality, he appealed to his neighbours; and for his conversation, he said that he suited it to his hearers. He talked of religion to religious men; to men of the world, he talked "of honest worldly things with godly intent." He saw no folly in having his horse decently appointed; and as to walking to parliament, it was indifferent to him whether he walked or rode. God had given him a child, after lawful prayer, begotten in honest marriage; he had therefore named him Samuel, and presented him to the minister as a poor member of Christ's Church; it was done openly in the cathedral, without offending any one. The crime of whistling he admitted, "thinking it better to bring up his son with loving entertainment," to encourage him to receive afterwards more serious lessons. He had whistled to the seal; and "such as meant folly might turn it to their purpose." He had said that the destruction of the fry of fish prevented fish from multiplying, because he believed it to be true.

Answered or unanswered, it is scarcely credible that such accusations should have received attention; but the real offence behind, and is indicated in a vague statement that he had supposed himself to a premunire. The exquisite iniquity of the Northumberland administration could not endure a bishop who had opposed the corrupt administration of patronage; and the explanation being held as insufficient, Ferrars was summoned to London and thrown into prison, where Mary's accession found him.

Cut off in this way from the opportunities of escape which were long open to others, the bishop remained in confinement till the opening of the persecution. He was deposed from his see by Gardiner's first commission, as having been married; otherwise, however, Ferrars was unobnoxious politically and personally. Being in prison, he had been incapable of committing any fresh offence against the queen, and might reasonably have been forgotten or passed over. But he had been a bishop, and he was ready caught to the hands of the authorities; and Mary had been compelled unwillingly to release a more conspicuous offender, Miles Coverdale, at the intercession of the King of Denmark. Ferrars was therefore brought before Gardiner on the 4th of February. On the 14th he was sent into Wales to be tried by Morgan, his successor at St. David's, and Constantine, the notary of the diocese, who had been one of his accusers. By these judges, on the 11th of March, he was condemned and degraded; he appealed to the legate, but the legate never listened to the prayer of heretics; the legate's mission was to extirpate them. On Saturday the 30th of March, Ferrars was brought to the stake in the market-place in Carmarthen. [460]

Rawlins White, an aged Cardiff fisherman, followed Ferrars. In the course of April, George Marsh, a curate, was burnt at Chester; and on the 20th of April, a man named William Flower, who had been once a monk of Ely, was burnt in Palace-yard, at Westminster. Flower had provoked his own fate. He appeared on Easter day in St. Margaret's Church, while mass was being said; and provoked, as he persuaded himself, by the Holy Spirit, he flew upon the officiating priest, and stabbed him with a dagger in the hand; when to the horror of pious Catholics, the blood spurted into the chalice, and was mixed with the consecrated elements.

Sixteen persons had now been put to death, and there was again a pause for the sharp surgery to produce its effects.

While Mary was destroying the enemies of the church, Julius the Third had died at the end of March, and Reginald Pole was again a candidate for the vacant chair. The courts of Paris and Brussels alike promised him their support, but alike gave their support to another. They flattered his virtues, but they permitted Marcellus Cervino, the Cardinal of St. Cross, to be elected unanimously; and the English legate was told that he must be contented with the event which God had been pleased to send. [461] An opportunity, however, seemed to offer itself to him of accomplishing a service to Europe.

For thirty-five years the two great Catholic powers had been wrestling with but brief interruption. The advantage to either had been as trifling as the causes of their quarrel were insignificant. Their revenues were anticipated, their credit was exhausted, yet year after year languid armies struggled into collision. Across the Alps in Italy, and along the frontiers of Burgundy and the Low Countries, towns and villages, and homesteads were annually sacked, and peasants and their families destroyed—for what it were vain to ask, except it was for some poor shadow of imagined honour. Two mighty princes believed themselves justified in the sight of Heaven in squandering their subjects' treasure and their subjects' blood, because the pride of each forbade him to be the first in volunteering insignificant concessions. France had conquered Savoy and part of Piedmont, and had pushed forward its northern frontier to Marienbourg and Metz: the emperor held Lombardy, Parma, and Naples, and Navarre was annexed to Spain. The quarrel might have easily been ended by mutual restitution; yet the Peace of Cambray, the Treaty of Nice, and the Peace of Crépy, lasted only while the combatants were taking breath; and those who would attribute the extravagances of human folly to supernatural influence might imagine that the great discord between the orthodox powers had been permitted to give time for the Reformation to strike its roots into the soil of Europe. But a war which could be carried on only by loans at sixteen per cent. was necessarily near its conclusion. The apparent recovery of England to the church revived hopes which the Peace of Passau and the dissolution of the Council of Trent had almost extinguished; and, could a reconciliation be effected at last, and could Philip obtain the disposal of the military strength of England in the interests of the papacy, it might not even yet be too late to lay the yoke of orthodoxy on the Germans, and, in a Catholic interpretation of the Parable of the Supper, "compel them to come in."

Mary, who had heard herself compared to the Virgin, and Pole, who imagined the Prince of Spain to be the counterpart of the Redeemer of mankind, indulged their fancy in large expectations. Philip was the Solomon who was to raise up the temple of the Lord, which the emperor, who was a man of war, had not been allowed to build: and France, at the same time, was not unwilling to listen to proposals. The birth of Mary's child was expected in a few weeks, when England would, as a matter of course, become more decisively Imperialist, and Henry, whose invasion of the Netherlands had failed in the previous summer, was ready now to close the struggle while it could be ended on equal and honourable terms.

A conference was, therefore, agreed upon, in which England was to mediate. A village in the Calais Pale was selected as the place of assembly, and Pole, Gardiner, Paget, and Pembroke were chosen to arrange the terms of a general peace, with the Bishop of Arras, the Cardinal of Lorraine, and Montmorency. The time pitched upon was that at which, so near as the queen could judge, she would herself bring into the world the offspring which was to be the hope of England and mankind; and the great event should, if possible, precede the first meeting of the plenipotentiaries.

The queen herself commenced her preparations with infinite earnestness, and, as a preliminary votive offering, she resolved to give back to the church such of the abbey property as remained in the hands of the crown. Her debts were now as high as ever. The Flanders correspondence was repeating the heavy story of loans and bills. Promises to pay were falling due, and there were no resources to meet them, and the Israelite leeches were again fastened on the commonwealth. [462] Nevertheless, the sacrifice should be made; the more difficult it was, the more favourably it would be received; and, on the 28th of March, she sent for the Lord Treasurer, and announced her intention. "If he told her that her estate would not bear it, she must reply," she said, "that she valued the salvation of her soul beyond all earthly things." [463] As soon as parliament could meet and give its sanction, she would restore the first-fruits also to the Holy See. She must work for God as God had worked for her.

About the 20th of April she withdrew to Hampton Court for entire quiet. The rockers and the nurses were in readiness, and a cradle stood open to receive the royal infant. Priests and bishops sang Litanies through the London streets; a procession of ecclesiastics in cloth of gold and tissue marched round Hampton Court Palace, headed by Philip in person; Gardiner walked at his side, while Mary gazed from a window. [464] Not only was the child assuredly coming, but its sex was decided on, and circulars were drawn and signed both by the king and queen, with blanks only for the month and day, announcing to ministers of state, to ambassadors, and to foreign sovereigns, the birth of a prince. [465]

On the 30th, the happy moment was supposed to have arrived; a message was sent off to London, announcing the commencement of the pains. The bells were set ringing in all the churches; *Te Deum* was sung in St. Paul's; priests wrote sermons; bonfires were piled ready for lighting, and tables were laid out in the streets. [466] The news crossed the Channel to Antwerp, and had grown in the transit. The great bell of the cathedral was rung for the actual birth. The vessels in the river fired salutes. "The regent sent the English mariners a hundred crowns to drink," and, "they made themselves in readiness to show some worthy triumph upon the waters." [467]

But the pains passed off without result; and whispers began to be heard, that there was, perhaps, a mistake of a more considerable kind. Mary, however, had herself no sort of misgiving. She assured her attendants that all was well, and that she felt the motion of her child. The physicians professed to be satisfied, and the priests were kept at work at the Litanies. Up and down the streets they marched, through city and suburb, park and square; torches flared along Cheapside at midnight behind the Holy Sacrament, and five hundred poor men and women from the almshouses walked two and two, telling their beads in their withered fingers: then all the boys of all the schools were set in motion, and the ushers and the masters came after them; clerks, canons, bishops, mayor, aldermen, officers of guilds. [468] Such marching, such chanting, such praying was never seen or heard before or since in London streets. A profane person ran one day out of the crowd, and hung about a priest's neck, where the beads should be, a string of puddings; but they whipped him, and prayed on. Surely, God would hear the cry of his people.

In the midst of the suspense the papal chair fell vacant again. The pontificate of Marcellus lasted three weeks, and Pole a third time offered himself to the suffrages of the cardinals. The courts were profuse of compliments as before. Noailles presented him with a note from Montmorency, containing assurances of the infinite desire of the King of France for the success of so holy a person. [469] Philip wrote to Rome in his behalf, and Mary condescended to ask for the support of the French cardinals. [470] But the fair speeches, as before, were but trifling. The choice fell on Pole's personal enemy, Cardinal Caraffa, who was French alike in heart and brain.

The choice of a pope, however, would signify little, if only the child could be born; but where was the child? The queen put it off strangely. The conference could be delayed no longer. It opened without the intended makeweight, and the court of France was less inclined to make concessions for a peace. The delay began to tell on the bourse at Antwerp. The Fuggers and the Schertzes drew their purse-strings, and made difficulties in lending more money to the emperor. [471] The plenipotentiaries had to separate after a few meetings, having effected nothing, to the especial mortification of Philip and Mary, who looked to the pacification to enable them to cure England of its unruly humours. The Duke of Alva (so rumour insisted) was to bring across the Spanish troops which were in the Low Countries, take possession of London, and force the parliament into submission. [472] The English were to be punished, for the infinite insolences in which they had indulged towards Philip's retinue, by being compelled, whether they liked it or not, to bestow upon him the crown. [473]

But the peace could not be, nor could the child be born; and the impression grew daily that the queen had not been pregnant at all. Mary herself, who had been borne forward to this, the crisis of her fortunes, on a tide of success, now suddenly found her exulting hopes closing over. From confidence she fell into anxiety, from anxiety into fear, from fear into wildness and despondency. She vowed that with the restoration of the estates, she would rebuild the abbeys at her own cost. In vain. Her women now understood her condition; she was sick of a mortal disease; but they durst not tell her; and she whose career had been painted out to her by the legate, as especial and supernatural, looked only for supernatural causes of her present state. Throughout May she remained in her apartments waiting — waiting — in passionate restlessness. With stomach swollen, and features shrunk and haggard, she would sit upon the floor, with her knees drawn up to her face, in an agony of doubt; and in mockery of her wretchedness, letters were again strewed about the place by an invisible agency, telling her that she was loathed by her people. She imagined they would rise again in her defence. But if they rose again, it would be to drive her and her husband from the country. [474]

After the mysterious quickening on the legate's salutation, she could not doubt that her hopes had been at one time well founded; but for some fault, some error in herself, God had delayed the fulfilment of his promise. And what could that crime be? The accursed thing was still in the realm. She had been raised up, like the judges in Israel, for the extermination of God's enemies; and she had smitten but a few here and there, when, like the evil spirits, their name was legion. [475] She had before sent orders round among the magistrates, to have their eyes upon them. On the 24th of May, when her distraction was at its height, she wrote a circular to quicken the over-languid zeal of the bishops.

"Right Reverend Father in God," it ran, "We greet you well; and where of late we addressed our letters unto the justices of the peace, within every of the counties within this our realm, whereby, amongst other good instructions given therein for the good order of the country about, they are willed to have special regard to such disordered persons as, forgetting their duty to Almighty God and us, do lean to any erroneous and heretical opinions; whom, if they cannot by good admonition and fair means reform, they are willed to deliver unto the ordinary, to be by him charitably travelled withal, and removed, if it may be, from their naughty opinions; or else, if they continue obstinate, to be ordered according to the laws provided in that behalf: understanding now, to our no little marvel, that divers of the said misordered persons, being, by the justices of the peace, for their contempt and obstinacy, brought to the ordinary, to be used as is aforesaid, are either refused to be received at their hands, or, if they be received, are neither so travelled with as Christian charity requireth, nor yet proceeded withal according to the order of justice, but are suffered to continue in their errors, to the dishonour of Almighty God, and dangerous example of others; like as we find this matter very strange, so have we thought convenient both to signify this our knowledge, and therewithal also to admonish you to have in this behalf such regard henceforth unto the office of a good pastor and bishop, as where any such offenders shall be, by the said justices of the peace, brought unto you, ye do use your good wisdom and discretion in procuring to remove them from their errors if it may be, or else in proceeding against them, if they continue obstinate, according to the order of the laws, so as, through your good furtherance, both God's glory may be the better advanced, and the commonwealth more quietly governed." [476]

Under the fresh impulse of this letter, fifty persons were put to death at the stake in the three ensuing months, — in the diocese of London, under Bonner; in the diocese of Rochester, under Maurice Griffin; in the diocese of Canterbury, where Pole, the archbishop designate, so soon as Cranmer should be despatched, governed through Harpsfeld, the archdeacon, and Thornton, the suffragan bishop of Dover. Of these sacrifices, which were distinguished all of them by a uniformity of quiet heroism in the sufferers, that of Cardmaker, prebendary of Wells, calls most for notice.

The people, whom the cruelty of the Catholic party was reconverting to the Reformation with a rapidity like that produced by the gift of tongues on the day of Pentecost, looked on the martyrs as soldiers are looked at who are called to accomplish, with the sacrifice of their lives, some great service for their country. Cardmaker, on his first examination, had turned his back and flinched. But the consciousness of shame, and the example of others, gave him back his courage; he was called up again under the queen's mandate, condemned, and brought out on the 30th of May, to suffer at Smithfield, with an upholsterer named Warne. The sheriffs produced the pardons. Warne, without looking at them, undressed at once, and went to the stake; Cardmaker "remained long talking;" "the people in a marvellous dump of sadness, thinking he would recant." He turned away at last, and knelt, and prayed; but he had still his clothes on; "there was no semblance of burning;" and the crowd continued nervously agitated, till he rose and threw off his cloak. "Then, seeing this, contrary to their fearful expectations, as men delivered out of great doubt, they cried out for joy with so great a shout as hath not been lightly heard a greater, God be praised; the Lord strengthen thee, Cardmaker. The Lord Jesus receive thy spirit." [477] Every martyr's trial was a battle; every constant death was a defeat of the common enemy; and the instinctive consciousness that truth was asserting itself in suffering, converted the natural emotion of horror into admiring pride.

Yet, for the great purpose of the court, the burnt-offerings were ineffectual as the prayers of the priests. The queen was allowed to persuade herself that she had mistaken her time by two months; and to this hope she clung herself, so long as the hope could last: but among all other persons concerned, scarcely one was any longer under a delusion; and the clear-eyed Renard lost no time in laying the position of affairs before his master.

The marriage of Elizabeth and Philibert had hung fire, from the invincible unwillingness on the part of Mary to pardon or in any way recognise her sister; [478] and as long as there was a hope of a child, she had not perhaps been pressed about it; but it was now absolutely necessary to do something, and violent measures towards the princess were more impossible than ever.

"The entire future," wrote Renard to the emperor, on the 27th of June, "turns on the accouchement of the queen; of which, however, there are no signs. If all goes well, the state of feeling in the country will improve. If she is in error, I foresee convulsions and disturbances such as no pen can describe. The succession to the crown is so unfortunately hampered, that it must fall to Elizabeth, and with Elizabeth there will be a religious revolution. The clergy will be put down, the Catholics persecuted, and there will be such revenge for the present proceedings as the world has never seen. I know not whether the king's person is safe; and the scandals and calumnies which the heretics are spreading about the queen are beyond conception. Some say that she has never been *enceinte*; some repeat that there will be a supposititious child, and that there would have been less delay could a child have been found that would answer the purpose. [479] The looks of men are grown strange and impenetrable; those in whose loyalty I had most dependence I have now most reason to doubt. Nothing is certain, and I am more bewildered than ever at the things which I see going on around me. There is neither government, nor justice, nor order; nothing but audacity and malice." [480]

The faint hopes which Renard expressed speedily vanished, and every one but the queen herself not only knew that she had no child at present, but that she never could have a child—that her days were numbered, and that if the Spaniards intended to secure the throne they must obtain it by other means than the order of inheritance. Could the war be brought to an end, Mary might live long enough to give her husband an opportunity of attempting violence; but of peace there was no immediate prospect, and it remained for the present to make the most of Elizabeth. Setting her marriage aside, it was doubtful whether the people would permit her longer confinement after the queen's disappointment; and, willingly or unwillingly, Mary must be forced to receive her at court again.

The princess was still at Woodstock, where she had remained for a year, under the harsh surveillance of Sir Henry Bedingfield. Lord William Howard's visit may have consoled her with the knowledge that she was not forgotten by the nobility; but her health had suffered from her long imprisonment, and the first symptom of an approaching change in her position was the appearance of the queen's physician to take charge of her.

A last effort was made to betray her into an acknowledgment of guilt. "A secret friend" entreated her to "submit herself to the queen's mercy." Elizabeth saw the snare. She would not ask for mercy, she said, where she had committed no offence; if she was guilty, she desired justice, not mercy; and she knew well she would have found none, could evidence have been produced against her: but she thanked God she was in no danger of being proved guilty; she wished she was as safe from secret enemies.

But the plots for despatching her, if they had ever existed, were laid aside; she was informed that her presence was required at Hampton Court. The rumour of her intended release spread abroad, and sixty gentlemen, who had once belonged to her suite, met her on the way at Colebrook, in the hope that they might return to attendance upon her; but their coming was premature; she was still treated as a prisoner, and they were ordered off in the queen's name.

On her arrival at Hampton Court, however, the princess felt that she had recovered her freedom. She was received by Lord William Howard. The courtiers hurried to her with their congratulations, and Howard dared and provoked the resentment of the king and queen by making them kneel and kiss her hand. [481] Mary could not bring herself at first to endure an interview. The Bishop of Winchester came to her on the queen's behalf, to repeat the advice which had been given to her at Woodstock, and to promise pardon if she would ask for it.

Elizabeth had been resolute when she was alone and friendless, she was not more yielding now. She repeated that she had committed no offence, and therefore required no forgiveness; she had rather lie in prison all her life than confess when there was nothing to be confessed.

The answer was carried to Mary, and the day after the bishop came again. "The queen marvelled," he said, "that she would so stoutly stand to her innocence;" if she called herself innocent, she implied that she had been "unjustly imprisoned;" if she expected her liberty "she must tell another tale."

But the causes which had compelled the court to send for her, forbade them equally to persist in an impotent persecution. They had desired only to tempt her into admissions which they could plead in justification for past or future severities. They had failed, and they gave way.

A week later, on an evening in the beginning of July, Lady Clarence, Mary's favourite attendant, brought a message, that the queen was expecting her sister in her room. The princess was led across the garden in the dusk, and introduced by a back staircase into the royal apartments. Almost two years had elapsed since the sisters had last met, when Mary hid the hatred which was in her heart behind a veil of kindness. There was no improvement of feeling, but the necessity of circumstances compelled the form of reconciliation.

Elizabeth dropped on her knees. "God preserve your majesty," she said; "you will find me as true a subject to your majesty as any; whatever has been reported of me, you shall not find it otherwise."

"You will not confess," the queen said; "you stand to your truth: I pray God it may so fall out."

"If it does not," said Elizabeth, "I desire neither favour nor pardon at your hands."

"Well," Mary bitterly answered, "you persevere in your truth stiffly; belike you will not confess that you have been wrongly punished?"

"I must not say so, your majesty," Elizabeth replied.

"Belike you will to others?" said the queen.

"No, please your majesty," answered the princess. "I have borne the burden, and I must bear it. I pray your majesty to have a good opinion of me, and to think me your true subject, not only from the beginning but while life lasteth."

The queen did not answer, she muttered only in Spanish, "*Sabe Dios*," "God knows," and Elizabeth withdrew. [482]

It was said that, during the interview, Philip was concealed behind a curtain, anxious for a sight of the captive damsel whose favour with the people was such a perplexity to him.

At this time, Elizabeth was beautiful; her haughty features were softened by misfortune; and as it is certain that Philip, when he left England, gave special directions for her good treatment, so it is possible that he may have envied the fortune which he intended for the Prince of Savoy; and the scheme which he afterwards attempted to execute, of making her his own wife on the queen's death, may have then suggested itself to him as a solution of the English difficulty. The magnificent girl, who was already the idol of the country, must have presented an emphatic contrast with the lean, childless, haggard, forlorn Mary; and he may easily have allowed his fancy to play with a pleasant temptation. If it was so, Philip was far too careless of the queen's feelings to conceal his own. If it was not so, the queen's haunting consciousness of her unattractiveness must have been aggravated by the disappointment of her hopes, and she may have tortured herself with jealousy and suspicion.

At all events, Mary could not overcome her aversion. Elizabeth was set at liberty, but she was not allowed to remain at the court. She returned to Ashridge, to be pursued, even there, with petty annoyances. Her first step when she was again at home was to send for her friend Mrs. Ashley; the queen instantly committed Mrs. Ashley to the Fleet, and sent three other officers of her sister's household to the Tower; while a number of gentlemen suspected of being her adherents, who had remained in London beyond their usual time of leaving for the country, were ordered imperiously to their estates. [483]

But neither impatience nor violence could conceal the fatal change which had passed over Mary's prospects. Not till the end of July could she part finally from her hopes. Then, at last, the glittering dream was lost for the waking truth; then at once from the imagination of herself as the virgin bride who was to bear a child for the recovery of a lost world, she was precipitated into the poor certainty that she was a blighted and a dying woman. Sorrow was heaped on sorrow; Philip would stay with her no longer. His presence was required on the continent, where his father was about to anticipate the death which he knew to be near, and, after forty years of battling with the stormy waters, to collect himself for the last great change in the calm of a monastery in Spain.

It was no new intention. For years the emperor had been in the habit of snatching intervals of retreat; for years he had made up his mind to relinquish at some time the labours of life before relinquishing life itself. The vanities of sovereignty had never any particular charm for Charles V.; he was not a man who cared "to monarchise and kill with looks," or who could feel a pang at parting with the bauble of a crown; and when the wise world cried out in their surprise, and strained their fancies for the cause of conduct which seemed so strange to them, they forgot that princes who reign to labour, grow weary like the peasant of the burden of daily toil.

Many influences combined to induce Charles to delay no longer in putting his resolution in effect.

The Cortes were growing impatient at the prolonged absence both of himself and Philip, and the presence of the emperor, although in retirement, would give pleasure to the Spanish people. His health was so shattered, that each winter had been long expected to be his last; and although he would not flinch from work as long as he was required at his post, there was nothing to detain Philip any more in England, unless, or until, the succession could be placed on another footing. To continue there the husband of a childless queen, with authority limited to a form, and with no recognised interest beyond the term of his wife's life, was no becoming position for the heir of the throne of Spain, of Naples, the Indies, and the Low Countries.

Philip was therefore now going. He concealed his intention till it was betrayed by the departure of one Spanish nobleman after another. The queen became nervous and agitated, and at last he was forced to avow part of the truth. He told her that his father wanted to see him, but that his absence would not be extended beyond a fortnight or three weeks; she should go with him to Dover, and, if she desired, she could wait there for his return. [484] Her consent was obtained by the mild deceit, and it was considered afterwards that the journey to Dover might be too much for her, and the parting might take place at Greenwich.

On the 3rd of August, the king and queen removed for a few days from Hampton Court to Oatlands; on the way Mary received consolation from a poor man who met her on crutches, and was cured of his lameness by looking on her. [485]

On the 26th, the royal party came down the river in their barge, attended by the legate; they dined at Westminster on their way to Greenwich, and as rumour had said that Mary was dead, she was carried through the city in an open litter, with the king and the cardinal at her side. To please Philip, or to please the people, Elizabeth was invited to the court before the king's departure; but she was sent by water to prevent a demonstration, while the archers of the guard who attended on the queen, were in corslet and morion. [486]

On the 28th, Philip went. Parliament was to sit again in October. It would then be seen whether anything more could be done about the succession. On the consent or refusal of the legislature his future measures would depend. To the queen he left particular instructions, which he afterwards repeated in writing, to show favour to Elizabeth; and doubting how far he could rely upon Mary, he gave a similar charge to such of his own suite as he left behind him. [487] Could he obtain it, he would take the princess's crown for himself; should he fail, he might marry her; or should this too be impossible, he would win her gratitude, and support her title against the dangerous competition of the Queen of Scots and Dauphiness of France.

On these terms the pair who had been brought together with so much difficulty separated after a little more than a year. The cardinal composed a passionate prayer for the queen's use during her husband's absence. [488] It is to be hoped that she was spared the sight of a packet of letters soon after intercepted by the French, in which her husband and her husband's countrymen expressed their opinions of the marriage and its consequences. [489] The truth, however, became known in England, although in a form under which the queen could turn from it as a calumny.

Before the meeting of parliament, a letter was published, addressed to the Lords of the Council, by a certain John Bradford. [490] The writer accounted for his knowledge of the secrets which he had to tell, by saying that he had lived in the household of one of the Spanish noblemen who were in attendance on Philip; that he had learnt the language unknown to his master, and had thus overheard unguarded conversations. He had read letters addressed to Philip, and letters written by him and by his confidential friends; and he was able to say, as a thing heard with his own ears, and seen with his own eyes, that the "Spaniards minded nothing less than the subversion of the English commonwealth." In fact, he repeated the rumours of the summer, only more circumstantially, and with fuller details. Under pretence of improving the fortifications, Philip intended to obtain command of the principal harbours and ports; he would lay cannon on the land side, and gradually bring in Spanish troops, the queen playing into his hands; and as soon as peace could be made with France, he would have the command of the fleet and the sea, and could do what he pleased. [491]

"I saw," the writer continued, "letters sent from the emperor, wherein was contained these privities, — that the king should make his excuse to the queen that he would go to see his father in Flanders, and that immediately he would return — seeing the good simple queen is so jealous over my son. (I term it," said Bradford, "as the letter doth.") "We," said the emperor, "shall make her agree unto all our requests before his return, or else keep him exercised in our affairs till we may prevail with the council, who, doubtless, will be won with fair promises and great gifts, politicly placed in time." "In other letters I have read the cause disputed, that the queen is bound by the laws of God to endue her husband in all her goods and possessions, so far as in her lieth; and they think she will do it indeed to the uttermost of her power. No man can think evil of the queen, though she be somewhat moved when such things are beaten into her head with gentlemen; but whether the crown belongs to the queen or the realm, the Spaniards know not, nor care not, though the queen, to her damnation, disherit the right heir apparent, or break her father's entail, made by the whole consent of the realm, which neither she nor the realm can justly alter." [492]

Struggle as the queen might against such a representation of her husband's feelings towards her, it was true that he had left her with a promise to return; and the weeks went, and he did not come, and no longer spoke of coming. The abdication of the emperor would keep him from her, at least, till the end of the winter. And news came soon which was harder still to bear; news, that he, whom she had been taught to regard as made in the image of our Saviour, [493] was unfaithful to his marriage vows, [494] Bradford had spoken generally of the king's vulgar amours; other accounts convinced her too surely that he was consoling himself for his long purgatory in England, by miscellaneous licentiousness. Philip was gross alike in all his appetites; bacon fat was the favourite food with which he gorged himself to illness; [495] his intrigues were on the same level of indelicacy, and his unhappy wife was forced to know that he preferred the society of abandoned women of the lowest class to hers.

The French ambassador describes her as distracted with wretchedness, speaking to no one except the legate. The legate was her only comfort; the legate and the thing which she called religion.

Deep in the hearts of both queen and cardinal lay the conviction that if she would please God, she must avoid the sin of Saul. Saul had spared the Amalekites, and God had turned his face from him. God had greater enemies in England than the Amalekites. Historians have affected to exonerate Pole from the crime of the Marian persecution; although, without the legate's sanction, not a bishop in England could have raised a finger, not a bishop's court could have been opened to try a single heretic. If not with Pole, with whom did the guilt rest? Gardiner was jointly responsible for the commencement, but after the first executions, Gardiner interfered no further; he died, and the bloody scenes continued. Philip's confessor protested; Philip himself left the country; Renard and Charles were never weary of advising moderation, except towards those who were politically dangerous. Bonner was an instrument whose zeal more than once required the goad; and Mary herself, when she came to the throne, was so little cruel, that she would have spared even Northumberland himself. When the persecution assumed its ferocious aspect, she was exclusively under the direction of the dreamer who believed that he was born for England's regeneration. All evidence concurs to show that, after Philip's departure, Cardinal Pole was the single adviser on whom Mary relied. Is it to be supposed that, in the horrible crusade which thenceforward was the business of her life, the papal legate, the sovereign director of the ecclesiastical administration of the realm, was not consulted, or, if consulted, that he refused his sanction? But it is not a question of conjecture or probability. From the legate came the first edict for the episcopal inquisition; under the legate every bishop held his judicial commission; while, if Smithfield is excepted, the most frightful scenes in the entire frightful period were witnessed under the shadow of his own metropolitan cathedral. His apologists have thrown the blame on his archdeacon and his suffragan: the guilt is not with the instrument, but with the hand which holds it. An admiring biographer [496] has asserted that the cruelties at Canterbury preceded the cardinal's consecration as archbishop, and the biographer has been copied by Dr. Lingard. The historian and his authority have exceeded the limits of permitted theological misrepresentation. The administration of the see belonged to Pole as much before his consecration as after it; but it will be seen that eighteen men and women perished at the stake in the town of Canterbury alone, — besides those who were put to death in other parts of the diocese — and five were starved to death in the gaol there — after the legate's installation. He was not cruel; but he believed that, in the catalogue of human iniquities, there were none greater than the denial of the Roman Catholic Faith, or the rejection of the Roman bishop's supremacy; and that he himself was chosen by Providence for the re-establishment of both. Mary was driven to madness by the disappointment of the grotesque imaginations with which he had inflated her; and where two such persons were invested by the circumstances of the time with irresponsible power, there is no occasion to look further for the explanation of the dreadful events of the three ensuing years.

The victims of the summer were chiefly undistinguished persons: Cardmaker and Bradford alone were in any way celebrated; and the greater prisoners, the three bishops at Oxford, the court had paused upon — not from mercy — their deaths had been long determined on; but Philip, perhaps, was tender of his person; their execution might occasion disturbances; and he and his suite might be the first objects on which the popular indignation might expend itself. Philip, however, had placed the sea between himself and danger, and if this was the cause of the hesitation, the work could now go forward.

A commission was appointed by Pole in September, consisting of Brookes, Bishop of Gloucester, Holyman, Bishop of Bristol, and White, Bishop of Lincoln, to try Cranmer, Ridley, and Latimer, for obstinate heresy. The first trial had been irregular; the country was then unreconciled. The sentence which had been passed therefore was treated as non-existent, and the tedious forms of the papacy continued still to throw a shield round the archbishop.

On Saturday, the 7th of September, [497] the commissioners took their places under the altar of St. Mary's Church, at Oxford. The Bishop of Gloucester sat as president, Doctors Story and Martin appeared as proctors for the queen, and Cranmer was brought in under the custody of the city guard, in a black gown and leaning on a stick.

"Thomas, Archbishop of Canterbury," cried an officer of the court, "appear here, and make answer to that which shall be laid to thy charge; that is to say, for blasphemy, incontinency, and heresy; make answer to the Bishop of Gloucester, representing his holiness the pope."

The archbishop approached the bar, bent his head and uncovered to Story and Martin, who were present in behalf of the crown, then drew himself up, put on his cap again, and stood fronting Brookes. "My lord," he said, "I mean no contempt to your person, which I could have honoured as well as any of the others; but I have sworn never to admit the authority of the Bishop of Rome in England, and I must keep my oath."

The president remonstrated, but without effect, and then proceeded to address the archbishop, who remained covered: [498] —

"My lord, we are come hither at this present to you, not intruding ourselves by our own authority, but sent by commission, as you know, by the pope's holiness partly; partly from the king's and queen's most excellent majesties; not utterly to your discomfort, but rather to your comfort if you will yourself. For we are come not to judge you immediately, but to put you in remembrance of that which you have been partly judged of before, and shall be thoroughly judged of ere long.

"Neither our coming or commission is to dispute with you, but to examine you in matters which you have already disputed in, taught, and written; and of your resolute answers in those points and others, to make relation to them that shall give sentence on you. If you, of your part, be moved to come to a uniformity, then shall not only we take joy of our examination, but also they that have sent us. Remember yourself then, *unde excideris*, from whence you have fallen. You have fallen from the unity of your mother, the Holy Catholic Church, and that by open schism. You have fallen from the true and received faith of the same Catholic Church, and that by open heresy. You have fallen from your fidelity and promise towards God, in breaking your orders and vow of chastity, and that by open apostasy. You have fallen from your fidelity and promise towards God's vicar-general, the pope, in breaking your oath made to his holiness at your consecration, and that by open perjury. You have fallen from your fidelity and allegiance towards God's magistrate, your prince and sovereign lady the queen, and that by open treason, whereof you are already attainted and convicted. Remember, *unde excideris*, from whence you have fallen, and in what danger you have fallen.

"You were sometime, as I and other poor men, in mean estate. God hath called you from better to better, from higher to higher, and never gave you over till he made you, *legatum natum*, Metropolitan Archbishop, Primate of England. Who was more earnest then in defence of the real presence of Christ's body and blood in the sacrament of the altar than ye were? Then was your candle shining to be a light to all the world, set on high on a pinnacle. But after you began to fall from the unity of the Catholic Church by open schism, and would no longer acknowledge the supremacy of the pope's holiness by God's word and ordinance; — and that by occasion, that you, in whose hands then rested the sum of all, being primate, as was aforesaid, would not, according to your high vocation, stoutly withstand the most ungodly and unlawful request of your prince touching his divorce, as that blessed martyr, St. Thomas of Canterbury, sometime your predecessor, did withstand the unlawful requests of the prince of his time, but would still not only yield and bear with things not to be borne withal, but also set a-flame the fire already kindled — then your perfections diminished; then began you, for your own part, to fancy unlawful liberty. Then decayed your conscience of your former faith, your former promise, the vow of chastity and discipline after the order of priesthood; and when good conscience was once cast off, then followed after, as St. Paul noteth, a shipwreck in the faith. Then fell you from the faith, and out of the Catholic Church, as out of a sure ship, into a sea of dangerous desperation; for out of the church, to say with St. Cyprian, there is no hope of salvation at all. To be brief; when you had forsaken God, his Spouse, his faith, and fidelity to them both, then God forsook you; and as the apostle writeth of the ingrate philosophers, delivered you up *in reprobum sensum*, and suffered you to fall from one inconvenience to another, as from perjury into schism, from schism into a kind of apostasy, from apostasy into heresy, from heresy into traitory, and so, in conclusion, from traitory into the highest displeasure and worthiest indignation of your most benign and gracious queen." [499]

When the bishop ceased, the crown proctors rose, and demanded justice against the prisoner in the names of the king and queen.

"My lord," Cranmer replied, "I do not acknowledge this session of yours, nor yet yourself my mislawful judge; neither would I have appeared this day before you, but that I was brought hither; and therefore here I openly renounce you as my judge, protesting that my meaning is not to make any answer as in a lawful judgment, for then I would be silent; but only for that I am bound in conscience to answer every man of that hope which I have in Jesus Christ."

He then knelt, and turning towards the west with his back to the court and the altar, he said the Lord's Prayer. After which, he rose, repeated the creed, and said —

"This I do profess as touching my faith, and make my protestation, which I desire you to note; I will never consent that the Bishop of Rome shall have any jurisdiction in this realm."

"Mark, Master Cranmer," interrupted Martin, "you refuse and deny him by whose laws you do remain in life, being otherwise attainted of high treason, and but a dead man by the laws of the realm."

"I protest before God I was no traitor," said the archbishop. "I will never consent to the Bishop of Rome, for then I should give myself to the devil. I have made an oath to the king, and I must obey the king by God's law. By the Scripture, the king is chief, and no foreign person in his own realm above him. The pope is contrary to the crown. I cannot obey both, for no man can serve two masters at once. You attribute the keys to the pope and the sword to the king. I say the king hath both."

Continuing the same argument, the archbishop entered at length into the condition of the law and the history of the Statutes of Provisors and Premunire: he showed that the constitution of the country was emphatically independent, and he maintained that no English subject could swear obedience to a foreign power without being involved in perjury.

The objection was set aside, and the subject of oaths was an opportunity for a taunt, which the queen's proctors did not overlook. Cranmer had unwillingly accepted the archbishopric when the Act of Appeals was pending, and when the future relations of England with the See of Rome, and the degree of authority which (if any) the pope was to retain, were uncertain. In taking the usual oaths, therefore, by the advice of lawyers, he made an especial and avowed reservation of his duty to the crown; [500] and this so-called perjury Martin now flung in his teeth.

"It pleased the king's highness," Cranmer replied, "many and sundry times to talk with me of the matter. I declared that, if I accepted the office of archbishop, I must receive it at the pope's hands, which I neither would nor could do, for his highness was the only supreme governor of this church in England. Perceiving that I could not be brought to acknowledge the authority of the Bishop of Rome, the king called Doctor Oliver and other civil lawyers, and devised with them how he might bestow it on me, enforcing me nothing against my conscience, who informed him I might do it by way of protestation. I said, I did not acknowledge the Bishop of Rome's authority further than as it agreed with the word of God, and that it might be lawful for me at all times to speak against him; and my protestation did I cause to be enrolled, and there I think it remaineth."

"Let your protestation, with the rest of your talk, give judgment against you," answered Martin. "*Hinc prima mali labes*: of that your execrable perjury, and the king's coloured and too shamefully suffered adultery, came heresy and all mischief into the realm."

The special charges were then proceeded with.

In reply to a series of questions, the archbishop said, that he had been twice married—once before, and once after he was in orders. In the time of Henry, he had kept his wife secretly, "affirming that it was better for him to have his own wife, than to do like other priests, having the wives of others;" and he was not ashamed of what he had done.

He admitted his writings upon the Eucharist; he avowed the authorship of the Catechism, of the Articles, and of a book against the Bishop of Winchester; and these books, and his conduct generally as Archbishop of Canterbury, he maintained and defended. His replies were entered by a notary, to be transmitted to the pope, and for the present the business of the court with him was over.

"Who can stay him that willingly runneth into perdition?" said Brookes. "Who can save that will be lost? God would have you to be saved, and you refuse it."

The archbishop was cited to appear at Rome within eighty days to answer to the charges which would there be laid against him; and in order that he might be able to obey the summons he was returned to his cell in Bocardo prison, and kept there in strict confinement.

Ridley and Latimer came next, and over them the papal mantle flung no protection.

They had been prisoners now for more than two years. What Latimer's occupation had been for all that time, little remains to show, except three letters:—one, of but a few lines, was to a Mrs. Wilkinson, thanking her for some act of kindness: [501] another, was a general exhortation to "all unfeigned lovers of God's truth," to be constant in their faith: the third, and most noteworthy, was to some one who had an opportunity of escaping from arrest, and probable martyrdom, by a payment of money, and who doubted whether he might lawfully avail himself of the chance: there was no question of recantation; a corrupt official was ready to accept a bribe and ask no questions.

Latimer had not been one of those fanatics who thought it a merit to go in the way of danger and court persecution; but in this present case he shared the misgiving of his correspondent, and did "highly allow his judgment in that he thought it not lawful to redeem himself from the crown, unless he would exchange glory for shame, and his inheritance for a mess of pottage."

"We were created," Latimer said, "to set forth God's glory all the days of our life, which we, as unthankful sinners, have forgotten to do, as we ought, all our days hitherto; and now God, by affliction, doth offer us good occasion to perform one day of our life, our duty. If any man perceive his faith not to abide the fire, let such an one with weeping buy his liberty until he hath obtained more strength, lest the gospel suffer by him some shameful recantation. Let the dead bury the dead. Do you embrace Christ's cross, and Christ shall embrace you. The peace of God be with you for ever." [502]

Ridley's pen had been more busy: he had written a lamentation over the state of England; he had written a farewell letter, taking leave of his friends, and taking leave of life, which, clouded as it was, his sunny nature made it hard to part from: he had written comfort to the afflicted for the gospel, and he had addressed a passionate appeal to the Temporal Lords to save England from the false shepherds who were wasting the flock of Christ. But both he and Latimer had looked death steadily in the face for two years, expecting it every day or hour. It was now come.

On the 30th of September, the three bishops took their seats in the Divinity school. Ridley was led in for trial, and the legate's commission was read, empowering them to try him for the opinions which he had expressed in the disputation at Oxford the year before, and "elsewhere in the time of perdition." They were to degrade him from the priesthood if he persisted in his heresies, and deliver him over to the secular arm.

On being first brought before the court, Ridley stood bareheaded. At the names of the cardinal and the pope, he put on his cap, like Cranmer, declining to acknowledge their authority. But his scruples were treated less respectfully than the archbishop's. He was ordered to take it off, and when he refused, it was removed by a beadle.

He was then charged with having denied transubstantiation, and the propitiatory sacrifice of the mass, and was urged at length to recant. His opinions on the real presence were peculiar. Christ, he said, was not the sacrament, but was really and truly in the sacrament, as the Holy Ghost was with the water at baptism and yet was not the water. The subtlety of the position was perplexing, but the knot was cut by the crucial question, whether, after the consecration of the elements, the substance of bread and wine remained. He was allowed the night to consider his answer, but he left no doubt what that answer would be. "The bishops told him that they were not come to condemn him, their province was to condemn no one, but only to cut off the heretic from the church, for the temporal judge to deal with as he should think fit." The cowardly sophism had been heard too often. Ridley thanked the court "for their gentleness," "being the same which Christ had of the high priest:" "the high priest said it was not lawful for him to put any man to death, but committed Christ to Pilate; neither would suffer him to absolve Christ, though he sought all the means therefore that he might."

Ridley withdrew, and Latimer was then introduced—eighty years old now—dressed in an old threadbare gown of Bristol frieze, a handkerchief on his head with a night-cap over it, and over that again another cap, with two broad flaps buttoned under the chin. A leather belt was round his waist, to which a Testament was attached; his spectacles, without a case, hung from his neck. So stood the greatest man perhaps then living in the world, a prisoner on his trial, waiting to be condemned to death by men professing to be the ministers of God. As it was in the days of the prophets, so it was in the Son of man's days; as it was in the days of the Son of man, so was it in the Reformers' days; as it was in the days of the Reformers, so will it be to the end, so long and so far as a class of men are permitted to hold power, who call themselves the commissioned and authoritative teachers of truth. Latimer's trial was the counterpart of Ridley's: the charge was the same, and the result was the same, except that the stronger intellect vexed itself less with nice distinctions. Bread was bread, said Latimer, and wine was wine; there was a change in the sacrament, it was true, but the change was not in the nature, but the dignity. He too was reprieved for the day. The following morning, the court sat in St. Mary's Church, with the authorities of town and university, heads of houses, mayor, aldermen, and sheriff. The prisoners were brought to the bar. The same questions were asked, the same answers were returned, and sentence was pronounced upon them, as heretics obstinate and incurable.

Execution did not immediately follow. The convictions for which they were about to die had been adopted by both of them comparatively late in life. The legate would not relinquish the hope of bringing them back into the superstition in which they had been born, and had lived so long; and Soto, a Spanish friar, who was teaching divinity at Oxford in the place of Peter Martyr, was set to work on them.

But one of them would not see him, and on the other he could make no impression. Those whom God had cast away, thought Pole, were not to be saved by man; [503] and the 16th of October was fixed upon as the day on which they were to suffer. Ridley had been removed from Bocardo, and was under the custody of the mayor, a man named Irish, whose wife was a bigoted and fanatical Catholic. On the evening of the 15th there was a supper at the mayor's house, where some members of Ridley's family were permitted to be present. He talked cheerfully of his approaching "marriage;" his brother-in-law promised to be in attendance, and, if possible, to bring with him his wife, Ridley's sister. Even the hard eyes of Mrs. Irish were softened to tears, as she listened and thought of what was coming. The brother-in-law offered to sit up through the night, but Ridley said there was no occasion; he "minded to go to bed, and sleep as quietly as ever he did in his life." In the morning he wrote a letter to the queen. As Bishop of London he had granted renewals of certain leases, on which he had received fines. Bonner had refused to recognise them, and he entreated the queen, for Christ's sake, either that the leases should be allowed, or that some portion of his own confiscated property might be applied to the repayment of the tenants. [504] The letter was long; by the time it was finished, the sheriff's officers were probably in readiness.

The place selected for the burning was outside the north wall of the town, a short stone's throw from the southward corner of Balliol College, and about the same distance from Bocardo prison, from which Cranmer was intended to witness his friends' sufferings.

Lord Williams of Thame was on the spot by the queen's order; and the city guard were under arms to prevent disturbance. Ridley appeared first, walking between the mayor and one of the aldermen. He was dressed in a furred black gown, "such as he was wont to wear being bishop," a furred velvet tippet about his neck, and a velvet cap. He had trimmed his beard, and had washed himself from head to foot; a man evidently nice in his appearance, a gentleman, and liking to be known as such. The way led under the windows of Bocardo, and he looked up; but Soto, the friar, was with the archbishop, making use of the occasion, and Ridley did not see him. [505] In turning round, however, he saw Latimer coming up behind him in the frieze coat, with the cap and handkerchief — the workday costume unaltered, except that under his cloak, and reaching to his feet, the old man wore a long new shroud.

"Oh! be ye there?" Ridley exclaimed.

"Yea," Latimer answered. "Have after as fast as I can follow."

Ridley ran to him and embraced him. "Be of good heart, brother," he said. "God will either assuage the flame, or else strengthen us to abide it." They knelt and prayed together, and then exchanged a few words in a low voice, which were not overheard.

Lord Williams, the vice-chancellor, and the doctors were seated on a form close to the stake. A sermon was preached, "a scant one," "of scarce a quarter of an hour;" and then Ridley begged that for Christ's sake he might say a few words.

Lord Williams looked to the doctors, one of whom started from his seat, and laid his hand on Ridley's lips —

"Recant," he said, "and you may both speak and live."

"So long as the breath is in my body," Ridley answered, "I will never deny my Lord Christ and his known truth. God's will be done in me. I commit our cause," he said, in a loud voice, turning to the people, "to Almighty God, who shall indifferently judge all."

The brief preparations were swiftly made. Ridley gave his gown and tippet to his brother-in-law, and distributed remembrances among those who were nearest to him. To Sir Henry Lee he gave a new groat, to others he gave handkerchiefs, nutmegs, slices of ginger, his watch, and miscellaneous trinkets; "some plucked off the points of his hose;" "happy," it was said, "was he that might get any rag of him."

Latimer had nothing to give. He threw off his cloak, stood bolt upright in his shroud, and the friends took their places on either side of the stake.

"O Heavenly Father," Ridley said, "I give unto thee most humble thanks, for that thou hast called me to be a professor of thee even unto death. Have mercy, O Lord, on this realm of England, and deliver the same from all her enemies."

A chain was passed round their bodies, and fastened with a staple.

A friend brought a bag of powder and hung it round Ridley's neck.

"I will take it to be sent of God," Ridley said. "Have you more, for my brother?"

"Yea, sir," the friend answered. "Give it him betimes then," Ridley replied, "lest ye be too late."

The fire was then brought. To the last moment, Ridley was distressed about the leases, and, bound as he was, he entreated Lord Williams to intercede with the queen about them.

"I will remember your suit," Lord Williams answered. The lighted torch was laid to the faggots. "Be of good comfort, Master Ridley," Latimer cried at the crackling of the flames; "Play the man: we shall this day light such a candle, by God's, grace, in England, as I trust shall never be put out."

"*In manus tuas, Domine, commendo spiritum meum,*" cried Ridley. "*Domine, recipe spiritum meum.*"

"O Father of Heaven," said Latimer, on the other side, "receive my soul."

Latimer died first: as the flame blazed up about him, he bathed his hands in it, and stroked his face. The powder exploded, and he became instantly senseless.

His companion was less fortunate. The sticks had been piled too thickly over the gorse that was under them; the fire smouldered round his legs, and the sensation of suffering was unusually protracted. "I cannot burn," he called; "Lord have mercy on me; let the fire come to me; I cannot burn." His brother-in-law, with awkward kindness, threw on more wood, which only kept down the flame. At last some one lifted the pile with "a bill," and let in the air; the red tongues of fire shot up fiercely, Ridley wrested himself into the middle of them, and the powder did its work.

The horrible sight worked upon the beholders as it has worked since, and will work for ever, while the English nation survives—being, notwithstanding, as in justice to those who caused these accursed cruelties, must never be forgotten—a legitimate fruit of the superstition, that, in the eyes of the Maker of the world, an error of belief is the greatest of crimes; that while for all other sins there is forgiveness, a mistake in the intellectual intricacies of speculative opinion will be punished not with the brief agony of a painful death, but with tortures to which there shall be no end.

But martyrdom was often but a relief from more barbarous atrocities. In the sad winter months which were approaching, the poor men and women, who, untried and uncondemned, were crowded into the bishops' prisons, experienced such miseries as the very dogs could scarcely suffer and survive. They were beaten, they were starved, they were flung into dark, fetid dens, where rotting straw was their bed, their feet were fettered in the stocks, and their clothes were their only covering, while the wretches who died in their misery were flung out into the fields where none might bury them. [506]

Lollard's Tower and Bonner's coal-house were the chief scenes of barbarity. Yet there were times when even Bonner loathed his work. He complained that he was troubled with matters that were none of his; the bishops in other parts of England thrust upon his hands offenders whom they dared not pardon and would not themselves put to death; and, being in London, he was himself under the eyes of the court, and could not evade the work. [507] Against Bonner, however, the world's voice rose the loudest. His brutality was notorious and unquestionable, and a published letter was addressed to him by a lady, in which he was called the "common cut-throat and general slaughter-slave to all the bishops in England." [508] "I am credibly informed," said this person to him, "that your lordship doth believe, and hath in secret said, there is no hell. The very Papists themselves begin now to abhor your bloodthirstiness, and speak shame of your tyranny. Every child can call you by name, and say, 'Bloody Bonner is Bishop of London!' and every man hath it as perfect upon his fingers' ends as his Paternoster, how many you for your part have burned with fire and famished in prison this three-quarters of a year. Though your lordship believe neither heaven nor hell, neither God nor devil, yet if your lordship love your own honesty, you were best to surcease from this cruel burning and murdering. Say not but a woman gave you warning. As for the obtaining your popish purpose in suppressing of the truth, I put you out of doubt, you shall not obtain it so long as you go this way to work as you do. You have lost the hearts of twenty thousand that were rank Papists within this twelve months."

In the last words lay the heart of the whole matter. The martyrs alone broke the spell of orthodoxy, and made the establishment of the Reformation possible.

In the midst of such scenes the new parliament was about to meet. Money was wanted for the crown debts, and the queen was infatuated enough still to meditate schemes for altering the succession, or, at least, for obtaining the consent of the legislature to Philip's coronation, that she might bribe him back to her side. [509]

As the opening of the session approached, Elizabeth was sent again from the court to be out of sight and out of reach of intrigue; and Mary had the mortification of knowing that her sister's passage through London was a triumphal procession. The public enthusiasm became so marked at last that the princess was obliged to ride forward with a few servants, leaving the gentlemen who were her escort to keep back the people. Fresh alarms, too, had risen on the side of the papacy. Cardinal Caraffa, Paul IV. as he was now named, on assuming the tiara, had put out a bull among his first acts, reasserting the decision of the canons on the sanctity of the estates of the church, and threatening laymen who presumed to withhold such property from its lawful owners with anathemas. In a conversation with Lord Montague, the English ambassador at Rome, he had used language far from reassuring on the concessions of his predecessor; and some violent demonstration would undoubtedly have been made in parliament, had not Paul been persuaded to except England especially from the general edict.

Even then the irritation was not allayed, and a whole train of sorrows was in store for Mary from the violent character of Caraffa. Political popes have always been a disturbing element in the European system. Paul IV., elected by French influence, showed his gratitude by plunging into the quarrel between France and the Empire. He imprisoned Imperialist cardinals in St. Angelo; he persecuted the Colonnas on account of their Imperialist tendencies, levelled their fortresses, and seized their lands. The Cardinal of Lorraine hastened to Rome to conclude an alliance offensive and defensive on behalf of France; and the queen, distracted between her religion and her duty as a wife, saw Philip on the point of being drawn into parricidal hostility with his and her spiritual father. Nay, she herself might be involved in the same calamity; for so bitter was the English humour that the liberal party in the council were inclined to take part in the war, if they would have the pope for an enemy; and Philip would be too happy in their support to look too curiously to the motives of it. [510]

A calamity of a more real kind was also approaching Mary. She was on the point of losing the only able minister on whose attachment she could rely. Gardiner's career on earth was about to end.

On the 6th of October, Noailles described the Bishop of Winchester as sinking rapidly, and certain to die before Christmas, [511] yet still eager and energetic, perfectly aware of his condition, yet determined to work till the last.

Noailles himself had two hours' conversation with him on business: when he took his leave, the chancellor conducted him through the crowded ante-chamber to the door, leaning heavily on his arm. "The people thought he was dead," he said, "but there was some life in him yet."

Notwithstanding his condition, he roused himself for the meeting of parliament on the 21st; he even spoke at the opening, and he was in his place in the House of Lords on the second day of the session; but his remaining strength broke down immediately after, and he died at Whitehall Palace on the 13th of November. The Protestants, who believed that he was the author of the persecution, expected that it would cease with his end; they were deceived in their hopes, for their sufferings continued unabated. In their opinion of his conduct they were right, yet right but partially.

Stephen Gardiner, Bishop of Winchester, was the pupil of Wolsey, and had inherited undiminished the pride of the ecclesiastical order. If he went with Henry in his separation from the papacy, he intended that the English Church should retain, notwithstanding, unimpaired authority and undiminished privileges. The humiliations heaped upon the clergy by the king had not discouraged him, for the Catholic doctrine was maintained unshaken, and so long as the priesthood was regarded as a peculiar order, gifted with supernatural powers, so long as the sacraments were held essential conditions of salvation, and the priesthood alone could administer them, he could feel assured that, sooner or later, their temporal position would be restored to them.

Thus, while loyal to the royal supremacy, the Bishop of Winchester had hated heresy, and hated all who protected heresy with a deadly hatred. He passed the Six Articles Bill; he destroyed Cromwell; he laboured with all his might to destroy Cranmer; and, at length, when Henry was about to die, he lent himself, though too prudently to be detected, to the schemes of Surrey and the Catholics upon the regency. The failure of those schemes, and the five years of arbitrary imprisonment under Edward, had not softened feelings already more than violent. He returned to power exasperated by personal injury; and justified, as he might easily believe himself to be, in his opinion of the tendencies of heresy, by the scandals of the Protestant administration, he obtained, by unremitting assiduity, the re-enactment of the persecuting laws, which he himself launched into operation with imperious cruelty.

Yet there was something in Gardiner's character which was not wholly execrable. For thirty years he worked unweariedly in the service of the public; his judgment as a member of council was generally excellent; and Somerset, had he listened to his remonstrances, might have saved both his life and credit. He was vindictive, ruthless, treacherous, but his courage was indomitable. He resisted Cromwell till it became a question which of the two should die, and the lot was as likely to have fallen to him as to his rival. He would have murdered Elizabeth with the forms of law or without, but Elizabeth was the hope of all that he most detested. He was no dreamer, no high-flown enthusiast, but he was a man of clear eye and hard heart, who had a purpose in his life which he pursued with unflagging energy. Living as he did in revolutionary times, his hand was never slow to strike when an enemy was in his power; yet in general when Gardiner struck, he stooped, like an eagle, at the nobler game, leaving the linen-drapers and apprentices to "the mousing owls." His demerits were vast; his merits were small, yet something.

"Well, well," as some one said, winding up his epitaph, "Mortuus est, et sepultus est, et descendit ad inferos; let us say no more about him." [512]

To return to the parliament. On the 23rd of October a bull of Paul IV, confirming the dispensation of Julius, was read in the House of Commons. [513] On the 29th the crown debts were alleged as a reason for demanding a subsidy. The queen had been prevented from indulging her desire for a standing army. The waste and peculation of the late reign had been put an end to; and the embarrassments of the treasury were not of her creation. Nevertheless the change in social habits, and the alteration in the value of money, had prevented the reduction of the expenditure from being carried to the extent which had been contemplated; the marriage had been in many ways costly, and large sums had been spent in restoring plundered church plate. So great had been the difficulties of the treasury, that, although fresh loans had been contracted with the Jews, the wages of the household were again two years in arrear.

Parliament showed no disposition to be illiberal; they only desired to be satisfied that if they gave money it would be applied to the purpose for which it was demanded. The Subsidy Bill, when first introduced, was opposed in the House of Commons on the ground that the queen would give the keys of the treasury to her husband; and after a debate, a minority of a hundred voted for refusing the grant. [514] The general spirit of the Houses, however, was, on the whole, more generous. Two fifteenths were voted in addition to the subsidy, which the queen, on her side, was able to decline with thanks. [515] The money question was settled quietly, and the business of the session proceeded.

If her subjects were indifferent to their souls, Mary was anxious about her own. On the 11th of November, a bill was read a first time in the House of Lords, "whereby the king's and queen's majesties surrendered, and gave into the hands of the pope's holiness the first-fruits and tenths of all ecclesiastical benefices." The reception of the measure can be traced in the changes of form which it experienced. The payment of annates to the See of Rome was a grievance, both among clergy and laity, of very ancient standing. The clergy, though willing to be relieved from paying first-fruits to the crown, were not so loyal to the successors of St. Peter as to desire to restore their contributions into the old channel; while the laity, who from immemorial time had objected on principle to the payment of tribute to a foreign sovereign, were now, through their possession of the abbey lands and the impropriation of benefices, immediately interested parties. On the 19th of November fifty members of the House of Commons waited, by desire, upon the queen, to hear her own resolutions, and to listen to an admonition from the cardinal. [516] On the 20th a second bill was introduced, "whereby the king's and queen's majesties surrendered and gave the first-fruits and tenths into the hands of the laity." [517] The crown would not receive annates longer in any form; and as laymen liable to the payment of them could not conveniently be required to pay tribute to Rome, it was left to their consciences to determine whether they would follow the queen's example in a voluntary surrender.

Even then, however, the original bill could not pass so long as the pope's name was in it, or so long as the pope was interested in it. As it left the Lords, it was simply a surrender, on behalf of the crown, of all claims whatever upon first-fruits of benefices, whether from clergy or laity. The tenths were to continue to be paid. Lay impropriators should pay them to the crown. The clergy should pay them to the legate, by whom they were to be applied to the discharge of the monastic pensions, from which the crown was to be relieved. The crown at the same time set a precedent of sacrifice by placing in the legate's hands unreservedly every one of its own impropriations. [518]

In this form the measure went down to the Commons, where it encountered fresh and violent opposition. To demand a subsidy in one week, and in the next to demand permission to sacrifice a sixth part of the ordinary revenue, was inconsistent and irrational. The laity had no ambition to take upon themselves the burdens of the clergy. On the 27th there was a long discussion; [519] on the 3rd of December the bill was carried, but with an adverse minority of a hundred and twenty-six, against a majority of a hundred and ninety-three. [520]

Language had been heard in both Houses, during the debates, of unusual violence. Bradford's letter on the succession was circulating freely among the members, and the parliament from which the queen anticipated so much for her husband's interests proved the most intractable with which she had had to deal. [521] After the difficulty which she had experienced with the first-fruits, she durst not so much as introduce the question of the crown. [522] She attempted a bill for the restoration of the forfeited lands of the Howards, but it was lost. [523] The Duchess of Suffolk, [524] with several other persons of rank, had lately joined the refugees on the Continent; she attempted to carry a measure for the confiscation of their property, and failed again. [525] A sharp blow was dealt also at the recovered privileges of ecclesiastics. A man named Benet Smith, who had been implicated in a charge of murder, and was escaping under plea of clergy, was delivered by a special act into the hands of justice. [526] The leaven of the heretical spirit was still unsubdued. The queen dissolved her fourth parliament on the 9th of December; and several gentlemen who had spoken out with unpalatable freedom were seized and sent to the Tower. She was unwise, thought Noailles; such arbitrary acts were only making her day by day more detested, and, should opportunity offer, would bring her to utter destruction.

Unwise she was indeed, and most unhappy. When the poor results of the session became known to Philip, he sent orders that such of his

Spanish suite as he had left behind him should no longer afflict themselves with remaining in a country which they abhorred; he summoned them all to come to him except Alphonso, his confessor. "The queen wept and remonstrated; more piteous lamentations were never heard from woman." "How," exclaimed a brother of Noailles, [527] "is she repaid now for having quarrelled with her subjects, and set aside her father's will! The misery which she suffers in her husband's absence cannot so change her but that she will risk crown and life to establish him in the sovereignty, and thus recall him to her side. Nevertheless, she will fail, and he will not come. He is weary of having laboured so long in a soil so barren; while she who feels old age stealing so fast upon her, cannot endure to lose what she has bought so dearly."

Nothing now was left for Mary but to make such use as she was able of the few years of life which were to remain to her. If Elizabeth, the hated Anne Boleyn's hated daughter, was to succeed her on the throne, and there was no remedy, it was for her to work so vigorously in the restoration of the church that her labours could not afterwards be all undone. At her own expense she began to rebuild and refound the religious houses. The Grey Friars were replaced at Greenwich, the Carthusians at Sheene, the Brigittines at Sion. The house of the Knights of St. John in London was restored; the Dean and Chapter of Westminster gave way to Abbot Feckenham and a college of monks. Yet these touching efforts might soften her sorrow but could not remove it. Philip was more anxious than ever about the marriage of Elizabeth; and as Mary could not overcome her unwillingness to sanction by act of her own Elizabeth's pretensions, Philip wrote her cruel letters, and set his confessor to lecture her upon her duties as a wife. [528] These letters she chiefly spent her time in answering, shut up almost alone, trusting no one but Pole, and seeing no one but her women. If she was compelled to appear in public, she had lost her power of self-control; she would burst into fits of violent and uncontrollable passion; she believed every one about her to be a spy in the interest of the Lords. So disastrously miserable were all the consequences of her marriage, that it was said, the pope, who had granted the dispensation for the contraction of it, had better grant another for its dissolution. [529] Unfortunately there was one direction open in which her frenzy could have uncontrolled scope.

The Archbishop of Canterbury, after his trial and his citation to Rome, addressed to the queen a singular letter; he did not ask for mercy, and evidently he did not expect mercy: he reasserted calmly the truth of the opinions for which he was to suffer; but he protested against the indignity done to the realm of England, and the degradation of the royal prerogative, "when the king and queen, as if they were subjects in their own realm, complained and required justice at a stranger's hand against their own subjects, being already condemned to death by their own laws." "Death," he said, "could not grieve him much more than to have his most dread and gracious sovereigns, to whom under God he owed all obedience, to be his accusers in judgment before a stranger and outward power." [530]

The appeal was intended perhaps to provoke the queen to let him die with his friends, in whose example and companionship he felt his strength supported. But it could not be; he was the spectator of their fate, while his own was still held at a distance before him. He witnessed the agonies of Ridley; and the long imprisonment, the perpetual chafing of Soto the Spanish friar, and the dreary sense that he was alone, forsaken of man, and perhaps of God, began to wear into the firmness of a many-sided susceptible nature. Some vague indication that he might yield had been communicated to Pole by Soto before Christmas, [531] and the struggle which had evidently commenced was permitted to protract itself. If the Archbishop of Canterbury, the father of the Reformed Church of England, could be brought to a recantation, that one victory might win back the hearts which the general constancy of the martyrs was drawing off in tens of thousands. Time, however, wore on, and the archbishop showed no definite signs of giving way. On the 14th of December, a mock trial was instituted at Rome; the report of the examination at Oxford was produced, and counsel were heard on both sides, or so it was pretended. Paul IV. then pronounced the final sentence, that Thomas Cranmer, Archbishop of Canterbury, having been accused by his sovereigns of divers crimes and misdemeanours, it had been proved against him that he had followed the teachings of John Wicliff and Martin Luther of accursed memory; [532] that he had published books containing matters of heresy, and still obstinately persisted in those his erroneous opinions: he was therefore declared to be anathema, to be deprived of his office, and having been degraded, he was to be delivered over to the secular arm.

There was some delay in sending the judgment to England. It arrived at the beginning of February, and on the 14th, Thirlby and Bonner went down to finish the work at Oxford. The court sat this time in Christ Church Cathedral. Cranmer was brought to the bar, and the papal sentence was read. The preamble declared that the cause had been heard with indifference, that the accused had been defended by an advocate, that witnesses had been examined for him, that he had been allowed every opportunity to answer for himself. "O Lord," he exclaimed, "what lies be these! that I, being in prison and never suffered to have counsel or advocate at home, should produce witness and appoint counsel at Rome; God must needs punish this shameless lying."

Silence would perhaps have been more dignified; to speak at all was an indication of infirmity. As soon as the reading was finished, the archbishop was formally arrayed in his robes, and when the decoration was completed, Bonner called out in exultation:

"This is the man that hath despised the pope's holiness, and now is to be judged by him; this is the man that hath pulled down so many churches, and now is come to be judged in a church; this is the man that hath contemned the blessed sacrament of the altar, and now is come to be condemned before that blessed sacrament hanging over the altar; this is the man that, like Lucifer, sat in the place of Christ upon an altar [533] to judge others, and now is come before an altar to be judged himself." [534]

Thirlby checked the insolence of his companion. The degradation was about to commence, when the archbishop drew from his sleeve an appeal "to the next Free General Council that should be called." It had been drawn after consultation with a lawyer, in the evident hope that it might save or prolong his life, [535] and he attempted to present it to his judges. But he was catching at straws, as in his clearer judgment he would have known. Thirlby said sadly that the appeal could not be received; his orders were absolute to proceed.

The robes were stripped off in the usual way. The thin hair was clipped. Bonner with his own hands scraped the finger points which had been touched with the oil of consecration; "Now are you lord no longer," he said, when the ceremony was finished. "All this needed not," Cranmer answered; "I had myself done with this gear long ago."

He was led off in a beadle's threadbare gown, and a tradesman's cap; and here for some important hours authentic account of him is lost. What he did, what he said, what was done or what was said to him, is known only in its results, or in Protestant tradition. Tradition said that he was taken from the cathedral to the house of the Dean of Christ Church, where he was delicately entertained, and worked upon with smooth words, and promises of life. "The noblemen," he was told, "bare him good-will; he was still strong, and might live many years, why should he cut them short?" The story may contain some elements of truth. But the same evening, certainly, he was again in his cell; and among the attempts to move him which can be authenticated, there was one of a far different kind; a letter addressed to him by Pole to bring him to a sense of his condition.

"Whosoever transgresseth, and abideth not in the doctrine of Christ," so the legate addressed a prisoner in the expectation of death, [536] "hath not God. He that abideth in the doctrine of Christ, he hath both the Father and the Son. If there come any unto you and bring not this doctrine, receive him not into your house, neither bid him God speed; for he that biddeth him God speed is partaker of his evil deeds. There are some who tell me that, in obedience to this command, I ought not to address you, or to have any dealings with you, save the dealings of a judge with a criminal. But Christ came not to judge only, but also to save; I call upon you, not to enter into your house, for so I should make myself a partaker with you; my desire is only to bring you back to the church which you have deserted.

"You have corrupted Scripture, you have broken through the communion of saints, and now I tell you what you must do; I tell you, or rather not I, but Christ and the church through me. Did I follow my own impulse, or did I speak in my own name, I should hold other language; to you I should not speak at all; I would address myself only to God; I would pray him to let fall the fire of Heaven to consume you, and to consume with you the house into which you have entered in abandoning the church. [537]

"You pretend that you have used no instruments but reason to lead men after you; what instrument did the devil use to seduce our parents in Paradise? you have followed the serpent; with guile you destroyed your king, the realm, and the church, and you have brought to perdition thousands of human souls.

"Compared with you, all others who have been concerned in these deeds of evil, are but objects of pity; many of them long resisted temptation, and yielded only to the seductions of your impious tongue; you made yourself a bishop—for what purpose, but to mock both God and man? Your first act was but to juggle with your king, and you were no sooner primate, than you plotted how you might break your oath to the Holy See; you took part in the counsels of the evil one, you made your home with the wicked, you sat in the seat of the scornful. You exhorted your king with your fine words, to put away his wife; you prated to him of his obligations to submit to the judgment of the church; [538] and what has followed that unrighteous sentence? You parted the king from the wife with whom he had lived for twenty years; you parted him from the church, the common mother of the faithful; and thenceforth throughout the realm law has been trampled under foot, the people have been ground with tyranny, the churches pillaged, the nobility murdered one by the other.

"Therefore, I say, were I to make my own cries heard in heaven, I would pray God to demand at your hands the blood of his servants. Never had religion, never had the church of Christ a worse enemy than you have been; now therefore, when you are about to suffer the just reward of your deeds, think no more to excuse yourself; confess your sins, like the penitent thief upon the cross.

"Say not in your defence that you have done no violence, that you have been kind and gentle in your daily life. Thus I know men speak of you; but cheat not your conscience with so vain a plea. The devil, when called to answer for the souls that he has slain, may plead likewise that he did not desire their destruction; he thought only to make them happy, to give them pleasure, honour, riches—all things which their hearts desired. So did you with your king: you gave him the woman that he lusted after; you gave him the honour which was not his due, and the good things which were neither his nor yours; and, last and worst, you gave him poison, in covering his iniquities with a cloak of righteousness. Better, far better, you had offered him courtesans for companions; better you and he had been open thieves and robbers. Then he might have understood his crimes, and have repented of them; but you tempted him into the place where there is no repentance, no hope of salvation.

"Turn then yourself, and repent. See yourself as you are. Thus may you escape your prison. Thus may you flee out of the darkness wherein you have hid yourself. Thus may you come back to light and life, and earn for yourself God's forgiveness. I know not how to deal with you. Your examination at Oxford has but hardened you; yet the issue is with God. I at least can point out to you the way. If you, then, persist in your vain opinions, may God have mercy on you."

The legate, in his office of guide, then travelled the full round of controversy, through Catholic tradition, through the doctrine of the sacraments and of the real presence, where there is no need to follow him. At length he drew to his conclusion:

"You will plead Scripture to answer me. Are you so vain, then, are you so foolish, as to suppose that it has been left to you to find out the meaning of those Scriptures which have been in the hands of the fathers of the church for so many ages? Confess, confess that you have mocked God in denying that he is present on the altar; wash out your sins with tears; and in the abundance of your sorrow you may find pardon. May it be so. Even for the greatness of your crimes may it be so, that God may have the greater glory. You have not, like others, fallen through simplicity, or fallen through fear. You were corrupted, like the Jews, by earthly rewards and promises. For your own profit you denied the presence of your Lord, and you rebelled against his servant the pope. May you see your crimes. May you feel the greatness of your need of mercy. Now, even now, by my mouth, Christ offers you that mercy; and with the passionate hope which I am bound to feel for your salvation, I wait your answer to your Master's call."

The exact day on which this letter reached the archbishop is uncertain, but it was very near the period of his sentence. He had dared death bravely while it was distant; but he was physically timid; the near approach of the agony which he had witnessed in others unnerved him; and in a moment of mental and moral prostration Cranmer may well have looked in the mirror which Pole held up to him, and asked himself whether, after all, the being there described was his true image—whether it was himself as others saw him. A faith which had existed for centuries, a faith in which generation after generation have lived happy and virtuous lives; a faith in which all good men are agreed, and only the bad dispute—such a faith carries an evidence and a weight with it beyond what can be looked for in a creed reasoned out by individuals—a creed which had the ban upon it of inherited execration; which had been held in abhorrence once by him who was now called upon to die for it. Only fools and fanatics believe that they cannot be mistaken. Sick misgivings may have taken hold upon him in moments of despondency, whether, after all, the millions who received the Roman supremacy might not be more right than the thousands who denied it; whether the argument on the real presence, which had satisfied him for fifty years, might not be better founded than his recent doubts. It is not possible for a man of gentle and modest nature to feel himself the object of intense detestation without uneasy pangs; and as such thoughts came and went, a window might seem to open, through which there was a return to life and freedom. His trial was not greater than hundreds of others had borne, and would bear with constancy; but the temperaments of men are unequally constituted, and a subtle intellect and a sensitive organisation are not qualifications which make martyrdom easy.

Life, by the law of the church, by justice, by precedent, was given to all who would accept it on terms of submission. That the archbishop should be tempted to recant, with the resolution formed, notwithstanding, that he should still suffer, whether he yielded or whether he was obstinate, was a suspicion which his experience of the legate had not taught him to entertain.

So it was that Cranmer's spirit gave way, and he who had disdained to fly when flight was open to him, because he considered that, having done the most in establishing the Reformation, he was bound to face the responsibility of it, fell at last under the protraction of the trial.

The day of his degradation the archbishop had eaten little. In the evening he returned to his cell in a state of exhaustion: [539] the same night, or the next day, he sent in his first submission, [540] which was forwarded on the instant to the queen. It was no sooner gone than he recalled it, and then vacillating again, he drew a second, in slightly altered words, which he signed and did not recall. There had been a struggle in which the weaker nature had prevailed, and the orthodox leaders made haste to improve their triumph. The first step being over, confessions far more humiliating could now be extorted. Bonner came to his cell, and obtained from him a promise in writing, "to submit to the king and queen in all their laws and ordinances, as well touching the pope's supremacy, as in all other things;" with an engagement further "to move and stir all others to do the like," and to live in quietness and obedience, without murmur or grudging; his book on the sacrament he would submit to the next general council.

These three submissions must have followed one another rapidly. On the 16th of February, two days only after his trial, he made a fourth, and yielding the point which he had reserved, he declared that he believed all the articles of the Christian religion as the Catholic Church believed. But so far he had spoken generally, and the court required particulars. In a fifth and longer submission, [541] he was made to anathematise particularly the heresies of Luther and Zuinglius; to accept the pope as the head of the church, out of which was no salvation; to acknowledge the real presence in the Eucharist, the seven sacraments as received by the Roman Catholics, and purgatory. He professed his penitence for having once held or taught otherwise, and he implored the prayers of all faithful Christians, that those whom he had seduced might be brought back to the true fold.

The demands of the church might have been satisfied by these last admissions; but Cranmer had not yet expiated his personal offences against the queen and her mother, and he was to drain the cup of humiliation to the dregs.

A month was allowed to pass. He was left with the certainty of his shame, and the uncertainty whether, after all, it had not been encountered in vain. On the 18th of March, one more paper was submitted to his signature, in which he confessed to be all which Pole had described him. He called himself a blasphemer, and a persecutor; being unable to undo his evil work, he had no hope, he said, save in the example of the thief upon the cross, who when other means of reparation were taken from him, made amends to God with his lips. He was unworthy of mercy, and he deserved eternal vengeance. He had sinned against King Henry and his wife; he was the cause of the divorce, from which, as from a seed, had sprung up schism, heresy, and crime; he had opened a window to false doctrines of which he had been himself the most pernicious teacher; especially he reflected with anguish that he had denied the presence of his Maker in the consecrated elements. He had deceived the living and he had robbed the souls of the dead by stealing from them their masses. He prayed the pope to pardon him; he prayed the king and queen to pardon him; he prayed God Almighty to pardon him, as he had pardoned Mary Magdalen; or to look upon him as, from his own cross, He had looked upon the thief. [542]

The most ingenious malice could invent no deeper degradation, and the archbishop might now die. One favour was granted to him alone of all the sufferers for religion—that he might speak at his death; speak, and, like Northumberland, perish with a recantation on his lips.

The hatred against him was confined to the court. Even among those who had the deepest distaste for his opinions, his character had won affection and respect; and when it was known that he was to be executed, there was a widespread and profound emotion. "Although," says a Catholic who witnessed his death, "his former life and wretched end deserved a greater misery, if any greater might have chanced to him; yet, setting aside his offence to God and his country, beholding the man without his faults, I think there was none that pitied not his case and bewailed not his fortune, and feared not his own chance, to see so noble a prelate, so grave a councillor, of so long-continued honours, after so many dignities, in his old years to be deprived of his estate, adjudged to die, and in so painful a death to end his life." [543]

On Saturday, the 21st of March, Lord Williams was again ordered into Oxford to keep the peace, with Lord Chandos, Sir Thomas Brydges, and other gentlemen of the county. If they allowed themselves to countenance by their presence the scene which they were about to witness, it is to be remembered that but a few years since, these same gentlemen had seen Catholic priests swinging from the pinnacles of their churches. The memory of the evil days was still recent, and amidst the tumult of conflicting passions, no one could trust his neighbour, and organised resistance was impracticable.

The March morning broke wild and stormy. The sermon intended to be preached at the stake was adjourned, in consequence of the wet, to St. Mary's, where a high stage was erected, on which Cranmer was to stand conspicuous. Peers, knights, doctors, students, priests, men-at-arms, and citizens, thronged the narrow aisles, and through the midst of them the archbishop was led in by the mayor. As he mounted the platform many of the spectators were in tears. He knelt and prayed silently, and Cole, the Provost of Eton, then took his place in the pulpit.

Although, by a strained interpretation of the law, it could be pretended that the time of grace had expired with the trial; yet, to put a man to death at all after recantation was a proceeding so violent and unusual, that some excuse or some explanation was felt to be necessary.

Cole therefore first declared why it was expedient that the late archbishop should suffer, notwithstanding his reconciliation. One reason was "for that he had been a great causer of all the alterations in the realm of England; and when the matter of the divorce between King Henry VIII and Queen Catherine was commenced in the court of Rome, he, having nothing to do with it, sate upon it as a judge, which was the entry to all the inconvenients which followed." "Yet in that Mr. Cole excused him—that he thought he did it, not out of malice, but by the persuasion and advice of certain learned men."

Another occasion was, "for that he had been the great setter-forth of all the heresy received into the church in the latter times; had written in it, had disputed, had continued it even to the last hour; and it had never been seen in the time of schism that any man continuing so long had been pardoned, and that it was not to be remitted for example's sake."

"And other causes," Cole added, "moved the queen and council thereto, which were not meet and convenient for every one to understand." [544]

The explanations being finished, the preacher exhorted his audience to take example from the spectacle before them, to fear God, and to learn that there was no power against the Lord. There, in their presence, stood a man, once "of so high degree—sometime one of the chief prelates of the church—an archbishop, the chief of the council, the second person of the realm: of long time, it might be thought, in great assurance, a king on his side;" and now, "notwithstanding all his authority and defence, debased from a high estate unto a low degree—of a councillor become a caitiff, and set in so wretched estate that the poorest wretch would not change conditions with him."

Turning, in conclusion, to Cranmer himself, Cole then "comforted and encouraged him to take his death well by many places in Scripture; bidding him nothing mistrust but that he should incontinently receive that the thief did, to whom Christ said, To-day shalt thou be with me in Paradise. Out of Paul he armed him against the terrors of fire, by the words, The Lord is faithful, and will not suffer you to be tempted beyond that which you are able to bear; by the example of the three Children, to whom God made the flame seem like a pleasant joy; by the rejoicing of St. Andrew on his cross; by the patience of St. Lawrence on the fire." He dwelt upon his conversion, which, he said, was the special work of God, because so many efforts had been made by men to work upon him, and had been made in vain. God, in his own time, had reclaimed him, and brought him home.

A dirge, the preacher said, should be sung for him in every church in Oxford; he charged all the priests to say each a mass for the repose of his soul; and finally, he desired the congregation present to kneel where they were, and pray for him.

The whole crowd fell on their knees, the archbishop with them; and "I think," says the eye-witness, [545] "that there was never such a number so earnestly praying together; for they that hated him before, now loved him for his conversion, and hopes of continuance: they that loved him before could not suddenly hate him, having hope of his confession; so love and hope increased devotion on every side."

"I shall not need," says the same writer, "to describe his behaviour for the time of sermon, his sorrowful countenance, his heavy cheer, his face bedewed with tears; sometimes lifting his eyes to heaven in hope, sometimes casting them down to the earth for shame—to be brief, an image of sorrow, the dolour of his heart bursting out of his eyes, retaining ever a quiet and grave behaviour, which increased the pity in men's hearts."

His own turn to speak was now come. When the prayer was finished, the preacher said, "Lest any man should doubt the sincerity of this man's repentance, you shall hear him speak before you. I pray you, Master Cranmer," he added, turning to him, "that you will now perform that you promised not long ago; that you would openly express the true and undoubted profession of your faith."

"I will do it," the archbishop answered.

"Good Christian people," he began, "my dear, beloved brethren and sisters in Christ, I beseech you most heartily to pray for me to Almighty God, that he will forgive me all my sins and offences, which be many and without number, and great above measure; one thing grieveth my conscience more than all the rest, whereof, God willing, I shall speak more; but how many or how great soever they be, I beseech you to pray God of his mercy to pardon and forgive them all."

Falling again on his knees: —

"O Father of heaven," he prayed, "O Son of God, Redeemer of the world, O Holy Ghost, three Persons and one God, have mercy upon me, most wretched caitiff and miserable sinner. I have offended both heaven and earth more than my tongue can express; whither then may I go, or whither should I flee for succour? To heaven I am ashamed to lift up mine eyes, and in earth I find no succour nor refuge. What shall I do? Shall I despair? God forbid! Oh, good God, thou art merciful, and refusest none that come to thee for succour. To thee, therefore, do I come; to thee do I humble myself, saying, O Lord, my sins be great, yet have mercy on me for thy great mercy. The mystery was not wrought that God became man, for few or little offences. Thou didst not give thy Son, O Father, for small sins only, but for all and the greatest in the world, so that the sinner return to thee with a penitent heart, as I do at this present. Wherefore have mercy upon me, O Lord, whose property is always to have mercy; although my sins be great, yet is thy mercy greater; wherefore have mercy upon me, O Lord, for thy great mercy. I crave nothing, O Lord, for mine own merits, but for thy Name's sake, and, therefore, O Father of heaven, hallowed be thy Name."

Then rising, he went on with his address: —

"Every man desireth, good people, at the time of his death, to give some good exhortation that others may remember after his death, and be the better thereby; for one word spoken of a man at his last end [546] will be more remembered than the sermons made of them that live and remain. So I beseech God grant me grace, that I may speak something at my departing whereby God may be glorified and you edified.

"But it is an heavy case to see that many folks be so doted upon the love of this false world, and be so careful for it, that of the love of God or the world to come, they seem to care very little or nothing; therefore this shall be my first exhortation — that you set not over-much by this glozing world, but upon God and the world to come; and learn what this lesson meaneth which St. John teacheth, that the love of the world is hatred against God.

"The second exhortation is, that next unto God, you obey your king and queen willingly, without murmur or grudging, not for fear of them only, but much more for the fear of God, knowing that they be God's ministers, appointed of God to rule and govern you, and therefore whosoever resisteth them resisteth God's ordinance.

"The third exhortation is, that you live all together like brethren and sisters: but, alas! pity it is to see what contention and hatred one man hath against another, not taking each other for brethren and sisters, but rather as strangers and mortal enemies. But I pray you learn and bear well away the lesson, to do good to all men as much as in you lieth, and hurt no man no more than you would hurt your own natural brother or sister. For this you may be sure, that whosoever hateth his brother or sister, and goeth about maliciously to hinder or hurt him, surely, and without all doubt, God is not with that man, although he think himself never so much in God's favour.

"The fourth exhortation shall be to them that have great substance and riches of this world, that they may well consider and weigh these three sayings of the Scriptures. One is of our Saviour Christ himself, who saith that it is a hard thing for a rich man to come to heaven; a sore saying, and spoken of Him that knoweth the truth. The second is of St. John, whose saying is this: He that hath the substance of this world, and seeth his brother in necessity, and shutteth up his compassion and mercy from him, how can he say he loveth God? The third is of St. James, who speaketh to the covetous and rich men after this manner: Weep and howl for the misery which shall come upon you; your riches doth rot, your clothes be moth-eaten, your gold and silver is cankered and rusty, and the rust thereof shall bear witness against you, and consume you like fire; you gather and hoard up treasure of God's indignation against the last day. I tell them which be rich, ponder these sentences; for if ever they had occasion to show their charity, they have it now at this present; the poor people being so many, and victuals so dear; for although I have been long in prison, yet have I heard of the great penury of the poor."

The people listened breathless, "intending upon the conclusion."

"And now," he went on, "forasmuch as I am come to the last end of my life, whereupon hangeth all my life past and all my life to come, either to live with my Saviour Christ in joy, or else to be ever in pain with wicked devils in hell; and I see before mine eyes presently either heaven" — and he pointed upwards with his hand—"or hell," and he pointed downwards, "ready to swallow me. I shall therefore declare unto you my very faith, without colour or dissimulation; for now it is no time to dissemble. I believe in God the Father Almighty, Maker of heaven and earth; in every article of the Catholic faith; every word and sentence taught by our Saviour Christ, his apostles, and prophets, in the Old and New Testament.

"And now I come to the great thing that troubleth my conscience more than any other thing that ever I said or did in my life, and that is the setting abroad of writings contrary to the truth, which here I now renounce and refuse, [547] as things written with my hand contrary to the truth which I thought in my heart, and written for fear of death to save my life, if it might be; and that is, all such bills and papers as I have written and signed with my hand since my degradation, wherein I have written many things untrue; and forasmuch as my hand offended in writing contrary to my heart, my hand therefore shall first be punished; for if I may come to the fire, it shall be the first burnt. As for the pope, I utterly refuse him, as Christ's enemy and Anti-Christ, with all his false doctrine; and as for the sacrament, I believe as I have taught in my book against the Bishop of Winchester."

So far the archbishop was allowed to continue, before his astonished hearers could collect themselves. "Play the Christian man," Lord Williams at length was able to call; "remember yourself; do not dissemble." "Alas! my lord," the archbishop answered, "I have been a man that all my life loved plainness, and never dissembled till now, which I am most sorry for." He would have gone on; but cries now rose on all sides, "Pull him down," "Stop his mouth," "Away with him," and he was borne off by the throng out of the church. The stake was a quarter of a mile distant, at the spot already consecrated by the deaths of Ridley and Latimer. Priest and monks "who did rue [548] to see him go so wickedly to his death, ran after him, exhorting him, while time was, to remember himself." But Cranmer, having flung down the burden of his shame, had recovered his strength, and such words had no longer power to trouble him. He approached the stake with "a cheerful countenance," undressed in haste, and stood upright in his shirt. Soto and another Spanish friar continued expostulating; but finding they could effect nothing, one said in Latin to the other, "Let us go from him, for the devil is within him." An Oxford theologian—his name was Ely— being more clamorous, drew from him only the answer that, as touching his recantation, "he repented him right sore, because he knew that it was against the truth."

"Make short, make short!" Lord Williams cried, hastily.

The archbishop shook hands with his friends; Ely only drew back, calling, "Recant, recant," and bidding others not approach him.

"This was the hand that wrote it," Cranmer said, extending his right arm; "this was the hand that wrote it, therefore it shall suffer first punishment." Before his body was touched, he held the offending member steadily in the flame, "and never stirred nor cried." The wood was dry and mercifully laid; the fire was rapid at its work, and he was soon dead. "His friends," said a Catholic bystander, "sorrowed for love, his enemies for pity, strangers for a common kind of humanity, whereby we are bound to one another."

So perished Cranmer. He was brought out, with the eyes of his soul blinded, to make sport for his enemies, and in his death he brought upon them a wider destruction than he had effected by his teaching while alive. Pole was appointed the next day to the See of Canterbury; but in other respects the court had overreached themselves by their cruelty. Had they been contented to accept the recantation, they would have left the archbishop to die broken-hearted, pointed at by the finger of pitying scorn; and the Reformation would have been disgraced in its champion. They were tempted, by an evil spirit of revenge, into an act unsanctioned even by their own bloody laws; and they gave him an opportunity of redeeming his fame, and of writing his name in the roll of martyrs. The worth of a man must be measured by his life, not by his failure under a single and peculiar trial. The apostle, though forewarned, denied his Master on the first alarm of danger; yet that Master, who knew his nature in its strength and its infirmity, chose him for the rock on which He would build His church.

CHAPTER V-CALAIS

Not far from Abingdon, on the London road, was a house belonging to a gentleman named Christopher Ashton. Here, on their way to and fro between the western counties and the capital, members of parliament, or other busy persons, whom the heat of the times tempted from their homes, occasionally called; and the character of the conversation which was to be heard in that house, may be gathered from the following depositions. On the 4th of January, Sir Nicholas Arnold looked in, and found Sir Henry Dudley there.

"Well, Sir Nicholas, what news?" said Ashton.

"None worth hearing," Arnold answered.

"I am sure you hear they go about a coronation," Dudley said.

"I hear no such matter," said Arnold. "The news that are worth the hearing, are in such men's heads that will not utter them, and the rest are not to be credited." [549]

"There be news come out of Flanders, as I heard from Sir Peter Mewtas," said Ashton, laughing, to another visitor: [550] "The king has written to the queen that he will not come hither a great while, or, as men think, any more; and the queen was in a rage, and caused the king's picture to be carried out of the privy chamber, and she in a wonderful storm, and could not be in any wise quieted." [551]

"They have put me in the Tower for their pleasures," said Sir Anthony Kingston; "but so shall they never do more." [552]

At another time Sir Henry Peckham was alone with Ashton. Peckham [553] had been one of the sharers in the forfeited estates of the Duke of Norfolk. He was obliged to relinquish his grant, with but small compensation, and he complained of his treatment. Ashton bade him "be of good cheer."

"If you will keep my counsel," Ashton said, "I will tell you news that will bring your land again or it be long."

Peckham promised to be secret.

"Sir Anthony Kingston," Ashton continued, "and a great many of the western gentlemen, are in a confederacy to send the queen's highness over to the king, and make the Lady Elizabeth queen, and to marry the Earl of Devonshire to the said Lady Elizabeth. The laws of the realm will bear it, that they may do it justly; and Sir Anthony Kingston hath required me to hearken to King Henry VIII.'s will; for there is sufficient matter for our purpose, as Sir Anthony doth tell me. I pray, if you can, help me to it."

Peckham said it was to be had in the Rolls. Ashton did not like to put himself in the way of suspicion by asking to see it publicly, and begged Peckham to obtain a copy for him elsewhere.

"I will show you a token," he then said, and took out half a broken penny; "the other half is with Sir Anthony, and whensoever I do send this same to Sir Anthony, then will he be in readiness with ten thousand men within three days upon receipt of this token." If Lord Pembroke's men made resistance on the Marches, Kingston would cut them off, and would be in London in twenty days at furthest. And "when this is done," Ashton continued, "your father shall be made a duke; for I tell you true, that the Lady Elizabeth is a jolly liberal dame, and nothing so unthankful as her sister is; and she taketh this liberality of her mother, who was one of the bountifullest women in all her time or since; and then shall men of good service and gentlemen be esteemed."

Peckham, who had not anticipated so dangerous a confidence, looked grave and uneasy; Ashton said he hoped he would not betray him. "No," Peckham answered, and gave him his hand with his promise.

"I will tell you more, then," his friend went on; "we shall have that will take our part, the Earl of Westmoreland, who will not come alone, and we shall have my Lord Williams." [554]

"That cannot be," Peckham said; "he hath served the queen right well, and by her highness was made lord."

"I can better tell than you," Ashton answered; "the Lord Williams is a good fellow, and is as unthankfully dealt with as you, Sir Henry. I tell you that he is sure on our side; and Sir Henry Dudley hath spoken with all the gentlemen that be soldiers, that be about the town, and they be all sure ours, so that we have left the queen never a man of war that is worth a button." [555]

The scene changes. Readers of the earlier volumes of this history will remember Arundel's, in Lawrence Poultney Lane, where Lord Surrey and his friends held their nightly festivities. Times had changed, and so had Arundel's. It was now the resort of the young liberal members of parliament, where the opposition tactics in the House of Commons were discussed and settled upon. Here during the late session had met the men whose names have been mentioned in the preceding conversation, and who had crossed the queen's purposes; Kingston, Peckham, Ashton, Dudley, and with them Sir John Perrot, Sir William Courtenay, Sir Hugh Pollard, Sir John Chichester, and two young Tremaynes of Colacombe in Devonshire, one of whom had been concerned with Wyatt and Carew. Here also came John Daniel, in the service at one time of Lord Northampton, who, not being in parliament, was excluded from the more private consultations, but heard much of the general talk; "how they, with great wilfulness, as might be perceived by their behaviour, did sore mislike such Catholic proceedings as they saw the queen went about, and did intend to resist such matters as should be spoken of in the Parliament House other than liked them." [556]

The party broke up with the dissolution. Some of them, however, came back to London, and Daniel, one afternoon in March, was waiting for his dinner in the public room, when a ruffling cavalier named Ned Horsey came in, humming a catch of "Good man priest, now beware your pallet," "and bringing out a rhyme thereto of 'Fire and faggot,' and 'helm and sallet.'"

"I desire to live no longer than Whitsuntide next," Horsey said to Daniel; "for if I live so long, I mistrust not but my deeds shall be chronicled."

"Tush, my boy," he went on, "be of good cheer; for when thou shalt hear what the matter is, thou wilt take up thy hand and bless thee, and marvel that such young heads could ever bring such a matter as this to pass. I tell thee, the matter hath been a-brewing this quarter of a year at least, when thou wast in the country like a lout. Well, well, man, we shall either be men shortly, or no men; yea, and that very shortly, too."

"Tell me what you mean," said Daniel.

"Alas! good lout," quoth Horsey, "and do you not know, I pray you? hath not Harry Dudley told you of it?"

"No, by the faith of a Christian man," said Daniel, "Harry Dudley told me nothing except that he was going into France. But I pray thee, good Ned Horsey, tell me."

"By God's blood!" said Horsey, "then I will not tell you; for we have all taken an oath on the Testament, that no man should break it to any man, except as told first by Harry Dudley."

Horsey went on to talk of preparations, in which Daniel had been concerned, for an expedition to Southampton. Daniel, being a man of property, had undertaken to provide the horses, and had deposited a sum of money for the purpose; but, from Horsey's words, he perceived that schemes were on foot, which, having something to lose, he had better keep clear of. "His heart," he said, "rys in his body as big as a loaf;" he left the table, went down into the garden, and walked up and down an alley to collect himself; at last he ran into an arbour, where he knelt and said his prayers.

"What, man!" said Sir John Harrington, looking in, "you are well occupied on your knees so soon after dinner."

Daniel made up his mind that his friends were bringing him into a fool's paradise; "as they did brew, so they should bake for him," he thought, "and those heads that had studied it before he came to town should work the end of it." He stole away, therefore, and crossed the river to Southwark, where he took into his confidence a surgeon named Blacklock. Daniel pretended a broken leg, which Blacklock pretended to set: and thus the expedition to Southampton went off without him; the object of it being the despatch of one of the party into France, and the arrangement of the details of the conspiracy with the Captain of the Isle of Wight.

The characters of the persons who were concerned in this new plot against Mary's throne will not require much further elucidation. Sir Henry Dudley was Northumberland's cousin—the same who had been employed by the duke as an agent with the French court; the rest were eager, headstrong, not very wise young men, who, in the general indignation of the country at the barbarity of the government, saw an opportunity of pushing themselves into distinction. Lord Willoughby, Lord Westmoreland, and Lord Oxford were suspected by the queen of being unsound in religion; they had been reprimanded, and Oxford was thought likely to lose his lands. [557] If the first move could be made successfully, the conspirators counted on general support from these noblemen, and indeed from the whole body of the lay peers.

The plan was identical with that of Wyatt and Suffolk and Carew. Kingston was to march on London from Wales, and the force of the western counties was to join him on the Severn. One of the Throgmortons, called "Long John," had been at the French court, and made arrangements with Henry. Throgmorton returned to England, and Henry Dudley crossed the Channel in his place. The French promised to supply ships and money, while Dudley undertook to furnish them with crews from among the refugees or the western privateers, as Carew had done two years before. The Captain of the Isle of Wight, Uvedale, undertook to betray the island and Hurst Castle to the French. Dudley was to attack Portsmouth, where he would find the cannon "pegged;" [558] and when Portsmouth was taken, Hampshire, Sussex, and Kent were expected to rise.

Although known to so many persons, the secret was well kept. On Dudley's disappearance, inquiries were made about him. It was pretended that he was in debt, and had gone abroad to escape from his creditors. Some suspicion attached to the Tremaynes, who had long been connected with the privateers at Scilly. Strangways, the pirate, happened to be taken prisoner, and told something to the council about them which led to their arrest; but though the matter was "true enough," they bore down their accuser by mere courageous audacity of denial; and their resolution and fidelity were held up as an example in the secret meetings of the conspirators. [559]

The active co-operation of France was an essential element in the chances of success. From France, however, it became suddenly uncertain whether assistance was to be looked for. The English mediation in the European war had failed, because, after Mary's disappointment, France refused to part with Savoy; and the emperor could not bring himself to make a peace where the sacrifices would be wholly on his own side. But the negotiations between the principals were never wholly let fall; the emperor had now resigned. Philip, with an embarrassed treasury, with his eye on the English crown, and with trouble threatening him from the Turks, was anxious to escape from the exhausting conflict; and at the beginning of February a truce for five years was concluded at Vaucelles, by which Henry was left in undisturbed possession of all his conquests.

Terms so advantageous to the court of France could not be rejected; but past experience forbade, nevertheless, any very sanguine hope that the truce would last out its term. Unquestionably, in the opinion of the French king, it would be broken without scruple could Philip obtain the active help of England; and Henry would not, therefore, relinquish his correspondence with the conspirators. He instructed Noailles only to keep them quiet for the present till Philip's intentions should be revealed more clearly. [560]

The "young heads," of whom Horsey had spoken to Daniel, were not, however, men whom it was easy to keep quiet. Noailles replied, that they were so anxious to make an effort for liberty, and felt so certain of success, that he found great difficulty in restraining them; if the King of France would give them some slight assistance at the outset, [561] they undertook to do the rest themselves.

Dudley, therefore, remained in France, whither he was followed by Ashton and Horsey, and Henry admitted them to a midnight audience. He said that, for the moment, he could not act with them openly; but he would throw no difficulty in their way; if they were as strong as they professed to be (and they said that members of the privy council were in the confederacy), he would have them go forward with their project; and if he found Philip occupied, as he expected that he would be with the Turks in Hungary, he would assist them with men, money, and other things. Meanwhile, he gave Dudley 1500 crowns, distributed considerable sums among his companions, and advised them to go, as Carew had done before, to the coast of Normandy, and keep up their communications with their friends.

The interview and the promises of Henry were betrayed to Wotton, and by him reported in cypher to Mary; [562] but the fear or treachery of one of the party had already placed the government in possession of information, as the first step was about to be taken. Fifty thousand pounds were in the treasury: to embarrass the court, and to provide the insurrection with funds, a party of four or five—Rosey, keeper of the Star Chamber, Heneage, an officer of the Chapel Royal, a man named Derick, and one or two others—were chosen to carry off the money. Before the enterprise could be undertaken, Thomas White—perhaps one of the five, in alarm at the danger—communicated with the council; and on the 18th of March, Throgmorton, Peckham, Daniel, Rosey, and twelve or fourteen others, were seized suddenly, and sent to the Tower. Dudley was traced to Southampton; he was himself beyond pursuit, but Uvedale was discovered, and brought to London; Kingston was sent for, but died on his way up from Wales, probably by his own hand, in despair.

Information was, of course, the great object of the court; and they would shrink from nothing which would enable them to extort confessions. The prisoners knew what was before them, and prepared themselves according to their courage.

Throgmorton, when locked into the room which was allotted to him in the Tower, found that Derick was in the chamber underneath. He loosened a board in the floor, and "required him that, in any case, he should not be the destruction of others besides himself;" "for look," Throgmorton said, "how many thou dost accuse, so many thou dost wilfully murder."

Derick, it seems, was already thinking whether he could not, perhaps, save his own life. None of the party as yet knew how much of their secret had been discovered, or the value, therefore, which the government would place upon a full confession.

"He would do nothing," Derick answered, "but that which God had appointed; and if God would that he should do it, there was no remedy."

When a man has made up his mind that it is God's will that he should be a rogue, he has small chance of recovering himself. Throgmorton tried to reason him into manliness, and thought he had succeeded. Derick even promised to "abide the torture," "whereupon Master Throgmorton did sup his porridge to him, in token of his truth." But the torture was used or threatened, and Derick did not "abide" it; promises of pardon were also used, which the prisoners knew to mean nothing, and yet were worked on by them. [563]

Derick turned approver, so did Rosey, so did Bedyll: Uvedale, who was ill and feeble, yielded to the rack; and, piece by piece, the whole conspiracy was drawn out. The investigation was committed exclusively to the queen's clique, Rochester, Englefield, Waldegrave, Jerningham, and Hastings. The rest of the council refused to meddle, [564] for reasons which, perhaps, the queen hoped to learn from one or other of the prisoners. Throgmorton, however, who could tell the most, would tell nothing, though the rack was used freely to open his lips. How much he suffered may be gathered from a few words which he used to a Mr. Walpole, who was one of his examiners.

"Tell me, I pray you, Mr. Walpole," he said, "if the council may rack me, or put me to torment, after the time I am condemned, or no?"

"They may," Walpole answered, "if it shall please them."

"Then," said Throgmorton, "I fear I shall be put to it again; and, I will assure you, it is terrible pain." [565]

When torture would not answer, promises were tried, and promises apparently of an emphatic kind.

"I pray you, pray for me," Throgmorton said to his brother prisoners; "for I shall not be long with you. I cannot live without I should be the death of a number of gentlemen; and therewithal the said Throgmorton recited a story of the Romans, commending much an old man that was taken prisoner by the enemy, whom the Romans would have redeemed with a great number of young men, which would have been much more worth to the Romans; but this old man would in no case agree thereto, but received his death at the enemies' hand very patiently, considering his old years, and also what profit these young men should be to the Romans." [566]

The inquiry lasted till June, and much was learnt from those who had not Throgmorton's courage. Matters came out implicating Lord Bray and Lord Delaware. Lord Bray was arrested and examined; Lord Delaware was tried and found guilty. But they were powerful, and had powerful friends. [567] The court were forced to content themselves with smaller game. Successive batches of the conspirators were despatched, as their confessions were exhausted or despaired of. Throgmorton, silent to the last, was sentenced on the 21st of April, and suffered on the 28th. On the 19th of May, Captain Stanton was hanged; on the 2nd of June, Derick followed—his cowardice had not saved him—with Rosey and Bedyll. On the 7th of July, Sir Henry Peckham was disposed of, and with him John Daniel, who was guilty, if not of worse, yet of having concealed machinations dangerous to the state. [568]

But the danger did not pass off with the execution of a few youths. An inveterate conviction had taken hold of men of all ranks, that Philip was coming over with an army to destroy English liberty. Paget went to Flanders to entreat him to come back unattended, to dispel the alarm by his presence, and to comfort the queen; but Paget returned with a letter instead of Philip, and the poor queen looked ten years older on the receipt of it. She durst not stir abroad to face the execration with which the people now received her. She passed her time in frenzied extremities of passion, "because she could neither enjoy the presence of her husband, nor the affection of her subjects; and dreading every moment that her life might be attempted by her own attendants." [569] A fleet was fitted out in the Channel. A bishop in the queen's confidence was asked the reason by another bishop. "To overawe rebels," was the answer, "and to carry off Elizabeth into Flanders or Spain." [570] The government was conducted entirely by the legate and the small knot of Catholic fanatics who had adhered to the queen's fortunes in the late reign. Lord William Howard told Noailles that he and the other lords lived in perpetual dread and suspicion; if his honour would allow him, he would throw up his office, and retire, with those who had gone before him, as a poor gentleman, to France.

The general suffering was aggravated by a likelihood of famine. The harvest of 1555 had failed, and bread, with all other articles of food, was daily rising. The conspiracy exasperated the persecution, which was degenerating into wholesale atrocity. On the 23rd of April, six men were burnt at Smithfield; on the 28th, six more were burnt at Colchester; on the 15th of May, an old lame man and a blind man were burnt at Stratford-le-Bow. In the same month three women suffered at Smithfield, and a blind boy was burnt at Gloucester. In Guernsey, a mother and her two daughters were brought to the stake. One of the latter, a married woman with child, was delivered in the midst of her torments, and the infant just rescued was tossed back into the flames. [571] Reason, humanity, even common prudence, were cast to the winds. On the 27th of June, thirteen unfortunates, eleven men and two women, were destroyed together at Stratford-le-Bow, in the presence of twenty thousand people. [572] A schoolmaster, in Norfolk, in July read an inflammatory proclamation in a church. He and three others were instantly hanged. Ferocity in the government and lawlessness in the people went hand in hand. Along the river bank stood rows of gibbets, with bodies of pirates swinging from them in the wind. In the autumn, sixty men were sentenced to be hanged together, for what crime is unknown, at Oxford; [573] and as a symbol at head-quarters of the system of the administration, four corpses of thieves hung as a spectacle of terror before the very gates of St. James's Palace. [574]

On the 20th of August, twenty-three men and women were brought to London from Colchester, tied in a string with ropes to furnish another holocaust. A thousand people cheered them through the streets as they entered the city; and the symptoms of disorder were so significant and threatening, that Bonner wrote to Pole for instructions how he should proceed. The government was alarmed; "the council, not without good consideration," decided that it would be dangerous to go on with the executions; and Pole, checking Bonner's zeal, allowed the prisoners to escape for the time, under an easy form of submission which they could conscientiously make. They were dismissed to their homes, only, however, for several of them to be slaughtered afterwards, under fresh pretexts, in detail; [575] and Pole took an occasion, as will be presently seen, of reprimanding the citizens of London for their unnatural sympathy with God's enemies. That he had no objection to these large massacres, when they could be ventured safely, he showed himself in the following year, when fourteen heretics, of both sexes, were burnt in two days at Canterbury and Maidstone. [576]

Why, it may well be asked, did not the lords and gentlemen of England rise and trample down the perpetrators of these devilish enormities? It is a grave question, to which, nevertheless, some tolerable answer is possible.

On the 21st of January, 1557, the English ambassador in Paris wrote in cypher to Sir William Petre, of "a matter" which he desired should not be communicated to the queen, "lest it should disquiet her." A refugee had informed him, "that there was a great conspiracy in hand against the queen, which without doubt would deprive her of her estate." He had asked for names, but these his informant would not give, saying merely, "the best of England were in it," and "such a number agreed thereupon, that it was impossible but that it would take effect." There was no chance of discovery; "the matter had been in hand for a year or thereabouts," yet no one "had uttered a word of it;" should it become known, the conspirators were so strong that the catastrophe would only be precipitated. They would have moved already, "but for one man who had stayed them for a while."

Entreaties for more explicitness were fruitless. "By no means," wrote Wotton, "would he name any man unto me; but only said that the chiefest of them were such as had never offended the queen's highness before; that the matter should begin in the evening, and the next day by eight in the morning it should be done."

The queen was not to be killed; at least, not immediately. "They will not kill her," the man said, "but deprive her of her estate, and then might she chance to be used as she used Queen Jane;" and he added, "*that they who went about the matter would not agree that any foreign prince should have any meddling in it; neither Dudley nor any of the English gentlemen in France were privy to the matter.*" [577]

That any such combination as this letter described ever really menaced Mary's throne cannot be affirmed with certainty. The last two sentences, however, point to the difficulty which had embarrassed all attempts which had been hitherto ventured. The vice of the previous conspiracies had been the intrigues with France. The better order of English statesmen refused to connect themselves with movements which would give the court of Paris a dangerous influence in England, and would entitle the French king to press the claims of the Queen of Scots upon the English crown. If there was truth in the refugee's story, if there really was a conspiracy of "the best of England," clear of all such mischievous elements, it must have consisted of the body of the nobility, whom Lord William Howard described to Noailles as equally dissatisfied with himself. The heresy acts had been restored by the help of the bishops against the sustained opposition of the majority of the lay peers. For the hundred and fifty years during which those acts had been upon the Statute Book, they had expressed the general feeling of the country, yet during all that time, fewer persons had suffered under them than had been sacrificed during the last twelve months. Having failed to destroy her sister, having been unable to alter the succession, the queen was desperate; the Spaniards were watching their opportunity to interfere by force, and would want no encouragement which she could give them; and every honest English statesman must have watched her with the most jealous distrust. Yet, on the other hand, she was childless; her life must necessarily soon close by the course of nature, and with her life the tyranny would end. If force was attempted, she would not fall without a struggle; the clergy would stand by her, and all whom the clergy could influence. Philip would have the pretext, for which he was longing, for sending Spanish troops; and though liberty might and would prevail in the end, thousands of lives might be sacrificed, and Elizabeth's succession would be stained. The appeal to strength was, and is, the last to which good men will allow themselves to be driven. The lords understood one another: they would not be the first to commence; but if an attempt were made to carry off Elizabeth, or to throw on land a single Spanish battalion, they would know how to act.

Meantime, Dudley, Ashton, Horsey, the brothers Tremayne, and "divers others," were safe in France, and were hospitably entertained there. In England they were proclaimed traitors. At Paris they were received openly at court. The queen wrote to Wotton with her own hand, commanding him to demand their surrender. [578] She sent for Noailles, and required that "those wretches, those heretics, those traitorous execrable villains," who had conspired against her throne should be placed in her hands. [579] Henry, with unembarrassed coolness, promised Wotton that they should be apprehended, while he furnished them with ships, which they openly fitted for sea at the mouth of the Seine; and one of their number, Henry Killegrew, went to Italy to look for Courtenay, who was in honourable exile there, to entreat him to put himself at their head. Courtenay promised to come, so Killegrew reported on his return; [580] his name would have given them strength, his presence weakness; but if he really thought again of mixing himself in conspiracies his intentions were frustrated. The last direct heir of the noblest family in England died at the end of the summer, of an ague caught among the lagoons at Venice. [581]

The refugees, however, could do their work without Courtenay. The Killegrews, the Tremaynes, young Stafford, and many more, put to sea with three or four vessels, and treated all Spaniards with whom they could fall in as their natural enemies. Before the summer was out, they had "taken divers good prizes," and "did trust they should take more." "In case the worst fell, the gain thereof would find them all;" and on the 4th of August it was reported that they had taken a fort "on one of her majesty's islands," probably in Scilly, where the dangerous and intricate navigation placed them beyond risk of capture. Making war on their own account, half as pirates, half as crusaders, these youthful adventurers seized the Spanish caracks on their way to Flanders, sailed openly with their prizes into Rochelle or La Hogue, sold them, and bought arms and ammunition. Their finances were soon prosperous. Wild spirits of all nations—Scots, English, French, whoever chose to offer—found service under their flag. They were the first specimens of the buccaneering chivalry of the next generation—the germ out of which rose the Drakes, the Raleighs, the Hawkinses, who harried the conquerors of the New World.

In vain Wotton protested. The French king affected to be sorry. The Constable said that France was large; things happened which ought not to happen, yet could not be helped; the adventurers should be put down, if possible.

"These men brought nothing with them out of England," Wotton doggedly replied, "and were in such good credit with the people in France that nobody would lend them a shilling, and yet had they found ships which they had armed, and manned with good numbers of soldiers. What would the queen's highness think?"

The French court, in affected deference to such complaints, armed vessels, which they pretended were to pursue the privateers to their nest; but, as Wotton ascertained, they were intended really to act as their consorts. [582]

It was plain that the French king did not anticipate any long continuance to the truce of Vaucelles. In fact, Paul IV., whose schemes in Italy that truce had arrested, had succeeded in inducing him to break it. Lest his oath should make a difficulty, the pope had an ever-ready dispensation; and Paul's nephew, Cardinal Caraffa, came to Paris in July to make arrangements for the expulsion of the Spaniards from Naples. [583]

To insure Henry the continued support of the papacy, Paul undertook to create French cardinals on so large a scale as would give him the command of the next election. Henry, in spite of the entreaties of Montmorency, promised, on his side, to send an army to Paul's support; and the pope, without waiting for the arrival of the French troops, seized the Duchy of Paleano, and excommunicated the Colonnas, as the friends of the enemies of the Holy See. Scarcely caring to look for a pretext, he declared the Spanish prince deprived of the kingdom of Naples; and himself attempted to put in force his sentence against the Duke of Alva, who was acting there as Philip's viceroy.

The event had thus actually arrived, of which the expectation the year before had appeared so alarming. The most orthodox sovereign in Europe found himself forced into war with his spiritual father. The parent was become insane; the faithful child was obliged, in consequence, to place him under restraint, with as much tenderness and respect as the circumstances permitted. To the English council Philip explained the hard necessity under which he was placed. [584]

The Duke of Alva crossed the Neapolitan frontier into the States of the Church with twelve thousand men, taking the towns that lay in his way; and protesting while he did it that he was the most faithful servant of the Holy See. Individually a pious Catholic, officially a military machine, Alva obeyed orders with mechanical inflexibility, and, irresistible as destiny, advanced towards Rome. The college of cardinals, who remembered the occupation of the city by Bourbon's army, implored the pope to have pity on them. The pope had been too precipitate in commencing operations without waiting for the French. He was forced to submit his pride, and sue for an armistice, to which Alva, in the moderation of conscious strength, consented.

The French, on the other hand, were preparing to strike a blow in a quarter where as yet they were unlooked for.

The pastoral anxieties of the English legate had extended to Calais, where the Protestants were in considerable numbers. A commission was sent thither which proceeded with the usual severities, [585] and the sufferers, or those among the garrisons in Calais and Guisnes whose sympathy with the Reformation was stronger than their patriotism, placed themselves in correspondence with Sir Henry Dudley, at Paris. The pay of the troops was long in arrear, and they were all mutinous and discontented. Neither Guisnes, Hammes, nor Calais itself were provisioned for more than three or four weeks; and the refugees, caring only to revenge themselves on Mary, were laying a train in connection with several of the "chiefest officers" in the three fortresses, to betray them into the hands of France. The existence of a conspiracy became known by accident to some one, who placed Wotton on his guard; and Wotton, by vigilance and by the help of spies, ascertained gradually the nature of the scheme. In the beginning of October he discovered that Senarpont, the governor of Boulogne, was silently increasing the garrison of the Boullonnois. Then he heard of troops collecting at Rouen, of large preparations of military stores, of sappers' and miners' tools, and "great files, which would cut in two without noise the largest [harbour] chains." [586] Next, it seemed that the leader of the adventurous party, which fourteen years before "took the town of Marano by practise and subtlety," was in Calais in disguise. Finally, he learnt that Henry himself was going to Rouen, to conduct the enterprise in person.

The disaffection had penetrated so deeply into the English garrisons that caution was required in dealing with them; while for some weeks either the queen disbelieved the danger, or the council took no steps to obviate it. The Catholic clique had, in fact, not a soldier among them, and possibly knew not in which direction to turn. The honour of his country at last recalled Lord Pembroke to the public service in time to save Calais for a few more months.

By the middle of November eighteen ensigns of French infantry and a thousand horse were at Abbeville. Dudley, with the refugee fleet, was in readiness to blockade the harbour, while Henry was to march upon the town. If possible, he would find the gates open: at all events he would meet with no protracted resistance. But the move had been anticipated. Reinforcements and supplies were sent from England, money was despatched to pay up the arrears of the troops, and Pembroke himself went over in command. [587] No open inquiry was ventured, but the suspected persons were quietly removed. The French withdrew, and the queen's government, through the bad patriotism of the refugees, recovered a momentary strength.

The faint good fortune came opportunely; for in England the harvest had again failed, and the threat of famine had become the reality. On the

23rd of December malt was sold in London for forty shillings a quarter, and white flour at six shillings a bushel. The helpless remedy was attempted of crying up the base money, but the markets answered only by a further rise. [588] In the utter misery of the people, some were feeding upon acorns; some, in London, more piteously, left their infant children at the doors of their wealthy neighbours, to save them from starvation.

A famine was considered to be the immediate work of Heaven, and to be sent for an immediate moral cause. And yet the monasteries were rising from their ruins. Westminster was again an abbey. Feckenham was installed abbot on the 29th of November, with the ancient ceremonies, and walked in sad procession round the cloisters at the head of his friars. [589] The remnant of the monks of Glastonbury had crawled back into the ruins of their home. The queen had spared no effort and no sacrifice where her own power extended; and she had exhorted and advised where she was unable to act. Yet enough had not been done. In Ireland, indeed, the Catholic spirit had life in it. The Earl of Desmond had allowed no stone to be thrown down from the religious houses which had fallen to his share in the distribution. He had sheltered and supported the monks in the bad times, he now replaced them at his private cost; [590] and the example was telling among the chiefs. But in England, unfortunately, the lay owners of the church lands, orthodox and unorthodox alike, were hopelessly impenitent.

This, perhaps, was one cause of God's displeasure — the heretics were another; the heretics, and the sympathy with heresy displayed by the inhabitants of London, which had compelled the temporary release of the prisoners sent up from Essex.

It has been mentioned that the legate took occasion to admonish the citizens for their behaviour. In the present or the following year [591] he issued a pastoral letter, laying before them, and before the educated inhabitants of England generally, their duty at the present crisis; with an explanation, not entirely accurate, of the spirit in which the church had hitherto dealt with them. "That by license and dispensation," he said, "you do enjoy, and keep, and possess such goods and lands of the church as were found in your hands, this was done of the church your mother's tenderness unto you, considering your imbecility and weakness after so sore a sickness that you had in the schism, at the which time your appetite served you to no meat, but to that fruit that came from the lands of the church; and by that you lived, which she was content you should keep still, and made promise it should not be taken from you. And so it was left in your hand, as it were an apple in a child's hand given by the mother, which she, perceiving him to feed too much of, and knowing it should do him hurt if he himself should eat the whole, would have him give her a little piece thereof, which the boy refusing, and whereas he would cry out if she would take it from him, letteth him alone therewith. But the father, her husband, coming in, if he shall see how the boy will not let go one morsel to the mother that hath given him the whole, she asking it with so fair means, he may peradventure take the apple out of the boy's hand, and if he cry, beat him also, and cast the apple out of the window."

The maternal tenderness, under this aspect of the secularisation, had been more weak than wise.

"As the English laity had dishonoured the ministers of the church above all people," continued the legate, "so must they now honour them above all people, remembering Christ's words—'He that despiseth you despiseth Me.' They must obey the priests, therefore, implicitly; they must be careful to pay their tithes honestly; what they denied their priests they denied their God; and they must show their repentance especially where they had especially offended, touching the injuries they had done to the ministers of God, whom God had set over them, to be honoured as they would their natural father."

"And this," he said, coming to the heart of the matter, "this you cannot do if you favour heretics, who being the very enemies of God and man, yet specially their enmity extendeth against priests. Here is another point that you must show worthy of a repentant mind: that whereas you have sore offended God by giving favour to heretics, now temper your favour under such manner that if you can convert them by any ways unto the unity of the church, then do it, for it is a great work of mercy. But if ye cannot, and ye suffer or favour them, there cannot be a work of greater cruelty against the commonwealth than to nourish or favour any such. *For be you assured, there is no kind of men so pernicious to the commonwealth as they be; there are no thieves, no murderers, no adulterers, nor no kind of treason, to be compared to theirs, who, as it were, undermining the chief foundation of all commonwealths, which is religion, maketh an entry to all kinds of vices in the most heinous manner.*"

... "You specially of the City of London, you being the first that received the fruit of grace in the new plantation, the seed of benediction being first cast upon you, to make you a ground to bring forth all fruit of sanctity and justice; ... shall I say, that after all this done, more briars and thorns hath grown here among you than in all the realm besides? I cannot say so, nor I will not; albeit it might so seem, for a greater multitude of these brambles and briars were cast in the fire here among you than in any place besides; but many of them being grown in other places, and brought in and burned among you, may give occasion that you have a worse name without your desert. The thing standeth not in the name—bethink you yourselves how it standeth.... Wherefore cometh this, that when any heretic shall go to execution, he shall lack no comforting of you, and encouraging to die in his perverse opinion? that when he shall be put in prison he shall have more cherishing?... As it is now, this may not be suffered.... For their boldness in their death, it is small argument of grace to be in them; Christ himself showing more heaviness and dolour at his dying hour than did the thieves that hung beside him, which did blaspheme Christ, setting nought by him, specially one of them, showing no further fear. So do the heretics at their deaths like the blasphemer." [592]

Cruel and savage as the persecution had become, it was still inadequate. The famine lasted, and therefore God was angry.

The new year opened with the appointment of a commission, consisting of Bonner, Thirlby, and twenty other peers, gentlemen, and canon lawyers, on whom the court could rely. "Wicked persons" had invented slanders against the queen's person, and had sown "pestilent heresies" in the realm. The queen, therefore, "minding to punish such enormities," and having especial trust in the wisdom of these persons, gave them power to institute inquiries at their pleasure into the conduct and opinions of every man and woman in all parts of the kingdom. The protection of the law was suspended. The commissioners might arrest any person at any place. Three of them were enough to form a court; and mayors, sheriffs, and magistrates were commanded to assist at their peril.

The object of the commission was "to search and find out" the sellers of heretical books, or those who in any way professed heresy or taught it; to ascertain who refused to attend mass, to walk in procession, to use holy water, or in any way betrayed disrespect for the established religion. Those who "persisted in their bad opinions" were to be given up to their ordinary, to be punished according to law. The commissioners were themselves empowered to punish with fine or imprisonment those who yielded, or those whose offences were in the second degree, taking care to collect the fines which they inflicted, and to certify the exchequer of their receipts. They were not embarrassed by a necessity of impanelling juries; they might call juries if they pleased; they might use "all other means and politic ways that they could devise." No Spanish inquisition possessed larger or less tolerable powers; no English sovereign ever more entirely set aside the restrictions of the law. [593] The appointment of the commission was followed up by Pole in a visitation of the diocese of Canterbury. Persons were nominated to examine into the doctrines of the clergy; to learn whether those who had been married held communication with their wives; whether the names of those who had not been reconciled had been registered as he had ordered; and from every clergyman to ascertain the habits, beliefs, and opinions of every resident, male or female, in his parish. [594]

Other commissioners again were sent to the universities, with powers extending, not over the living only, but the dead.

Scot, Bishop of Chester, Watson, Bishop of Lincoln, and Christopherson, Master of Trinity and Bishop of Chichester, went in January to Cambridge, accompanied by Ormaneto, the Venetian, a confidential friend of the legate. Bucer and Fagius slept in St. Mary's and St. Michael's. The 10th of January, the day after the bishops' arrival, the two churches were laid under an interdict, as defiled with the presence of unhallowed bodies. On the 15th a summons was fixed to St. Mary's door, citing Martin Bucer and Paul Fagius, or any other who would plead on their behalf, to make answer three days after, before the commission, on a charge of heresy. The court sate, and no one appeared. The session was adjourned for a week, while the colleges were searched, and Primers, Prayer-books, Bibles, or other interdicted volumes, were hunted out and brought together. On the 26th the bishops met again; the accused remained undefended, and the heresy was taken to be proved; sentence was passed therefore, that the bodies should be disinterred and burnt. On the 6th of February the coffins were taken out of the graves, and chained to a stake in the market-place; the Bibles and prayer-books were heaped round them with a pile of faggots, and books and bodies were reduced to ashes.

Having purged Cambridge, Ormaneto proceeded to Oxford, on business of the same description.

Peter Martyr, when he came into residence as divinity professor at Christ Church, had outraged the orthodox party in the university by bringing a wife within the college walls; and Catherine Cathie, so the wife was named, had, like the wife of Luther, been a professed nun. She had died before Mary's accession, and had been buried in the cathedral. A process has now instituted against her similar to that at Cambridge.

An unforeseen difficulty occurred in the conduct of the prosecution. Catherine Cathie had lived quietly and unobtrusively; she had taught nothing and had written no books; and no evidence could be found to justify her conviction on a charge of heresy.

Ormaneto wrote to the legate for instructions; and as burning was not permissible, the legate replied that, "forasmuch as Catherine Cathie, of detestable memory, had called herself the wife of Peter Martyr, a heretic, although both he and she had before taken vows of religion; forasmuch as she had lived with him in Oxford in fornication, and after her death was buried near the sepulchre of the Holy Virgin St. Frideswide, Ormaneto should invite the dean of the cathedral to cast out the carcase from holy ground, and deal with it according to his discretion."

Catherine Cathie, therefore, was dug up, taken out of her coffin, and flung into a cesspool at the back of the dean's house, and it was hoped that by this means the blessed St. Frideswide would be able to rest again in peace. Human foresight is imperfect; years passed and times changed; and Elizabeth, when she had the power to command, directed that the body should be restored to decent burial. The fragments were recovered with difficulty, and were about to be replaced in the earth under the floor of the cathedral, when some one produced the sacred box which contained the remains of St. Frideswide. Made accessible to the veneration of the faithful by Cardinal Pole, the relics had been concealed on the return of heresy by some pious worshipper. They were brought out at the critical moment, and an instant sense of the fitness of things consigned to the same resting-place the bones of the wife of Peter Martyr. The married nun and the virgin saint were buried together, and the dust of the two still remains under the pavement inextricably blended. [595]

But Pole did not live to see the retribution. Convinced, if ever there was a sincere conviction in any man, that the course which he was pursuing was precisely that which God required of him, he laboured on in his dark vocation. Through the spring and summer the persecution, under the new commission, raged with redoubled fury.

The subject is one to which it will not be necessary to return, except with some brief details. In this place, therefore, shall be given an extract from a tract in circulation among the Protestants who were expecting death; and it may be judged, from the sentiments with which these noble-natured men faced the prospect of their terrible trial, with what justice Pole called them brambles and briars only fit to be burnt — criminals worse than thieves, or murderers, or adulterers. [596]

"The cross of persecution, if we will put childishness apart, and visibly weigh the worthiness thereof, is that sovereign, tried medicine that quencheth the daily digested poison of self-love, worldly pleasure, fleshly felicity. It is the only worthy poison of ambition, covetousness, extortion, uncleanness, licentiousness, wrath, strife, sedition, sects, malice, and such other wayward worms: it is the hard hammer that breaketh off the rust from the anchor of a Christian faith. O profitable instrument! O excellent exercise, that cannot be spared in a Christian life! with what alacrity of mind, with what desirous affection, with what earnest zeal, ought we to embrace this incomparable jewel, this sovereign medicine, this comfortable cup of tribulation.

"When a piece of ground is limited and bounded, it doth not only signify that it goeth no further, but also it tendeth and stretcheth to the bound. It is not enough to consider that we shall not pass the time that God hath limited and determined us to live, but we must assuredly persuade ourselves that we shall live as long as He hath ordained us to live; and so shall we do, in despite of all our enemies.

"And tell me, have men given us our life? No, forsooth. No more can they take it away from us. God hath given it, and God only doth take it away, for He is the Lord of death as well as of life; wherefore when the appointed time of our death is come, let us assure ourselves, that it is God only and none other that doth kill us, for He saith, It is I that kill and make alive again.

"Let us follow the example of Christ, our Master, who seeing His death approaching, said to God, My Father, not as I will, but as thou wilt; thy will be done, and not mine. — Let us offer then, unto God our Father, ourselves for a sacrifice, whose savour, although it be evil in the nose of the world, yet it is good and agreeable unto God, by Jesus Christ his Son, in the faith of whom we do dedicate and offer ourselves, when we perceive our hour to approach.

"And, whatsoever betide, let us not fear men; let us not fear them. God doth inhibit and forbid us in the same, saying, by his prophet, Fear them not, for I am with you; and seeing God doth forbid us to fear men, can we fear them without sin? No truly. To what purpose do we fear them? Men of themselves can do nothing, and if at any time they have any power, the same only cometh unto them from God, and is given unto them only to accomplish the will of God. But peradventure ye will say to me that Jesus Christ himself, in the time of his cross, did fear death, and therefore it is no marvel though we do fear it, in whom is no such perfection and constancy. Truly the flesh doth always abuse herself with the example of Jesus Christ; she doth abuse it, for she cannot rightfully use it, inasmuch as the flesh is in all ways repugnant unto the spirit and the good will of God. Forasmuch as ye will herein follow Christ — well, I am contented — fear death, but fear it as he did fear it. If you will say that Christ had fear of death, consider the same also to be on such sort as the fear did not keep him back from the voluntary obedience of his Father, and from saying, with unfeigned lips, Thy will be done.

"Ye will say, We fear not death for any fear we have to be damned, neither for any diffidence that we have of eternal life; but we fear death for the human understanding that we have of the great pain that some do suffer in dying, and especially in dying by fire; for we suppose that pain to surmount all patience. O fond flesh, thy voice is always full of love of thyself, and of a secret diffidence and mistrust of the Almighty power, wisdom, and goodness of God."

While the true heroes of the age were fighting for freedom with the weapons of noble suffering, the world was about to recommence its own battles, with which it is less easy to sympathise. The attempt on Calais having failed, it became a question at the French court, whether, after having given so just cause of quarrel to England, wisdom would not suggest an abandonment of the intention of recommencing the war with Philip. Noailles crossed to Paris in December, where the king questioned him whether Mary would be able to declare war. Noailles assured him, "that out of doubt she would not; for if she should send those whom she trusted out of the realm, then would they whom she trusted not, not fail to be busy within the realm." [597] Reassured by the ambassador's opinion, Henry resumed his intentions. In March, the Duke of Guise led an army into Italy. The pope recovered courage, defied Alva, and again laid claim to Naples; and it was to be seen now whether Noailles was right — whether the English people would unite with the court to resent the French king's conduct sufficiently to permit Mary at last to join in the quarrel.

Philip, anxious and hopeful, paid England the respect of returning for a few weeks, and in the same month of March came over to sue the council in person. The affair at Calais was a substantial ground for a rupture, but the attack, though intended, had not been actually made. The story might seem, to the suspicions of the country, to have been invented by the court; and, in other respects, Mary's injuries were not the injuries of the nation. The currency was still prostrate; the people in unexampled distress. The Flanders debts were as heavy as ever, and the queen had insisted on abandoning a fifth of her revenues. A war would inevitably be most unpopular. The attempt nevertheless was made. The queen produced the treaty of 1546, between England and the empire; and, in compliance with its provisions, laid before the privy council a proposal, if not to declare war with France, yet to threaten a declaration, in the event of an invasion of the Netherlands.

The privy council considered the queen's request; their conclusion was not what she desired.

The treaty of 1546, the council replied, had been abrogated by the treaty of marriage, so far as it might involve England in a war with France. "Her majesty would be unable to maintain a war, and, therefore, to say to the French king that she would aid her husband, according to the treaty, and not being able to perform it, indeed would be dishonourable, and many ways dangerous." "It was to be considered further, that, if by these means the realm should be drawn into war, the fault would be imputed to the king's majesty." "The common people of the realm were at present many ways grieved — some pinched with famine, some for want of payment of money due to them, some discontented for matters of religion; and, generally, all yet tasting the smart of the late wars. It would be hard to have any aid of money of them. And in times past," the council added, significantly, "although the prince found himself able to make and maintain wars, yet the causes of those wars were opened for the most part in parliament." [598]

Objections so decided and so just would have hardly been overcome, but for an injudicious enterprise of the refugees, under French auspices. The French court believed that, by keeping Mary in alarm at home, they would make it the less easy for her to join in the war. They mistook the disposition of the people, who resented and detested the interference of France in their concerns.

Among the exiles at the court of Paris, the most distinguished by birth, if not by ability, was Sir Thomas Stafford, Lord Stafford's second son, and grandson of the Duke of Buckingham, who was put to death under Henry VIII. On the 27th of April, Wotton sent notice to the queen that Stafford had sailed from the mouth of the Seine with two vessels well manned and appointed. His destination was unknown; but it was understood that he intended to take some fortress on the English coast, and that the refugees, in a body, intended to follow him. Before Wotton's letter arrived, the scheme, such as it was, had been already executed. Stafford, with thirty Englishmen and one Frenchman, had surprised Scarborough Castle, and sent his proclamations through Yorkshire. He was come, he said, to deliver his country from foreign tyranny. He had sure evidence that an army of Spaniards was about to land, and that Philip intended to seize the crown by force. The queen, by her marriage with a stranger, had forfeited her own rights; and he himself, as the protector of English liberty, intended to bestow the crown on the next rightful heir, and to restore all such acts, laws, liberties, and customs as were established in the time of that most prudent prince, King Henry VIII. "He did not mind," he thought it necessary to add, "to work his own advancement touching possession of the crown, but to restore the blood and house of the Staffords to its pristine estate, which had been wrongfully suppressed by Cardinal Wolsey." [599]

The landing of Edward IV., at Ravenspurg, had made any wild enterprise seem feasible, and Stafford had counted on the notorious hatred of the people for the queen.

But if the Spaniards meditated a descent upon England, it was not by adventurers like the refugees that their coming would be either prevented or avenged; and the good sense of the country had determined once for all to give no countenance to revolution supported by France. The occupation of Scarborough lasted two days, at the end of which Stafford and his whole party were taken by the Earl of Westmoreland. Thirty-two prisoners were sent to London; thirty-one were put to death; and the council reluctantly withdrew their opposition to the war. A hundred and forty thousand pounds were in the exchequer, being part of the subsidy granted by parliament to pay the crown debts. [600] With this the court prepared to commence, trusting to fortune for the future. War was to be declared on the 7th of June, and, while seven thousand men were to cross the Channel and join Pembroke in the Low Countries, [601] Howard was to cruise with the fleet in the Channel to use his discretion in annoying the enemy, and, if possible, to destroy the French ships at Dieppe. [602]

Happy, however, in having succeeded in gratifying her husband, the queen brought at once upon herself a blow which she had little foreseen, and from a quarter from which an injury was most painful. In her desire to punish France for assisting her rebellious heretical subjects, she seemed to have forgotten that France had an ally beyond the Alps. No sooner did Paul IV. learn that England was about to declare on the side of Philip, than, under the plausible pretence that he could have no ambassador residing in a country with which he was at war, he resolved to gratify his old animosity against Cardinal Pole, and cancel his legation.

Sir Edward Karne, the English resident at Rome, waited on the pope to remonstrate. He urged Paul to recollect how much the Holy See owed to the queen, and how dangerous it might be to re-open a wound imperfectly healed. The pope at first was obstinate. At length he seemed so far inclined to yield as to say that, if the queen would herself expressly desire it, he would distinguish between her and her husband. [603] But the suspension of the legation, though not at first published, was carried through the Consistory; and so ingeniously was it worded, that not only the formal and especial commission was declared at an end, but the legatine privileges, attached by immemorial custom to the archbishopric of Canterbury, were cancelled with it. The pope chose to leave himself without representative, ordinary or extraordinary, at the English court.

The queen was in despair. Before Karne's letter reached her, she had heard what was impending, and she wrote a letter of passionate expostulation, in which she expatiated on her services to religion, and on the assistance which Pole had rendered her. She said that, in the unsettled condition of England, the presence of a legate with supreme authority was absolutely necessary; and she implored Paul to reconsider a decision so rash and so unkind.

The council added their separate protest. [604] "They had heard with infinite grief that the legate was to be taken from them. There was no precedent for the recall of a legate who had been once commissioned, unless from fault of his own; and for themselves, they were unconscious of having misconducted themselves in any way since the reconciliation. Cardinal Pole had been the saviour of religion. Before his coming to England, the queen, with the best intentions to do good, had failed to arrest the growth of heresy, and the name of the Holy See was held in detestation. Pole, the noblest and most distinguished of the cardinals, had made what was crooked straight; he had introduced reforms everywhere; in a few years the wound would heal, and all would be well. If, however, he were now removed, the convalescent, deserted too soon by his physician, would relapse, and be worse than before. They entreated his holiness, therefore, to listen to them, and allow him to remain. When they were reconciled, the pope then reigning had promised that the customary privileges and immunities of the English nation should be maintained. It was the special prerogative of English sovereigns to have a legate perpetually resident in the person of the Archbishop of Canterbury; and from immemorial time there was no record of any archbishop to whom the legatine character had not attached as of right. The queen, who had risked her life for the faith of the church, did not deserve that the first exception should be made in her disfavour. The bishops did not deserve it. The few who, in the late times of trial, had remained faithful, did not deserve it. Even if the queen would consent and give way, they would themselves be obliged to remonstrate." [605]

Karne's letter produced a brief hope that the pope would relent. But the partial promise of reconsidering his resolution had been extorted from Paul, while it was uncertain whether England would actually join in the conflict; the intended declaration of war had in the interval become a reality, and the pope, more indignant than ever, chose to consider Pole personally responsible for the queen's conduct. Since a point was made of the presence of a papal legate in England, he was so far ready to give way; but so far only. The king left England the first week in July. Mary accompanied him to Dover, and there a papal nuncio met her, bringing a commission by which Pole was reduced into the ordinary rank of archbishop; and the office of papal representative was conferred on Peto, the Greenwich friar. For his objections to the present legate, the pope gave the strange but wounding reason, that his orthodoxy was not above suspicion.

The queen, with something of her father's temper in her, ordered the nuncio to return to Calais till she could again communicate with Rome. She interdicted Peto from accepting the commission, and desired Pole to continue to exercise his functions till the pope had pronounced again a final resolution. Pole, however, was too faithful a child of the church to disobey a papal injunction; he relinquished his office, but he sent Ormaneto to Rome with his own entreaties and protests.

Never had a legate of the Holy See been treated as he was treated, he said; there was no precedent, therefore, to teach him how to act, nor was ever charge of heresy urged with less occasion than against one whose whole employment had been to recover souls to Christ and his church, and to cut off those that were obstinate as rotten members. His services to the church, he passionately exclaimed, transcended far the services of any legate who had been employed for centuries, and, nevertheless, he found himself accused of heresy by the Vicar of Christ upon earth. Such an insult was unjust and unprovoked; and his holiness should consider also what he was doing in bringing the queen, the mother of obedience, into heaviness and sorrow. Mother of obedience the Queen of England might well be called, whom God had made a mother of sons who were the joy of the whole church. How was the pope rewarding this sainted woman, when with the thunder of his voice he accused the king, her husband, of schism, and himself, the legate, of heresy? [606]

Scarcely in his whole troubled life had a calamity more agitating overtaken Reginald Pole. To maintain the supremacy of the successor of St. Peter, he had spent twenty years in treason to his native country. He had held up his sovereign to the execration of mankind for rejecting an authority which had rewarded him with an act of enormous injustice; and to plead his consciousness of innocence before the world against his spiritual sovereign, would be to commit the same crime of disobedience for which he had put to death Cranmer, and laboured to set Europe on fire. Most fatal, most subtle retribution — for he knew that he was accused without cause; he knew that the pope after all was but a peevish, violent, and spiteful old man; he knew it — yet even to himself he could not admit his own conviction.

Fortune, however, seemed inclined for a time to make some amends to Mary in the results of the war.

The French usually opened their summer campaigns by an advance into Lorraine or the Netherlands. This year their aggressive resources had been directed wholly into Italy, and at home they remained on the defensive. Philip, with creditable exertion, collected an army of 50,000 men, to take advantage of the opportunity. Fixing his own residence at Cambray, he gave the command in the field to the Duke of Savoy; and Philibert, after having succeeded in distracting the attention of the enemy, and leading them to expect him in Champagne, turned suddenly into Picardy, and invested the town of St. Quentin. The garrison must soon have yielded, had not Coligny, the Admiral of France, broken through the siege lines and carried in reinforcements. Time was thus gained, and the constable, eager to save a strong place, the possession of which would open to the Spaniards the road to Paris, advanced with all the force which he could collect, not meaning to risk a battle, but to throw provisions and further supplies of men into St. Quentin. Montmorency had but 20,000 men with him. His levies consisted of the reserved force of the kingdom — princes, peers, knights, gentlemen, with their personal retinues, the best blood in France. It was such an army as that which lost Agincourt, and a fate not very different was prepared for it.

On the 10th of August, the constable was forced by accident into an engagement, in which he had the disadvantage of position as well as of numbers. Mistaken movements caused a panic in the opening of the battle, and the almost instant result was a confused and hopeless rout. The Duke d'Enghien fell on the field with four thousand men; the constable himself, the Duke de Montpensier, the Duke de Longueville, the Marshal St. André, three hundred gentlemen, and several thousand common soldiers, were taken; the defeat was irretrievably complete, and to the victors almost bloodless. The English did not share in the glory of the battle, for they were not present; but they arrived two days after to take part in the storming of St. Quentin, and to share, to their shame, in the sack and spoiling of the town. They gained no honour; but they were on the winning side. The victory was credited to the queen as a success, and was celebrated in London with processions, bonfires, and *Te Deums*.

Nor was the defeat at St. Quentin the only disaster which the French arms experienced. Henry sent in haste to Italy for the Duke of Guise to defend Paris, where Philibert was daily expected. Guise was already returning after a failure less conspicuous, but not less complete, than that of the constable. The pope had received him on his arrival with enthusiasm, but the promised papal contingent for the campaign had not been provided; the pope was contented to be the soul of the enterprise of which France was to furnish the body. Guise advanced alone for the conquest of Naples, and he found himself, like De Lautrec in 1528, baffled by an enemy who would not meet him in the field, and obliged to waste his time and the health of his army in a series of unsuccessful sieges, till in a few months the climate had done Alva's work. The French troops perished in thousands, and Guise at last drew off his thinned ranks and fell back on Rome. Here the news of St. Quentin reached him, and the duke, leaving Paul to his fate, amid a storm of mutual reproaches, hurried back to his own country.

The pontiff had now no resource but to yield; and the piety of the Spaniards, whom he had compelled against their will to be his enemies, softened the ignominy of his compelled submission. Cardinal Caraffa and the Duke of Alva met at Cava, where, in a few words, it was agreed that his holiness should relinquish his alliance with France, and cease to trouble the Colonnas. Alva, on his side, restored the papal towns which he had taken; he went to Rome to ask pardon on his knees, in Philip's name, for the violence which he had used to his spiritual father; and the pope gave him gracious absolution.

This bad business, which had tried Mary so severely, was thus well finished, and on the 6th of October London was again illuminated for the peace between the king and the papacy. But the shadow which had been thrown on Pole was maliciously permitted to remain unremoved; on him, perhaps from personal ill-feeling, Paul visited his own disappointment. With the return of peace there was no longer any plausible reason for the recall of the legation; Peto was dead, having survived his unpropitious honours but a few months: yet, unmoved by Pole's entreaties, the pope refused to permit him to resume his legatine functions, except so far as they were inherent in the archbishopric. The odious accusation of heresy was not withdrawn; and the torturing charge was left to embitter the peace of mind, and poison the last days of the most faithful servant of the church who was then living. [607]

And again, though there was peace with the pope, there was still war with France; there was still war with Scotland. The events which had taken place in Scotland will be related hereafter. It is enough for the present to say that the Scots had been true as usual to their old allies; no sooner was an English army landed in France, than a Scotch army was wasting and burning on the Border. A second force had to be raised and kept in the field to meet them, and the scantily supplied treasury was soon empty.

Money had to be found somewhere. The harvest, happily, had been at last abundant, and wheat had fallen from fifty shillings a quarter to four or five. The country was in a condition to lend, and a commission was sent out for a forced loan, calculated on the assessment of the last subsidy. Lists of the owners of property in each county were drawn out, with sums of money opposite to their names, and the collectors were directed "to travail by all the best ways they might for obtaining the sums noted." Persons found conformable were to receive acknowledgments. Should "any be froward" they were to find securities to appear when called on before the privy council, or to be arrested on the spot and sent to London. [608] A hundred and ten thousand pounds were collected under the commission, in spite of outcry and resistance; [609] but it was not enough for the hungry consumption of the war, and the court was driven to call a parliament.

The writs went out at the beginning of December, accompanied with the usual circulars; to which the queen added a promise, that if the mayors and sheriffs [610] would consult her wishes she would remember their services. In a second address she said her pleasure was that when the privy council, or any of them within their jurisdiction, should recommend "men of learning and wisdom," their directions should "be regarded and followed." [611] Yet there was not perhaps any wish to have the House of Commons unfairly packed. Mary desired, probably with sincerity, "to have the assembly of the most chiefest men in the realm for advice and counsel."

How the parliament would have acted in the circumstances under which the meeting was anticipated, is very uncertain. The intense unpopularity of the war had been little relieved by the victory at St. Quentin, and the general state of suffering made a fresh demand for money infinitely grievous. But between the issue of the writs and the 20th of January a blow had fallen on England which left room for no other thought.

For the last ten years the French had kept their eyes on Calais. The recovery of Boulogne was an insufficient retaliation for the disgrace which they had suffered in the loss of it, while the ill success with which the English maintained themselves in their new conquest, suggested the hope, and proved the possibility, of expelling them from the old. The occupation of a French fortress by a foreign power was a perpetual insult to the national pride; it was a memorial of evil times; while it gave England inconvenient authority in the "narrow seas." Scarcely a month had passed since Mary had been on the throne, without a hint from some quarter or other to the English government to look well to Calais; and the recent plot for its surprise was but one of a series of schemes which had been successively formed and abandoned.

In 1541 the defences of Guisnes, Hammes, and Calais, had been repaired by Henry VIII. The dykes had been cleared and enlarged, the embankments strengthened, and the sluices put in order. [612] But in the wasteful times of Edward, the works had fallen again into ruin; and Mary, straitened by debt, by a diminished revenue, and a supposed obligation to make good the losses of the clergy, had found neither means nor leisure to attend to them.

In the year 1500, the cost of maintaining the three fortresses was something less than £10,000 a-year; [613] and the expense had been almost or entirely supported by the revenue of the Pale. The more extended fortifications had necessitated an increase in the garrison; two hundred men were now scarcely sufficient to man the works; [614] while, owing to bad government, and the growing anomaly of the English position, the wealthier inhabitants had migrated over the frontiers, and left the Pale to a scanty, wretched, starving population, who could scarcely extract from the soil sufficient for their own subsistence. [615] While the cost of the occupation was becoming greater, the means of meeting it became less. The country could no longer thrive in English hands, and it was time for the invaders to begone.

The government in London, however, seemed, notwithstanding warnings, to be unable to conceive the loss of so old a possession to be a possibility; and Calais shared the persevering neglect to which the temporal interests of the realm were subjected. The near escape from the Dudley treason created a momentary improvement. The arrears of wages were paid up, and the garrison was increased. Yet a few months after, when war was on the point of being declared, there were but two hundred men in Guisnes, a number inadequate to defend even the castle; and although the French fleet at that time commanded the Channel, Calais contained provisions to last but for a few weeks. [616] Lord Grey, the governor of Guisnes, reported in June, after the declaration, that the French were collecting in strength in the neighbourhood, and that unless he was reinforced, he was at their mercy. A small detachment was sent over in consequence of Grey's letter; but on the 2nd of July Sir Thomas Cornwallis informed the queen that the numbers were still inadequate. "The enemy," Cornwallis said, "perceiving our weakness, maketh daily attempts upon your subjects, who are much abashed to see the courage of your enemies, whom they are not able to hurt nor yet defend themselves." He entreated that a larger force should be sent immediately, and maintained in the Pale during the war. The charge would be great, but the peril would be greater if the men were not provided; and as her majesty had been pleased to enter into the war, her honour must be more considered than her treasure. [617]

The arrival of the army under Pembroke removed the immediate ground for alarm; and after the defeat of the French, the danger was supposed to be over altogether. The queen was frightened at the expenses which she was incurring, and again allowed the establishment to sink below the legitimate level. Lord Wentworth was left at Calais with not more than five hundred men. Grey had something more than a thousand at Guisnes, but a part only were English; the rest were Burgundians and Spaniards. More unfortunately also, a proclamation had forbidden the export of corn in England, from which Calais had not been excepted. Guisnes and Hammes depended for their supplies on Calais, and by the middle of the winter there was an actual scarcity of food. [618]

Up to the beginning of December, notwithstanding, there were no external symptoms to create uneasiness; military movements lay under the usual stagnation of winter, and except a few detachments on the frontiers of the Pale, who gave trouble by marauding excursions, the French appeared to be resting in profound repose. On the 1st of December, the governor of Guisnes reported an expedition for the destruction of one of their outlying parties, which had been accomplished with ominous cruelty.

"I advertised your grace," Lord Grey wrote to the queen, "how I purposed to make a journey to a church called Bushing, strongly fortified by the enemy, much annoying this your majesty's frontier. It may please your majesty, upon Monday last, at nine of the clock at night, having with me Mr. Aucher marshal of Calais, Mr. Alexander captain of Newnham Bridge, Sir Henry Palmer, my son, [619] and my cousin Louis Dives, with such horsemen and footmen as could be conveniently spared abroad in service, leaving your majesty's pieces in surety, I took my journey towards the said Bushing, and carried with me two cannon and a sacre, for that both the weather and the ways served well to the purpose, and next morning came hither before day. And having before our coming enclosed the said Bushing with two hundred footmen harquebuziers, I sent an officer to summon the same in the king's highness' and your majesty's name; whereunto the captain there, a man of good estimation, who the day before was sent there with twelve men by M. Senarpont, captain of Boulogne, answered that he was not minded to render, but would keep it with such men as he had, which were forty in number or thereabouts, even to the death; and further said, if their fortune was so to lose their lives, he knew that the king his master had more men alive to serve, with many other words of French bravery. Upon this answer, I caused the gunners to bring up their artillery to plank, and then shot off immediately ten or twelve times. But yet for all this they would not yield. At length, when the cannon had made an indifferent breach, the Frenchmen made signs to parley, and would gladly have rendered; but I again, weighing it not meet to abuse your majesty's service therein, and having Sir H. Palmer there hurt, and some others of my men, refused to receive them, and, according to the law of arms, put as many of them to the sword as could be gotten at the entry of the breach, and all the rest were blown up with the steeple at the rasing thereof, and so all slain." [620]

The law of arms forbade the defence of a fort not rationally defensible; but it was over hardly construed against a gallant gentleman. Grey was a fierce, stern man. It was Grey who hung the priests in Oxfordshire from their church towers. It was Grey who led the fiery charge upon the Scots at Musselburgh, and with a pike wound, which laid open cheek, tongue, and palate, he "pursued out the chase," till, choked by heat, dust, and his own blood, he was near falling under his horse's feet. [621]

Three weeks passed, and still the French had made no sign. On the 22nd an indistinct rumour came to Guisnes that danger was near. The frost had set in; the low damp ground was hard, the dykes were frozen; and in sending notice of the report to England, Grey said that Calais was unprovided with food; Guisnes contained a few droves of cattle brought in by forays over the frontier, [622] but no corn. On the 27th, the intelligence became more distinct and more alarming. The Duke of Guise was at Compiègne. A force of uncertain magnitude, but known to be large, had suddenly appeared at Abbeville. Something evidently was intended, and something on a scale which the English commanders felt ill prepared to encounter. In a hurried council of war held at Calais, it was resolved to make no attempt to meet the enemy in the field until the arrival of reinforcements, which were written for in pressing haste. [623]

But the foes with whom they had to deal knew their condition, and were as well aware as themselves that success depended on rapidity. Had the queen paid attention to Grey's despatch of the 22nd there was time to have trebled the garrison and thrown in supplies; but it was vague, and no notice was taken of it. The joint letter of Grey and Wentworth written on the 27th, was in London in two days, and there were ships at Portsmouth and in the Thames, which ought to have been ready for sea at a moment's warning. Orders were sent to prepare; the Earl of Rutland was commissioned to raise troops; and the queen, though without sending men, sent a courier with encouragements and promises. But when every moment was precious, a fatal slowness, and more fatal irresolution hung about the movements of the government. On the 29th Wentworth wrote again, that the French were certainly arming and might be looked for immediately. On the 31st, the queen, deceived probably by some emissary of Guise, replied, that "she had intelligence that no enterprise was intended against Calais or the Pale," and that she had therefore countermanded the reinforcements. [624]

The letter containing the death sentence, for it was nothing less, of English rule in Calais was crossed on the way by another from Grey, in which he informed the queen that there were thirty or forty vessels in the harbour at Hambletue, two fitted as floating batteries, the rest loaded with hurdles, ladders, and other materials for a siege. Four-and-twenty thousand men were in the camp above Boulogne; and their mark he knew to be Calais. For himself, he would defend his charge to the death; but help must be sent instantly, or it would be too late to be of use.

The afternoon of the same day, December 31, he added, in a postscript, that flying companies of the French were at that moment before Guisnes; part of the garrison had been out to skirmish, but had been driven in by numbers; the whole country was alive with troops.

The next morning (January 1, 1558) Wentworth reported to the same purpose, that, on the land side, Calais was then invested. The sea was still open, and the forts at the mouth of the harbour on the Rysbank were yet in his hands. Heavy siege cannon, however, were said to be on their way from Boulogne, and it was uncertain how long he could hold them.

The defences of Calais towards the land, though in bad repair, had been laid out with the best engineering skill of the time. The country was intersected with deep muddy ditches; the roads were causeways, and at the bridges were bulwarks and cannon. Guisnes, which was three miles from Calais, was connected with it by a line of small forts and "turnpikes." Hammes lay between the two, equidistant from both. Towards the sea the long line of low sandhills, rising in front of the harbour to the Rysbank, formed a natural pier; and on the Rysbank was the castle, which commanded the entrance and the town. The possession of the Rysbank was the possession of Calais.

The approaches to the sandhills were commanded by a bulwark towards the south-west called the Sandgate, and further inland by a large work called Newnham Bridge. At this last place were sluices, through which, at high water, the sea could be let in over the marshes. If done effectually, the town could by this means be effectually protected; but unfortunately, owing to the bad condition of the banks, the sea water leaked in from the high levels to the wells and reservoirs in Calais.

The night of the 1st of January the French remained quiet; with the morning they advanced in force upon Newnham Bridge. An advanced party of English archers and musketeers who were outside the gate were driven in, and the enemy pushed in pursuit so close under the walls that the heavy guns could not be depressed to touch them. The English, however, bored holes through the gates with augers, fired their muskets through them, and so forced their assailants back. Towards Hammes and Guisnes the sea was let in, and the French, finding themselves up to their waists in water, and the tide still rising, retreated on that side also. Wentworth wrote in the afternoon in high spirits at the result of the first attack. The brewers were set to work to fill their vats with fresh water, that full advantage might be taken of the next tide. Working parties were sent to cut the sluices, and the English commander felt confident that if help was on the way, or could now be looked for, he could keep his charge secure. But the enemy, he said, were now thirty thousand strong; Guise had taken the Sandgate, and upwards of a hundred boats were passing backwards and forwards to Boulogne and Hambletue, bringing stores and ammunition. [625] If the queen had a body of men in readiness, they would come without delay. If she was unprepared, "the passages should be thrown open," and "liberty be proclaimed for all men to come that would bring sufficient victuals for themselves;" thus, he "was of opinion that there would be enough with more speed than would be made by order."

So far Wentworth had written. While the pen was in his hand, a message reached him, that the French, without waiting for their guns, were streaming up over the Rysbank, and laying ladders against the walls of the fort. He had but time to close his letter, and send his swiftest boat out of the harbour with it, when the castle was won, and ingress and egress at an end. The same evening, the heavy guns came from Boulogne, and for two days and nights the town was fired upon incessantly from the sandbank, and from "St. Peter's Heath."

The fate of Calais was now a question of hours; Wentworth had but 500 men to repel an army, and he was without provisions. Calais was probably gone, but Guisnes might be saved; Guisnes could be relieved with a great effort out of the Netherlands. On the night of the 4th, Grey found means to send a letter through the French lines to England. "The enemy," he said, "were now in possession of Calais harbour, and all the country between Calais and Guisnes." He was now "clean cut off from all relief and aid which he looked to have;" and there "was no other way for the succour of Calais" and the other fortresses, but "a power of men out of England or from the king's majesty, or from both," either to force the French into a battle or to raise the siege. Come what would, he would himself do the duty of a faithful subject, and keep the castle while men could hold it. [626]

The court, which had been incredulous of danger till it had appeared, was now paralysed by the greatness of it. Definite orders to collect troops were not issued till the 2nd of January. The Earl of Rutland galloped the same day to Dover, where the musters were to meet, flung himself into the first boat that he found, without waiting for them, and was half-way across the Channel when he was met by the news of the loss of the Rysbank. [627] Rutland therefore returned to Dover, happy so far to have escaped sharing the fate of Wentworth, which his single presence could not have averted. The next day, the 3rd, parties of men came in slowly from Kent and Sussex; but so vague had been the language of the proclamation, that they came without arms; and although the country was at war with France, there were no arms with which to provide them, either in Deal, Dover, or Sandwich. Again, so indistinct had been Rutland's orders, that although a few hundred men did come in at last tolerably well equipped, and the Prince of Savoy had collected some companies of Spaniards at Gravelines, and had sent word to Dover for the English to join him, Rutland was now obliged to refer to London for permission to go over. On the 7th, permission came; it was found by that time, or supposed to be found, that the queen's ships were none of them seaworthy, and an order of the council came out to press all competent merchant ships and all able seamen everywhere, for the queen's service. [628] Rutland contrived at last, by vigorous efforts, to collect a few hoys and boats, but the French had by this time ships of war in co-operation with them, and he could but approach the French coast near enough to see that he could venture no nearer, and again return. [629]

He would have been too late to save Calais at that time, however, even if he had succeeded in crossing.

The day preceding, the 6th of January, after a furious cannonade, Guise had stormed the castle. The English had attempted to blow it up when they could not save it, but their powder train was wetted, and they failed. The Spaniards, for once honourably careful of English interests, came along the shore from Gravelines alone, since no one joined them from England, and attempted in the face of overwhelming odds to force their way into the town; but they were driven back, and Wentworth, feeling that further resistance would lead to useless slaughter, demanded a parley, and after a short discussion accepted the terms of surrender offered by Guise. The garrison and the inhabitants of Calais, amounting in all, men, women, and children, to 5000 souls, were permitted to retire to England with their lives, and nothing more. Wentworth and fifty others were to remain prisoners; the town, with all that it contained, was to be given up to the conquerors.

On these conditions the English laid down their arms and the French troops entered. The spoil was enormous, and the plunder of St. Quentin was not unjustly revenged; jewels, plate, and money were deposited on the altars of the churches, and the inhabitants, carrying with them the clothes which they wore, were sent as homeless beggars in the ensuing week across the Channel.

Then only, when it was too late, the queen roused herself. As soon as Calais had definitely fallen, all the English counties were called on by proclamation to contribute their musters. Then all was haste, eagerness, impetuosity; those who had money were to provide for those who had none, till "order could be taken."

On the 7th of January, the vice-admiral, Sir William Woodhouse, was directed to go instantly to sea, pressing everything that would float, and promising indemnity to the owners in the queen's name. Thirty thousand men were rapidly on their way to the coast; the weather had all along been clear and frosty, with calms and light east winds, and the sea off Dover was swiftly covered with a miscellaneous crowd of vessels. On the 10th came the queen's command for the army to cross to Dunkirk, join the Duke of Savoy, and save Guisnes.

But the opportunity which had been long offered, and long neglected, was now altogether gone; the ships were ready, troops came, and arms came, but a change of weather came also, and westerly gales and storms. On the night of the 10th a gale blew up from the south-west which raged for four days: such vessels as could face the sea, slipped their moorings, and made their way into the Thames with loss of spars and rigging; the hulls of the rest strewed Dover beach with wrecks, or were swallowed in the quicksands of the Goodwin.

The effect of this last misfortune on the queen was to produce utter prostration. Storms may rise, vessels may be wrecked, and excellent enterprises may suffer hindrance, by the common laws or common chances of things; but the queen in every large occurrence imagined a miracle; Heaven she believed was against her. Though Guisnes was yet standing, she ordered Woodhouse to collect the ships again in the Thames, "forasmuch as the principal cause of their sending forth had ceased;" [630] and on the 13th she counter-ordered the musters, and sent home all the troops which had arrived at Dover. [631]

Having given way to despondency, the court should have communicated with Grey, and directed him to make terms for himself and the garrisons of Guisnes and Hammes. In the latter place there was but a small detachment; but at Guisnes were eleven hundred men, who might lose their lives in a desperate and now useless defence. The disaster, however, had taken away the power of thinking or resolving upon anything.

It must be said for Philip that he recognised more clearly and discharged more faithfully the duty of an English sovereign than the queen or the queen's advisers. Spanish and Burgundian troops were called under arms as fast as possible; and when he heard of the gale he sent ships from Antwerp and Dunkirk to bring across the English army. But when his transports arrived at Dover they found the men all gone. Proclamations went out on the 17th to call them back; [632] but two days after there was a counter-panic and a dread of invasion, and the perplexed levies were again told that they must remain at home. So it went on to the end of the month; the resolution of one day alternated with the hesitation of the next, and nothing was done.

The queen's government had lost their heads. Philip having done his own part, did not feel it incumbent on him to risk a battle with inferior numbers, when those who were more nearly concerned were contented to be supine. Guisnes, therefore, and its defenders, were left to their fate.

On Thursday, the 13th, the Duke of Guise appeared before the gates. The garrison could have been starved out in a month, but Guise gave England credit for energy, and would not run the risk of a blockade. To reduce the extent of his lines, Grey abandoned the town, burnt the houses, and withdrew into the castle. The French made their approaches in form. On the morning of Monday the 17th they opened fire from two heavily armed batteries, and by the middle of the day they had silenced the English guns, and made a breach which they thought practicable. A storming party ventured an attempt: after sharp fighting the advanced columns had to retreat; but as they drew back the batteries re-opened, and so effectively, that the coming on of night alone saved the English from being driven at once, and on the spot, from their defences. The walls were of the old sort, constructed when the art of gunnery was in its infancy, and brick and stone crumbled to ruins before the heavy cannon which had come lately into use.

Under shelter of the darkness earthworks were thrown up, which proved a better protection; but the French on their side planted other batteries, and all Tuesday and Wednesday the terrible bombardment was continued. The old walls were swept away; the ditch was choked with the rubbish, and was but a foot in depth; the French trenches had been advanced close to its edge, and on Wednesday afternoon (January 19), twelve companies of Gascons and Swiss again dashed at the breaches. The Gascons were the first; the Swiss followed "with a stately leisure;" and a hand-to-hand fight began all along the English works. The guns from a single tower which had been left standing causing loss to the assailants, it was destroyed by the batteries. The fight continued till night, when darkness as before put an end to it.

The earthworks could be again repaired, but the powder began to fail, and this loss was irreparable. Lord Grey, going his rounds in the dark, trod upon a sword point, and was wounded in the foot. The daylight brought the enemy again, who now succeeded in making themselves masters of the outer line of defence. Grey, crippled as he was, when he saw his men give way, sprung to the top of the rampart, "wishing God that some shot would take him." A soldier caught him by the scarf and pulled him down, and all that was left of the garrison fell back, carrying their commander with them into the keep. The gate was rammed close, but Guise could now finish his work at his leisure, and had the English at his mercy. He sent a trumpeter in the evening to propose a parley, and the soldiers insisted that if reasonable terms could be had, they should be accepted. The extremity of the position was obvious, and Grey, as we have seen, was no stranger to the law of arms in such cases. Hostages were exchanged, and the next morning the two commanders met in the French camp.

Better terms were offered by Guise than had been granted to Calais— Grey, Sir Henry Palmer, and a few officers should consider themselves prisoners; the rest of the garrison might depart with their arms, and "every man a crown in his purse." Grey, however, demanded that they should march out with their colours flying; Guise refused, and after an hour's discussion they separated without a conclusion.

But the soldiers were insensible to nice distinctions; if they had the reality, they were not particular about the form. Grey lectured them on the duties of honour; for his part, he said, he would rather die under the red cross than lose it. The soldiers replied that their case was desperate;

they would not be thrust into butchery or sell their lives for vain glory. The dispute was at its height when the Swiss troops began to lay ladders to the walls; the English refused to strike another blow; and Grey, on his own rule, would have deserved to be executed had he persisted longer.

Guise's terms were accepted. He had lived to repay England for his spear wound at Boulogne, and the last remnant of the conquests of the Plantagenets was gone.

Measured by substantial value, the loss of Calais was a gain. English princes were never again to lay claim to the crown of France, and the possession of a fortress on French soil was a perpetual irritation. But Calais was called the "brightest jewel in the English crown." A jewel it was, useless, costly, but dearly prized. Over the gate of Calais had once stood the insolent inscription: —

"Then shall the Frenchmen Calais win,When iron and lead like cork shall swim:"

and the Frenchmen had won it, won it in fair and gallant fight.

If Spain should rise suddenly into her ancient strength and tear Gibraltar from us, our mortification would be faint, compared to the anguish of humiliated pride with which the loss of Calais distracted the subjects of Queen Mary.

CHAPTER VI-DEATH OF MARY

The queen would probably have found the parliament which met on the 20th of January little better disposed towards her than its predecessor. The subsidy which should have paid the crown debts had gone as the opposition had foretold, and the country had been dragged after all into the war so long dreaded and so much deprecated. The forced loan of £100,000 had followed, and money was again wanted.

But ordinary occasions of discontent disappeared in the enormous misfortune of the loss of Calais; or rather, the loss of Calais had so humbled the nation in its own eyes, that it expected to be overrun with French armies in the approaching summer. The church had thriven under Mary's munificence, but every other interest had been recklessly sacrificed. The fortresses were without arms, the ships were unfit for service, the coast was defenceless. The parliament postponed their complaints till the national safety had been provided for.

On the 26th, a committee, composed of thirty members of both houses, met to consider the crisis. [633] "That no way or policy should be undevised or not thought upon," they divided themselves into three sub-committees; and after three days' separate consultation the thirty met again, and agreed to recommend the heaviest subsidy which had been ever granted to an English sovereign, equivalent in modern computation to an income-tax of 20 per cent, for two years. If levied fairly such a tax would have yielded a large return. Michele, the Venetian, says that many London merchants were worth as much as £60,000 in money; the graziers and the merchants had made fortunes while the people had starved. But either from hatred of the government, or else from meanness of disposition, the money-making classes generally could not be expected to communicate the extent of their possessions. The landowners, truly or falsely, declared that, "for the most part, they received no more rent than they were wont to receive," "yet, paying for everything, they provided thrice as much by reason of the baseness of the money." [634] It was calculated that the annual proceeds of the subsidy would be no more than £140,000; [635] and even this the House of Commons declared that the country would not bear for more than one year. They did not choose perhaps to leave the queen at liberty to abuse their confidence by giving her the full grant to squander on the clergy. They were unanimous that the country must and should be defended. They admitted that the sum which they were ready to vote would fall short of the indispensable outlay; nevertheless, when the report of the committee was laid before them they cut it down to half. They agreed to give four shillings in the pound for one year, and to pay it all at Midsummer. "They entreated her majesty to stay the demanding of more" until another session of parliament. Should circumstances then require it, they promised that they would add whatever might be necessary; but, for the present, "if any invasion should be in the realm, or if the enemy should seek to annoy them at home, they would have to employ themselves with all their powers, which would not be without their great charges." [636]

The resolution of parliament decided the council in the course which they must pursue with respect to Calais. Philip, unable to prevent the catastrophe alone, proposed to take the field at once with a united army of English and Spaniards, to avenge it, and effect a recapture. He laid his plans before the council. The council, in reply, thanked his majesty for his good affection towards the realm; they would have accepted his offer on their knees had it been possible, but the state of England obliged them to decline. The enemy, after the time which had been allowed them, "would be in such strength that it was doubtful if by force alone they could be expelled." If England sent out an army, it could not send less than twenty thousand men; and the troops would go unwillingly upon a service for which they had no heart, at a time of year when they were unused to exposure. Before the year was out £150,000 at the lowest would have to be spent in keeping the musters of the country under arms. The navy and the defences of the coast and of the isles, would cost £200,000, without including the losses of cannon and military stores at Guisnes and Calais, which would have to be made good. The campaign which Philip proposed could not cost less than a further £170,000; and so much money could not be had "without the people should have strange impositions set upon them, which they could not bear." There was but "a wan hope of recovering Calais," and "inconveniences might follow" if the attempt was made and failed. [637]

"The people have only in their heads," the council added, "the defence of the realm by land and sea." The hated connection with Spain had produced all the evils which the opponents of the marriage had foretold, and no good was expected from any enterprise pursued in common with Philip. Prone as the English were to explain events by supernatural causes, they saw, like the queen, in the misfortunes which had haunted her, an evidence that Heaven was not on her side, and they despaired of success in anything until it could be undertaken under better auspices. They would take care of themselves at home, and they would do no more. In reducing the subsidy, the Commons promised to defend the country "with the residue of their goods and life," to "provide every man armour and weapons according to his ability," and to insist by a special law that it should be done. [638]

Every peer, knight, or gentleman, with an income above £1000 a-year, was called on to furnish sixteen horses, with steel harness, forty corslets, coats of mail, and morions, thirty longbows, with sheaves of arrows, and as many steelcaps, halberds, blackbills, and haquebuts. All English subjects, in a descending scale, were required to arm others or arm themselves according to their property. [639]

In the levies of the past summer, men had shrunk from service, and muster-masters, after the fashion of Falstaff, had taken bribes to excuse them. On the present occasion no excuse was to be taken, and every able-bodied man, of any rank, from sixteen to sixty, was to be ready to take arms when called upon, and join his officers, under pain of death. [640] With these essential orders, the business of the legislature ended, and parliament was prorogued on the 7th of March till the following November.

The chief immediate difficulty was to find money for present necessities. The loan was gone. The subsidy would not come in for six months. Englefield, Waldegrave, Petre, Baker, and Sir Walter Mildmay, were formed into a permanent committee of ways and means, with instructions to sit daily "till some device had been arrived at." [641] Sir Thomas Gresham was sent again to Antwerp to borrow £200,000, if possible, at fourteen per cent. [642] The queen applied in person for a loan to the citizens of London. For security, she offered to bind the crown lands, "so assuredly as they themselves could cause to be devised;" [643] and she promised, further, that, if she could legally do it, she would dispense in their favour with the statute for the limitation of usury.

To this last appeal the corporation responded with a loan of £20,000, at twelve per cent.; the Merchant Adventurers contributed £18,000 more; and Gresham sent from Flanders from time to time whatever he could obtain. In this way dockyards and armouries were set in activity, and the castles on the coast were repaired.

Yet with the masses the work of arming went forward languidly. The nation was heavy at heart, and it was in vain that the noblemen and gentlemen endeavoured to raise men's spirits; the black incubus of the priesthood sat upon them like a nightmare. The burnings had been suspended while parliament was in session. On the 28th of March the work began again, and Cuthbert Simson, the minister of a protestant congregation, was put to death in Smithfield, having been first racked to extort from him the names of his supporters; [644] on the same day Reginald Pole, to clear himself of the charge of heresy, sent a fresh commission to Harpsfeld, to purge the diocese of Canterbury; [645] and the people, sick to their very souls at the abominable spectacles which were thrust before them, sank into a sullen despondency.

The musters for Derbyshire were set down at fifteen hundred. Lord Shrewsbury raised four hundred from among his own dependents on his estates. The magistrates declared that, owing to dearth, want, and waste of means in the war of the last year, the "poor little county" could provide but one hundred more.

The musters in Devonshire broke up and went to their homes. The musters in Lincolnshire mutinied. The ringleaders in both counties were immediately hanged; [646] yet the loyalty was none the greater. The exiled divines in Germany, believing that the people were at last ripe for insurrection, called on them to rise and put down the tyranny which was crushing them. Goodman published a tract on the obedience of subjects, and John Knox blew his "First Blast against the Monstrous Regimen of Women." The queen, as if the ordinary laws of the country had no existence, sent out a proclamation that any one who was found to have these books in his or her possession, or who, finding such books, did not instantly burn them, should be executed as a rebel by martial law. [647] "Affectionate as I be to my country and countrymen," said Sir Thomas Smith, "I was ashamed of both; they went about their matters as men amazed, that wist not where to begin or end. And what marvel was it? Here was nothing but firing, heading, hanging, quartering and burning, taxing and levying. A few priests in white rochets ruled all, who with setting up of six-foot roods and rebuilding of roodlofts, thought to make all sure."

With the summer, fever and ague set in like a pestilence, "God did so punish the realm," said Sir Thomas Smith again, "with quartan agues, and with such other long and new sicknesses, that in the last two years of the reign of Queen Mary, so many of her subjects was made away, what with the execution of sword and fire, what by sicknesses, that the third part of the men of England were consumed." [648] In the spring, the queen, misled by the same symptoms which had deceived her before, had again fancied herself *enceinte*. She made her will in the avowed expectation that she was about to undergo the perils of childbearing. She wrote for her husband to come to her. She sent the fleet into the Channel, and laid relays of horses along the roads to London from Dover and from Harwich, that he might choose at which port to land.

Philip so far humoured the fancy, which he must have known to be delusive, that he sent the Count de Feria to congratulate her. Her letter, he said, contained the best news which he had heard since the loss of Calais. But the bubble broke soon. Mary had parted from her husband on the 5th of the preceding July, and her suspense, therefore, was not long protracted. It is scarcely necessary to say in what direction her second disappointment vented itself.

Cranmer alone hitherto had suffered after recantation; to others, pardon had continued to be offered to the last moment. But this poor mercy was now extinguished. A man in Hampshire, named Bembridge, exclaimed at the point of execution that he would submit; a form was produced on the spot, which Bembridge signed, and the sheriff, Sir Richard Pexall, reprieved him by his own authority. But a letter of council came instantly to Pexall, that "the queen's majesty could not but find it very strange" that he had saved from punishment a man condemned for heresy: the execution was to proceed out of hand; and "if the prisoner continued in the Catholic faith, as he pretended," "some discreet and learned man might be present with him in his death, for the aiding of him to die God's servant." [649] Bembridge was accordingly burnt, and the sheriff, for the lenity which he had dare to show, was committed to the Fleet. Whole detachments of men and women were again slaughtered in London; and the queen, exasperated at the determination with which the populace cheered the sufferers with their sympathy, sent out a proclamation forbidding her subjects to approach, touch, speak to, or comfort heretics on their way to execution, under pain of death. Shortly after, a congregation of Protestants were detected at a prayer-meeting in a field near the city; thirteen were taken as prisoners before Bonner, and seven were burnt at Smithfield together on the 28th of June. The people replied to the queen's menaces by crowding about the stake with passionate demonstrations of affection, and Thomas Bentham, a friend of Lever the preacher, when the faggots were lighted, stood out in the presence of the throng, and cried:

"We know that they are the people of God, and therefore we cannot choose but wish well to them and say, God strengthen them. God almighty, for Christ's sake, strengthen them."

The multitude shouted, in reply, "Amen, Amen." [650]

Alarmed himself, this time, at the display of emotion, Bonner dared not outrage the metropolis with the deaths of the remaining six. Yet, not to let them escape him, he tried them privately in his own house at Fulham, and burnt them at Brentford at night in the darkness. [651]

So fared the Protestants, murdered to propitiate Providence, and, if possible, extort for the queen a return of the Divine favour. The alarm of invasion diminished as summer advanced. England had again a fleet upon the seas which feared no enemy, and could even act on the offensive. In May, two hundred and forty ships, large and small, were collected at Portsmouth; [652] and on the day of the burning at Brentford, accident gave a small squadron among them a share in a considerable victory.

Lord Clinton, who was now admiral in the place of Howard, after an ineffectual cruise in the south of the Channel, returned to Portsmouth on the 8th of July. A few vessels remained in the neighbourhood of Calais, when M. de Thermes, whom the Duke of Guise left in command there, with the garrison of Boulogne, some levies collected in Picardy, and his own troops, in all about 9000 men, ventured an inroad into the Low Countries, took Dunkirk, and plundered it. Not caring to penetrate further, he was retreating with his booty, when Count Egmont, with a few thousand Burgundians and Flemings, cut in at Gravelines between the French and their own frontiers. They had no means of passing, except at low water, between the town of Gravelines and the sea, and the English ships, which were in communication with Egmont, stood in as near as they could venture, so as to command the sands.

De Thermes, obliged to advance when the tide would permit him, dashed at the dangerous passage; the guns of Gravelines on one side, the guns of the English vessels on the other, tore his ranks to pieces, and Egmont charging when their confusion was at its worst, the French were almost annihilated. Five thousand were killed, De Thermes himself, Senarpont of Boulogne, the Governor of Picardy, and many other men of note, were taken. If Clinton had been at hand with the strength of the fleet, and a dash had been made at Calais by land and sea, it would have been recovered more easily than it had been lost. But fortune had no such favour to bestow on Queen Mary. Clinton was still loitering at Spithead, and when news of the action came it was too late.

The plan of the naval campaign for the season was to attack Brest with the united strength of England and Flanders, and hold it as a security for the restoration of Calais at the peace. It was for the arrival of his allies that Clinton had been waiting, and it was only at the end of the month that the combined fleet, a hundred and forty sail, left Portsmouth for the coast of Brittany. They appeared duly off Brest; yet, when their object was before them, they changed their minds on the feasibility of their enterprise; and leaving their original design they landed a force at Conquêt, which they plundered and burnt, and afterwards destroyed some other villages in the neighbourhood. The achievement was not a very splendid one. Four or five hundred Flemings who ventured too far from the fleet were cut off; and as the Duke d'Estampes was said to be coming up with 20,000 men, Clinton re-embarked his men in haste, returned to Portsmouth, after an ineffectual and merely mischievous demonstration, and then reported the sickness in the fleet so considerable, that the operations for the season must be considered at an end. [653]

In the meantime, the contending princes in their own persons, Philip with the powers of the Low Countries and Spain, Henry with the whole available strength of France, sate watching each other in entrenched camps upon the Somme. The French king, with the recollection of St. Quentin fresh upon him, would not risk a second such defeat. Philip would not hazard his late advantage by forcing an action which might lose for him all that he had gained. In the pause, the conviction came slowly over both, that there was no need for further bloodshed, and that the long, weary, profitless war might at last have an end. A mighty revolution had passed over Europe since Francis first led an army over the Alps. The world had passed into a new era; and the question of strength had to be tried, not any more between Spaniard and Frenchman, but between Protestant and Catholic. Already the disciples of Calvin threatened the Church of France; Holland was vexing the superstition of Philip, and the Protestants in Scotland were breaking from the hand of Mary of Guise: more and more the Catholic princes felt the want of a general council, that the questions of the day might be taken hold of firmly, and the Inquisition be set to work on some resolute principle of concert.

On September 21, the emperor passed away in his retirement at St. Just. With him perished the traditions and passions of which he was the last representative, and a new page was turning in the history of mankind. Essential ground of quarrel between Henry and Philip there was none; the outward accidental ground — the claims on Milan and Naples, Savoy and Navarre — had been rendered easy of settlement by the conquest of Calais, and by the marriage which was consummated a few weeks after Guise's victory, between the Dauphin and the Queen of Scots.

Satisfied with the triumph of a policy which had annexed the crown of Scotland to France, and with having driven the English by main strength from their last foothold on French soil, Henry could now be content to evacuate Savoy and Piedmont, if Philip, on his side, would repeat the desertion of Crêpy, and having brought England into the war, would leave her to endure her own losses, or avenge them by her single strength. With this secret meaning on the part of France, an overture for a peace was commenced in the autumn of 1558, through the mediation of the Duchess of Lorraine. An armistice was agreed upon, and the first conference was held at the abbey of Cercamp, where Arundel, Wotton, and Thirlby attended as the representatives of England.

How far Philip would consent to an arrangement so perfidious towards the country of which he was the nominal sovereign, depended, first, on the life of the queen. The titular King of England could by no fiction or pretext relieve himself of the duties which the designation imposed upon him; and if the English were deserted their resentment would explode in a revolution of which Mary would be the instant victim. [654]

Mary, indeed, would soon cease to be a difficulty. She was attacked in September by the fever which was carrying off so many of her subjects. The fresh disease aggravated her constitutional disorder, and her days were drawing fast to their end. But Philip's hold on England need not perish with the death of his wife, if he could persuade her sister to take her place. His policy, therefore, was for the present to linger out the negotiations; to identify in appearance his own and the English interests, and to wait the events of the winter.

At the opening of the conference it was immediately evident that France would not part with Calais. The English commissioners had been ordered to take no part in the discussion, unless the restitution was agreed on as a preliminary; and when they made their demand, Henry replied that "he would hazard his crown rather than forego his conquest." [655] The resolution was expressed decisively; and they saw, or thought they saw, so much indifference in the Spanish representatives, that they at first intended to return to England on the spot.

"To our minds," they wrote, "Calais is so necessary to be had again for the quieting of the world's mind in England, and it should so much offend and exasperate England, if any peace was made without restitution of it, that, for our part, no earthly private commodity nor profit could induce us thereto, nor nothing could be more grievous to us than to be ministers therein." [656]

They were on the point of departure, when a letter from Philip required them to remain at their posts. Contrary to their expectation, the king promised to support England in insisting on the restoration, and his own commissioners were instructed equally to agree to nothing unless it was conceded. [657] Thus for a time the negotiation remained suspended till events should clear up the course which the different parties would follow.

And these events, or the one great event, was now close, and the shadows were drawing down over the life of the unfortunate Mary. Amidst discontent and misery at home, disgrace and failure abroad, the fantastic comparisons, the delirious analogies, the child which was to be born of the Virgin Mary for the salvation of mankind — where were now these visionary and humiliating dreams?

On the 6th of October, the privy council were summoned to London "for great and urgent affairs." At the beginning of November three men and two women suffered at Canterbury. They were the last who were put to death, and had been presented by Pole in person to be visited "with condign punishment." [658] On the 5th, parliament met, and the promised second subsidy was demanded, but the session was too brief for a resolution. The queen's life, at the time of the opening, was a question perhaps of hours, at most of days; and aware of what was impending, Philip despatched the Count de Feria to her with a desire that she should offer no objections to the succession of Elizabeth.

The count reached London on the 9th of November. He was admitted to an interview, and the queen, too brave to repine at what was now inevitable, and anxious to the last to please her husband, declared herself "well content" that it should be as he wished; she entreated only that her debts might be paid, and that "religion" should not be changed.

Leaving Mary's deathbed, De Feria informed the council of the king's request, and from the council hastened to the house of Lord Clinton, a few miles from London, where Elizabeth was staying. In Philip's name, he informed her that her succession was assured; his master had used his influence in her favour, and no opposition need be anticipated.

Elizabeth listened graciously. That Philip's services to her, however, had been so considerable as De Feria told her, she was unable to allow. She admitted, and admitted thankfully, the good offices which he had shown to her when she was at Woodstock. She was perhaps ignorant that it was for the safety of Philip's life that her own had been so nearly sacrificed; that Philip's interest in her succession had commenced only when his own appeared impossible. But she knew how narrow had been her escape; she had neither forgotten her danger, nor ceased to resent her treatment. It was to the people of England, she told the count, that she owed her real gratitude. The people had saved her from destruction; the people had prevented her sister from changing the settlement of the crown. She would be the people's queen, and she would reign in the people's interest.

De Feria feared, from what she said, that "in religion she would not go right." The ladies by whom she was surrounded were suspected; Sir William Cecil, whose conformity was as transparent then as it is now, would be her principal secretary; and the count observed, with a foreboding of evil, that "she had an admiration for the king her father's mode of ruling;" and that of the legate she spoke with cold severity. [659]

It is possible that Pole was made acquainted with Elizabeth's feelings towards him. To himself personally, those feelings were of little moment, for he, too, like the queen, was dying—dying to be spared a second exile, and the wretchedness of seeing with his eyes the dissolution of the phantom fabric which he had given the labours of his life to build.

Yet what he did not live to behold he could not have failed to anticipate. The spirit of Henry VIII. was rising from the grave to scatter his work to all the winds; while he, the champion of Heaven, the destroyer of heresy, was lying himself under a charge of the same crime, with the pope for his accuser. Without straining too far the licence of imagination, we may believe that the disease which was destroying him was chiefly a broken heart. But it was painful to him to lie under the ill opinion of the person who was so soon to be on the throne of England; and possibly he wished to leave her, as a legacy, the warning entreaties of a dying man.

Three days after De Feria's visit, therefore, Pole sent the Dean of Worcester to Elizabeth with a message, the import of which is unknown; and a short letter, as the dean's credentials, saying only that the legate desired, before he should depart, to leave all persons satisfied of him, and especially her grace. [660]

This was the 14th of November. The same day, or the day after, a lady-in-waiting carried the queen's last wishes to her successor. They were the same which she had already mentioned to De Feria—that her debts should be paid, and that the Catholic religion might be maintained, with an additional request that her servants should be properly cared for. [661] Then, taking leave of a world in which she had played so ill a part, she prepared, with quiet piety, for the end. On the 16th, at midnight, she received the last rites of the church. Towards morning, as she was sinking, mass was said at her bedside. At the elevation of the Host, unable to speak or move, she fixed her eyes upon the body of her Lord; and as the last words of the benediction were uttered, her head sunk, and she was gone.

A few hours later (November 17), at Lambeth, Pole followed her, and the reign of the pope of England, and the reign of terror, closed together.

No English sovereign ever ascended the throne with larger popularity than Mary Tudor. The country was eager to atone to her for her mother's injuries; and the instinctive loyalty of the English towards their natural sovereign was enhanced by the abortive efforts of Northumberland to rob her of her inheritance. She had reigned little more than five years, and she descended into the grave amidst curses deeper than the acclamations which had welcomed her accession. In that brief time she had swathed her name in the horrid epithet which will cling to it for ever; and yet from the passions which in general tempt sovereigns into crime, she was entirely free: to the time of her accession she had lived a blameless, and, in many respects, a noble life; and few men or women have lived less capable of doing knowingly a wrong thing.

Philip's conduct, which could not extinguish her passion for him, and the collapse of the inflated imaginations which had surrounded her supposed pregnancy, it can hardly be doubted, affected her sanity. Those forlorn hours when she would sit on the ground with her knees drawn to her face; those restless days and nights when, like a ghost, she would wander about the palace galleries, rousing herself only to write tear-blotted letters to her husband; those bursts of fury over the libels dropped in her way; or the marchings in procession behind the host in the London streets — these are all symptoms of hysterical derangement, and leave little room, as we think of her, for other feelings than pity. But if Mary was insane, the madness was of a kind which placed her absolutely under her spiritual directors; and the responsibility for her cruelties, if responsibility be anything but a name, rests first with Gardiner, who commenced them, and, secondly, and in a higher degree, with Reginald Pole. Because Pole, with the council, once interfered to prevent an imprudent massacre in Smithfield; because, being legate, he left the common duties of his diocese to subordinates, he is not to be held innocent of atrocities which could neither have been commenced nor continued without his sanction; and he was notoriously the one person in the council whom the queen absolutely trusted. The revenge of the clergy for their past humiliations, and the too natural tendency of an oppressed party to abuse suddenly recovered power, combined to originate the Marian persecution. The rebellions and massacres, the political scandals, the universal suffering throughout the country during Edward's minority, had created a general bitterness in all classes against the Reformers; the Catholics could appeal with justice to the apparent consequences of heretical opinions; and when the reforming preachers themselves denounced so loudly the irreligion which had attended their success, there was little wonder that the world took them at their word, and was ready to permit the use of strong suppressive measures to keep down the unruly tendencies of uncontrolled fanatics.

But neither these nor any other feelings of English growth could have produced the scenes which have stamped this unhappy reign with a character so frightful. The parliament which re-enacted the Lollard statutes, had refused to restore the Six Articles as being too severe; yet under the Six Articles twenty-one persons only suffered in six years; while, perhaps, not twice as many more had been executed under the earlier acts in the century and a half in which they had stood on the Statute roll. The harshness of the law confined the action of it to men who were definitely dangerous; and when the bishops' powers were given back to them, there was little anticipation of the manner in which those powers would be misused.

And that except from some special influences they would not have been thus misused, the local character of the persecution may be taken to prove. The storm was violent only in London, in Essex, which was in the diocese of London, and in Canterbury. It raged long after the death of Gardiner; and Gardiner, though he made the beginning, ceased after the first few months to take further part in it. The Bishop of Winchester would have had a persecution, and a keen one; but the fervour of others left his lagging zeal far behind. For the first and last time the true Ultramontane spirit was dominant in England; the genuine conviction that, as the orthodox prophets and sovereigns of Israel slew the worshippers of Baal, so were Catholics rulers called upon, as their first duty, to extirpate heretics as the enemies of God and man.

The language of the legate to the city of London shows the devout sincerity with which he held that opinion himself. Through him, and sustained by his authority, the queen held it; and by these two the ecclesiastical government of England was conducted.

Archbishop Parker, who succeeded Pole at Canterbury, and had therefore the best opportunity of knowing what his conduct had really been, called him *Carnifex et flagellum Ecclesæ Anglicanæ*, the hangman and the scourge of the Church of England. His character was irreproachable; in all the virtues of the Catholic Church he walked without spot or stain; and the system to which he had surrendered himself had left to him of the common selfishnesses of mankind his enormous vanity alone. But that system had extinguished also in him the human instincts, the genial emotions by which theological theories stand especially in need to be corrected. He belonged to a class of persons at all times numerous, in whom enthusiasm takes the place of understanding; who are men of an "idea;" and unable to accept human things as they are, are passionate loyalists, passionate churchmen, passionate revolutionists, as the accidents of their age may determine. Happily for the welfare of mankind, persons so constituted rarely arrive at power: should power come to them, they use it, as Pole used it, to defeat the ends which are nearest to their hearts.

The teachers who finally converted the English nation to Protestantism were not the declaimers from the pulpit, nor the voluminous controversialists with the pen. These, indeed, could produce arguments which, to those who were already convinced, seemed as if they ought to produce conviction; but conviction did not follow till the fruits of the doctrine bore witness to the spirit from which it came. The evangelical teachers, caring only to be allowed to develop their own opinions, and persecute their opponents, had walked hand in hand with men who had spared neither tomb nor altar, who had stripped the lead from the church roofs, and stolen the bells from the church towers; and between them they had so outraged such plain honest minds as remained in England, that had Mary been content with mild repression, had she left the pope to those who loved him, and married, instead of Philip, some English lord, the mass would have retained its place, the clergy in moderate form would have resumed their old authority, and the Reformation would have waited for a century. In an evil hour, the queen listened to the unwise advisers, who told her that moderation in religion was the sin of the Laodicæans; and while the fanatics who had brought scandal on the Reforming cause, either truckled, like Shaxton, or stole abroad to wrangle over surplices and forms of prayer, the true and the good atoned with their lives for the crimes of others, and vindicated a noble cause by nobly dying for it.

And while among the Reformers that which was most bright and excellent shone out with preternatural lustre, so were the Catholics permitted to exhibit also the preternatural features of the creed which was expiring.

Although Pole and Mary could have laid their hands on earl and baron, knight and gentleman, whose heresy was notorious, although in the queen's own guard there were many who never listened to a mass, [662] they dared not strike where there was danger that they would be struck in return. They went out into the highways and hedges; they gathered up the lame, the halt, and the blind; they took the weaver from his loom, the carpenter from his workshop, the husbandman from his plough; they laid hands on maidens and boys "who had never heard of any other religion than that which they were called on to abjure;" [663] old men tottering into the grave, and children whose lips could but just lisp the articles of their creed; and of these they made their burnt-offerings; with these they crowded their prisons, and when filth and famine killed them, they flung them out to rot. How long England would have endured the repetition of the horrid spectacles is hard to say. The persecution lasted three years, and in that time something less than 300 persons were burnt at the stake. [664] "By imprisonment," said Lord Burghley, "by torment, by famine, by fire, almost the number of 400 were," in their various ways, "lamentably destroyed."

Yet, as has been already said, interference was impossible except by armed force. The country knew from the first that by the course of nature the period of cruelty must be a brief one; it knew that a successful rebellion is at best a calamity; and the bravest and wisest men would not injure an illustrious cause by conduct less than worthy of it, so long as endurance was possible. They had saved Elizabeth's life and Elizabeth's rights, and Elizabeth, when her time came, would deliver her subjects. The Catholics, therefore, were permitted to continue their cruelties till the cup of iniquity was full; till they had taught the educated laity of England to regard them with horror; and till the Romanist superstition had died, amidst the execrations of the people, of its own excess.

INDEX

Doria, Andrea .
Drury, Sir Wm. .
Dudley, Lord Ambrose .
Dudley, Sir Andrew .
Dudley, Lord Guilford .
Dudley, Lord Henry .
Dudley, Sir Henry .
Dudley, Lord Robert .
Dunkirk, plundering of .
Durham, Bishop of .
Dymocke, Sir Ed. .

Edgecumbe, Sir Richard .
EdwardVI. .
Egmont, Count .
Elder, John .
Elizabeth Tudor .
d'Enghien, Duc .
Englefield, Sir Francis .
d'Estampes, Duke .
Exeter, Marchioness of .

Fagius, Paul .
Famine in England .
Feckenham, Abbot .
Feria, Count de .
Ferrars, Robert .
Fitzgerald .
Fitzwalter, Lord .
Fitzwarren .
Flanders MSS. .
Flower, Wm. .
Foxe, quoted .
Framlingham .

Gage, Sir John .
Gardiner, Stephen .
Gates, Sir Henry .
Gates, Sir John .
Goldwell, Thos. .
Gomez, Ruy .

London Bridge, closing of .
Longueville, Duke de .
*Lords Journals*quoted .
Lorraine, Cardinal of .
Low Countries, campaign in .

Machyn .
Markham, Wm. .
Marsh, George .
Martin, Dr. .
Martyn, Peter .
Mary, Chronicles of Queen .
Mary, Queen of Scots .
Mason, Sir John .
Mendoza, Diego de .
Merchant adventurers, loan of the .
Mewtas, Sir Peter .
Michele, Giovanni .
Mildmay, Sir Walter .
Mohun's Ottery .
Money, shortage of .
Mordaunt, Lord .
Moreman, Dr. .
Montague, Judge .
Montague, Lord .
Montmorency .
Montpensier, Duke de .
Morgan, Bishop .
Morone, Cardinal .
Mortmain, Statute of
suspended .
Mountain, Thos. .

Namur attacked .
Navas, Marquis delas .
Newhall .
Newnham Bridge .
Nichols, John Gough .
de Nigry .
Noaillesreferred to .
Norfolk, Duke of .

Ponet, Bishop .
Potter, Gilbert .
Premunire, Act of .
Prideaux, John .
Property of Church .
Protestants, set-back to
hangingof .

Radcliff, Sir Humfrey .
Rampton, Thos. .
Regency Bill .
Register introduced .
Religious houses rebuilt .
Religious Persecution Bills .
Renard quoted .
Renty, attack on .
Repeal, Act of .
Rich, Lord .
Richmond, Mary at .
Ridley, Bishop .
Rochester, Sir Robert .
Rochester, rising at .
Rogers, Canon .
Rolls House MSS. .
Rome, supplication to .
Rosey .
Russell, Lord .
Rutland, Earl of .
Rymer quoted .
Rysbank .

St. André, Marshal .
St. Leger, Sir Anthony .
St. Lowe, Sir Wm. .
St. Mary Overy, Church of .
St. Quentin, battle of .
Salkyns quoted .
Sandars, Laurence .
Sanders, Ninian .
Sandgate .
Sandys, Edwin .

Thornton, Bishop .
Throgmorton, Sir Nicholas .
Throgmortons, the .
Toledo, Antonio de .
Tomkins .
Treason, Act of .
Tregonwell, Dr. .
Tremayne, Edmund .
Tremaynes of Colacombe, the .
Tucker, Lazarus .
Tunstal, Cuthbert .
Tytler quoted .

Underhill, Ed. .
Uvedale .

Valles, Marquisde los .
Vannes, Peter .
Vaughan, Cuthbert .
Villegaignon, Admiral .

Waldegrave, Sir Ed. .
Walpole .
Warne .
Warner, Sir Edmund .
Warwick, Earl of .
Watson, Bishop .
Watson, Dr. .
Wentworth, Lord .
Westmoreland, Lord .
Weston, Dr. .
Wharton, Lord .
White, Bishop .
White, Rawlins .
White, Thomas .
Wight, Isle of .
Wilkins quoted .
Wilkinson, Mrs. .
Williams, Lord, of Thame .
Willoughby, Lord .

Footnote 1: *Grey Friars' Chronicle*:
Machyn. (Back to Main Text)

Footnote 2: Baoardo's *History of the Revolution
in England on the Death of Edward VI.*, printed
at Venice, 1558. A copy of this rare book is in the
Bodleian Library at Oxford. (Back to Main Text)

Footnote 3: Avant nostre arrivée elle mist en delibération
avec aulcungs de ses plus confidens ce qu'elle debvroit faire,
advenant la dicte morte; la quelle treuva, que incontinant
la dicte morte decouverte, elle se debvoit publier royne
par lettres et escriptz, et qu'en ce faisant, elle conciteroit
plusieurs à se déclairer pour la maintenir telle, (et aussy
que y a quelque observance par de çà que celuy ou celle qui
est appelé à la couronne se doit incontinent tel déclairer et
publier) pour la haine qu'ilz portent audict duc, le tenant
tiran et indigne; s'estant absolument resolue qu'elle debvoit
suyvre ceste conclusion et conseil, aultrement elle tomberoit
en danger de sa personne plus grand qu'elle n'est et perdroit
l'espoir de parvenir à la couronne. La quelle conclusion
avons treuvé estrange, difficile, et dangereuse, pour les
raisons soubzcriptes: pour aultant que toutes les forces du
pays sont ès mains dudict duc: que la dicte dame n'a espoir
de contraires forces ny d'assistance pour donner pied à
ceulx qu'ilz adhérer luy vouldroient; que se publiant royne,
le roy et royne désignés par le dict testament (encores qu'il
soit mal) prendroient fondement, de l'invahir par la force
et que n'y aura moien d'y résister si vostre majesté ne s'en
empesche; ce que avons pesé pour les grands affaires et

empeschemens qu'elle a contre les Françoys et en divers lieux, que ne semble convenir que l'on concite en ceste saison les Angloys contre vostre Majesté et ses pays. Comme n'avons peu communiquer verbalement avec elle, l'avons advertie desdicts difficultés.... Que si la noblesse ses adhérens, ou le peuple la desiroit et maintenoit pour royne, il le pourroit démonstrer par l'effect; que la question estoit grande mêsme entre barbares et gens de telle condition que les Angloys ... luy touchant ces difficultez pour le respect de sa personne et pour suyvre la fin de la dicte instruction qu'est de non troubler le royaulme au désadvantaige de vostre Majesté — The Ambassadors in England to the Emperor: *Papiers d'État du Cardinal de Granvelle*, vol. iv. pp. 19, 20. (Back to Main Text)

Footnote 4: Nous avons veu par vos lectres l'advertissement qu'avez donné soubz main à Madame la princesse nostre cousine, affin qu'elle ne se laisse forcompter par ceulx qui luy persuadent qu'elle se haste de se déclairer pour royne, que nous a semblé tres bien pour les raisons et considerations touschez en vosdictes lectres. — The Emperor to the Ambassadors: Ibid. pp. 24, 25. (Back to Main Text)

Footnote 5: Ne se pouvoient faire grand fondement sur la faveur et affection que aulcuns particuliers et le peuple peuvent porter à nostredicte cousine, ne fust que y en y eust plus grant nombre ou des principaulx, n'estant cela souffisant pour contreminer la negociation si fondée et de si longue main que le dict duc de Northumberland a empris avec l'assistance que doubtez de France. — Ibid. pp. 25, 26. (Back to Main Text)

Footnote 6: Baoardo. (Back to Main Text)

Footnote 7: In the explanation given on the following Tuesday to the Emperor's ambassadors, Madame Marie was said — "N'estre capable dudict royaulme pour le divorce faict entre le feu Roy Henry et la Royne Katherine; se référant aux causes aians meu ledict divorce; *et mesme n'estre suffisante pour l'administration d'icelluy comme estant femme*, et pour la religion." — *Papiers d'État du Cardinal de Granvelle* , p. 28. Noailles was instructed to inform the King of France of the good affection of "the new King" ("le nouveaulx Roy"). He had notice of the approaching coronation of "the King;" and in the first communication of Edward's death to Hoby and Morryson in the Netherlands, a "king," and not a "queen," was described as on the throne in his place. (Back to Main Text)

Footnote 8: Letters of Lady Jane Grey to Bullinger: *Epistolæ Tigurinæ*, pp. 3-7. (Back to Main Text)

Footnote 9: Baoardo—who tells the story as it was told by Lady Jane herself to Abbot Feckenham. (Back to Main Text)

Footnote 10: La detta maestà haveva ben considerato un atto di Parliamento nel quale fu già deliberato che qualunque volesse riconoscere Maria overo Elizabetha sorelle per heredi della corona fusse tenuto traditore.—Baoardo. (Back to Main Text)

Footnote 11: Mr. John Gough Nichols, the accomplished editor of so many of the best publications of the Camden Society, throws a doubt on the authenticity of this scene, being unable to find contemporary authority for it. It comes to us, through Baoardo, from Lady Jane herself. (Back to Main Text)

Footnote 12: Edward Lord Courtenay was son of the executed Marquis of Exeter and great grandson of Edward IV. He was thrown into the Tower with his father when a little boy, and in that confinement, in fifteen years, he had grown to manhood. Of him and his fortunes all that need be said will unfold itself. (Back to Main Text)

Footnote 13: Scheyfne to Charles V., July 10: *MS. Rolls House.* (Back to Main Text)

Footnote 14: Noailles. (Back to Main Text)

Footnote 15: Renard to Charles V.: *Papiers d'État du Cardinal Granvelle*, vol. iv. (Back to Main Text)

Footnote 16: Holinshed. (Back to Main Text)

Footnote 17: Le quale parole io senti con mio gran dispiacere.—Baoardo. (Back to Main Text)

Footnote 18: Baoardo. (Back to Main Text)

Footnote 19: Se faisoit servir de mesme.—Renard to Charles V.: *MS. Rolls House.* (Back to Main Text)

Footnote 20: Renard to Charles V.: *MS. Rolls House.* (Back to Main Text)

Footnote 21: Ibid. (Back to Main Text)

Footnote 22: *Queen Jane and Queen Mary.* Renard to Charles V. (Back to Main Text)

Footnote 23: *Grey Friars' Chronicle.* (Back to Main Text)

Footnote 24: "Ille impigre quidem, utpote cujus res agebatur, proponit magna stipendia; conducit militem partim invitum partim perfidum; constabant enim majori ex parte satellitia nobilium qui secreto Mariæ favebant." —Julius Terentianus to John 'ab Ulmis: *Epistolæ Tigurinæ*, p. 243. (Back to Main Text)

Footnote 25: Renard to Charles V.: *Rolls House MSS.* (Back to Main Text)

Footnote 26: Ibid. (Back to Main Text)

Footnote 27: *Chronicle of Queen Jane.* (Back to Main Text)

Footnote 28: Noailles, vol. ii. (Back to Main Text)

Footnote 29: Ajoutant menace de la rigeur de leurs lois barbares. — Renard to Charles V.: *Granvelle Papers,* vol. iv. (Back to Main Text)

Footnote 30: *Chronicle of Queen Jane.* (Back to Main Text)

Footnote 31: Ibid. (Back to Main Text)

Footnote 32: "Aliqui subscripserunt, id quod postea compertum est, ut facilius fallerent Northumbrum, cujus consilio hæc omnia videbant fieri et tegerent conspirationem quam adornabant in auxilium Mariæ." — Julius Terentianus to John ab Ulmis: *Epistolæ Tigurinæ,* p. 242. John Knox allowed his vehemence to carry him too far against the Marquis of Winchester, who unquestionably was not one of those who advised the scheme of Northumberland. In the "aliqui" of Julius Terentianus, the letters of Renard, of Scheyfne, enable us to identify both him and Arundel; but there must have been many more, in the council or out of it, who were acting in concert with them. (Back to Main Text)

Footnote 33: Cecil's Submission, printed by Tytler, vol. ii. (Back to Main Text)

Footnote 34: Scheyfne to Charles V.: *Rolls House MSS.* (Back to Main Text)

Footnote 35: *Chronicle of Queen Jane.* (Back to Main Text)

Footnote 36: Ibid. (Back to Main Text)

Footnote 37: Cecil's Submission: Tytler, vol. ii. (Back to Main Text)

Footnote 38: Stow. (Back to Main Text)

Footnote 39: Account of a Sermon at Amersham: *Admonition to the Faithful in England,* by John Knox. (Back to Main Text)

Footnote 40: Some jest, perhaps, upon a shorn crown; at any rate, a euphemism for decapitation; for Foxe, who tells the story, says, "and even so it came to pass, for he and Sir John Gates, who was then at table, were made deacons ere it was long after on the Tower Hill." — Foxe, vol. viii. p. 590. (Back to Main Text)

Footnote 41: Foxe, vol. viii. p. 590. (Back to Main Text)

Footnote 42: Renard to Charles V.: *Rolls House MSS.* (Back to Main Text)

Footnote 43: La peine où se retreuve ledict due est qu'il ne se ose fier en personne, pour n'avoir faict où donné occasion à personne de l'aimer, — que a meu envoyer en France le Millor Dudley son frère, pour l'assurer du secours que luy a esté promis par le roy de France, et le prier en faire demonstration pour intimider ceulx de par deça. Car encores qu'il entende qu'il dégoustera davantage ceulx du pays pour y amener François, si est ce craignant d'estre rebouté de son emprinse, et d'estre massacré du peuple et sa generation, et que ma dicte dame Marie ne parvienne à la couronne, il ne respectera chose quelconque: plustôt donnera il pied aux François ou peys: tel est le couraige d'ung homme tiran, obstiné, et resolu, signamment quant il est question de se démesurer pour regner. — Renard to Charles V.: *Granvelle Papers*, vol. iv. p. 38. (Back to Main Text)

Footnote 44: The letter is among the *Lansdowne MSS*. It is in the hand of Sir John Cheke, and dated July 19. The signatures are Cranmer, Goodrich, Winchester, Bedford, Suffolk, Arundel, Shrewsbury, Pembroke, Darcy, Paget, Cheyne, Cotton, Petre, Cheke, Baker, Bowes. (Back to Main Text)

Footnote 45: Fronting the river, about three-quarters of a mile above London Bridge. The original castle of Baynard the Norman had fallen into ruins at the end of the fifteenth century. Henry VII. built a palace on the site of it, which retained the name. (Back to Main Text)

Footnote 46: E quando le persuasioni del conte d'Arundel non habiano luogo appresso di voi, o questa spada farà Reina Maria, o perderò io la vita. — Baoardo. (Back to Main Text)

Footnote 47: Renard had been prepared, by a singular notice, to expect their coming, and to suspect their good faith. Ce matin, he wrote, relating the counter-revolution to the Emperor; ce matin, à bonne heure, il y a venu une vieille femme de soixante ans en nostre logis pour nous advertir que l'on deust faire sçavoir à madicte dame Marie qu'elle se donna garde de ceulx de conseil car its la vouloient tromper soubz couleur de luy monstrer affection. — *Granvelle Papers*, vol. iv. (Back to Main Text)

Footnote 48: Baoardo to Charles V.: *Rolls House MSS.* (Back to Main Text)

Footnote 49: Narrative of Edward Underhill: *Harleian MSS*. 425. (Back to Main Text)

Footnote 50: Renard to Charles V.: *Rolls House MSS.* All authorities agree in the general description of the state of London. Renard, Noailles, and Baoardo are the most explicit and interesting. (Back to Main Text)

Footnote 51: This letter is among the *Tanner MSS.* in the Bodleian Library at Oxford. It was printed by Stowe. (Back to Main Text)

Footnote 52: "Our bounden duties most humbly remembered to your excellent Majesty. It may like the same to understand, that we, your most humble, faithful, and obedient subjects, having always, God we take to witness, remained your Highness's true and humble subjects in our hearts, ever since the death of our late Sovereign Lord and master your Highness's brother, whom God pardon, and seeing hitherto no possibility to utter our determination without great destruction and bloodshed, both of ourselves and others, till this time, have this day proclaimed in your city of London your Majesty to be our true natural sovereign liege Lady and Queen; most humbly beseeching your Majesty to pardon and remit our former infirmities, and most graciously to accept our meanings, which have been ever to serve your Highness truly, and so shall remain with all our power and force, to the effusion of our blood, as these bearers, our very good Lords, the Earls of Arundel and Paget, can, and be ready more particularly to declare—to whom it may please your excellent Majesty to give firm credence; and thus we do and shall daily pray to Almighty God for the preservation of your most royal person long to reign over us." —*Lansdowne MSS.* 3. Endorsed, in Cecil's hand, "Copy of the Letter of the Lords to the Queen Mary from Baynard's Castle." The signatures are, unfortunately, wanting. (Back to Main Text)

Footnote 53: Renard to Charles V.: *Rolls House MSS.* (Back to Main Text)

Footnote 54: Foxe, vol. viii. (Back to Main Text)

Footnote 55: Holinshed. (Back to Main Text)

Footnote 56: Foxe, vol. viii. pp. 591-2. (Back to Main Text)

Footnote 57: I must again remind my readers of the distinction between Catholic and Papist. Three-quarters of the English people were Catholics; that is, they were attached to the hereditary and traditionary doctrines of the Church. They detested, as cordially as the Protestants, the interference of a foreign power, whether secular or spiritual, with English liberty. (Back to Main Text)

Footnote 58: "Adversity is a good thing. I trust in the Lord to live to see the day her Grace to marry such an one as knoweth what adversity meaneth; so shall we have both a merciful queen and king to their subjects; and would to God I might live to have another virtuous Edward." — Epistle of Poor Pratt to Gilbert Potter, written July 13: *Queen Jane and Queen Mary*, Appendix, p. 116. The occasion of this curious epistle was the punishment of Gilbert on the pillory. The writer was a Protestant, and evidently thought the Reformation in greater danger from Northumberland than Mary. "We have had many prophets and true preachers," he said, "which did declare that our king shall be taken away from us, and a tyrant shall reign. The gospel shall be plucked away, and the right heir shall be dispossessed; and all for our unthankfulness. And, thinkest thou not, Gilbert, this world is now come? Yea! truly! and what shall follow, if we repent not in time? The same God will take from us the virtuous Lady Mary our lawful Queen, and send such a cruel Pharaoh as the Ragged Bear to rule us, which shall pull and poll us, and utterly destroy us, and bring us in great calamities and miseries." (Back to Main Text)

Footnote 59: *MS. Harleian*, 523. (Back to Main Text)

Footnote 60: Governor of Calais. (Back to Main Text)

Footnote 61: Noailles. (Back to Main Text)

Footnote 62: Charles V. to Renard, July 22: *Granvelle Papers*, vol. iv. (Back to Main Text)

Footnote 63: Elle sera odieuse, suspecte, et dangereuse. — Renard to the Emperor: *Rolls House MSS.* (Back to Main Text)

Footnote 64: Renard to Queen Mary, copy enclosed to Charles V.: *Rolls House MSS.* (Back to Main Text)

Footnote 65: Vous avez tres bien faict de desconseillier à la dicte Royne qu'elle fist les obsèques du feu Roy, ce qu'elle peult tant plus delaisser avecque le repos de sa conscience, puisque comme escripvez il est décédé soustenant jusques à la fin, selon, qu'il avoit esté persuadé de depuis sa jeunesse, les opinions de desvoyez de nostre ancienne religion: par ou l'on ne peult sans scrupule luy faire l'enterrement et obsèques accoustumez en nostre dicte religion. Et est bien que l'ayez persuadé par vostre dicte lettre à la dicte dilation. — Charles V. to Renard, July 29: *Granvelle Papers*, vol. iv. (Back to Main Text)

Footnote 66: Et il seroit a esperer que y appellant ceulx du Noort et de Cornuailles avec les autres comme ce sont ceulx qui sont demeurez plus ferme en la religion, et qui ont démonstré plus d'affection en son endroit qu'elle trouveroit envers iceulx pour tout ce qu'elle vouldroit ordonner plus de faveur. — Ibid. (Back to Main Text)

Footnote 67: Renard to Charles V.: *Rolls House MSS.* Baoardo. *Grey Friars' Chronicle.* (Back to Main Text)

Footnote 68: Renard to Charles V.: *Rolls House MSS.* (Back to Main Text)

Footnote 69: Ibid. (Back to Main Text)

Footnote 70: She, perhaps, imagined that she was not exceeding her statutable right in the refusal. The 17th of the 28th of Henry VIII. empowered any one of the heirs to the crown named in the king's will, on arriving at the age of twenty-four, to repeal laws passed not only in his or her own minority; but under circumstances such as those which had actually occurred, where the first heir had died before coming of age. The 11th of the 1st of Edward VI. modified the act of Henry, limiting the power of repeal to the sovereign in whose own reign the law to be repealed had been passed. But this act of Edward's was, itself, passed in a minority, and Mary might urge that she might repeal that as well as any other statute passed in his reign in virtue of the act of her father. (Back to Main Text)

Footnote 71: Renard to Charles V.: *Rolls House MSS.* (Back to Main Text)

Footnote 72: "La beauté de visage plus que médiocre," are Renard's words to Charles. (Back to Main Text)

Footnote 73: Renard; Noailles; Machyn; *Grey Friars' Chronicle.* (Back to Main Text)

Footnote 74: Renard to Charles V.: *Rolls House MSS.* (Back to Main Text)

Footnote 75: Et luy fust proposé l'exemple de Maximus et Victor son filz que Theodose l'Empereur feit mourir pour s'estre attribué le nom d'Empereur par tyrannie et l'avoir voulu continuer en son diet filz Victor, escripvant l'histoire que l'on feit mourir le filz pour le scandale et danger qu'en eust peu advenir. — Renard to Charles V.: *Rolls House MSS.* For the story, see Gibbon, cap. xxvii. (Back to Main Text)

Footnote 76: Renard to Charles V.: *Rolls House MSS.* (Back to Main Text)

Footnote 77: Signantment sembleroit que vostre majesté ne se deust confier en Madame Elizabeth que bien a point, et discouvrir sur ce qu'elle ne se voit en espoir d'entrer en règne, ne avoir voulu fleschir quant au point de la religion ny ouyr la messe; ce que l'on jugeoit elle deust faire pour la respect de vostre majesté, et pour les courtoysies dont elle use en son endroit encores qu'elle ny eust faict sinon l'assister et l'accompaigner. Et davantage l'on peult discouvrir comme elle se maintient en la nouvelle religion par practique, pour attirer et gaigner a sa dévotion ceulx quilz sont de la dicte religion en s'en aider, si elle avoit intention de maligner; et jaçois l'on se pourroit fourcompter quant à son intention, si est en ce commencement, qu'il est plus sure prévenir que d'estre prévenu et penser a ce que peult advenir; actendu que les objects sont evidens. — Les Ambassadeurs de l'Empereur à Marie, Reine d'Angleterre: *Granvelle Papers*, vol. ii. pp. 64-69. (Back to Main Text)

Footnote 78: *Chronicle of the Grey Friars of London*, p. 82. (Back to Main Text)

Footnote 79: August 1553. Debts of the crown. Irish debt, £36,094 18s. Household debts, £14,574 16s. Further household debts, £7450 5s. Berwick debt, with the wages of the officers, £16,639 18s. Calais debt, beside £17,000 of loans and other things, £21,184 10s. Ordnance Office, £3134 7s. Public works, £3200. Admiralty debt, £3923 4s. Debts in the Office of the Chamber, £17,968. Debts beyond the seas by Sir Thomas Gresham's particular bill, £61,068. Alderney's debt, £3028. Scilly debt, £3071. — *MS. Mary, Domestic*, vol. i. State Paper Office. (Back to Main Text)

Footnote 80: Note of things to be attended to: *MS. Mary, Domestic*, vol. i. (Back to Main Text)

Footnote 81: Another natural feature of these curious days was the arrest of suspected persons; one of whom, Edward Underhill, the Hot Gospeller, has left behind him, in the account of his own adventures, a very vivid picture of the time. Underhill was a yeoman of the guard. He had seen service in the French wars, but had been noted chiefly for the zeal which he had shown in the late reign in hunting Catholics into gaol. He had thus worked his way into Court favour. During the brief royalty of Jane Grey, his wife was confined. His child was christened at the Tower church, and Suffolk and Pembroke were "gossips," and Jane herself was godmother. The day that Mary was proclaimed, he put out a ballad, which, as he expected, brought him into trouble. "The next day," he is telling his own story, "after the queen was come to the Tower, the foresaid ballad came into the hands of Secretary Bourne, who straightway made inquiry for the said Edward, who dwelt in Lymehurst; which he having intelligence of, sent the sheriff of Middlesex with a company of bills and glaives, who came into my house, being in my bed, and my wife newly laid in childbed. The high constable, whose name is Thomas Joy, dwelled at the house next to me, whom the sheriff brought also with him. He being my very friend, desired the sheriff and his company to stay without for frighting of my wife, and he would go fetch me unto him; who knocked at the door, saying, he must speak with me. I, lying so near that I might hear him, called unto him, willing him to come unto me, for that he was always my very friend and earnest in the gospel, who declared unto me that the sheriff and a great company was sent for me. Whereupon I rose and made me ready to come unto him.

"Sir, said he, I have commandment from the council to apprehend you and bring you unto them.

"Why, said I, it is now ten of the clock at night; you cannot now carry me unto them.

"No, sir, said he, you shall go with me to my house in London, where you shall have a bed, and to-morrow I will bring you unto them in the Tower.

"In the name of God, quoth I, and so went with him, requiring him if I might understand the cause. He said he knew none."

Underhill, however, conjectured that it was the ballad. He "was nothing dismayed;" and in the morning went readily to the Tower, where he waited in the presence chamber talking to the pensioners.

Sir Edward Hastings passed through, and as he saw him, "frowned earnestly." "Are you come?" said Hastings, "we will talk with you ere you part, I warrant you." They were old acquaintances. Underhill had been controller of the ordnance at Calais when Lord Huntingdon was in command there. The earl being in bad health, his brother Sir Edward was with him, assisting in the duties of the office; and Underhill, being able to play and sing, had been a frequent visitor at the Government House. The earl, moreover, "took great delight to hear him reason" with Sir Edward, on points of controversy—chiefly on the real presence—where the controller of the ordnance (according to his own account) would quote Scripture, and Sir Edward would "swear great oaths," "especially by the Lord's foot;" on which Underhill would say, "Nay, then, it must needs be so, and you prove it with such oaths," and the earl would laugh and exclaim, "Brother, give him over, Underhill is too good for you."

Hastings, it seemed, could not forgive these passages of wit, and Underhill was too smart for them. While he stood waiting, Secretary Bourne came in, "looking as the wolf at the lamb," and seeing the man that he had sent for, carried him off into the council room. Hastings was gone, Bedford sat as President, "and Bedford," says Underhill, "was my friend, for that my chance was to be at the recovery of his son, my Lord Russell, when he was cast into the Thames by Lymehurst, whom I received into my house, and gate him to bed, who was in great peril of his life, the weather being very cold."

Bedford, however, made no sign of recognition. Bourne read the ballad; on which Underhill protested that there was no attack on the queen's title in it. No! Bourne said, but it maintains the queen's title with the help of an arrant heretic, Tyndal. Underhill used the word Papist. Sir John Mason asked what he meant by that: "Sir," he says that he replied, "I think, if you look among the priests in Paul's, you shall find some old mumpsimusses there.

"Mumpsimusses, knave, said he, mumpsimusses! Thou art an heretic knave, by God's blood!

"Yea! by the mass, said the Earl of Bath, I warrant him an heretic knave indeed.

"I beseech your honours," Underhill said, "speaking to the Lords that sat at the table (for those others stood by and were not of the council), be my good Lords. I have offended no laws. I have served the Queen's Majesty's father and brother long time, and spent and consumed my living therein. I went not forth against her Majesty, notwithstanding I was commanded."

He was interrupted by Arundel, who said that, "by his writing," "he wished to set them all by the ears." Hastings re-entered at the moment, telling the council that they must repair to the queen, and the Hot Gospeller was promptly ordered to Newgate.

The sheriff led him through the streets, his friend Joy "following afar off, as Peter followed Christ." He wrote a few words to his wife at the door of Newgate, asking her to send him "his nightgown, his Bible, and his lute;" and then entered the prison, his life in which he goes on to describe.

In the centre of Newgate was "a great open hall." "As soon as it was supper time," the board was covered in the same hall. The keeper, whose name was "Alisander," with his wife, came and sat down, and half a dozen prisoners that were there for felony, Underhill "being the first that for religion was sent unto that prison." One of the felons had served with him in France. "After supper," the story continues, "this good fellow, whose name was Bristow, procured me to have a bed in his chamber, who could play well upon a rebeck. He was a tall fellow, and after one of Queen Mary's guard; yet a Protestant, which he kept secret, for else, he said, he should not have found such favour as he did at the keeper's hands and his wife's, for to such as loved the gospel they were very cruel. Well, said Underhill, I have sent for my Bible, and, by God's grace, therein shall be my daily exercise; I will not hide it from them. Sir, said he, I am poor; but they will bear with you, for they see your estate is to pay well; and I will shew you the nature and manner of them; for I have been here a good while. They both do love music very well. Wherefore you with your lute, and I to play with you on my rebeck, will please them greatly. He loveth to be merry, and to drink wine, and she also. If you will bestow upon them, every dinner and supper, a quart of wine and some music, you shall be their white son, and have all the favour they can shew you."

The honour of being "white son" to the governor and governess of Newgate was worth aspiring after. Underhill duly provided the desired entertainments. The governor gave him the best room in the prison, with all other admissible indulgences.

"At last," however, "the evil savours, great unquietness, with over many drafts of air," threw the poor gentleman into a burning ague. He shifted "his lodgings," but to no purpose; the "evil savours" followed him. The keeper offered him his own parlour, where he escaped from the noise of the prison; but it was near the kitchen, and the smell of the meat was disagreeable. Finally, the wife put him away in her store-closet, amidst her best plate, crockery, and clothes, and there he continued to survive till the middle of September, when he was released on bail through the interference of the Earl of Bedford. — Underhill's Narrative: *Harleian MSS.* 425. (Back to Main Text)

Footnote 82: Strype. (Back to Main Text)

Footnote 83: Noailles, vol. ii. p. 111. (Back to Main Text)

Footnote 84: Monseigneur, je n'ay sceu trouver moien jusques à ceste heure de communiquer avec la royne, ce que je deliberois faire avec l'occasion des lectres de sa Majesté, si sans suspicion, j'eusse pen avoir accès, que n'a esté possible pour estre les portes en la Tour de Londres où elle este logée, si gardées que n'est possible y entrer que l'on ne soit congneu; elle m'avoit faict dire si je me pouvoys desguiser et prendre ung manteau, mais il m'a semblé pour le mieux et plus seur d'attendre qu'elle soit a Richemont. — Renard to Charles V.: *Granvelle Papers*, vol. iv. pp. 71, 72. (Back to Main Text)

Footnote 85: Renard to the Emperor: *Rolls House MSS. Queen Jane and Queen Mary*, p. 15. (Back to Main Text)

Footnote 86: Renard says it was at these words that the exasperation broke out. (Back to Main Text)

Footnote 87: Car si elle y avoit fantasie, elle ne laisseroit, si elle este du naturel des autres femmes, de passer oultre, et si se ressentiroit à jamais de ce que vous en pourriez avoir dit. — Arras to Renard: *Granvelle Papers*, vol. iv. p. 77. (Back to Main Text)

Footnote 88: Renard to the Bishop of Arras: *Granvelle Papers*, vol. iv. p. 79. Renard to Charles V., August 16: *Rolls House MSS.* (Back to Main Text)

Footnote 89: *Queen Jane and Queen Mary*. The anomaly in the constitution of the Court amused Renard, who commented upon it to the Emperor, as an illustration of England and the English character. — *Rolls House MSS.* (Back to Main Text)

Footnote 90: Renard to Charles V.: *Rolls House MSS. Queen Jane and Queen Mary*, Appendix. Baoardo says, Northampton pleaded — Ch' egli non si era mai messo in governo et che sempre attese alla caccia. (Back to Main Text)

Footnote 91: Ibid. (Back to Main Text)

Footnote 92: *Queen Jane and Queen Mary*, p 17, Renard says that he asked the council to intercede for his life. (Back to Main Text)

Footnote 93: So Renard states. The author of the *Chronicle of Queen Mary* says merely that he denied that he had borne arms against the queen, but admitted that he had been with the army. (Back to Main Text)

Footnote 94: The authority for this story is Parsons the Jesuit, who learnt it from one of the council who was present at the interview. Parsons says, indeed, that Mary would have spared the duke; but that some one wrote to the emperor, and that the emperor insisted that he should be put to death. This could not be, because there was no time for letters to pass and repass between Brussels and London, in the interval between the sentence and the execution; but Renard says distinctly that Mary did desire to pardon him, and that he was himself obliged to exert his influence to prevent it. (Back to Main Text)

Footnote 95: Gardiner. (Back to Main Text)

Footnote 96: *Harleian MSS.* 284. Compare the account of the chronicler, *Queen Jane and Queen Mary*, pp. 18, 19. (Back to Main Text)

Footnote 97: "Not for any hatred towards you," he added, "but for fear that harm might come thereby to my late young master." — *Queen Jane and Queen Mary*, p. 20. (Back to Main Text)

Footnote 98: Lady Jane Grey spoke a few memorable words on the duke's conduct at the scaffold. "On Tuesday, the 29th of August," says the writer of the *Chronicle of Queen Mary*, "I dined at Partridge's house (in the Tower) with my Lady Jane, she sitting at the board's-end, Partridge, his wife, and my lady's gentlewoman. We fell in discourse of religion. I pray you, quoth she, have they mass in London. Yea, forsooth, quoth I, in some places. It may so be, quoth she. It is not so strange as the sudden conversion of the late duke; for who could have thought, said she, he would have so done? It was answered her, perchance he thereby hoped to have had his pardon. Pardon! quoth she, woe worth him! He hath brought me and our stock in most miserable calamity by his exceeding ambition; but for the answering that he hoped for life by his turning, though other men be of that opinion, I utterly am not. For what man is there living, I pray you, although he had been innocent, that would hope of life in that case, being in the field in person against the queen, as general, and after his taking so hated and evil spoken of by the Commons; and at his coming into prison, so wondered at as the like was never heard by any man's time. Who can judge that he should hope for pardon whose life was odious to all men? But what will ye more? Like as his life was wicked and full of dissimulation, so was his end thereafter. I pray God I view no friend of mine die so. Should I, who am young and in my few years, forsake my faith for the love of life? Nay, God forbid! Much more he should not, whose fatal course, although he had lived his just number of years, could not have long continued. But life was sweet, it appeared. So he might have lived, you will say, he did not care how; indeed the reason is good; for he that would have lived in chains to have had his life, by like would leave no other means unattempted. But God be merciful to us, for he saith, whoso denyeth him before men, he will not know him in his Father's kingdom." — *Queen Jane and Queen Mary*, p. 24. (Back to Main Text)

Footnote 99: *Harleian MSS.* 284. (Back to Main Text)

Footnote 100: Renard to Charles V.: *Rolls House MSS.* (Back to Main Text)

Footnote 101: Ibid. (Back to Main Text)

Footnote 102: Noailles; Renard. (Back to Main Text)

Footnote 103: Renard to Queen Mary: *Granvelle Papers*, vol. iv. p. 65. (Back to Main Text)

Footnote 104: Renard to Charles V., September 9: *Rolls House MSS.* (Back to Main Text)

Footnote 105: Some of the Protestant bishops (Cranmer, Hooper, Ridley, and Ferrars were admirable exceptions) had taken care of themselves in the seven years of plenty. At the time of the deposition of the Archbishop of York an inventory was taken of the personal property which was then in his possession. He had five houses, three very well provided, two meetly well. At his house at Battersea he had, of coined gold, £300; plate gilt and parcel gilt, 1600 oz. Mitre, gold, with two pendants set with very fine diamonds, sapphires, and balists, and other stones and pearls, weight 125 oz.; six great gold rings, with very fine sapphires, emeralds, diamonds, turquoises. "At Cawood he had of money £900; mitres, 2. Plate gilt and parcel gilt, 770 oz; broken cross of silver gilt, 46 oz.; two thousand five hundred sheep; two Turkey carpets, as big and as good as any subject had; a chest full of copes and vestments. Household stores: wheat, 200 quarters; malt, 500 quarters; oats, 60 quarters; wine, five or six tuns; fish and ling, six or seven hundred; horses at Cawood, four or five score; harness and artillery sufficient for seven score men." —Strype's *Crammer*, vol. i. p. 440. (Back to Main Text)

Footnote 106: *Privy Council Register, MS. Mary.* (Back to Main Text)

Footnote 107: Foxe. (Back to Main Text)

Footnote 108: Strype's *Cranmer.* (Back to Main Text)

Footnote 109: Renard to Charles V.: *Rolls House MSS.* In these late times, when men whose temper has not been tried by danger, feel themselves entitled, nevertheless, by their own innocence of large errors, to sit in judgment on the greatest of their forefathers, Cranmer has received no tender treatment. Because, in the near prospect of a death of agony, his heart for a moment failed him, the passing weakness has been accepted as the key to his life, and he has been railed at as a coward and a sycophant. Considering the position of the writer, and the circumstances under which it was issued, I regard the publication of this letter as one of the bravest actions ever deliberately ventured by man.

Let it be read, and speak for itself.

"As the devil, Christ's antient adversary, is a liar and the father of lying, even so hath he stirred his servants and members to persecute Christ and his true word and religion, which he ceaseth not to do most earnestly at this present. For whereas the most noble prince, of famous memory, King Henry VIII., seeing the great abuses of the Latin masses, reformed some things therein in his time, and also our late sovereign lord King Edward VI. took the same wholly away, for the manifold errours and abuses thereof, and restored in the place thereof Christ's holy supper, according to Christ's own institution, and as the Apostles in the primitive Church used the same in the beginning, the devil goeth about by lying to overthrow the Lord's holy supper, and to restore the Latin satisfactory masses, a thing of his own invention and device. And to bring the same more clearly to pass, some have abused the name of me, Thomas, Archbishop of Canterbury, bruiting abroad that I have set up the mass at Canterbury, and that I offered to say mass before the Queen's Highness at Paul's Cross and I wot not where. I have been well exercised these twenty years, to suffer and to bear evil reports and lies, and have not been much grieved thereat, and have borne all things quietly; yet where untrue reports and lies turn to the hindrance of God's truth, they be in no ways to be tolerated and suffered. Wherefore these be to signify to the world that it was not I that did set up the mass at Canterbury, but a false, flattering, lying, and dissembling monk, which caused the mass to be set up there without my advice and counsel: and as for offering myself to say mass before the Queen's Highness, or in any other place, I never did, as her Grace knoweth well. But if her Grace will give me leave, I shall be ready to prove against all that will say the contrary, that the Communion-book, set forth by the most innocent and godly prince King Edward VI., in his High Court of Parliament, is conformable to the order which our Saviour Christ did both observe and command to be observed, which his Apostles and primitive Church used many years; whereas the mass in many things not only hath no foundation of Christ, his Apostles, nor the primitive Church, but also is contrary to the same, and containeth many horrible blasphemies." (Back to Main Text)

Footnote 110: Renard to Charles V., September 9: *Rolls House MSS.* (Back to Main Text)

Footnote 111: Before his embassy to Spain. (Back to Main Text)

Footnote 112: Opus in quatuor libros sum partitus. (Back to Main Text)

Footnote 113: "Scripta quæ nunc edo," are his own words in the apology, and therefore, in an earlier part of this work, I said that he published his book himself. There is no doubt, from the context, that in the word *scripta* he referred to that book and to no other. (Back to Main Text)

Footnote 114: "Eum ad te librum Catholice princeps nunc mitto, et sub nominis tui auspiciis cujus te strenuum pietatis ministrum præbes in lucem exire volo." — Epistola ad Regem Scotiæ: *Poli Epistolæ* , vol. i. p. 174. (Back to Main Text)

Footnote 115: "Qui si postea editus fuit magis id aliorum voluntate et illius qui mihi imperare potuit quam meâ est factum, mea vero fuit ut impressus supprimeretur." — Ibid. vol. iv. p. 85. (Back to Main Text)

Footnote 116: "Nam cum ad urbem ex Hispaniâ rediens libros injussu meo typis excusos reperissem, *toto volumine amicorum studio et operâ non sine ejus auctoritate qui jus imperandi haberet in plures libros disposito quod ego non feceram* quippe qui de ejus editione nunquam cogitâssem," etc. "Quid aliud hoc significavit nisi me ab his libris divulgandis penitus abhorruisse ut certe abhorrui." — Epistola ad Edwardum Sextum: Poli *Epistolæ*. The book being the sole authority for some of the darkest charges against Henry VIII., the history of it is of some importance.

This was not the only instance in which his recollection of his own conduct was something treacherous. In the apology to Charles V., speaking of a war against Henry, he had said: "Tempus venisse video, ad te primum missus, deinde ad Regem Christianissimum, ut hujus scelera per se quidem minime obscura detegam, et te Cæsar a bello Turcico abducere coner et quantum possum suadeam ut arma tua eo convertas si huic tanto malo aliter mederi non possis." For thus, "levying war against his country," Pole had been attainted. The name of traitor grated upon him. To Edward, therefore, he wrote: "I invited the two sovereigns rather to win back the king, by the ways of love and affection, as a fallen friend and brother, than to assail him with arms as an enemy. This I never desired nor did I urge any such conduct upon them. *Hoc ego nunquam profecto volui neque cum illis egi.*" — Epistola ad Edwardum Sextum; Ibid. (Back to Main Text)

Footnote 117: He remained fifteen days, and he left for Rome the day after the execution of Northumberland. — Pallavicino. (Back to Main Text)

Footnote 118: Cælitum ductu. (Back to Main Text)

Footnote 119: "Nec destiterat regina id ipsum Commendono indicare, eum percontata an existimaret Pontificem ad id legem Polo relaxaturum, cum is nondum sacerdos sed diaconus esset, extarentque hujusmodi relaxionum exempla ingentis alicujus emolumenti gratiâ." — Pallavicino. (Back to Main Text)

Footnote 120: Mary described her throne as, "acquistato per benevolenze di quei popoli, che per la maggior parte odiano a morte questa sancta sede, oltre gl' interessi dei beni ecclesiastici occupati da molti signori, che sono del suo consiglio." —Julius III. to Pole: *Poli Epistolæ*, vol. iv. (Back to Main Text)

Footnote 121: "Le parole che haveva inteso da lei disse di haver inteso da persone Catholice et digne di fede in quel paese." —Ibid. (Back to Main Text)

Footnote 122: "Et similmente espose l' opinione vostra con le ragioni che vi movano." —Ibid. (Back to Main Text)

Footnote 123: Julius III. to Pole: *Poli Epistolæ*, vol. iv. (Back to Main Text)

Footnote 124: "Onde se per questa molta diligenza nostra, le avvenisse qualche caso sinistro, si rovinarebbe forse (il che Dio non voglie) ogni speranza della reduttione di quella patria, levando se le forze a questa buona e Catholica regina, overo alienando la de noi par offesa ricevuta." —Ibid. (Back to Main Text)

Footnote 125: "Ayant le Cardinal Pole si expressement declairé qu'il n'a nul désir de soy marier, et que nous tenons, que pour avoir si longuement suivi l'état ecclesiastique, et s'accommodé aux choses duysant a icelluy et estant diacre." —Charles V. to Renard: *Granvelle Papers*, vol. iv. (Back to Main Text)

Footnote 126: Ibid. (Back to Main Text)

Footnote 127: "Elle jura que jamais elle n'avoit senti esquillon de ce que l'on appelle amour, ny entre en pensement de volupté, etc." —Renard to the Bishop of Arras: *Granvelle Papers*, vol. iv. (Back to Main Text)

Footnote 128: Renard to Charles V.: *Rolls House MSS.* (Back to Main Text)

Footnote 129: Noailles to the King of France: *Ambassades*, vol. ii. p. 147. (Back to Main Text)

Footnote 130: Renard to Charles V.: *Rolls House MSS.* (Back to Main Text)

Footnote 131: Ibid. (Back to Main Text)

Footnote 132: Renard to Charles V., September 23: Ibid. (Back to Main Text)

Footnote 133: Noailles. (Back to Main Text)

Footnote 134: Renard to Charles V., September 19: *Rolls House MSS.* (Back to Main Text)

Footnote 135: Noailles; Renard. (Back to Main Text)

Footnote 136: Renard to Charles V.: *Rolls House MSS.* (Back to Main Text)

Footnote 137: Ibid. (Back to Main Text)

Footnote 138: "Devant les quelz elle se mist à genoulx." — Renard to Charles V.: *Rolls House MSS.* (Back to Main Text)

Footnote 139: Ibid. (Back to Main Text)

Footnote 140: The Hot Gospeller, half-recovered from his gaol fever, got out of bed to see the spectacle, and took his station at the west end of St. Paul's. The procession passed so close as almost to touch him, and one of the train seeing him muffled up, and looking more dead than alive, said, There is one that loveth her majesty well, to come out in such condition. The queen turned her head and looked at him. To hear that any one of her subjects loved her just then was too welcome to be overlooked. — Underhill's Narrative: *MS. Harleian*, 425. (Back to Main Text)

Footnote 141: Arras to Renard: *Granvelle Papers*, vol. iv. p. 105. (Back to Main Text)

Footnote 142: Renard to the Regent Mary: *Rolls House MSS.* (Back to Main Text)

Footnote 143: "Mary, by the grace of God, Queen of England, etc.... to all mayors, sheriffs, justices of the peace, and other our subjects, these our letters, hearing or seeing: whereas we have appointed a certain number of able men to be presently levied for our service within our realm of Ireland, and to be transported hither with diligence, we let you wit that for that purpose we have authorised our trusty Sir George Stanley, Knight," etc. — October 5, 1553. From the original Commission: *Tanner MSS.* 90, Bodleian Library. (Back to Main Text)

Footnote 144: "J'estime qu'il desire presentment y veoir une bonne partie de l'Espaigne et Allemaigne, y tenir grosses et fortes garnisons, pour mortifier ce peuple, et s'en venger," etc. — Noailles to the King of France: *Ambassades*, vol. ii. p. 169. (Back to Main Text)

Footnote 145: A look at Gardiner, at this time, through contemporary eyes, assists much towards the understanding him. Thomas Mountain, parson of St. Michael's by the Tower, an ultra-Reformer, had been out with Northumberland at Cambridge. The following story is related by himself.

"Sunday, October 8," Mountain says, "I ministered service, according to the godly order set forth by that blessed prince King Edward, the parish communicating at the Holy Supper. Now, while I was even a breaking of bread at the table, saying to the communicants, Take and eat this, Drink this, there were standing by several serving-men, to see and hear, belonging to the Bishop of Winchester; among whom one of them most shamefully blasphemed God, saying:

"Yea, by God's blood, standest thou there yet, saying— Take and eat, Take and drink; will not this gear be left yet? You shall be made to sing another song within these few days, I trow, or else I have lost my mark."

A day or two after came an order for Mountain to appear before Gardiner at Winchester House. Mountain said he would appear after morning prayers; but the messenger's orders were not to leave him, and he was obliged to obey on the instant.

The bishop was standing when he entered, "in a bay window, with a great company about him; among them Sir Anthony St. Leger, reappointed Lord Deputy of Ireland."

"Thou heretic," the Bishop began; "how darest thou be so bold as to use that schismatical service still, seeing God hath sent us a Catholic queen. There is such an abominable company of you, as is able to poison a whole realm with heresies."

"My lord," Mountain replied, "I am no heretic, for in that way you count heresy, so worship we the living God."

"God's passion," said the Bishop, "did I not tell you, my Lord Deputy, how you should know a heretic. He is up with his living God as though there was a dead God. They have nothing in their mouths, these heretics, but the Lord liveth; the living God; the Lord! the Lord! and nothing but the Lord."

"Here," says Mountain, "he chafed like a bishop; and as his manner was, many times he put off his cap, and rubbed to and fro up and down the forepart of his head, where a lock of hair was always standing up."

"My good Lord Chancellor," St. Leger said to him, "trouble not yourself with this heretic; I think all the world is full of them; God bless me from them. But, as your Lordship said, having a Christian queen reigning over us, I trust there will shortly be a reformation and an order taken with these heretics." "Submit yourself unto my lord," he said to Mountain, "and you shall find favour."

"Thank you, sir," Mountain answered, "ply your own suit, and let me alone."

A bystander then put in that the parson of St. Michael's was a traitor as well as a heretic. He had been in the field with the duke against the queen.

"Is it even so?" cried Gardiner; "these be always linked together, treason and heresy. Off with him to the Marshalsea; this is one of our new broached brethren that speaketh against good works; your fraternity was, is, and ever will be unprofitable in all ages, and good for nothing but the fire." — Troubles of Thomas Mountain: printed by Strype.

The portraits of Gardiner represent a fine, vehement-looking man. The following description of him, by Ponet, his rival in the See of Winchester, gives the image as it was reflected in Ponet's antipathies.

"The doctor hath a swart colour, hanging look, frowning brows, eyes an inch within his head, a nose, hooked like a buzzard's, nostrils like a horse, ever snuffing in the wind; a sparrow mouth, great paws like the devil, talons on his feet like a gripe, two inches longer than the natural toes, and so tied with sinews that he cannot abide to be touched." (Back to Main Text)

Footnote 146: "Que s'il vouloit estre voluptueux ce n'est ce quelle desire pour estre de telle eaige." — Renard to the Emperor: *Rolls House MSS.* (Back to Main Text)

Footnote 147: Renard to the Emperor: *Rolls House MSS.* (Back to Main Text)

Footnote 148: "Vostre Majesté seit les humeurs des Angloys et leur voluntez estre forte discordantes, désireux de nouvelleté, de mutation, et vindicatifz, soit pour estre insulaires, ou pour tenir ce natural de la marine." — Renard to Mary: *Granvelle Papers,* vol. iv. p. 129. (Back to Main Text)

Footnote 149: "Les roys du passé on esté forcés de traicter en rigueur de justice et effusion de sang par l'execution de plusieurs du royaulme, voir du sang royal, pour s'asseurer et maintenir leur royaulme, dont ils out acquis le renom de tyrans et cruelz." — Ibid. (Back to Main Text)

Footnote 150: "Quanto grave peccato et irreparabil danno sia il differir cosa che pertenga alle salute di tante anime, le quale mentre quel regno sta disunito dalla Chiesa, si trovano in manifesto pericolo della loro dannatione." — Pole to the Emperor's Confessor: *MS. Germany,* bundle 16, State Paper Office. (Back to Main Text)

Footnote 151: God, he said, had joined the title to the Crown, "con l'obedientia della Sede Apostolica, che levata questa viene a cader in tutto, quella non essendo ella legitime herede del regno, se non per la legitimation del matrimonio della regina sua madre, et questa non valendo senon per l'autorita et dispensa del Papa." —Pole to the Emperor's Confessor: *MS. Germany,* bundle 16, State Paper office. (Back to Main Text)

Footnote 152: "Friday, October 13, it was declared by the commissioners that Alex. Nowel, being prebendary in Westminster, and thereby having a voice in the Convocation House, cannot be a member of this House, and so agreed by the House." —*Commons Journal,* 1 Mary. (Back to Main Text)

Footnote 153: Burnet and other Protestant writers are loud-voiced with eloquent generalities on the interference with the elections, and the ill-treatment of the Reforming members; but of interference with the elections they can produce no evidence, and of members ejected they name no more than the two bishops and the two prebends. Noailles, indeed, who had opportunities of knowing, says something on both points. "Ne fault douter, sire," he wrote to the King of France, "que la dicte dame n'obtienne presque tout ce qu'elle vouldra en ce parlement, de tant qu'elle a faict faire election de ceulx qui pourront estre en sa faveur, et jetter quelques uns à elle suspectz." The queen had probably done what she could; but the influence which she could exercise must obviously have been extremely small, and the event showed that the ambassador was entirely wrong in his expectations. (Back to Main Text)

Footnote 154: Renard to Charles V., October 19: *Rolls House MSS.* (Back to Main Text)

Footnote 155: Even the most reactionary clergy, men like Abbot Feckenham and Doctor Bourne, had no desire, as yet, to be re-united to Rome. In a discussion with Ridley in the Tower, on the real presence, Feckenham argued that "forty years before all the world was agreed about it. Forty years ago, said Ridley, all held that the Bishop of Rome was supreme head of the Universal Church. What then? was Master Feckenham beginning to say; but Master Secretary (Bourne) took the tale, and said that was a positive law. A positive law, quoth Ridley; he would not have it so; he challenged it by Christ's own word, by the words, 'Thou art Peter; thou art Cephas,' Tush, quoth Master Secretary, it was not counted an article of our faith." —Foxe, vol. vi. (Back to Main Text)

Footnote 156: Renard to Charles V., October 28: *Rolls House MSS.* (Back to Main Text)

Footnote 157: Ibid. October 15: *Rolls House MSS.* (Back to Main Text)

Footnote 158: Ibid. (Back to Main Text)

Footnote 159: Renard to Charles V., October 21: *Rolls House MSS.* (Back to Main Text)

Footnote 160: 1 Mary, cap. 1. (Back to Main Text)

Footnote 161: Report of the Disputation in the Convocation House. — Foxe, vol. v. p. 395. (Back to Main Text)

Footnote 162: Renard to Charles V., October 28: *Rolls House MSS.* (Back to Main Text)

Footnote 163: Ibid. November 8: *Rolls House MSS.* (Back to Main Text)

Footnote 164: Ibid. December 8. (Back to Main Text)

Footnote 165: Renard. (Back to Main Text)

Footnote 166: "Elle l'avoit toujours invoqué comme son protecteur, conducteur, et conseilleur." — Renard to Charles V., October 31: *Rolls House MSS.* (Back to Main Text)

Footnote 167: Renard to Charles V., October 31: *Rolls House MSS.* (Back to Main Text)

Footnote 168: "Il fauldra obtenir dispense du Pape, pour le parentage, qui ne pourra estre publique ains secrete, autrement le peuple se revolteroit, pour l'auctorité du Pape qu'il ne veult admettre et revoir." — Renard to Charles V., November 9: *Rolls House MSS.* (Back to Main Text)

Footnote 169: Renard to Charles V., November 4: *Rolls House MSS.* (Back to Main Text)

Footnote 170: "Visage intimidé et gestes tremblans." — Renard to Charles V.: *Rolls House MSS.* (Back to Main Text)

Footnote 171: Renard to Charles V., November 17: *Rolls House MSS.* (Back to Main Text)

Footnote 172: "Fort envieillie et agée." — Noailles. (Back to Main Text)

Footnote 173: Renard is the only authority for this speech, which he heard from the queen. Translated by him into French, and retranslated by myself into English, it has, doubtless, suffered much in the process. (Back to Main Text)

Footnote 174: "Ce seroit procurer l'inconvenient de sa mort." (Back to Main Text)

Footnote 175: Renard to Charles V., November 28: *Rolls House MSS.* (Back to Main Text)

Footnote 176: "Elle l'a faict quelquefois aller apres la Comtesse de Lennox, que l'on appelle icy Madame

Marguerite, et Madame Françoise, qu'est la susdicte Duchesse de Suffolk." — Noailles to the King of France, November 30. (Back to Main Text)

Footnote 177: Noailles to the King of France, December 6. (Back to Main Text)

Footnote 178: "La Reine a tres bien dissimulée, en son endroict." — Renard to Charles V., December 8: *Rolls House MSS.* (Back to Main Text)

Footnote 179: Noailles. (Back to Main Text)

Footnote 180: Renard to Charles V., December 8: *Rolls House MSS.* (Back to Main Text)

Footnote 181: Renard to Charles V.: *Rolls House MSS.* (Back to Main Text)

Footnote 182: "Le dict Paget me respondict qu'il n'estoit ja besoing d'entrer en si grande jalousie, et que tout ainsi que nous les avions faicts amys avecques les Escossoys, ce marriage seroit aussy cause que nous serions amys avecques l'Empereur." — Noailles to the King of France, December 26. Compare also the letter of December 23, *Ambassades*, vol. ii. pp. 334-356. (Back to Main Text)

Footnote 183: Renard to Charles V.: November 14, November 28, December 3, December 8, December 11: *Rolls House MSS.* (Back to Main Text)

Footnote 184: Renard to Charles V.: *Rolls House MSS.* The queen wrote to Wotton to learn his authority. The Venetian ambassador, Wotton said, was the person who had told him; but the quarter from which the information originally came, he believed, might be relied on. — Wotton to the Queen and Council: *MS. State Paper Office.* (Back to Main Text)

Footnote 185: "Un des principaulx qu'il a avec luy que se nomme William Peto, theologien, luy a escript luy donnant conseil de non se marrier, et vivre en celibat; meslant en ses lettres plusieurs allegations du Vieux et Nouveau Testament, repetant x ou xii fois qu'elle tombera en la puissance et servitude du mari, qu'elle n'aura enfans, sinon soubz danger de sa vie pour l'âge dont elle est." — Renard to Charles V.: Tytler, vol. ii. p. 303. (Back to Main Text)

Footnote 186: Instructions of Cardinal Pole to Thomas Goldwell: *Cotton MSS. Titus*, B. 11. (Back to Main Text)

Footnote 187: Renard dwelt much on this point as a reason for haste. (Back to Main Text)

Footnote 188: Marriage Treaty between Mary, Queen of England, and Philip of Spain: Rymer, vol. vi. (Back to Main Text)

Footnote 189: Renard to Charles V., December 11: *Rolls House MSS.* (Back to Main Text)

Footnote 190: "The English," he said, "sont si traictres, si inconstantes, si doubles, si malicieux, et si faciles à esmover qu'il ne se fault fier; et si l'alliance est grande, aussi est elle hazardeuse pour la personne de son Altesse." — Renard to Charles V., December 12: *Rolls House MSS.* (Back to Main Text)

Footnote 191: Charles V. to Renard, December 24: *Rolls House MSS.* (Back to Main Text)

Footnote 192: Renard to Charles V., December 20: Ibid. (Back to Main Text)

Footnote 193: The queen to Sir Thomas Gresham: *Flanders MSS. Mary*, State Paper Office. (Back to Main Text)

Footnote 194: Noailles to the King of France, December 6: *Ambassades*, vol. ii. (Back to Main Text)

Footnote 195: The Bishop of Arras to the Ambassadors in England: *Granvelle Papers*, vol. iv. p. 181, etc. (Back to Main Text)

Footnote 196: The 10th day of January the ambassadors rode into Hampton Court, and there they had as great cheer as could be had, and hunted and killed, tag and rag, with hounds and swords. — Machyn's *Diary*. (Back to Main Text)

Footnote 197: After dinner Lord William Howard entered, and, seeing the queen pensive, whispered something to her in English; then turning to us, he asked if we knew what he had said? The queen bade him not tell, but he paid no attention to her. He told us he had said he hoped soon to see somebody sitting there, pointing to the chair next her majesty. The queen blushed, and asked him how he could say so. He answered that he knew very well she liked it; whereat her majesty laughed, and the court laughed, etc. — Egmont and Renard to Charles V.: *Rolls House MSS.* (Back to Main Text)

Footnote 198: Noailles. (Back to Main Text)

Footnote 199: Ibid. (Back to Main Text)

Footnote 200: Noailles and d'Oysel to the King of France, January 15: *Ambassades*, vol. iii. (Back to Main Text)

Footnote 201: "Sire, tout maintenant en achevant cette lettre, les maire et aldermans de Plymouth, m'ont envoyé prier de vous supplier les vouloir prendre en votre protection, voulans et deliberans mettre leur ville entre vos mains, et y recepvoir dedans telle garrison qu'il vous plaira y envoyer; s'estans resoubz de ne recevoir aulcunement le Prince d'Espaigne, ne s'asservir en façon que ce soit à ses commandemens, et s'asseurans que tous les gentilz-hommes de l'entour d'icy en feroient de mesme." — Noailles to the King of France: *Ambassades*, vol. ii. p. 342. (Back to Main Text)

Footnote 202: One of the projects mooted was the queen's murder; a scheme suggested by a man from whom better things might have been expected, William Thomas, the late Clerk of the Council. Wyatt, however, would not stain the cause with dark crimes of that kind, and threatened Thomas with rough handling for his proposal. (Back to Main Text)

Footnote 203: The house of Sir Peter Carew. (Back to Main Text)

Footnote 204: Miscellaneous Depositions on the State of Devonshire: *MS. Domestic, Mary*, vol. ii. State Paper Office. (Back to Main Text)

Footnote 205: Instructions to la Marque: Noailles, vol. iii. p. 25, etc. (Back to Main Text)

Footnote 206: Noailles to the King of France: *Ambassades*, vol. iii. p. 31. (Back to Main Text)

Footnote 207: "On the morning of Christmas-day came twelve neighbours of Silverton, being the parish where Mr. Gybbes dwelleth, and they complained to me of a cross of latten, and of an altar-cloth stolen out of the church before that time; and that the cross was set up upon a gate or upon a hedge by the way, where the picture of Christ was dressed with a paste or such like tyre, and the picture of our Lady and St. John tied by threads to the arms of the cross, like thieves." "Mr. Gybbes" could not be actually convicted of having been the perpetrator, but he was "vehemently suspected," and, when examined, had used "vile words." — Depositions of John Prideaux: MS. *Mary, Domestic*, vol. ii. State Paper Office. (Back to Main Text)

Footnote 208: Depositions of John Prideaux: *MS. Mary, Domestic*, vol. ii. State Paper Office. (Back to Main Text)

Footnote 209: Ibid. (Back to Main Text)

Footnote 210: Noailles. (Back to Main Text)

Footnote 211: Confession of Anthony Norton: *MS. Mary, Domestic*, vol. iii. State Paper Office. (Back to Main Text)

Footnote 212: Confession of Anthony Norton: *MS. Mary, Domestic,* vol. iii. State Paper Office. (Back to Main Text)

Footnote 213: Renard to Charles V.: *Rolls House MSS.* (Back to Main Text)

Footnote 214: Ibid. (Back to Main Text)

Footnote 215: Charles V. to the Ambassadors in England, January 24 *Granvelle Papers,* vol. iv. (Back to Main Text)

Footnote 216: *Chronicle of Queen Mary.* Baoardo says that Suffolk was sent for to take command of the force which was to be sent against Wyatt. But Wyatt's insurrection had not commenced, far less was any resolution taken to send a force against him. Noailles is, doubtless, right in saying that he was to have been arrested.— *Ambassades,* vol. iii. p. 48. (Back to Main Text)

Footnote 217: Southwell to Sir William Petre: *MS. Mary. Domestic,* State Paper Office. (Back to Main Text)

Footnote 218: "You shall understand that Henry Lord of Abergavenny; Robert Southwell, knight, and George Clarke, gentleman, have most traitorously, to the disturbance of the commonwealth, stirred and raised up the queen's most loving subjects of this realm, to [maintain the] most wicked and devilish enterprise of certain wicked and perverse councillors, to the utter confusion of this her Grace's realm, and the perpetual servitude of all her most loving subjects. In consideration whereof, we Sir Thos. Wyatt, knight, Sir George Harper, knight, Anthony Knyvet, esq., with all the faithful gentlemen of Kent, with the trusty commons of the same, do pronounce and declare the said Henry Lord of Abergavenny, Robert Southwell, and George Clarke to be traitors to God, the Crown, and the commonwealth." — *MS. Mary, Domestic,* State Paper Office. (Back to Main Text)

Footnote 219: Renard to Charles V.: *Rolls House MSS.* (Back to Main Text)

Footnote 220: Strype, vol. v. p. 127. Mr. Tytler appeals to this letter as an evidence of the good feeling of the queen towards her sister; but many and genuine as were Mary's good qualities, she may not be credited with a regard for Elizabeth. Renard's letters explain her real sentiments, and account for her outward graciousness. She had already consulted with Renard and Gardiner on the necessity of sending her to the Tower; and, on the 29th of January, as the princess did not avail herself of the queen's proposal, Renard describes himself to the emperor as pressing her immediate arrest.— *Rolls House MSS.* (Back to Main Text)

Footnote 221: Renard to Charles V., January 29: *Rolls House MSS.* (Back to Main Text)

Footnote 222: A letter from Gardiner to Sir William Petre is in the State Paper Office, part of which he wrote with the cypher open under his eyes in the first heat of the discovery. The breadth and depth of the pen-strokes express the very pulsation of his passion: —

"As I was in hand with other matters," the paragraph runs, "was delivered such letters as in times past I durst not have opened; but now, somewhat heated with these treasons, I waxed bolder, wherein I trust I shall be borne with; wherein hap helpeth me, for they be worth the breaking up an I could wholly decypher them, wherein I will spend somewhat of my leisure, if I can have any. But this appeareth, that the letter written from my Lady Elizabeth to the Queen's Highness, now late in her excuse, is taken a matter worthy to be sent into France; for I have the copy of it in the French Ambassador's packet. I will know what can be done in the decyphering, and to-morrow remit that I cannot do unto you." — Gardiner to Petre: *MS. Mary, Domestic*, State Paper Office. (Back to Main Text)

Footnote 223: Norfolk to the Council from Gravesend, Sunday, January 28, Monday, January 29: *MS. Domestic, Mary*, State Paper Office. (Back to Main Text)

Footnote 224: "It is a great deal more than strange," he added, "to see the beastliness of the people, to see how earnestly they be bent in this their most devilish enterprise, and will by no means be persuaded the contrary but that it is for the commonweal of all the realm." — Cheyne to the Council: *MS. Mary, Domestic*, vol. iii. (Back to Main Text)

Footnote 225: Cowling Castle, a place already famous in English Reforming history as the residence of Sir John Oldcastle. (Back to Main Text)

Footnote 226: He contrived to send a letter to the queen the evening of the day on which his house was taken. After describing the scene, he added: "If your Grace will assemble forces in convenient numbers, they not being above 2000 men, and yet not 500 of them able and good armed men, but rascals and rakehells such as live by spoil, I doubt not but your Grace shall have the victory." — Cobham to the Queen: *MS. State Paper Office.* But Cobham under-estimated the numbers, and undervalued the composition of Wyatt's forces, perhaps intentionally. Renard, who is generally accurate, says that the rebels at this time amounted to three thousand; Noailles says, twelve or fifteen thousand. (Back to Main Text)

Footnote 227: Renard to the Emperor, January 29: *Rolls House MSS.* The Emperor to Renard, February 4: *Granvelle Papers*, vol. iv. p. 204. (Back to Main Text)

Footnote 228: Instructions to Sir Thomas Cornwallis and Sir Edward Hastings: *MS. State Paper Office.* (Back to Main Text)

Footnote 229: Renard to the Emperor: *Rolls House MSS.* (Back to Main Text)

Footnote 230: Holinshed; Noailles. (Back to Main Text)

Footnote 231: Vous, asseurant, sire, comme celluy qui l'a veu, que scaichant la dicte dame aller au diet lieu, je me deliberay en cape de veoir de quelle visaige elle et sa compaignie y alloient; que je congneus estre aussy triste et desplorée qu'il se peult penser. — Noailles to the King of France, Feb. 1. (Back to Main Text)

Footnote 232: La voce grossa et quasi di huomo. — Giovanni Michele: Ellis, vol. ii.] series ii. (Back to Main Text)

Footnote 233: "The Duke has raised evil-disposed persons, minding her Grace's destruction, and to advance the Lady Jane, his daughter, and Guilford Dudley, her husband." — Royal Proclamation: *MS. State Paper Office.* Printed in the additional Notes to Mr. Nichols's *Chronicle of Queen Mary.* Baoardo says that the duke actually proclaimed Lady Jane. (Back to Main Text)

Footnote 234: Rampton's Confession: *MS. Domestic. Mary*, vol. iii. State Paper Office. (Back to Main Text)

Footnote 235: Renard to the Emperor: *Rolls House MSS.* (Back to Main Text)

Footnote 236: I follow Baoardo in the account of the duke's capture. Renard says that he was found in the tree by a little dog: "qu'a esté grand commencement du miracle pour le succès prospere des affaires de la dicte dame." — Renard to the Emperor, February 8: *MS.* (Back to Main Text)

Footnote 237: Noailles. (Back to Main Text)

Footnote 238: Renard to Charles V.: *Rolls House MSS.* February 5. (Back to Main Text)

Footnote 239: The Regent Mary to the Ambassadors in England: *Granvelle Papers*, vol. iv. (Back to Main Text)

Footnote 240: Underhill's *Narrative.* (Back to Main Text)

Footnote 241: Underhill, however, was too notorious a person to be allowed to remain on duty at such a time of danger. "When Wyatt was come to Southwark," he says, "the pensioners were commanded to watch in armour that night at the Court.... After supper, I put on my armour, as the rest did, for we were appointed to watch all the night. So, being all armed, we came up into the chamber of presence with our pole-axes in our hands, wherewith the ladies were very fearful. Some lamenting, crying, and wringing their hands, said, Alas! there is some great mischief toward: we shall all be destroyed this night. What a sight is this, to see the Queen's chamber full of armed men: the like was never seen nor heard of! Mr. Norris, chief usher of Queen Mary's privy chamber, was appointed to call the watch to see if any were lacking; unto whom, Moore, the clerk of our check, delivered the book of our names; and when he came to my name, What, said he, what doth he here? Sir, said the clerk, he is here ready to serve as the rest be. Nay, by God's body, said he, that heretic shall not watch here. Give me a pen. So he struck my name out of the book." (Back to Main Text)

Footnote 242: Renard to Charles V., February 8: *Rolls House MSS.* (Back to Main Text)

Footnote 243: Letter of William Markham: *Tanner MSS.* Bodleian Library. Compare Stow. (Back to Main Text)

Footnote 244: Renard to Charles V., February 8: *Rolls House MSS.* (Back to Main Text)

Footnote 245: Holinshed. (Back to Main Text)

Footnote 246: The dress of the Londoners who came with Wyatt being the city uniform, they were distinguished by the dirt upon their legs from their night march. The cry of Pembroke's men in the fight was "Down with the daggle-tails!" (Back to Main Text)

Footnote 247: "On Sunday, the 11th of February, the Bishop of Winchester preached in the chapel before the queen." "The preachers for the seven years last past, he said, by dividing of words and other their own additions, had brought in many errours detestable unto the Church of Christ." "He axed a boon of the Queen's Highness, that, like as she had beforetime extended her mercy particularly and privately, [and] so through her lenity and gentleness much conspiracy and open rebellion was grown ... she would now be merciful to the body of the commonwealth and conservation thereof, which could not be unless the rotten and hurtful members thereof were cut off and consumed." — *Chronicle of Queen Mary*, p. 54. (Back to Main Text)

Footnote 248: *Rolls House MSS.* (Back to Main Text)

Footnote 249: Renard to Charles V., February 12: *Rolls House MSS.* (Back to Main Text)

Footnote 250: Baoardo. The writer of the *Chronicle of Queen Mary*, says, "She was appointed to have been put to death on Friday, but was stayed — for what cause is not known." Baoardo supplies the explanation. (Back to Main Text)

Footnote 251: Vol. vi. pp. 415-417. (Back to Main Text)

Footnote 252: The story told by Baoardo, to whom, it would seem, Feckenham related it. (Back to Main Text)

Footnote 253: Foxe, vol. vi. (Back to Main Text)

Footnote 254: *Chronicle of Queen Mary*, p. 57, note. In the same manual are a few words in Guilford Dudley's hand, addressed to Suffolk, and a few words also addressed to Suffolk by Lady Jane. Mr. Nichols supposes that the book (it is still extant among the *Harleian MSS.*) was used as a means of communicating with the duke when direct intercourse was unpermitted. If this conjecture is right, Lady Jane's letter, perhaps, never reached her father at all. There is some difficulty about the memorial which the Lieutenant of the Tower obtained from her. Baoardo says, that she gave him a book, in which she had written a few words in Greek, Latin, and English.

"La Greca era tale. La morte dara la pena al mio corpo del fallo ma la mia anima giustificara inanzi al conspetto di Dio la innocenza mia.

"La Latina diceva. Se la giustitia ha luogo nel corpo mio l'anima mia l'havera nella misericordia di Dio.

"La Inglese. Il fallo e degno di morte ma il modo della mia ignoranza doueva meritar pieta e excusatione appresso il mondo e alle leggi." (Back to Main Text)

Footnote 255: Andate: che nostro Signore Dio vi contenti d'ogni vostro desiderio, e siate sempre infinitamente ringratiato della compagnia che m'havete fatta avenga che da quella sia stata molto piu noiata che hora non mi spaventa la morte. — Baoardo. (Back to Main Text)

Footnote 256: The 51st: "Have mercy on me, oh Lord, after thy goodness." (Back to Main Text)

Footnote 257: *Chronicle of Queen Mary*, pp. 58, 59. (Back to Main Text)

Footnote 258: Renard says: "A hundred were hanged in London and a hundred in Kent." Stow says: "Eighty in London and twenty-two in Kent." *The Chronicle of Queen Mary* does not mention the number of executions in London, but agrees with Stow on the number sent to Kent. The smaller estimate, in these cases, is generally the right one. (Back to Main Text)

Footnote 259: On Sunday the 11th of February, the day on which he exhorted the queen to severity from the pulpit, Gardiner wrote to Sir William Petre, "To-morrow, at your going to the Tower, it shall be good ye be earnest with one little Wyatt there prisoner, who by all likelihood can tell all. He is but a bastard, and hath no substance; and it might stand with the Queen's Highness's pleasure there were no great account to be made whether ye pressed him to say truth by sharp punishment or promise of life." —*MS. Domestic, Mary,* vol. iii. State Paper Office. I do not know to whom Gardiner referred in the words "little Wyatt." (Back to Main Text)

Footnote 260: Renard to the Emperor: *Rolls House MSS.* (Back to Main Text)

Footnote 261: The Order of my Lady Elizabeth's Grace's Voyage to the Court: *MS. Mary, Domestic* vol. iii. State Paper Office. (Back to Main Text)

Footnote 262: Renard to the Emperor: February 17: *Rolls House MSS.* (Back to Main Text)

Footnote 263: "Pour desguyser le regret qu'elle a," says Renard, unable to relinquish his first conviction. (Back to Main Text)

Footnote 264: Renard was instructed to exhort the queen: "Que l'execution et chastoy de ceulx qui le meritent se face tost; usant à l'endroit de Madame Elizabeth et de Cortenay comme elle verra convenir à sa seureté, pour après user de clémence en l'endroit de ceulx qu'il luy semblera, afin de tost reassurer le surplus." —The Emperor to Renard: *Granvelle Papers,* vol. iv. pp. 224, 225. (Back to Main Text)

Footnote 265: Il est certain l'enterprinse estoit en sa faveur. Et certes, sire, si pendant que l'occasion s'adonne elle ne la punyt et Cortenay, elle ne sera jamais asseurée.—Renard to Charles V.: Tytler, vol. ii. p. 311. (Back to Main Text)

Footnote 266: Renard to the Emperor, March 8: *Rolls House MSS.* (Back to Main Text)

Footnote 267: La quelle me respondit et afferme qu'elle ne dort ny repose pour le soucy elle tient de la seuré venue de son Altesse. — Renard to the Emperor: Tytler, vol. ii. (Back to Main Text)

Footnote 268: *Granvelle Papers*, vol. iv. p. 267. (Back to Main Text)

Footnote 269: Renard to Charles V., March 8: *Rolls House MSS.* (Back to Main Text)

Footnote 270: Arundel nous dit qu'il convenoit que son alteze amena ses cuyseniers, sommeliers du cave, et autres officiers pour son bouche, que quant aux autres luy y pourvoyeroit selon les coustumes d'Angleterre. — Renard to Charles V.: *Rolls House MSS.* (Back to Main Text)

Footnote 271: Puis par la main de l'Évesque de Winchester les promesses et paroles de præsenti, furent dictes et prononcées intelligiblement par la diet Egmont seul et la dicte Dame. — Ibid. Compare Tytler, vol. ii. p. 327. The great value of Mr. Tytler's work is diminished by the many omissions which he has permitted himself to make in the letters which he has edited. (Back to Main Text)

Footnote 272: Pole's first commission granted him powers only "concordandi et transigendi cum possessoribus bonorum ecclesiasticorum, (restitutis prius si expedire videtur immobilibus per eos indebite detentis,) super fructibus male perceptis ac bonis mobilibus consumptis." — Commission granted to Reginald Pole: Wilkins's *Concilia*, vol. iv. Cardinal Morone, writing to Pole as late as June, 1554, said that the pope was still unable to resolve on giving his sanction to the alienation. — Burnet's *Collectanea*. (Back to Main Text)

Footnote 273: Paget to Renard: Tytler, vol. ii. (Back to Main Text)

Footnote 274: Par feug et sang. — Renard to Charles V., March 14: *Rolls House MSS.*; partially printed by Tytler. (Back to Main Text)

Footnote 275: Ibid. (Back to Main Text)

Footnote 276: Establir forme d'Inquisition contre les hérétiques. — Renard to Charles V.: *Rolls House MSS.* (Back to Main Text)

Footnote 277: Ibid. (Back to Main Text)

Footnote 278: La chaleur exhorbitante. — Charles V. to Renard: *Granvelle Papers*, vol. iv. p. 229. (Back to Main Text)

Footnote 279: Pour estre la plus part des Angloys sans foy, sans loy, confuz en la religion, doubles,

inconstans, et de nature jaloux et abhorrissans
estrangiers. — *Rolls House MSS.* (Back to Main Text)

Footnote 280: The French and Calais correspondence in
the State Paper Office contains a vast number of letters on
this subject. The following extracts are specimens: —

On the 24th of March Thomas Corry writes to Lord Grey that
"two hundred vessels be in readiness" in the French harbours.
"There is lately arrived at Caen in Normandy Sir Peter Carew,
Sir William Pickering, Sir Edward Courtenay, John Courtenay,
Brian Fitzwilliam, and divers other English gentlemen. It is
thought Sir Peter Carew shall have charge of the fleet. There
be three ships of Englishmen, which be already gone to sea
with Killegrew, which do report that they serve the king to
prevent the coming of the King of Spain." — *Calais MSS.*

On the 28th of March, Edgar Hormolden writes
from Guisnes to Sir John Bourne: "The number of Sir Peter
Carew's retinue increaseth in France by the confluence of such
English *qui potius alicujus præclari facinoris quam artis bonæ
famam quærunt*; and they be so entreated there as it cannot
be otherwise conjectured but that they practise with France:
insomuch I have heard credible intelligence that the said
Carew used this persuasion, of late, to his companions: Are
not we, said he, allianced with Normandy; yea! what ancient
house is either there or in France, but we claim by them and
they by us? why should we not rather embrace their love than
submit ourselves to the servitude of Spain?" — *Calais MSS.*

April 17, Dr. Wotton writes in cypher from Paris to the queen:
"Yesterday, an Italian brought a letter to my lodging, and
delivered it to a servant of mine, and went his way, so that I
know not what he is. The effect of his letter is, that for because
he taketh it to be the part of every good Christian man to
further your godly purpose and Catholic doings, he hath
thought good to advertise me that those fugitives of England
say to their friends here that they have intelligence of great
importance in England with some of the chiefest on the realm,
which shall appear on the arrival of the Prince of Spain. Within
few days they go to Normandy to embark themselves there,
so strong, that, if they do not let the Prince of Spain to land,
as they will attempt to do, yet they will not fail, by the help
of them that have intelligence with them, to let him come to
London." — *French MSS.* bundle xi. (Back to Main Text)

Footnote 281: Wotton to the
Queen: *French MSS.* bundle xi. State
Paper Office. (Back to Main Text)

Footnote 282: Noailles to the King of France: *Ambassades*, vol. iii. (Back to Main Text)

Footnote 283: "When the Ambassador replied that his master minded to do justly, her Grace remembering how those traitors be there aided, especially such of them as had conspired her death and were in arms in the field against her; and being not able to bear those words, so contrary to their doings, told the Ambassador that, for her own part, her Majesty minded simply and plainly to perform as she had promised, and might with safe conscience swear she ever meant so; but, for their part, her Grace would not swear so, and being those arrant traitors so entertained there as they be, she could not have found in her heart to have used, in like matter, the semblable part towards his master for the gain of two realms, and with those words she departed." —Gardiner to Wotton: *French MSS.* bundle xi. (Back to Main Text)

Footnote 284: On the 29th of April Wotton wrote in a cypher to Mary; "Towards the end of the summer the French king, by Peter Carew's provocation, intendeth to land the rebels, with a number of Scots, in Essex, and in the Isle of Wight, where they mean to land easily, and either go on, if any number of Englishmen resort unto them, as they say many will, or else fortify themselves there. They council the French king to make war against your Highness in the right and title of the young Queen of Scots." —*French MSS.* bundle xi. (Back to Main Text)

Footnote 285: The execution was commenced in earnest. The prince, says Noailles, "fust souldainement mesné au gibet par ceulx de la part du Roy et de M. Wyatt; et sans quelques hommes qui tout à propoz y accoururent, ils l'eussent estranglé; ce que se peult clairement juger par les marques qu'il en a et aura encores d'icy à long temps au col." —Noailles to Montmorency: *Ambassades*, vol. iii. (Back to Main Text)

Footnote 286: Dict on qu'elle veult que l'ung d'eulx soit sacrifié pour tout le peuple. —Ibid. (Back to Main Text)

Footnote 287: Ce qui faict juger à beaulcoup de gens que Wyatt ne mourra point, mais que la dicte dame le rendra tant son obligé par ceste grace de luy rendre la vie qu'elle en pourra tirer beaulcoup de bons et grandes services. Ce qui se faict par le moyen dudict ambassadeur de l'Empereur par l'advis duquel se conduisent aujourdhuy toutes les opinions d'icelle dame, et lequele traice ceste composition avecques la femme dudict Wyatt à laquelle comme l'on diet il a asseuré la vie de son dict mari. —Noailles to the Constable of France, March 31. Renard's secrets were betrayed to Noailles by "a corrupt secretary" of the Flemish embassy. — Wotton to the Queen: *French MSS.* bundle xi. State Paper Office. (Back to Main Text)

Footnote 288: Noailles says: Wyatt a esté condamné à mourir; toutesfois il n'est encores executé et avant que luy prononçer sa sentence on luy avoit promis tant de belles choses que vaincu par leur doulces paroles oultre sa deliberation, il a accusé beaulcoup de personnages et parlé au desadvantage de mylord de Courtenay et de Madame Elizabeth. — Noailles to d'Oysel, March 29. The different parties were so much interested in Wyatt's confession, that his very last words are so wrapped round with contradictions, that one cannot tell what they were. It is certain, however, that he did implicate Elizabeth to some extent; it is certain, also, that he did not say enough for the purposes of the court, and that the court believed he could say more if he would, for, on Easter Sunday he communicated, and the queen was distressed that he should have been allowed to partake, while his confession was incomplete. As to Courtenay, Renard said he had communicated enough, "mais quant à Elizabeth l'on ne peult encores tomber en preuves suffisantes pour les loys d'Angleterre contre elle." — Renard to Charles V.: *Rolls House MSS.* (Back to Main Text)

Footnote 289: Holinshed says that a certain lord exclaimed that there would be no safety for the realm until Elizabeth's head was off her shoulders; and either Holinshed himself, or his editor, wrote in the margin opposite, the words: "The wicked advice of Lord Paget." — Renard describes so distinctly the attitude of Paget, that there can be no doubt whatever of the injustice of such a charge against him. (Back to Main Text)

Footnote 290: *MS. Mary, Domestic,* vol. iv. Printed by Ellis, 2nd series, vol. ii. p. 255. (Back to Main Text)

Footnote 291: As soon as Noailles learnt that his enclosure formed part of the case against Elizabeth, he came forward to acquit her of having furnished him with it; "jurant et blasphémant tous les sermens du monde pour la justification de la dicte Dame Elizabeth." — Renard to Charles V., April 3: *Rolls House MSS.* (Back to Main Text)

Footnote 292: Renard. (Back to Main Text)

Footnote 293: Contemporary Narrative: *Harleian MSS.* 419. *Chronicle of Queen Mary,* p. 71. Holinshed. (Back to Main Text)

Footnote 294: Renard to Charles V., March 22; *Rolls House MSS.* (Back to Main Text)

Footnote 295: Il me repliqua que vivant Elizabeth il n'a espoir à la tranquillité du Royaulme, que quant à luy si chascun alloit si rondement en besoyn comme il fait, les choses se porteroient mieux. — Renard to the Emperor, April 3: *Rolls House MSS.* From these dark plotters, what might not be feared? Holinshed says that while Elizabeth was in the Tower, a writ was sent down for her execution devised, as was believed, by Gardiner; and that Lord Chandos (Sir John Brydges, the Lieutenant of the Tower) refused to put it in force. The story has been treated as a fable, and in the form in which it is told by Holinshed, it was very likely untrue: yet in the presence of these infernal conversations, I think it highly probable that, as the hope of a judicial conviction grew fainter, schemes were talked of, and were perhaps tried, for cutting the knot in a decisive manner. In revolutionary times men feel that if to-day is theirs, to-morrow may be their enemies'; and they are not particularly scrupulous. The anxious words of Sussex did not refer to the merely barring a prisoner's door. (Back to Main Text)

Footnote 296: Renard. (Back to Main Text)

Footnote 297: Noailles, vol. iii. p. 141. (Back to Main Text)

Footnote 298: Renard to Charles V., April 7. (Back to Main Text)

Footnote 299: 1 Mary, cap. ii. (Back to Main Text)

Footnote 300: See the treaty of marriage between Philip and Mary in Rymer. (Back to Main Text)

Footnote 301: 1 Mary, cap. i. (Back to Main Text)

Footnote 302: Y a telle confusion que l'on n'attend sinon que la querelle se demesle par les armes et tumults. — Renard to Charles V., April 22. (Back to Main Text)

Footnote 303: Holinshed says, Edmund Tremayne was racked, and I have already quoted Gardiner's letter to Petre, suggesting the racking of "little Wyatt." (Back to Main Text)

Footnote 304: Her grace's cook said to him, My lord, I will never suffer any stranger to come about her diet but her own sworn men as long as I live. — *Harleian MSS.* 419, and see Holinshed. (Back to Main Text)

Footnote 305: L'Admiral s'est coleré au grand chamberlain de la Royne que a la garde de la dicte Elizabeth et luy a dit qu'elle feroit encores trancher tant de testes que luy et autres s'en repentiroient. — Renard to Charles V., April 7: *Rolls House MSS.* (Back to Main Text)

Footnote 306: Lord Chandos stated the same day in the House of Lords that he threw himself at Courtenay's feet and implored him to confess the truth. The sheriffs of London, on the other hand, said that he entreated Courtenay to forgive him for the false charges which he had brought against him and against Elizabeth. — Foxe, vol. vi. Compare *Chronicle of Queen Mary*, p. 72, note. (Back to Main Text)

Footnote 307: So far the *Chronicle of Queen Mary*, Holinshed, Stow, and the narratives among the *Harleian MSS.* essentially agree. But the chronicle followed by Stow makes Wyatt add, "As I have declared no less to the Queen's council;" whereas Foxe says that he admitted that he had spoken otherwise to the council, but had spoken untruly. Noailles tells all that was really important in a letter to d'Oysel: "M. Wyatt eust la teste coupée, dischargeant advant que de mourir Madame Elizabeth et Courtenay qu'il avoit aulparavant chargé de s'estre entendus en son entreprinse sur promesses que l'on luy avoit faictes de luy saulver la vie." — Noailles, vol. iii. (Back to Main Text)

Footnote 308: Courtenay, however, certainly *was* guilty; and had Wyatt acquitted Elizabeth without naming Courtenay, his words would have been far more effective than they were. This, however, it was hard for Wyatt to do, as it would have been equivalent to a repetition of his accusations. (Back to Main Text)

Footnote 309: Les gens de loy ne treuvent matière pour la condamner. — Renard to Charles V., April 22: Tytler, vol. ii. (Back to Main Text)

Footnote 310: Ibid. And see a passage in the MS., which Mr. Tytler has omitted. (Back to Main Text)

Footnote 311: It is printed at length in Holinshed. (Back to Main Text)

Footnote 312: Que tant altère la dicte dame qu'elle a esté trois jours malade, et n'est encore bien d'elle. — Renard to Charles V.: Tytler, vol. ii. p. 374. (Back to Main Text)

Footnote 313: He whom you wrote of comes to me with a sudden and strange proposal, that, since matters against Madame Elizabeth do not take the turn which was wished, there should be an Act brought into Parliament to disinherit her. I replied that I would give no consent to such a scheme. — Paget to Renard: Tytler, vol. ii. p. 382. (Back to Main Text)

Footnote 314: *Lords Journals.* (Back to Main Text)

Footnote 315: Renard complains of Paget's conduct bitterly. — Renard to Charles V., May 1: Tytler, vol. ii. (Back to Main Text)

Footnote 316: *Commons Journals.* (Back to Main Text)

Footnote 317: Paget to Renard; Tytler, vol. ii. p. 382. And compare Renard's correspondence with the emperor during the month of April.—*Rolls House MSS.* (Back to Main Text)

Footnote 318: Pour ce qui ordinairement les humeurs des Angloys boulissent plus en l'esté que en autre temps. (Back to Main Text)

Footnote 319: Quant l'on a parlé de la peyne des hérétiques, il a sollicité les sieurs pour non y consentir, y donner lieu à peyne de mort.—Renard to Charles V., May 1. (Back to Main Text)

Footnote 320: *Lords Journals.* (Back to Main Text)

Footnote 321: There can, I think, be no doubt that it was this which the peers said. The statute of Henry IV. was not passed; yet the queen told Renard, "que le peyne antienne contre les hérétiques fut agrée par toute la noblesse, et qu'ilz fairent dire expressement et publiquement qu'ilz entendoient l'hérésie estre extirpée et punie." The chancellor informed Renard that, "Although the Heresy Bill was lost, there were penalties of old standing against heretics which had still the form of law, and could be put in execution." And, on the 3rd of May, the privy council directed the judges and the queen's learned counsel to be called together, and their opinions demanded, "what they think in law her highness may do touching the cases of Cranmer, Ridley, Latimer, being already, by both the Universities of Oxford and Cambridge, judged to be obstinate heretics, which matter is the rather to be consulted upon, for that the said Cranmer is already attainted."—*MS. Privy Council Register.* The answer of the judges I have not found, but it must have been unfavourable to the intentions of the court. Joan Bocher was burnt under the common law, for her opinions were condemned by all parties in the church, and were looked upon in the same light as witchcraft, or any other profession definitely devilish. But it was difficult to treat as heresy, under the common law, a form of belief which had so recently been sanctioned by act of parliament. (Back to Main Text)

Footnote 322: Renard to Charles V., May 13: *Rolls House MSS.* (Back to Main Text)

Footnote 323: Noailles. (Back to Main Text)

Footnote 324: Renard to Charles V., May 13: Tytler, vol. ii. (Back to Main Text)

Footnote 325: Les ont provoqué à debatz, les cerrans et poulsans.—Renard to Charles V.: Tyler vol. ii. p. 413. (Back to Main Text)

Footnote 326: Samedy dernier Elizabeth fut tirée de la Tour et menée a Richmond; et dois ledict Richmond l'on l'a conduit à Woodstock pour y estre gardée surement jusques l'on la fasse aller à Pomfret. Et s'est resjouy le peuple de sa departye, pensant qu'elle fut en liberté, et passant par devant la Maison des Stillyards ilz tirerent trois coups d'artillerie en signe d'allegrie, que la reyne et son conseil ont prins a desplaisir et regret, et estimons que l'on en fera demonstration. —Renard to Charles V.: *Granvelle Papers*, vol. iv. (Back to Main Text)

Footnote 327: Machyn's Diary; Strype's *Memorials of the Reformation*. (Back to Main Text)

Footnote 328: Le doubte luy est souvent augmentée par plusieurs marchants mariniers et aultres malcontens de son marriage qui venans de France et Espaign luy desguisent et luy controuvent un infinité de nouvelles estranges, les ungs du peu de volunté que le prince a de venir par deçà, les aultres d'avoir ouy et entendus combats sur la mer, et plusieurs d'avoir descouvert grand nombre de voisles Françoises avec grand appareil. —Noailles to the King of France: *Ambassades*, vol. iii. p. 253. (Back to Main Text)

Footnote 329: L'on m'a dict que quelques heures de la nuict elle entre en telle resverie de ses amours et passions que bien souvent elle se met hors de soy, et croy que la plus grande occasion de sa douleur vient du desplaisir qu'elle a de veoir sa personne si diminuée et ses ans multiplier en telle nombre qu'ilz luy courent tous les jours à grande interest. —Noailles to the King of France: *Ambassades*, vol. iii. p. 252. (Back to Main Text)

Footnote 330: Ibid. p. 255. (Back to Main Text)

Footnote 331: Nuper cum litterarum studia pene extincta jacerent cum salus omnium exiguâ spe dubiâque penderet quis non fortunæ incertos eventus extimescebat? Quis non ingemuit et arsit dolore? Pars studia deserere cogebantur; pars huc illucque quovis momento rapiebantur; nec ulli certus ordo suumve propositum diu constabat. —The happy change of the last year was then contrasted with proper point and prolixity. —The University of Oxford to the Queen: *MS. Domestic, Mary*, vol. iv. (Back to Main Text)

Footnote 332: "Homme d'esprit." —Instructions données à Philippe, Prince d'Espagne: *Granvelle Papers*, vol. iv. p. 267. (Back to Main Text)

Footnote 333: Gresham's Correspondence: *Flanders MSS*. State Paper Office. The bullion was afterwards drawn in procession in carts through the London streets. (Back to Main Text)

Footnote 334: Wotton's Correspondence: *French MSS*. State Paper Office. The title of the Queen of Scots was, perhaps, the difficulty; or Carew may have felt that he could do nothing of real consequence, while he might increase the difficulty of protecting Elizabeth. (Back to Main Text)

Footnote 335: Noailles to the King of France, July 23: *Ambassades*, vol. iii. (Back to Main Text)

Footnote 336: Antiquaries dispute whether Philip received the Garter on board his own vessel or after he came on shore. Lord Shrewsbury himself settles the important point. "I, the Lord Steward," Shrewsbury wrote to Wotton, "at his coming to land, presented the Garter to him." — *French MSS. Mary*, State Paper Office. (Back to Main Text)

Footnote 337: John Elder to the Bishop of Caithness: *Queen Jane and Queen Mary*, appendix 10. Elder adds that his stature was about that of a certain "John Hume, my Lord of Jedward's kinsman," which does not help our information. Philip, however, was short. (Back to Main Text)

Footnote 338: Baoardo. (Back to Main Text)

Footnote 339: Non havendo mai levato la berretta a persona. — Baoardo. (Back to Main Text)

Footnote 340: Noailles. (Back to Main Text)

Footnote 341: Crudele pioggia. — Baoardo. (Back to Main Text)

Footnote 342: La Dominica Mattina se n'ando a messa et tornato a casa mangio in publico servito da gli officiali che gli haveva data la Reina con mala satisfattione degli Spagnuoli, i quali dubitando che la cosa non andasse a lungo, mormoravano assai tra di loro. — Baoardo. (Back to Main Text)

Footnote 343: "Sire, la Nostra Reina ama tanto l'Altezza vostra ch'ella non vorebbe che pigliasse disagio di caminar per tempi cosi tristi." — Baoardo. (Back to Main Text)

Footnote 344: Wotton to the Queen; cypher: *French MSS. Mary*, bundle xi. (Back to Main Text)

Footnote 345: "You shall understand that the Emperor hath suddenly caused his army to march towards Namur, and that himself is gone after in person; the deliberation whereof, both of the one and the other, is against the advice of his council, and all other men to the staying of him. Wherein Albert the Duke of Savoy, John Baptiste Castaldo, Don Hernando de Gonzaga, and Andrea Doria have done their best, as well by letter as by their coming from the camp to this town, *vivâ voce* alleging to him the puissance of his enemy, the unableness as yet of his army to encounter with them, the danger of the chopping of them between him and this town, the hazard of himself, his estate, and all these countries, in case, being driven to fight, their army should have an overthrow; in the preservation whereof standeth the safety of the whole, and twenty other arguments. Yet was there no remedy, but forth he would, and commanded them that they should march *sans plus répliquez*. His headiness hath often put him to great hindrance, specially at Metz, and another time at Algiers. This enterprise is more dangerous than they both. God send him better fortune than *multi ominantur*." — Mason to Petre, Brussels, July 10; *German MSS. Mary,* bundle 16, State Paper Office. (Back to Main Text)

Footnote 346: "The Emperor, in these nine or ten days following of his enemy, hath showed a great courage, and no less skilfulness in the war; but much more notably showed the same when, with so small an army as he then had, he entered into Namur, a town of no strength, but commodious for the letting of his enemy's purpose, against the advice and persuasion of all his captains; which, if he had not done, out of doubt first Liége, and after, these countries, had had such a foil as would long after have been remembered. By his own wisdom and unconquered courage the enemy's meaning that way was frustrated." — Mason to the Council, Aug. 13: *German MSS. Mary,* bundle 16, State Paper Office. (Back to Main Text)

Footnote 347: Renard. (Back to Main Text)

Footnote 348: Que pourroit estre l'on auroit mis en avant au consistoire cette commission par affection particulière pour plustôt nuire, que servir aux consciences; attendu qu'ilz sont partiaulx pour les princes Chrestiens, et souvent meslent les choses séculières et prophanes avec les conseils divins et ecclésiastiques. — Renard to Philip: *Granvelle Papers,* vol. iv. (Back to Main Text)

Footnote 349: He begged Morone not to suppose him ignorant, "quale sia il mare d'Inghilterra nel quale io ho da navigare et che fortuna et travagli potrei haver a sostinere per condurre la navi in porto." — Pole to Morone: *Epist.* Reg. Pol. vol. iv. I have not seen Morone's first letter. The contents are to be gathered, however, from Pole's answer, and from a second letter of apology which Morone wrote two months later. (Back to Main Text)

Footnote 350: Scrissi alla Regina non la volendo contristare condolermi di cio, che lo interpretava et intendeva che questa tardita non venisse tanto da lei quanto delle Providentia di Dio, il qual habbia ordinato che si come per discordia matrimoniale d'un Re Inglese et d'una Regina Hispana fu levata l'obedientia della chiesa de quel Regno cosi dalla concordia matrimoniale d'un Re Hispano et d'una Regina Inglese ella vi doverse ritornare. — Pole to Morone: *Epist. Reg. Pol.* vol. iv. (Back to Main Text)

Footnote 351: E benchè S. Sanctità non havesse patienza secundo l'ordinario suo di leggere o di udir la lettera, nondimeno le dissi talmente la summa che nostro restare satisfattissima, e disse esser più che certa che quella non haveva dato causa ne all' Imperatore ne ad altri d'usar con lei termini cosi extravaganti. — Morone to Pole: Burnet's *Collectanea.* (Back to Main Text)

Footnote 352: Ibid. (Back to Main Text)

Footnote 353: Powers granted by the Pope to Cardinal Pole: Burnet's *Collectanea.* (Back to Main Text)

Footnote 354: Charles V. to Renard: *Granvelle Papers,* vol. iv. (Back to Main Text)

Footnote 355: Che gran differenza sarebbe se fosse stata commessa la cosa o al S. Cardinale, o alli Serenissimi Principi. — Ormaneto to Priuli, July 31: Burnet's *Collectanea.* (Back to Main Text)

Footnote 356: Salvo tamen in his, in quibus propter rerum magnitudinem et gravitatem hæc sancta sedes merito tibi videretur consulenda, nostro et præfatæ sedis beneplacito et confirmatione. — Powers granted by the Pope to Cardinal Pole: Ibid. (Back to Main Text)

Footnote 357: Nondimeno non si risolveva in tutto, com anco non si risolveva nella materia delli beni ecclesiastici, sopra la qual sua Sanctità ha parlato molte volte variamente. — Morone to Pole, July 13: Ibid. (Back to Main Text)

Footnote 358: Il sçauroit bien user de modération quant aux biens occupez; mais que toutesfois il fauldroit que se fust de sorte que la reste de la Chrestienté n'en prînt malvais exemple; et signamment que aucuns Catholiques qui tiennent biens ecclésiastiques soubz leur main ne voulsissent pretendre d'eulx approprier avec cest exemple; et que de vouloir laisser les biens à ceulx qui les occupent, il ne conviendroit pour ce qu'il sembleroit que ce seroit racheter, comme à deniers comptans l'auctorité du siége apostolique en ce coustel-là. The Emperor to Renard: *Granvelle Papers,* vol. iv. pp. 282, 283. (Back to Main Text)

Footnote 359: Nous sçavons que le diet Cardinal n'a commission de presser si chauldement en cette affaire — ains avons heu soubz main advertissement du nunce propre de sa Saincteté que la résolution de la commission dudict Cardinal est que toutes choses se traictent comm'il nous semblera pour le mieulx et qu'il tienne cecy pour règle. — *Granv. Papers*, vol. iv. (Back to Main Text)

Footnote 360: Trop plus chastolleux que celuy de la vraye religion. — Renard to the Emperor: Ibid. p. 287. (Back to Main Text)

Footnote 361: Ibid. (Back to Main Text)

Footnote 362: Pole to Philip: *Epist.* Reg. Pol. vol. iv. (Back to Main Text)

Footnote 363: Avecques d'aultres petits depportements de mocquerie qui croissent tous les jours d'ung cousté et d'aultre. — Noailles to the King of France, August 1. (Back to Main Text)

Footnote 364: Noailles, and compare Pole to Miranda, Oct. 6: *Epist.* Reg. Pol. vol. v. (Back to Main Text)

Footnote 365: *Chronicle of Queen Mary.* Contemporary Narrative: *MS. Harleian*, 419. (Back to Main Text)

Footnote 366: *Chronicle of Queen Mary.* (Back to Main Text)

Footnote 367: Tant et si longuement que se seroit l'utilité et commodité de ce dict Royaulme d'Angleterre. — Noailles to the King of France. (Back to Main Text)

Footnote 368: Renard to Charles V.: *Granvelle Papers*, vol. iv. p. 294. (Back to Main Text)

Footnote 369: Renard to the Bishop of Arras: Ibid. p. 330. (Back to Main Text)

Footnote 370: Renard to the Emperor: *Granvelle Papers*, vol. iv. p. 321. (Back to Main Text)

Footnote 371: Entre les seigneurs et gens de la noblesse et de credit et administration, il y a telle partialité que l'un ne se fie de l'autre. — Ibid. (Back to Main Text)

Footnote 372: Les choses se vont accommoder à quoy sert la saison de l'hiver et ce que en la court l'on y danse souvent; que les Espaignolz et Angloys commencent à converser les ungs avec les aultres ... et n'y a personne qui puisse imaginer que Dieu ait voulu ung si grand marriage et de telz princes, pour en esperer sinon ung grand bien publique pour la Chrestienté, et pour restablir et asseurer les estatz de vostre majesté troublez par ses ennemis. — Renard to the Emperor: *Granvelle Papers*, vol. iv. p. 319. (Back to Main Text)

Footnote 373: *Granvelle Papers*, vol. iv. p. 320. (Back to Main Text)

Footnote 374: Royal Circular; printed in Burnet's *Collectanea*. (Back to Main Text)

Footnote 375: Les lettres de la convocation du parlement sont esté pourjectées sur la vieille forme dont l'on usoit au temps du Roy Henry septième pour avoir en icelluy gens de bien Catholiques: et à propos et selon ce ceulx de Londre en publique assemblée ont choisiz quatre personnaiges que l'on tient estre fort saiges et modestes. — Renard to the Emperor: *Granvelle Papers*, vol. iv. p. 324. (Back to Main Text)

Footnote 376: Le mandement et declaration que vostre Majesté a faict publier sur le point de la religion, laissant la liberté à ung chacun pour tenir quelle religion l'on vouldra. — Renard to Philip and Mary: *Granvelle Papers*, vol. iv. p. 327. (Back to Main Text)

Footnote 377: Et que sa Saincteté le fonde in pietate Christianâ et ecclesiasticâ quia, nunquam Ecclesia claudit gremium, semper indulget exemplo Salvatoris, et Evangelium semper consolatur, semper remittit, et sur plusieurs aultres fondemens generaulx. — Ibid. p. 326. (Back to Main Text)

Footnote 378: Perciocche quanto alla Doctrina disse che poco se ne curavano questo tali non credendo ne all' una ne all' altra via. — Pole to the Pope, October 13: Burnet's *Collectanea*. (Back to Main Text)

Footnote 379: Disse anche che essendo stati questi beni dedicati a Dio non era da concedere cosi ogna cosa a quelli che la tenevano. — Burnet's *Collectanea*. (Back to Main Text)

Footnote 380: The greatest and only means to procure the agreement of the noblemen and others of our council was our promise that the Pope's Holiness would, at our suit, dispense with all possessors of any lands or goods of monasteries, colleges, or other ecclesiastical houses, to hold and enjoy their said lands and goods without any trouble or scruple; without which promise it had been impossible to have had their consent, and shall be utterly impossible to have any fruit and good concord ensue. For which purpose you shall earnestly pray our said cousin to use all possible diligence, and say that if he have not already, he may so receive authority from the See Apostolic to dispense in this manner as the same, being now in good towardness, may so in this Parliament take the desired effect; whereof we see no likelihood except it may be therewithal provided for this matter of the lands and goods of the Church. — Instructions to Paget and Hastings, November 5; Tytler, vol. ii. p. 446. (Back to Main Text)

Footnote 381: Tytler, vol. ii. p. 446. (Back to Main Text)

Footnote 382: Cecil had taken no formal part in Mary's government, but his handwriting can be traced in many papers of State, and in the Irish department he seems to have given his assistance throughout the reign. In religion Cecil, like Paget, was a latitudinarian. His conformity under Mary has been commented upon bitterly; but there is no occasion to be surprised at his conduct — no occasion, when one thinks seriously of his position, to blame his conduct. There were many things in the Catholic creed of which Cecil disapproved; and when his opportunity came, he gave his effectual assistance for the abolition of them; but as long as that creed was the law of the land, as a citizen he paid the law the respect of external obedience.

At present religion is no longer under the control of law, and is left to the conscience. To profess openly, therefore, a faith which we do not believe is justly condemned as hypocrisy. But wherever public law extends, personal responsibility is limited. A minority is not permitted to resist the decisions of the legislature on subjects in which the legislature is entitled to interfere; and in the sixteenth century opinion was as entirely under rule and prescription as actions or things. Men may do their best to improve the laws which they consider unjust. They are not, under ordinary circumstances, to disobey them so long as they exist. However wide the basis of a government, questions will ever rise between the individual and the state — questions, for instance, of peace or war, in which the conscience has as much a voice as any other subject; where, nevertheless, individuals, if they are in the minority, must sacrifice their own opinions; they must contribute their war taxes without resistance; if they are soldiers, they must take part as combatants for a cause of which they are convinced of the injustice. That is to say, they must do things which it would be impious and wicked in them to do, were they as free in their obligations as citizens as they are *now* free in the religion which they will profess.

This was the view in which the mass was regarded by statesmen like Cecil, and generally by many men of plain straightforward understanding, who believed transubstantiation as little as he. In Protestantism, as a constructive theology, they had as little interest as in Popery; when the alternative lay between the two, they saw no reason to sacrifice themselves for either.

It was the view of common sense. It was not the view of a saint. To Latimer, also, technical theology was indifferent—indifferent in proportion to his piety. But he hated lies—legalised or unlegalised—he could not tolerate them, and he died sooner than seem to tolerate them. The counsels of perfection, however, lead to conduct neither possible, nor, perhaps, desirable for ordinary men. (Back to Main Text)

Footnote 383: Charles was particular in his inquiries of Mary's prospect of a family. He spoke to Sir John Mason about it, who was then the resident ambassador:—

"Sir, quoth I," so Mason reported the conversation, "I have from herself nothing to say, for she will not confess the matter till it be proved to her face; but by others I understand, to my great joy, that her garments wax very straight. I never doubted, quoth he, of the matter, but that God, that for her had wrought so many miracles, would make the same perfect to the assisting of nature to his good and most desired work: and I warrant it shall be, quoth he, a man-child. Be it man, quoth I, or be it woman, welcome it shall be; for by that we shall be at the least come to some certainty to whom God shall appoint by succession the government of our estates." —Mason to the King and Queen, November 9: Tytler, vol. ii. p. 444. (Back to Main Text)

Footnote 384: Paget and Hastings to the Queen: Ibid. p. 459 (Back to Main Text)

Footnote 385: Neantmoins il sera necessaire achever avec elle selon l'advis de vostre Majesté. —Renard to the Emperor: *Granvelle Papers*, vol. iv. (Back to Main Text)

Footnote 386: Dio gran tempo perduto e hora ritrovato. —Descriptio Reductionis Angliæ: *Epist.* Reg. Pol. vol. v. (Back to Main Text)

Footnote 387: Imbarcatosi adunque sua S. R. ad un hora di giorno, passo a Doure nell' Isola in tre hore et mezza che fu camino di quaranta miglia fatto con extraordinaria prestezza. —*Epist.* Reg. Pol. vol. v. (Back to Main Text)

Footnote 388: "Tu es Polus, qui aperis nobis Polum regni cælorum. Aer, flumina, terra, parietes ipsi, omnia denique te desiderant. Quamdiu abfuisti omnia fuerunt tristia et adversa. In adventu tuo, omnia rident, omnia læta, omnia tranquilla." I have endeavoured to preserve the play on the word Polus, altering the meaning as little as the necessities of translation would allow. It has been suggested to me that the word "parietes" implies properly *internal* walls, and the allusion was to the defacement of the cathedral. (Back to Main Text)

Footnote 389: "Cardinalis cum reginam salutaret, nec ulla humana verba occurrerent tali muliere digna, Sanctis Scripturarum verbis abuti non verebatur, sed in primo congressu iisdem quibus matrem Dei salutavit Angelus, Reginam Polus alloquitur, Ave Maria," etc. — Salkyns to Bullinger: *Epistolæ* Tigurinæ, p. 169. (Back to Main Text)

Footnote 390: "Il Signor Legato rispose che Dio havea voluto, che fusse tardato a tempo piú maturo, perchè egli havesse potuto dire a sua Altezza come diceva Benedictus fructus ventris tui." — Descriptio Reductionis Angliæ. (Back to Main Text)

Footnote 391: Descriptio Reductionis Angliæ. (Back to Main Text)

Footnote 392: The queen's assurances respecting her child were so emphatic, that even Noailles believed her. Profane persons were still incredulous. On Sunday the 25th, the day after the *Te Deums*, Noailles says, "S'est trouve ung placard attaché à la porte de son palais, y estant ces mots en substance: 'serons nous si bestes, oh nobles Angloys, que croy renotre reyne estre enciente si non d'un marmot ou d'un dogue?'" (Back to Main Text)

Footnote 393: Contemporary Diary: *MS. Harleian*, iv. 19. (Back to Main Text)

Footnote 394: The writer of the Italian "Description" says that Bagenall gave way the next day. The contemporary narrative among the *Harleian MSS.* says that he persisted, and refused to kneel at the absolution. (Back to Main Text)

Footnote 395: "Mentre la casa alta mandava a far sapere la sua conclusione alla casa bassa, la casa bassa mandava anch' ella per fare intendere il medesimo alla casa alta, sicchè i messi s' incontrarono per via; segno evidentissimo che lo Spirito di Dio lavorava in amendue i luoghi in un tempo i di una medesima conformita." — Descriptio Reductionis Angliæ. (Back to Main Text)

Footnote 396: Foxe, vol. vi. p. 571. The petition was in Latin; but, as I have nowhere seen the original, I have not ventured to interfere with Foxe's translation. Foxe, who could translate very idiomatically when he pleased, perhaps relieved his indignation on the present occasion by translating as awkwardly as possible. (Back to Main Text)

Footnote 397: Descriptio Reductionis Angliæ: *Epist.* Reg. Pol. vol. v. (Back to Main Text)

Footnote 398: This amazing comparison (for one cannot forget what Philip had been, was, and was to be) must be given in the original words of the legate:

"Quam sancte sanctitas vestra omni auctoritate studioque huic matrimonio favit; quod sane videtur præ se ferre magnam summi illius regis similitudinem, qui mundi hæres a regalibus sedibus a patre demissus fuit, ut esset virginis sponsus et filius, et hâc ratione universum genus humanum consolaretur ac servaret. Sic enim hic rex maximus omnium qui in terris sunt hæres, patriis relictis regnis de illis quidem amplissimis ac felicissimis in hoc turbulentum regnum de contulit, hujusque virginis sponsus et filius est factus; ita enim erga illam se gerit tanquam filius esset cum sit sponsus, ut quod jam plane perfecit sequestrem se atque adjutorem ad reconciliandos Christo et Ecclesiæ hos populos præberet." — Pole to the Pope: *Epist*. Reg. Pol. vol. v. (Back to Main Text)

Footnote 399: Pallavicino. (Back to Main Text)

Footnote 400: Renard to the Emperor: *Granvelle Papers*, vol. iv. (Back to Main Text)

Footnote 401: "It was this morning told me by one of the Emperor's council, who misliked much the matter, that a preacher of ours whose name he rehearsed, beateth the pulpit jollily in England for a restitution of abbey lands. It is a strange thing in a well-ordered commonwealth that a subject should be so hardy to cry unto the people openly such learning, whereby your winter work may in the summer be attempted with some storm. These unbridled preachings were so much misliked in the ill-governed time as men trusted in this good governance it should have been amended; and so may it be when it shall please my Lords of the Council as diligently to consider it, as it is more than necessary to be looked unto. The party methinketh might well be put to silence, if he were asked now, being a monk, and having professed and vowed solemnly wilful poverty, he can with conscience keep a deanery and three or four benefices." — Mason to Petre: *MS. Germany*, bundle 16, *Mary*, State Paper Office. It is not clear who the offender was. Perhaps it was Weston, Dean of Westminster and Prolocutor of Convocation. (Back to Main Text)

Footnote 402: Demands of the Lower House of Convocation, December, 1554; printed in Wilkins's *Concilia*. (Back to Main Text)

Footnote 403: "La chambre haulte y faict difficulté pour ce que l'auctorité et jurisdiction des evesques est autorizée et renouvellée, et que le peine semble trop griefve. Mais l'on tient qu'ilz s'accorderont par la pluralité." —Renard to the Emperor, December 21: *Granvelle Papers*, vol. iv. (Back to Main Text)

Footnote 404: "Le parlement faict instance que, en statut de la dicte obedience la dicte dispense soit inserée, ce que le dict cardinal ne veult admettre, à ce que ne semble la dicte obedience avoir este rachetée; et est passée si avant la dicte difficulté que le dict cardinal a déclaré qu'il retourneroit plutôt à Rome et delaisseront la chose imparfaite que consentir à chose contre l'auctorité dudict S. Siège, et de si grande préjudice." —Renard to the Emperor, December: *Granvelle Papers*, vol. iv. (Back to Main Text)

Footnote 405: "Ces jours passez, il y eust ung personnaige de la haulte chambre, auquel il sembla pour ne perdre temps debvoir porter, (comme il fist) un billette à la basse par laquelle il mettait en advant s'il n'estoit pas raisonnable que le filz secourust le père, voullant dire de ce roy a l'Empereur. Ce qui fut si bien recueilly du tiers estat, si promptment et avecques grande raison respondu, comme par le dernier parlement et le traité de mariaige d'entre ce roy et royne cela avoit esté et estoit tellement considéré, qu'il n'estoit plus besoing mettre telles choses en advant pour les faire entrer à la guerre." —Noailles to the King of France: *Ambassades*, vol. iv. p. 76. (Back to Main Text)

Footnote 406: "Je vous puis dire, Sire, que toutes ces choses ont passé bien loing de l'espérance qu'il avoit, puisqu'il s'attendoit de se faire couronner, comme despuis six jours il en avoit particulièrement faict rechercher ceulx de la basse chambre dudict parlement qui luy out tous d'une voix rejetté." —Noailles to the King of France: *Ambassades*, vol. iv. p. 137. (Back to Main Text)

Footnote 407: 1 and 2 Philip and Mary, cap. 8. (Back to Main Text)

Footnote 408: 21 Henry VIII. cap. 13. (Back to Main Text)

Footnote 409: 23 Henry VIII. cap. 9. (Back to Main Text)

Footnote 410: 24 Henry VIII. cap. 12. (Back to Main Text)

Footnote 411: 23 Henry VIII. cap. 20. The Act was repealed, but the annates were not restored. (Back to Main Text)

Footnote 412: 25 Henry VIII. cap. 19. (Back to Main Text)

Footnote 413: 25 Henry VIII. cap. 20. (Back to Main Text)

Footnote 414: 25 Henry VIII. cap. 21. (Back to Main Text)

Footnote 415: 26 Henry VIII. cap. 1. (Back to Main Text)

Footnote 416: 26 Henry VIII. cap. 14. (Back to Main Text)

Footnote 417: 27 Henry VIII. cap. 15. (Back to Main Text)

Footnote 418: 28 Henry VIII. cap. 10. (Back to Main Text)

Footnote 419: 28 Henry VIII. cap. 16. (Back to Main Text)

Footnote 420: 31 Henry VIII. cap. 9. (Back to Main Text)

Footnote 421: 33 Henry VIII. cap. 38. (Back to Main Text)

Footnote 422: 35 Henry VIII. cap. 3. (Back to Main Text)

Footnote 423: 37 Henry VIII. cap. 17. (Back to Main Text)

Footnote 424: 28 Henry VIII. cap. 7; 35 Henry VIII. cap. 1. (Back to Main Text)

Footnote 425: "Albeit, by the laws of the Church, the bishops and clergy were the defenders and protectors of all ecclesiastical rights, and would therefore in nature be bound to use their best endeavours for the recovery of the lands and goods lost to the Church during the late schism, they, nevertheless, perceiving the tenures of those lands and goods were now complicated beyond power of extrication, and that the attempt to recover them might promote disaffection in the realm, and cause the overthrow of the present happy settlement of religion, preferring public peace to private commodity, and the salvation of souls to worldly possessions, did consent that the present disposition of those lands and goods should remain undisturbed. They besought their Majesties to intercede with the legate for his consent, and, for themselves, they requested, in return, that the lawful jurisdiction of the Church might be restored." —1 and 2 Philip and Mary, cap. 8, sec. 31. (Back to Main Text)

Footnote 426: "Et licet omnes res mobiles ecclesiarum indistincte iis qui eas tenent relaxaverimus, eos tamen admonitos esse volumus ut ante oculos habentes divini judicii severitatem contra Balthazarem Regem Babylonis, qui vasa sacra non a se sed a patre a templo ablata in profanos usus convertit, ea propriis ecclesiis si extant vel aliis restituant, hortantes etiam et per viscera misericordiæ Jesu Christi obtestantes eos omnes quos hæc res tangit, ut salutis suæ non omnino immemores hoc saltem efficiant, ut ex bonis ecclesiasticis maxime iis quæ ratione personatuum et vicariatuum populi ministrorum sustentationi fuerint specialiter destinata, seu aliis cathedralibus et aliis quæ nunc extant inferioribus ecclesiis curam animarum exercentibus, ita provideatur, ut eorum pastores commode et honeste juxta eorum qualitatem et statum sustentari possint, et curam animarum laudabiliter exercere." —1 and 2 Philip and Mary, cap. 8, sec. 31. (Back to Main Text)

Footnote 427: Ibid. (Back to Main Text)

Footnote 428: 1 and 2 Philip and Mary, cap. 8, sec. 31. (Back to Main Text)

Footnote 429: "It was suspected," says Renard, "que le dict act se proposoit à maulvais fin, qu'il estoit contre les traictez et capitulation de marriage pour hereder la couronne qui venoit de maulvais auteurs quilz plustôt desiroient le mal dudict S. roy et inquietude dudict royaulme que le bien." — Renard to the Emperor: *Granvelle Papers*, vol. iv. p. 347. (Back to Main Text)

Footnote 430: Ibid. vol. iv. p. 348. (Back to Main Text)

Footnote 431: "Et que en son absence il y pourra nommer qui luy plaira." — Ibid. vol. iv. p. 348. (Back to Main Text)

Footnote 432: "Aulcuns particuliers proposaient en ladicte chambre basse que le dict S. roy deust demeurer roy absolut dudict royaulme mourant ladicte dame sans hoirs sa vie durant." — Ibid. vol. iv. p. 348. (Back to Main Text)

Footnote 433: "Ruy Gomez est allé vers l'Empereur pour faire entendre les difficultez qu'ilz trouvent de faire demeurer ceste couronne à son dict filz, au cas que la royne sa femme allast de vie à trespaz sans enfans, et d'aultant qu'ilz ont congneu la volunté de ceulx cy estre bien loin de leur intention; et pour ce scavoir par quelz moyens il semblera bon audict Empereur qu'on puisse mettre cela en termes devant la fin de ce parlement." — Noailles. (Back to Main Text)

Footnote 434: "Et quant à la declaration de bastardise l'on n'est d'opinion qu'elle se doige entamer aux dict parlement, puisque l'apparence d'heretier est certaine et pour l'evident et congneue contrarieté que seroit en toute le royaulme." — Renard to the Emperor: *Granvelle Papers*, p. 348. (Back to Main Text)

Footnote 435: Ibid. (Back to Main Text)

Footnote 436: 1 and 2 Philip and Mary, cap. 10. (Back to Main Text)

Footnote 437: "Ilz sont pour cejourdhuy bien esloignez de ce qu'ilz pensoient faire il y a six sepmaines en ce parlement, ou ilz faisoient compte que ne pouvant couronner ce roy ou luy faire succeder ce royaulme, à tout le moings de luy en faire tumber l'administration, avecques tel pouvoir sur les forces et finances qu'il en eust pen disposer à sa volunté. Toutefois la chose a prins telle issue que pour ce coup il fault qu'il se contente à beaucoup moings qu'il ne s'attendoit.

"Ce qui a tellement despleu à cedict roy et royne, que le 16 de ce mois ilz allerent par eau tous deulx clorre et terminer ledict parlement, sur les quatre heures du soir, assez petitement accompaignez et sans aulcune ceremonie, monstrans et faisans congnoistre à ung chascun avoir quelque grand mescontentement contre l'assemblé d'icelluy." —Noailles to the Constable: *Ambassades*, vol. iv. p. 153. (Back to Main Text)

Footnote 438: Instructions of Cardinal Pole to the Bishops: Burnet's *Collectanea*. (Back to Main Text)

Footnote 439: The opinion of Pole, on the propriety of putting men to death for nonconformity, was strictly orthodox. He regarded heretics, he said, as rebellious children, with whom persuasion and mild correction should first be tried. "Nec tamen, negârim fieri posse," he continued, "ut alicujus opiniones tam perniciosæ existant, ipseque jam corruptus tam sit ad corrumpendos alios promptus ac sedulus ut non dubitârim dicere eum e vitâ tolli oportere et tanquam putridum membrum e corpore exsecari. Neque id tamen priusquam ejus sanandi causâ omnis leviter medendi tentata sit ratio." —Pole to the Cardinal of Augsburg: *Epist. Reg. Pol.* vol. iv. (Back to Main Text)

Footnote 440: *Privy Council Register,* Edward VI. *MS.* (Back to Main Text)

Footnote 441: Correspondence between Hooper and Ridley: Foxe, vol. vi. (Back to Main Text)

Footnote 442: Account of Hooper's Imprisonment, by himself: Foxe, vol. vi. (Back to Main Text)

Footnote 443: Bradford to Cranmer, Ridley, and Latimer: Foxe. (Back to Main Text)

Footnote 444: "Cejourdhuy a esté faicte la confirmation de l'alliance entre le Pape et ce Royaulme par ung sacrifice publique et solempnel d'ung docteur predicant nommé Rogerus, lequel a esté brulé tout vif pour estre Lutherien; mais il est mort persistant en son opinion, à quoy la plus grand part de ce peuple a prins tel plaisir qu'ilz n'ont eu craincte de luy faire plusieurs acclamations pour comforter son courage; et mesmes ses enfans y ont assistés le consolantes de telle façon qu'il sembloit qu'on le menast aux nopces." —Noailles to Montmorency: *Ambassades*, vol. iv. (Back to Main Text)

Footnote 445: Mandate for the execution of Hooper: Burnet's *Collectanea*. (Back to Main Text)

Footnote 446: Foxe. (Back to Main Text)

Footnote 447: Hooper to his friends: Foxe, vol. vi. (Back to Main Text)

Footnote 448: "L'évesque de Londres avec les autres évesques assembléez en ce lieu pour l'exécution du statut conclu en dernier Parlement sur le faict de la religion, a fait brusler trois hérétiques; l'ung en ce lieu et les deux autres en pays; et sont après pour continuer contre les obstinez: dont les nobles et le peuple hérétique murmure et s'altère; selon que l'ay faict entendre au roy par ung billet par escript duquel la copie va avec les présentes; et la noblesse tousjours désire d'avoir occasion d'attirer le peuple et le faire joindre à révolte avec elle; et prévoys si Dieu n'y remédie, ou que telle précipitation ne se modère, les choses prendront dangereux succès, et signamment les partiaulx, contre le chancelier ne perdront ceste commodité de vengeance.... Les dictes conseilliers se retirent de négoces. Paget se voyant en la male grâce de la royne, et de la pluspart du conseil, se trouve souvent au quartier dudict Sieurroy ... le peuple parle contre la royne estrangement.... Comme j'entendz que l'on parle pour me faire demeurer, et séjourner par deçà après le départ du roy, je n'ay pen délaisser de supplier très humblement vostre majesté me excuser ... je suys certain l'on me tueroit incontinant après ledict parlement," etc.—Renard to Charles V.: *Granvelle Papers*, vol. iv. pp. 400-402. (Back to Main Text)

Footnote 449: "Et a l'on dict que plusieurs ... se sont voulu voluntairement mettre sur le bûche à costé de ceulx que l'on brusloit." —Ibid. p. 404. (Back to Main Text)

Footnote 450: "Un bourgeois estant interrougé par ledict évesque de Londres se souffriroit bien le feug, respondist qu'il en fist l'expérience: et aiant fait apporter une chandelle allumée, il meit la main dessus sans la retirer ny se mouvoir." —Renard to Charles V.: *Granvelle Papers*, vol. vi. p. 404. The man's name was Tomkins. Foxe, who tells the story as an illustration of Bonner's brutality, says that the Bishop himself held the hand. But Renard's is probably the truer version. (Back to Main Text)

Footnote 451: Renard to Charles V.: *Granvelle Papers*, vol. iv. p. 403. (Back to Main Text)

Footnote 452: Renard to Charles V.: Ibid. pp. 404, 405. (Back to Main Text)

Footnote 453: "Et combien l'on pouvoit requérir plus de civilité en la Reyne.—Renard to Philip: *Granvelle Papers*, vol. iv. p. 394. (Back to Main Text)

Footnote 454: "Les gens d'église ne sont reformées, il y a plusieurs abuz qui donnent scandale et maulvaise impression, et ilz ne respondent aux offices auxquelz ilz sont appellez."—Ibid. p. 395. (Back to Main Text)

Footnote 455: "Donner ce contentement à la royne d'avoir intention de asseurer et establir ses affaires et la secourir comme bon Seigneur et mari." (Back to Main Text)

Footnote 456: "Que ès choses de la religion l'on ne use de précipitation par punition cruelle, ains avec la modération, et mansuétude requise, et dont l'église a tousjours usé; retirant le peuple de l'erreur par doctrine et prédication, et que si ce n'est un acte scandaleux l'on ne passe oultre en chastoy que puisse altérer le peuple et le désgouter, que la reformation requise pour le bon example, soit introduicte sur les gens de l'église comme le légat advisera pour le mieulx."—Renard to Philip: *Granvelle Papers*, vol. iv. p. 395. (Back to Main Text)

Footnote 457: Foxe, vol. vi. (Back to Main Text)

Footnote 458: The story of Hunter was left in writing by his brother, and was printed by Foxe. I have already said that whenever Foxe prints documents instead of relating hearsays, I have found him uniformly trustworthy; so far, that is to say, as there are means of testing him. (Back to Main Text)

Footnote 459: Wherefore it came to pass that Hannah bare a son, and called his name Samuel, saying, Because I have asked him of the Lord. 1 *Samuel* i. 20. (Back to Main Text)

Footnote 460: Foxe, vol. vii. (Back to Main Text)

Footnote 461: Noailles to the King of France, April 5 and April 17. Montmorency to Noailles, April 21. Noailles to Montmorency, April 30: *Ambassades*, vol. iv. (Back to Main Text)

Footnote 462: Letters to and from Sir Thomas Gresham: *MS. Flanders, Mary,* State Paper Office. (Back to Main Text)

Footnote 463: Strype's *Memorials.* (Back to Main Text)

Footnote 464: Machyn's *Diary.* (Back to Main Text)

Footnote 465: These curious records of disappointed expectations remain in large numbers in the State Paper Office. The following is the letter addressed to Pole: —

Philip. — Mary the Queen. — Most Reverend Father in God, our right trusty and right entirely beloved cousin, We greet you well: And whereas it hath pleased Almighty God, of His infinite goodness, to add unto the great number of other His benefits bestowed upon us, the gladding of us with the happy deliverance of a prince, for the which we do most humbly thank Him; knowing your affections to be such towards us as whatsoever shall fortunately succeed unto us, the same cannot be but acceptable unto you also; We have thought good to communicate unto you these happy news of ours, to the intent you may rejoice with us; and praying for us, give God thanks for this his work accordingly. Given under our signet, at our house of Hampton Court, the — — of — —, the 1st and 2nd year of our and my Lord the King's reign. — *MS. Mary, Domestic,* vol. v. State Paper Office. (Back to Main Text)

Footnote 466: Noailles to Montmorency, April 30: *Ambassades,* vol. iv. (Back to Main Text)

Footnote 467: Sir Thomas Gresham to the Council: *MS. Flanders, Mary,* State Paper Office. (Back to Main Text)

Footnote 468: Machyn's *Diary.* (Back to Main Text)

Footnote 469: Noailles to Montmorency, May 15: *Ambassades,* vol. iv. (Back to Main Text)

Footnote 470: Philip and Mary to Gardiner, Arundel, and Paget: Burnet's *Collectanea.* (Back to Main Text)

Footnote 471: Noailles: *Ambassades,* vol. iv. p. 313. (Back to Main Text)

Footnote 472: "Et là où ladicte paix ou trefve adviendront ledict seigneur (l'Empereur) fera bientost après repasser en ce royaulme le duc d'Alva avecque la plus grande

part de sesdictes forces pour y fabvoriser les affaires de
ce roy." — Noailles, vol. iv. p. 330. (Back to Main Text)

Footnote 473: "Il n'est rien que l'Empereur ne fasse pour
venir à la paix, tant il désire avant de retourner en Espaigne
de faire couronner son filz, roy de ce pays. Et pensera par
même moyen se saisir des places fortes d'icelluy et chastier
des Angloys d'infinies injures qu'ilz out faict recepvoir aux
Espagnols, mettant grosses garnisons en ceste ville de Londres,
et aultres lieux, à quoy ces roy et royne proposent ... s'y faire
obéir absolument aux parlemens, suyvant ce qu'ilz n'ont
peu faire par cydevant." — Noailles, vol. iv. pp. 332, 333.

In these reports the truth was anticipated but not
exceeded. It will be seen that such projects were really
formed at a later period. (Back to Main Text)

Footnote 474: "Ladicte dame plusieurs fois de le jour demeure
longtemps assise à terre, les genoulx aussy haultz que la teste.

"Se trouva hier fort malade et plus que de coustume, et
pour la soulager, fust trouvé à mesme heure en sa court
plusieurs lettres semées contre son honneur," etc. —
Noailles, vol. iv. p. 342. (Back to Main Text)

Footnote 475: "The Queen said she could not be safely
and happily delivered, nor could anything succeed
prosperously with her, unless all the heretics in prison
were burnt *ad unum*." — Burnet. (Back to Main Text)

Footnote 476: Burnet's *Collectanea*. This letter is addressed
to Bonner, and was taken from Bonner's *Register*; but,
from the form, it was evidently a circular. The Bishop of
London had not deserved to be singled out to be especially
admonished for want of energy. (Back to Main Text)

Footnote 477: Foxe, vol. vii. (Back to Main Text)

Footnote 478: A letter of Mary's to Philip on the
subject will be given in the following chapter, which
reveals the disagreement which had arisen between
them about this marriage. (Back to Main Text)

Footnote 479: The impression was very generally
spread. Noailles mentions it, writing on the 20th of June to
the King of France; and Foxe mentions a mysterious attempt
of Lord North to obtain a new-born child from its mother, as
having happened within his own knowledge. The existence

of the belief, however, proves nothing. At such a time it was inevitable, nor was there any good evidence to connect Lord North, supposing Foxe's story true, with the court. The risk of discovery would have been great, the consequences terrible, and few people have been more incapable than Mary of knowingly doing a wrong thing. (Back to Main Text)

Footnote 480: Renard to the Emperor, June 27: *Granvelle Papers*, vol. vi. (Back to Main Text)

Footnote 481: Joanna of Castille, the emperor's mad mother, dying soon after, masses were said for her with some solemnity at St. Paul's. "Aux obsèques que la royne commanda estre faictes à Londres, l'admiral d'Angleterre démontra ouvertement avoir quelque ressentment, de ce qu'il disoit le roy ne luy faisoit si bonne chiere et démonstration si favorable qu'il avoit accoustumé, disant qu'il sçavoit bien pourquoy s'estoit, inférant que ce fust pour ce qu'il avoit faict baiser les mains de Elizabetz aux gentilhommes qui l'avoient visitez." (Back to Main Text)

Footnote 482: Foxe; Holinshed. (Back to Main Text)

Footnote 483: Le dict conseil voyant que plusieurs gentilhommes s'assembloient à Londres, et communicquoient par ensemble, qu'ils se tenoient à Londres, contre ce qu'est accoustumé en Angleterre, qu'est que ceulx qu'ilz eu moien ne demeurent à Londres en l'esté, ains au pays pour la chaleur et maladies ordinaires qu'ilz y reignent, et que toutes les dicts gentilhommes sont hérétiques, ains esté pour le plus part rebelles, les autres parens et adhérens de Elizabetz, leur a faict faire commandement de se retirer chascun en sa maison et se separer; qu'ilz ont prins mal et en out fait grandes doleances, en prétendant qu'ilz estoient gens de bien, qu'ilz n'estoient traistres. — Renard to the Emperor: *Granvelle Papers*, vol. iv. (Back to Main Text)

Footnote 484: Noailles, vol. v. pp. 77-82. (Back to Main Text)

Footnote 485: Machyn's *Diary*. (Back to Main Text)

Footnote 486: Noailles, vol. v. pp. 98, 99, 123. (Back to Main Text)

Footnote 487: Elle a bonne part en la grace dudict Seigneur Roy, lequel par plusieurs lettres qu'il escript à la royne sa femme la luy recommende, comme aussy il a faict particulièrement et par soubz main aux principaux seigneurs Espaignolz qui sont demourez en ce lieu. — Ibid. p. 127. (Back to Main Text)

Footnote 488: Domine Jesu Christe, qui es verus sponsus animæ meæ, verus Rex ac Dominus meus qui me ad Regni hujus gubernacula singulari tuâ providentiâ ac benignitate vocatam, cum antea essem derelicta et tanquam mulier ab adolescentiâ abjecta, eum virum in matrimonium et regni societatem expetere voluis ti, *qui plus cæteris imaginem tuam quam in sanctitate et justitiâ mundo ostendisti in suis meisque actionibus dirigendis exprimeret, et expetitum dedisti,* cujus nunc discessum mœrens defleo — quæso per illum pretiosissimum sanguinem quem pro me sponsâ tuâ proque illo et omnibus in arâ crucis effudisti, ut hunc meum dolorem ita lenias, ita purges, ita temperes, ut quoties ille sanctis suis consiliis mihi adest, quoties per litteras quæ ad salutem hujus populi tui pertinent commendat, toties illum præsentem esse, teque unicum consolatorem in medio nostro adesse sentiam, utque in illo te semper amem atque glorificem. Obsecro, Domine, ut in nobis tua imago sic indies per tuam gratiam renovetur in conspectu populi tui, quern nobis gubernandum commisisti, ut cum is justitiæ tuæ severitatem, in iis quæ amiserat dum hi regnarent qui a rectâ fide declinantes sanctitatem et justitiam expulerunt, jam pridem senserit, quæ nunc per tuam misericordiam recuperaverit sub illorum Regno quos nunquam a rectâ fide declinare es passus, cum gratiarum actione lætus intelligat ut uno ore tarn nos quam populus noster Deum patrem per te ejus unicum filium in unitate Spiritûs glorificemus, ad nostram ipsorum et piorum omnium salutem et consolationem. Amen. — *Epist.* Reg. Pol. vol. v. (Back to Main Text)

Footnote 489: Il me fauldroit faire ung merveilleux discours pour vous rendre compte de tous les propoz qui font dans les dictes lettres. Je vous diray seulment ce qui plus tousche et regarde le lieu où vous estes. Et premièrement la royne a tant enchanté et ensorcelé ce beau jeune prince son mary que de luy avoir faict croyre ung an entier qu'elle estoit grosse pour le retenir près d'elle, dont il se trouve à présent si confus et fasché qu'il n'a plus délibéré de retourner habiter ceste terre, promettant à tous ses serviteurs que s'il peult estre une fois en Espaigne qu'il n'en sortira plus à si maulvaise occasion, etc....—Le Protonotaire de Noailles à M. de Noailles: *Ambassades*, vol. v. p. 136. (Back to Main Text)

Footnote 490: Not the martyr; he had been despatched by Bonner among the victims of the summer; but a person otherwise-known. (Back to Main Text)

Footnote 491: "Ye will say, How could this fellow know their counsel?—I was chamberlain to one of the privy council, and with all diligence gave myself to write and read Spanish, which thing once obtained I kept secret from my master and my fellow-servants, because I might be trusted in my master's closet or study, where I might read such writing as I saw daily brought into the council chamber."—John Bradford to the Lords of the Council: Strype's *Memorials of the Reformation*. (Back to Main Text)

Footnote 492: Elizabeth, when she came to the throne, refused to admit that she was under any real obligation to Philip. She was entirely right in her refusal. The Spaniards had sworn, if possible, to make away "with all those which by any means might lay claim to the crown."

"I call God to record," Bradford continues, "I have heard it with mine ears, and seen the said persons with mine eyes, that have said, if ever the king obtain the crown, he would make the Lady Elizabeth safe from ever coming to the same, or any of our cursed nation. For they say, that if they can find the means to keep England in subjection, they would do more with the land than with all the rest of his kingdoms. I speak not of any fool's communication, but of the wisest, and that no mean persons. Yea, and they trust that there shall means be found before that time to despatch the Lady Elizabeth well enough by the help of assured traitors, as they have already in England plenty, and then they may the more easier destroy the others when she is rid out of the way.

2. I speak not this, as some men would take it, to move dissension; for that were the best way for the Spaniards to come to their prey. Such a time they look for, and such a time they say some nobleman hath promised to provide for them.

3. God is my witness that my heart will not suffer me for very shame to declare such vile reports as I have heard them speak against the queen, and yet her Grace taketh them for her faithful friends. The Spaniards say, that if they obtain not the

crown, they may curse the time that ever the king was married to a wife so unmeet for him by natural course of years; but and if that may be brought to pass that was meant in marriage-making, they shall keep old rich robes for high festival days.

"Alas, for pity! Ye be yet in such good estate that ye may, without loss of any man's life, keep the crown and realm quietly. If ye will hear a fool's counsel, keep still the crown to the right succession in your hands, and give it to no foreign princes. Peradventure her Grace thinketh the king will keep her the more company and love her the better, if she give him the crown. Ye will crown him to make him chaste contrary to his nature. They have a saying—'The baker's daughter is better in her gown than Queen Mary without the crown.' They say, 'Old wives must be cherished for their young fair gifts.' 'Old wives,' they say, 'for fair words will give all that they have.' But how be they used afterwards? Doth the queen think the king will remain in England with giving him the realm? The council of Spain purposeth to establish other matters; to appoint in England a viceroy with a great army of Spanish soldiers, and let the queen live at her beads like a good antient lady."—John Bradford to the Earls of Arundel, Shrewsbury, Derby, and Pembroke: Strype's *Memorials*, vol. vi. p. 340, etc. (Back to Main Text)

Footnote 493: Prayer written by Cardinal Pole for Queen Mary: *supra*. (Back to Main Text)

Footnote 494: Noailles to the King of France, October 21: *Ambassades*, vol. v. (Back to Main Text)

Footnote 495: Noailles to Montmorency, December 5: Ibid. (Back to Main Text)

Footnote 496: Phillips. (Back to Main Text)

Footnote 497: Foxe says the 12th; but this is wrong.—See Cranmer's letter to the Queen: Jenkins, vol. i. p. 369. (Back to Main Text)

Footnote 498: Exhortation of the Bishop of Gloucester to Thomas Cranmer: *Cotton MSS., Vespasian*, A. 25. A copy, more rounded and finished, is given by Foxe, in his account of Cranmer's trial: but the latter has the appearance of having been touched up afterwards. (Back to Main Text)

Footnote 499: The address concluded with a prolix exhortation to repentance, which I omit. It may be read in a form sufficiently accurate in Foxe. (Back to Main Text)

Footnote 500: Although the circumstances of the time called properly for an open declaration of this kind on the part of Cranmer, yet every one of his predecessors, from the time of Edward I., must have been inducted with a tacit understanding of the same kind. If a bishop had been prosecuted under the Statutes of Provisors, his oath to the Papacy would have been no more admitted as an excuse by the Plantagenet sovereigns, than the oath of a college Fellow to obey the statutes of the founder would have saved him from penalties under the House of Hanover had he said mass in his college chapel. Because Cranmer, foreseeing an immediate collision between two powers, which each asserted claims upon him, expressed in words a qualification which was implied in the nature of the case—it was, and is (I regret to be obliged to speak in the present tense), but a shallow sarcasm to taunt him with premeditated perjury. (Back to Main Text)

Footnote 501: If the gift of a pot of cold water shall not be in oblivion with God, how can God forget your manifold and bountiful gifts, when He shall say unto you. "I was in prison, and you visited me." God grant us all to do and suffer while we be here as may be to His will and pleasure. — Latimer to Mrs. Wilkinson, from Bocardo: Latimer's *Remains*, p. 444. (Back to Main Text)

Footnote 502: Latimer's *Remains*, p. 429. (Back to Main Text)

Footnote 503: A Rev. P. Soto accepi litteras Oxonio datas quibus me certiorem facit quid cum duobus illis hæreticis egerit qui jam erant damnati, quorum alter ne loqui quidem cum eo voluit: cum altero est locutus sed nihil profecit, ut facile intelligatur a nemine servari posse quos Deus projecerit. Itaque de illis supplicium est sumptum. — Pole to Philip: *Epist.* Reg. Pol. vol. v. p. 47. (Back to Main Text)

Footnote 504: Foxe, vol. vii. p. 545. It is to the discredit of Mary that she paid no attention to this appeal, and left Bonner's injustice to be repaired by the first parliament of Elizabeth. *Commons Journals*, 1 Elizabeth. (Back to Main Text)

Footnote 505: The execution, however, was doubtless appointed to take place on that spot, that Cranmer might see it. An old engraving in Foxe's *Martyrs* represents him as on the leads of the Tower while the burning was going forward, looking at it, and praying. (Back to Main Text)

Footnote 506: Foxe, vols. vii. viii., *passim,* especially vol. vii. p. 605. Philpot's Petition, Ibid. p. 682; and an account of the Prisons at Canterbury, vol. viii. p. 255. At Canterbury, *after* Pole became archbishop, his archdeacon, Harpsfeld, had fifteen prisoners confined together, of whom five were starved to death; the other ten were burnt. But before they suffered, and while one of those who died of hunger still survived, they left on record the following account of their treatment, and threw it out of a window of the castle:—

"Be it known to all men that shall read, or hear read, these our letters, that we, the poor prisoners of the castle of Canterbury, for God's truth, are kept and lie in cold irons, and our keeper will not suffer any meat to be brought to us to comfort us. And if any man do bring in anything—as bread, butter, cheese, or any other food—the said keeper will charge them that so bring us anything (except money or raiment), to carry it thence again; or else, if he do receive any food of any for us, he doth keep it for himself, and he and his servants do spend it; so that we have nothing thereof: and thus the keeper keepeth away our victuals from us; insomuch that there are four of us prisoners there for God's truth famished already, and thus it is his mind to famish us all. And we think he is appointed thereto by the bishops and priests, and also of the justices, so to famish us; and not only us of the said castle, but also all other prisoners in other prisons for the like cause to be also famished. Notwithstanding, we write not these our letters to that intent we might not afford to be famished for the Lord Jesus' sake, but for this cause and intent, that they having no law so to famish us in prison, should not do it privily, but that the murderers' hearts should be openly known to all the world, that all men may know of what church they are, and who is their father."—Foxe, vol. viii. p. 255. (Back to Main Text)

Footnote 507: See especially his conversation with Philpot: Foxe, vol. vii. p. 611. (Back to Main Text)

Footnote 508: Godly Letter addressed to Bonner: Ibid. p. 712. (Back to Main Text)

Footnote 509: Pour le faire plustost retourner elle fera toutes choses incrédible en ce dict parlement en faveur dudict Sieur.... L'on dict que l'occasion pour laquelle le dict parlement a esté assemblé, ne tend à aultre fin que pour faire s'il est possible tomber le gouvernement absolu de ce royaulme entre les mains de ce roy. — Noailles to the King of France, October 21: *Ambassades*, vol. v. (Back to Main Text)

Footnote 510: Ce soit ung argument plus grand que tout aultre pour faire entrer ceulx cy à la guerre ouverte; estant ceste nation comme ung chascung sçait fort ennemie de sadict Sainctité. — Noailles to Montmorency: *Ambassades*, vol. v. p. 188. (Back to Main Text)

Footnote 511: Same to the same. — Ibid. p. 150. (Back to Main Text)

Footnote 512: Special Grace appointed to have been said at York on the Accession of Elizabeth. — *Tanner MSS.*, Bodleian Library. (Back to Main Text)

Footnote 513: *Commons Journals*, 2nd and 3rd Philip and Mary. (Back to Main Text)

Footnote 514: *Commons Journals*, 2nd and 3rd Philip and Mary. — Noailles to the Constable, October 31. (Back to Main Text)

Footnote 515: *Commons Journal.* Noailles says that the queen demanded the fifteenths, and that the Commons refused to grant them. The account in the *Journals* is confirmed by a letter of Lord Talbot to the Earl of Shrewsbury. — Lodge's *Illustrations*, vol. i. p. 207. (Back to Main Text)

Footnote 516: Mr. Speaker declared the queen's pleasure to be spoken yesterday, for to depart with the first-fruits and tenths; and my Lord Cardinal spake for the tithes and impropriations of benefices to be spiritual. — *Commons Journals*, November 20: 2nd and 3rd Philip and Mary. (Back to Main Text)

Footnote 517: *Lords Journals.* (Back to Main Text)

Footnote 518: 2nd and 3rd Philip and Mary, cap. iv. (Back to Main Text)

Footnote 519: *Commons Journals.* (Back to Main Text)

Footnote 520: Ibid. The temper of the opposition may be gathered from the language of a pamphlet which appeared on the accession of Elizabeth.

The writer describes the clergy as "lads of circumspection, and verily *filii hujus sæculi*." He complains of their avarice in inducing the queen, "at one chop, to give away fifty thousand pounds and better yearly from the inheritance of her crown unto them, and many a thousand after, unto those idle hypocrites besides."

He then goes on: —

"And yet this great profusion of their prince did so smally serve their hungry guts, like starven tikes that were never content with more than enough; at all their collations, assemblies, and sermons, they never left yelling and yelping in pursuit of their prey, Restore! Restore! These devout deacons nothing regarded how some for long service and travail abroad, while they sat at home — some for shedding his blood in defence of his prince's cause and country, while they with safety, all careless in their cabins, in luxe and lewdness, did sail in a sure port — some selling his antient patrimony for purchase of these lands, while they must have all by gift a God's name — they nothing regarding, I say, what injury to thousands, what undoing to most men, what danger of uproar and tumult throughout the whole realm, and what a weakening to the State, should thereby arise; with none of these matters were they moved a whit, but still held on their cry, Restore! Restore!"

"And that ye may be sure they meant nothing more than how to have all, and that with all haste; after that their Pope, this seditious Paul IV., that now is, had sent hither his bulls and his thunderbolts for that cause, and other (and yet little restored, because the world, indeed, would not be so faced out of their livelihood) sundry of our prelates, like hardy champions, slacke not a whit themselves to thrust lords out of their lands, and picked quarrels to their lawful possessions. Well. Let nobility consider the case as they list; but, as some think, if the clergy come to be masters again, they will teach them a school point. Christ taught the young man that perfection was in *vade, vende, et da*, not in *mane, acquire, accumula*." — Grace to be said at the Accession of Elizabeth: *Tannes MSS.*, Bodleian Library. (Back to Main Text)

Footnote 521: Noailles. (Back to Main Text)

Footnote 522: Michele, the Venetian ambassador, in his curious but most inaccurate account of England during this reign, states that the queen had it in her power to cut off Elizabeth from the succession, but that she was prevented from doing it by Philip. Michele's information suffered from the policy of Venice. Venice held aloof from the complications of the rest of Europe, and her representatives were punished by exclusion from secrets of state. The letters of Noailles might be suspected, but the correspondence of Renard with Charles V. leaves no doubt whatever either as to the views of the Spaniards towards Elizabeth, of their designs on the crown, or of the causes by which they were baffled. (Back to Main Text)

Footnote 523: Noailles to the King of France, December 16. (Back to Main Text)

Footnote 524: The witty Katherine Brandon, widow of Henry VIII.'s Charles Brandon, married to Richard Bertie. She was a lady of advanced opinions, between whom and the Bishop of Winchester there were some passages-at-arms. She dressed a dog in a rochet on one occasion, and called it Bishop Gardiner.

Gardiner himself said that he was once at a party at the Duke of Suffolk's, and it was a question who should take the duchess down to dinner. She wanted to go with her husband; but as that could not be, "My lady," said Gardiner, "taking me by the hand, for that my lord would not take her himself, said that, forasmuch as she could not sit down with my lord whom she loved best, she had chosen me whom she loved worst." — Holinshed. (Back to Main Text)

Footnote 525: Et de mesme fust rejetté audict parlement à la grande confusion de ladicte dame ung aultre bill, par lequel elle vouloit confisquer les personnes et biens de ceulx qui sont transfuges de ce royaulme depuis son advènement à la couronne. — Noailles to the King of France, December 16: *Ambassades*, vol. v. (Back to Main Text)

Footnote 526: 2nd and 3rd Philip and Mary, cap. 17. (Back to Main Text)

Footnote 527: François de Noailles to Madame de Roye: *Ambassades*, vol. v. (Back to Main Text)

Footnote 528: Among the surviving memorials of Mary, none is more affecting than a rough copy of an answer to one of these epistles, which is preserved in the Cotton Library. It is painfully scrawled, and covered with erasures and corrections, in which may be traced the dread in which she stood of offending Philip. *Demander license de votre Haultesse,* is crossed through and altered into *Supplier très humblement.* Where she had described herself as *obeissante,* she enlarged the word into *très obeissante;* and the tone throughout is most piteous. She entreats the king to appoint some person or persons to talk with her about the marriage. She says that the conscience which she has about it she has had for twenty-four years; that is to say, since Elizabeth's birth. Nevertheless, she will agree to Philip's wish, if the realm will agree. She is ready to discuss it; but she complains, so far as she dares complain, of the confessor. The priests trouble her, she says. "Alfonsez espécialement me proposoit questions si obscures que mon simple entendement ne les pouvoit comprehendre, comme pour exemple il me demandoit qui estoit roy au temps de Adam, et disoit comme j'estoy obligée de faire ceste marriage par ung article de mon Credo, mais il ne l'exposoit.... Aultres choses trop difficiles pour moy d'entendre ... ainsy qu'il estoit impossible en si peu de temps de changer ... conscience.... Votre Haultesse escript en ses dictes lettres que si le consent de ce royaulme iroyt au contraire, Votre Haultesse en imputeroit la coulpe en moy. Je supplie en toute humilité votre Haultesse de différer ceste affaire jusques à votre retour; et donques Votre Haultesse sera juge si je seray coulpable ou non. Car autrement je vinray en jalousie de Votre Haultesse la quelle sera pire à moy que mort; car j'en ay commencé déjà d'en taster trop à mon grand regret," etc. — *Cotton MSS., Titus,* B. 2: printed very incorrectly in Strype's *Memorials,* vol. vi. 418. (Back to Main Text)

Footnote 529: Noailles. (Back to Main Text)

Footnote 530: Cranmer to Queen Mary: Jenkins, vol. i. p. 369. This protest was committed to Pole to answer, who replied to it at length.

The authority of the pope in a secular kingdom, the legate said, was no more a foreign power than "the authority of the soul of man coming from heaven in the body generate on earth." "The pope's laws spiritual did no other but that the soul did in the body, giving life to the same, confirming and strengthening the same;" and that it was which the angel signified in Christ's conception, declaring what his authority should be, that he should sit *super domum David*, which was a temporal reign, *ut confirmet illud et corroboret*, as the spiritual laws did.

The quotation is inaccurate. The words in the Vulgate are, *Dabit illi Dominus sedem David patris ejus: et regnabit in domo Jacob in æternum.*

The letter contains another illustration of Pole's habit of mind. "There was never spiritual man," he says, "put to execution according to the order of the laws of the realm but he was first by the canon laws condemned and degraded; whereof there be as many examples afore the time of breaking the old order of the realm these last years, as hath been delinquents. Let the records be seen. And specially this is notable of the Bishop of — —, which, being imprisoned for high treason, the king would not proceed to his condemnation and punishment afore he had the pope's bull given him...."

The historical argument proceeded smoothly up to the name, which, however, was not and is not to be found. Pole was probably thinking of Archbishop Scrope, who, however, unfortunately for the argument, was put to death *without* the pope's sanction. — Draft of a Letter from Cardinal Pole to Cranmer: *Harleian MSS.* 417. (Back to Main Text)

Footnote 531: Pole to Philip: *Epistolæ* Reg. Pol., vol. v. p. 47. (Back to Main Text)

Footnote 532: *Damnatæ memoriæ.* Sentence Definitive against Thomas Cranmer: Foxe, vol. viii. (Back to Main Text)

Footnote 533: An allusion to a scaffold in St. Paul's Church, on which Cranmer had sat as a commissioner; said to have been erected over an altar. (Back to Main Text)

Footnote 534: Foxe, vol. viii. p. 73. (Back to Main Text)

Footnote 535: Cranmer to a Lawyer: Jenkins, vol. i. p. 384. (Back to Main Text)

Footnote 536: *Epist.* Reg. Pol., vol. v. p. 248. I am obliged to abridge and epitomise. (Back to Main Text)

Footnote 537: Car se je n'écourtois que les mouvemens de la nature, se je ne vous parlois qu'en mon nom, je vous tiendrois un autre langage au plutôt je ne vous dirois rien;

je m'entretiendrois avec Dieu seul at je lui demanderois de faire tomber le feu du ciel pour vous consumer avec cette maison où vous avez passé en abandonnant l'Église. The letter was only known to the editor of Pole's remains in a French translation. I do not know whether the original exists, or whether it was in Latin or in English. (Back to Main Text)

Footnote 538: The innumerable modern writers who agree with Pole on the iniquity of the divorce of Catherine forget that, according to the rule which most of us now acknowledge, the marriage of Henry with his brother's wife *really was incestuous* — really was forbidden by the laws of God and nature; that the pope had no more authority to dispense with those laws then than he has now; and that if modern law is right, Cranmer did no more than his duty. (Back to Main Text)

Footnote 539: Jenkins, vol. iv. p. 129. (Back to Main Text)

Footnote 540: Forasmuch as the king's and queen's majesties, by consent of parliament, have received the pope's authority within this realm, I am content to submit myself to their laws herein, and to take the pope for chief head of this Church of England so far as God's laws and the customs of this realm will permit. — Thomas Cranmer. (Back to Main Text)

Footnote 541: Of this fifth submission there is a contemporary copy among the MSS. at Corpus Christi College, Oxford. It was the only one known to Foxe; and this, with the fact of its being found in a separate form, gives a colour of probability to Mr. Southey's suspicion that the rest were forgeries. The whole collection was published by Bonner, who injured his claims to credit by printing with the others a seventh recantation, which was never made, and by concealing the real truth. But the balance of evidence I still think is in favour of the genuineness of the first six. The first four lead up to the fifth, and the invention of them after the fifth had been made would have been needless. The sixth I agree with Strype in considering to have been composed by Pole, and signed by Cranmer. (Back to Main Text)

Footnote 542: Recantations of Thomas Cranmer: Jenkins, vol. iv. p. 393. (Back to Main Text)

Footnote 543: Death of Cranmer, related by a Bystander: *Harleian MSS.*, 442. Printed, with some inaccuracies, by Strype. (Back to Main Text)

Footnote 544: Narrative of the Execution of Thomas Cranmer: *MS. Harleian*, 422. Another account gives among the causes which Cole mentioned, that "it seemed meet, according to the law of equality, that, as the death of the Duke of Northumberland of late made even with Sir Thomas More, Chancellor, that died for the Church, so there should be one that should make even with Fisher, Bishop of Rochester; and because that Ridley, Hooper, and Ferrars were not able to make even with that man, it seemed that Cranmer should be joined with them to fill up their part of equality." — Foxe, vol. viii. p. 85. Jenkins, vol. iv. p. 133. (Back to Main Text)

Footnote 545: *MS. Harleian*, 422. (Back to Main Text)

Footnote 546: Shakspeare was perhaps thinking of this speech of Cranmer when he wrote the magnificent lines which he placed in the mouth of the dying Gaunt: —

rrr"O, but they say, the tongues of dying men
Enforce attention, like deep harmony:
Where words are scarce, they are seldom spent in vain:
For they breathe truth, that breathe their words in pain.
He, that no more must say, is listened more
Than they whom youth and ease have taught to gloze;
More are men's ends marked, than their lives before:
The setting sun, and music at the close,
As the last taste of sweets, is sweetest last;
Writ in remembrance more than things
long past." (Back to Main Text)

Footnote 547: There are two original contemporary accounts of Cranmer's words — *Harleian MSS.*, 417 and 422 — and they agree so far almost word for word with "The Prayer and Saying of Thomas Cranmer a little before his Death," which was published immediately after by Bonner. But we now encounter the singular difficulty, that the conclusion given by Bonner is altogether different. The archbishop is made to repeat his recantation, and express especial grief for the books which he had written upon the Sacrament.

There is no uncertainty as to what Cranmer really said; but, inasmuch is Bonner at the head of his version of the speech has described it as "written with his own hand," it has been inferred that he was required to make a copy of what he intended to say — that he actually wrote what

Bonner printed, hoping to the end that his life would be spared; and that he would have repeated it publicly, had he seen that there was a chance of his escape. Finding, however, that his execution had been irrevocably determined on, he made the substitution at the last moment.

There are many difficulties in this view, chiefly from the character of the speech itself, which has the stamp upon it of too evident sincerity to have been composed with any underhand intentions. The tone is in harmony throughout, and the beginning leads naturally to the conclusion which Cranmer really spoke.

There is another explanation, which is to me more credible. The Catholics were furious at their expected triumph being snatched from them. Whether Cranmer did or did not write what Bonner says he *wrote*, Bonner knew that he had not *spoken* it, and yet was dishonest enough to print it as having been spoken by him, evidently hoping that the truth could be suppressed, and that the Catholic cause might escape the injury which the archbishop's recovered constancy must inflict upon it. A man who was capable of so considerable a falsehood would not have hesitated for the same good purpose to alter a few sentences. Pious frauds have been committed by more religious men than Edmund Bonner. See the Recantation of Thomas Cranmer, reprinted from Bonner's original pamphlet: Jenkins, vol. iv. p. 393. (Back to Main Text)

Footnote 548: *Harleian MS.*, 422. Strype has misread the word into "run," losing the point of the expression. (Back to Main Text)

Footnote 549: Saying of Sir Nicholas Arnold: *MS. Mary, Domestic*, vol. vii. (Back to Main Text)

Footnote 550: The conversations with Ashton were sometimes at his own house; sometimes at an inn by the waterside, near Lambeth; sometimes at other places. The localities are not always easy to make out. (Back to Main Text)

Footnote 551: Deposition of Thomas White: *MS. Mary, Domestic*, vol. vii. (Back to Main Text)

Footnote 552: Wotton to the Queen, cypher: *French MSS.*, bundle 13. State Paper Office. Kingston was one of the members of the House of Commons who was imprisoned at the close of the late session, for the freedom of his language in parliament. He was "Vice-Admiral of the Ports about the Severn," and a man of large influence in the Welsh Marches. (Back to Main Text)

Footnote 553: Younger son of Sir Edward Peckham, Cofferer of the Household, and Member of Council under Edward VI. (Back to Main Text)

Footnote 554: Lord Williams of Thame, who superintended the executions of Ridley, Latimer, and Cranmer. (Back to Main Text)

Footnote 555: Confession of Sir Henry Peckham: *Mary, Domestic, MS.* vol. viii. (Back to Main Text)

Footnote 556: Confession of John Daniel: *MS. Mary, Domestic,* vol. viii. (Back to Main Text)

Footnote 557: Noailles to the King of France, March 12: *Ambassades,* vol. v. (Back to Main Text)

Footnote 558: Uvedale's Confession: *Mary, Domestic, MS.,* vol. vii.; Peckham's Confession, vol. viii. (Back to Main Text)

Footnote 559: John Throgmorton said to Bedyll, Derick, and me, on this wise: "Whatsoever becomes of any of us in this dangerous enterprise, we will here promise, that albeit, I, you, and your nannye, every of us, by name, should accuse any of us of this, or any part touching this enterprise, bye and bye to revile him with most taunting and naughty rebukes that may be devised. And thereby setting a stern countenance, and for our couraging and better comfort herein, he shewed us of a matter that was most true, and accused by Strangways against two brethren, meaning [the] Tremaynes, who being but little men in personage, so reviled Strangways, accusing them before your honours, that because Strangways had no further proof but his only saying, and they so stoutly denying it, even to the threatening of the rack (or whether they were anything thereto constrained or no, as he said, I do not perfectly remember); but at length Strangways was in effect ready to weep, and think he had accused them wrongfully, and so they dismissed, and Strangways much of your honours rebuked." —Thomas White to the Council: *MS. Mary, Domestic,* vol. vii. (Back to Main Text)

Footnote 560: The Constable
to Noailles, Feb. 7: *Ambassades,* vol. v. (Back to Main Text)

Footnote 561: De leur prêtur un peu
d'espaule. (Back to Main Text)

Footnote 562: Wotton to the Queen: *French MSS.,*
bundle 13. (Back to Main Text)

Footnote 563: Although they be promised by your
means to move the queen's majesty to be gracious
lady to them, they know that it is not so meant; but
to suck out of others all ye may, and yet thereby
to have no mercy shewed. — Thomas White to the
Council: *MS. Mary, Domestic,* vol. vii. (Back to Main Text)

Footnote 564: Robert Swift to Lord Shrewsbury:
Lodge's *Illustrations,* vol. i. (Back to Main Text)

Footnote 565: Walpole's
Deposition: *MS.* Lodge's *Illustrations,* vol. viii.
(Back to Main Text)

Footnote 566: Peckham's
Confession: *MS.* Lodge's *Illustrations,* vol. viii.
(Back to Main Text)

Footnote 567: Swift to Lord Shrewsbury: Ibid., vol. i.;
Machyn's *Diary.* (Back to Main Text)

Footnote 568: Daniel was supposed, like Throgmorton, to
know more than he had told; and to quicken his confession
he was confined in a dungeon, of which he has left his own
description in an appeal to the mercy of the commissioners.
"I beseech your honours be good to me," he wrote, "for I
am a sick man, laid here in a dungeon where I am fain to
do — — and — — in the place that I do lie in, and if I do lie
here all this night, I think I shall not be alive to-morrow.
Mr. Binifield [perhaps an examiner] as he cometh to me
is ready to cast his gorge, so he saith; and I have no light
all day so much as to see my hands perfectly. Pity me, for
God's sake — Your honours' footstool, John Daniel. Good
Master of the House, good Mr. Controller, good Mr. Vice-
Chamberlain, good Mr. Englefield, good Mr. Waldegrave!"

Again in another letter, he writes: —

"For God's sake, be my honourable masters, and rid me out of this dungeon, for I do lie here a man sore pained with the stone, and among the newts and spiders. For the love of God, I ask it; for I do all things in the place that I do lie in. My good and honourable masters, for God's sake, be good to me, and consider that I did never give my consent to do no evil. Good Mr. Englefield, consider my meaning, and be good master to me, and consider the place I lie in, and the pain of the stone." —Daniel's Confessions: *MS. Mary, Domestic,* vol. viii.

The effect, however, apparently was what the examiners desired. A note of the council remains to the effect that—

"Daniel being yesterday removed, to a worse lodging, beginneth this day to be more open and plain than he hath been, whereby we perceive he knoweth all, and we trust and think verily he will utter the same." — Privy Council Minutes, Ibid. (Back to Main Text)

Footnote 569: Estant en continuel fureur de ne pouvoir jouir de la présence de son mary ny de l'amour de son peuple, et dans une fort grande peur d'estre offensée de sa propre vie par aulcungs des siens. —Noailles to the King of France, May 7: *Ambassades,* vol. v. (Back to Main Text)

Footnote 570: Same to Montmorency, April 21: Ibid. (Back to Main Text)

Footnote 571: Foxe. This hideous story was challenged by Harding, the controversialist, in the next reign. He was unfortunate in calling attention to it, for the case was inquired into, and the account was found too certainly true. (Back to Main Text)

Footnote 572: Machyn's *Diary.* (Back to Main Text)

Footnote 573: Machyn. (Back to Main Text)

Footnote 574: Ibid. (Back to Main Text)

Footnote 575: See their stories: Foxe, vol. viii. (Back to Main Text)

Footnote 576: Foxe, vol. viii. (Back to Main Text)

Footnote 577: Wotton to Petre, cypher: *French MSS., Mary,* bundle 13. State Paper Office. (Back to Main Text)

Footnote 578: The Queen to Wotton: *MS. France,* bundle 13. (Back to Main Text)

Footnote 579: Gens abominables, hérétiques et traistres villains et exécrables. — Noailles to the King, May 7: *Ambassades,* vol. v. (Back to Main Text)

Footnote 580: Wotton to Petre, cypher: *French MSS.* State Paper Office, bundle 13. (Back to Main Text)

Footnote 581: His death was of course attributed by the world to poison. Courtenay's birth, and the fortune which was so nearly thrust upon him, give his fate a kind of interest, and an authentic account of it may not be unwelcome.

On the 18th of September, Peter Vannes, the English resident at Venice, wrote to the queen from Padua: —

"It hath pleased Almighty God, as the Author of all goodness, and as One that doth nothing in vain, to call the Earl of Devonshire to his mercy, even about the hour, or little more or less, that I am writing of this present; and being very sorry to trouble your Highness with this kind of news, yet forasmuch as the providence of God must be fulfilled in all things, I shall somewhat touch his sickness till the hour of death. True it is that he, as I have perceived, for the avoiding all suspicion from himself, hath chosen a life more solitary than needed, saving the company of certain gentlemen, Venetians, among whom he was much made of. It chanced him upon three weeks agone, for his honest recreation, to go to a place called Lio, a piece of an island five miles from Venice, for to see his hawks fly upon a wasted ground, without any houses; and there he was suddenly taken with a great tempest of wind and rain, insomuch that his boat, called [a] gondola, could not well return to Venice: and he was fain, for his succour, to take a certain searcher's boat that by chance there arrived, and so to Venice he came, being body and legs very thinly clothed, refusing to change them with any warmer garment. And upon that time, or within few days after, as he told me, had a fall upon the stairs of his house, and after seeming to himself to be well, and finding no pain, took his journey hither unto Padua; and for the avoiding of the weariness of the water, and the labouring of horses, chose the worse way coming; and so by certain waggons called coaches, very shaking and uneasy to my judgment, came to Padua upon Saturday at night. Of whose coming being advertised, I went to visit him on the morrow after, and found him very weak; and since that time he began to appear every day worse and worse, avoiding friends' visitations; and drew himself to the counsel of two of the best physicians of this town, and entered into a continued hot ague, sometimes more vehement than at another; and as I have seen and heard, he hath been always diligently attended. I have charged his servants in your name, and as they will avoid your displeasure, that a true inventory shall be made of such small movables as he had here, and that especially all kind of writings and letters that he had either here or at Venice, shall be put in assurance, abiding for your commandment. I am now about to see the order of his burial, with as much sparing and as much honour as can be done; for the merchantmen on whom, by your Grace's commandment, he had a credit of 3 or 4 thousand crowns, are not as yet willing to disburse any money without a sufficient discharge of my Lord of Devonshire's hand, the doing whereof is past. I shall shift to see him buried as well as I can; notwithstanding, I beseech your Grace not to be discontented with me that I am at the next door to go a begging.

"My said Lord of Devonshire is dead, in mine opinion a very good Christian man; for after that I had much exhorted him to take his communion and rites of the Church as a thing most necessary, and by whose means God giveth unto His chosen people health, both bodily and ghostly, he answered me, by broken words, that he was well content so to do: and in token thereof, and in repentance for his sins, he lift up his eyes and knocked himself upon the heart; and after I had suffered him to pause a good while, I caused the Sacrament to be brought, and after the priest's godly exhortation, he forced himself to receive the blessed Communion; but his tongue had so stopped his mouth, and his teeth so clove together, that in no wise he could receive that same; and after this sort this gentleman is gone, as I do not doubt, to God his mercy.

"I shall not let to say to your Grace, that since his coming to Padua, by way of communication, he showed unto me, that it had been reported unto him that some one had said that he was better French than English, and if God did recover him and send him his health so that he might come to the knowledge of his misreporter, he was minded to try that quarrel by the sword."

In a letter written a few days later, Vannes said that, in consequence of rumours having gone abroad that the earl had been poisoned, the Podesta, at his request, had ordered the body to be opened, and examined by physicians, which was accordingly done. — Peter Vannes to the Queen: *Venetian MSS.* State Paper Office. (Back to Main Text)

Footnote 582: Letters of Wotton to the Queen: *French MSS.*, bundle 13, State Paper Office. (Back to Main Text)

Footnote 583: Wotton to Petre: *MS.* Ibid. Compare Sir James Melville's *Memoirs*, p. 38. (Back to Main Text)

Footnote 584: "Pontifex, tantum abest ut mollissimis obsequiis atque officiis acquieverit, non potuit tandem sibi obtemperare quin pleno Cardinalium Senatu Regni Neapolitani privationem per suum fiscalem proposuerit, cum nullius nos in ipsum Pontificem, aut sedem apostolicam contumaciæ, summæ quin potius uti fas est observantiæ nobis simus conscii, ac ne in præfractâ quidem ejus obstinatione a solitis officiis destitum est, donec cum nullâ molliore ope malum posset mitigari; magisque indies ac magis propagaretur videretque Albæ Dux copias eum undique contrahere, apparatum facere, tempus ducere, quoscumque principes quibuscumque conditionibus sollicitare, ut ingruenti rerum omnium ruinæ occurreret, ad hoc extremum remedium invitus coactusque descendit. Quæ omnia quanquam vobis comperta quando in eorum mentionem per vestras litteras incidistis, per nos etiam vobis significanda duximus; atque id præterea eâ temperantiâ ac modestiâ hoc bellum a duce geri atque administrari, ut nihil nisi orbis Christiani tranquillitas, sedis apostolicæ dignitas, et nostrorum regnorum securitas procuretur, neque ullum nos ex hoc bello gloriæ aucupemur, summum potius dolorem animique ægritudinem percipiamus." — Philip to the English Council: *MS. Mary, Domestic*, vol. ix. State Paper Office. (Back to Main Text)

Footnote 585: "There is a faction or dissension within Calais for religion's sake, whereof it seemeth that a commission of late sent thither, I cannot tell whether somewhat rigorously used, may have given occasion." — Wotton to the Queen, cypher: *French MSS.*, bundle 13, State Paper Office. (Back to Main Text)

Footnote 586: Wotton to the Queen, cypher: *French MSS.*, bundle 13, State Paper Office. (Back to Main Text)

Footnote 587: The Council to Philip, November 22nd: *MS. Domestic, Mary*, vol. ix. (Back to Main Text)

Footnote 588: Machyn. (Back to Main Text)

Footnote 589: The new monks did not do credit to their restoration. Anne of Cleves died the next year, and lay in state in the abbey.

"The 22nd of August," says Machyn, "was the herse of my Lady Anne Cleves taken down at Westminster, the which the monks by night had spoiled of all velvet cloth, arms, banners, penselles, of all the majesty and valence, the which was never seen afore so done." — *Diary*, p. 148. (Back to Main Text)

Footnote 590: Desmond to the Queen: *Irish MSS*. State Paper Office. (Back to Main Text)

Footnote 591: "Three years and more after the restoration of the people to the church," the legate says in the body of the letter. The date of it will be December, 1556, or December, 1557, as the three years are calculated from the restoration of Orthodoxy, or from the reunion with Rome. (Back to Main Text)

Footnote 592: Address of Cardinal Pole to the citizens of London: Strype's Memorials, vol. vi. (Back to Main Text)

Footnote 593: Royal Commission printed in Foxe, vol. viii. p. 301, and by Burnet in his *Collectanea*. (Back to Main Text)

Footnote 594: Articles of the visitation of Cardinal Pole: Foxe, vol. iii. (Back to Main Text)

Footnote 595: Wood's *Annals of the University of Oxford.* — The story is authentic. The following is the Roman Catholic version of it: — "Oxonii sepulta fuerat digna Petro Martyre concubina, parthenonis et ipsa desertrix sacrilega ut ille cœnobii. Ejus ossa refodi jusserat Maria et sterquilinio ut par erat condi. Nunc æmulo plane sanctitatis et virginitatis in Elizabâthe ingenio requisita sunt inter sordes sterquilinii publici quarum fœdissima pars erant, et incredibili studio inventa purgata lota in thecam eandem reponuntur in quâ S. Frideswidæ reliquiæ colebantur, et cum his adeo confusa ut nullâ unquam possunt diligentiâ secerni. Clauditur loculus et cubitalibus litteris hoc epitaphio decoratur, 'Hic jacet religio cum superstitione,' meliore titulo meretrici hæretici pessimi concubinæ; proh nefas! deteriore ancillæ Christi sanctissimæ virgini attributo." — Foxe, vol. viii. Editor's note. (Back to Main Text)

Footnote 596: An excellent epistle, translated from French into English by Thomas Pownell, with a preface, A.D. 1556. The copy from which I make my extract is in the Bodleian Library at Oxford; it is marked in the margin in various places with a finger ☐ apparently almost as old as the printing; and this finger was perhaps drawn by some one whom the words were consoling or inspiriting in the hour of his own trial. (Back to Main Text)

Footnote 597: Wotton to Petre: *French MSS.*, bundle 13, State Paper Office. (Back to Main Text)

Footnote 598: Answer of the Privy Council to the queen's question whether England shall enter the wars with France. — *Sloane MSS.* 1786, British Museum. (Back to Main Text)

Footnote 599: Proclamation of Thomas Stafford, son to the Lord Henry, rightful Duke of Buckingham. — Strype's *Memorials*, vol. vi. p. 515. (Back to Main Text)

Footnote 600: Exchequer Accounts: *MS. Mary, Domestic*, vol. xii. State Paper Office. (Back to Main Text)

Footnote 601: Bitterly hating their work that they were sent upon, "the people went to the musters, said Sir Thomas Smith, with kerchiefs on their heads — they went to the wars hanging down their looks; they came from them as men dismayed and forlorn." — Strype's *Life of Sir Thomas Smith*, Appendix, p. 249. (Back to Main Text)

Footnote 602: Instructions to the Lord Admiral: *MS. Mary, Domestic*, vol. xi. (Back to Main Text)

Footnote 603: Sir Edward Karne to the Queen: Burnet's *Collectanea*. (Back to Main Text)

Footnote 604: Printed by Strype, *Memorials of the Reformation*, vol. vi. p. 476, and described by him as a letter of the parliament. But at this time there was no parliament in existence; the last had been dissolved eighteen months before, the next did not meet till the ensuing January. The queen's letter is dated the 21st May, and the letter which I suppose to have been from the council, and another, said also to have been from "the nobility," were evidently written under the same impression, and at the same time, when the idea of the recall was new. (Back to Main Text)

Footnote 605: Letters to the Pope: Strype, vol. vi. pp. 476-482. The drafts of the letters are not signed, nor does it appear what names were attached to them. It is not even certain that they were sent. (Back to Main Text)

Footnote 606: Pole to the Pope: Strype's *Memorials*, vol. vi. p. 34, etc. (Back to Main Text)

Footnote 607: Pole's sufferings in consequence were really piteous. "Your holiness," he wrote on the 30th of March, 1558, "is taking my life from me when you take from me the reputation of orthodoxy. You told the English ambassador it was God's doing; God has told you, like Abraham, to kill your son; and that your holiness intends that kind of death for me, I know far more certainly than Isaac seemed to know his father's purpose. When I see the fire and the knife in the hands of your holiness, and the wood laid upon my shoulders, there is no need for me to ask where is the victim.

"When I was yet a lamb, I gave myself as a sacrifice to the pontiff, who chose me for a cardinal. Thus I thought of myself; thus I spoke when I lay prostrate before the altar. Little did I then think the time would come, when I should be offered up by my father's hands a second time, especially when the Bishop of Rochester was here hanging as a ram among the briars ready to be immolated," etc. — Pole to the Pope: *Epistolæ*, vol. v. p. 31. (Back to Main Text)

Footnote 608: Commission for the Loan: *MS. Mary, Domestic*, vol. xi. (Back to Main Text)

Footnote 609: Ibid. vol. xii. (Back to Main Text)

Footnote 610: The queen to all sheriffs, mayors, etc. — For the well choosing of the knights of the shire and burgesses: "Trusty and well-beloved, we greet you well: and whereas for certain great and weighty causes touching both the honour of Almighty God, and the wealth and good government of this our realm, we have summoned our High Court of Parliament, to be holden at Westminster, the 20th of January next: and forasmuch as we consider that a great part of the furthering of such things, as shall be treated in our said parliament, and bringing them to good effect, shall consist in the well appointing and choosing of such as shall be knights of shires, citizens of any city, or burgesses of other towns corporate, we have thought good to require you to have good regard, and so far forth as in you may lie, to provide that such as shall be appointed may be men given to good order, Catholic, and discreet, and so qualified, as the antient law of this realm requireth; giving the freeholders, citizens, burgesses within our said county to understand, what our will and pleasure is in that behalf. Hereby as you shall do good service unto God and this your country, so shall you also do us right acceptable pleasure, which we shall consider towards you as any occasion may shew. Given under our signet, December 10, 1557." —*MS. Mary, Domestic*, vol. xii. (Back to Main Text)

Footnote 611: *MS.* Ibid. (Back to Main Text)

Footnote 612: A complete account of the repairs at Calais, with the cost of work, and the wages of the workmen, is printed in an appendix to the *Chronicle of Calais*, published by the Camden Society. (Back to Main Text)

Footnote 613: *Chronicle of Calais* . (Back to Main Text)

Footnote 614: Lord Grey to the Queen, June 13, 1557: *Calais MSS.* bundle 10, State Paper Office. (Back to Main Text)

Footnote 615: In 1550, Sir John Mason wrote to the council, "I have heard say that, not long sythen the Low Countries were able to set to the field 300 able men on horseback; I think there lacketh of that number at this present a great many, the occasion whereof, by the report of the king's ministers on this side, is for that the king's lands are so raised as no man is able to live thereupon unless it is a sort of poor dryvells, that must dig their living with their nails out of the ground, and be not able scarce to maintain a jade to carry their corn to market." *French MSS.* Edward VI. bundle 9. (Back to Main Text)

Footnote 616: *Calais MSS.* bundle 10. (Back to Main Text)

Footnote 617: Cornwallis to the Queen: *Calais MSS.* bundle 10. (Back to Main Text)

Footnote 618: When all your majesty's pieces on this side make account to be furnished of victuals and other necessaries from hence, it is so that of victuals your highness hath presently none here, and the town hath none; by reason that the restraint in the realm hath been so strait, and the victuallers as were wont to bring daily hither good quantities of butter, cheese, bacon, wheat, and other things, might not of late be suffered to have any recourse hither, whereby is grown a very great scarcity. — Wentworth to the Queen: *Calais MSS.* bundle 10. (Back to Main Text)

Footnote 619: Sir Arthur Grey. (Back to Main Text)

Footnote 620: Grey to the Queen: *Calais MSS.* bundle 10. (Back to Main Text)

Footnote 621: He was held up by the Earl of Warwick, who sprang from his own horse, and "did lift a firkin of ale" to Grey's mouth. *Life of Lord Grey of Wilton*, by his son. (Back to Main Text)

Footnote 622: Grey to the Queen: *Calais MSS.* bundle 10. (Back to Main Text)

Footnote 623: Wentworth and Grey to the Queen: *Calais MSS.* bundle 10. (Back to Main Text)

Footnote 624: The Queen to Wentworth: Ibid. (Back to Main Text)

Footnote 625: "Surely," Wentworth wrote to the queen, "if your majesty's ships had been on the shore, they might either have letted this voyage, or, at the least, very much hindered it, and not unlike to have distressed them, being only small boats. Their ordnance that comes shall be conveyed in the same sort. It may therefore please your majesty to consider it. I am, as a man may be, most sure that they will first attempt upon Rysbank, and that way chiefly assail the town. Marry, I think that they lie hovering in the country for the coming of their great artillery and also to be masters of the sea, and therefore I trust your highness will haste over all things necessary with all expedition." — Wentworth to the Queen: *Calais MSS.* bundle 10. (Back to Main Text)

Footnote 626: Grey to the Queen: *Calais MSS.* The letter was dated January 4, seven o'clock at night. The messenger was to carry it to Gravelines under cover of darkness. It is endorsed, "Haste, haste, haste! post haste for thy life, for thy life." (Back to Main Text)

Footnote 627: Rutland to the
Queen: *Calais MSS.* (Back to Main Text)

Footnote 628: *MS. Council Records.* (Back to Main Text)

Footnote 629: *MS. Mary, Domestic,* vol. xi. (Back to Main Text)

Footnote 630: The Queen to Sir William Woodhouse, January
12: *MS. Mary, Domestic,* vol. xii. (Back to Main Text)

Footnote 631: Circular for Staying of the Musters: *MS. Mary,
Domestic,* vol. xii. (Back to Main Text)

Footnote 632: *MS. Mary, Domestic,* vol. xii.,
January 17. (Back to Main Text)

Footnote 633: *Commons Journals.* (Back to Main Text)

Footnote 634: Ibid. The famous graziers and other people,
how well willing soever they be taken to be, will not be
known of their wealth, and by miscontentment of their
loss, be grown stubborn and liberal of talk. The Council
to Philip: *Cotton. MS. Titus,* B. 2. (Back to Main Text)

Footnote 635: Estimate of the money to be provided
for the furniture and charges of the war: *MS. Mary,
Domestic,* vol. xii. (Back to Main Text)

Footnote 636: Discourse on the order that was
used in granting of the Subsidy: *MS. Mary,
Domestic,* vol. xii. (Back to Main Text)

Footnote 637: The Council to Philip:
Cotton. *MSS. Titus,* B. 2. (Back to Main Text)

Footnote 638: *MS. Mary, Domestic,* vol. xii.
(Back to Main Text)

Footnote 639: 4 and 5 Philip and Mary,
statute 2. (Back to Main Text)

Footnote 640: Ibid. statute 3. (Back to Main Text)

Footnote 641: *MS. Mary, Domestic,* vol. xii.
(Back to Main Text)

Footnote 642: *Flanders MSS. Mary.* The aggregate of the debts
to the Flanders Jews, which Elizabeth inherited, cannot be
prudently guessed at; and I have not yet found any complete
account on which I can rely. It cost her, however, fifteen
years of economy to pay them off. (Back to Main Text)

Footnote 643: Queen Mary to the Aldermen of the City of London: *MS.* Ibid. (Back to Main Text)

Footnote 644: Foxe: Burnet. (Back to Main Text)

Footnote 645: Strype's *Memorials*, vol. vi. p. 120. (Back to Main Text)

Footnote 646: *Privy Council Register, MS. Mary.* (Back to Main Text)

Footnote 647: Royal Proclamation, June 6, 1558: Strype's *Memorials*, vol. vi.; Foxe, vol. xiii. (Back to Main Text)

Footnote 648: Oration on the Queen's Marriage: Strype's *Life of Sir Thomas Smith.* (Back to Main Text)

Footnote 649: *Privy Council Register, MS.* (Back to Main Text)

Footnote 650: Bentham to Lever: Strype's *Memorials*, vol. vi. (Back to Main Text)

Footnote 651: "This fact," says Foxe, "purchased him more hatred than any that he had done of the common people." (Back to Main Text)

Footnote 652: Swift to the Earl of Shrewsbury: Lodge's *Illustrations.* (Back to Main Text)

Footnote 653: *MS. Mary, Domestic*, vol. xiii. (Back to Main Text)

Footnote 654: Renard found it necessary to warn Philip of this, in a despatch written in October: *Granvelle Papers*, vol. v. p. 225. (Back to Main Text)

Footnote 655: Arundel, Thirlby, and Wotton to the Council: *French MSS.*, bundle 13. (Back to Main Text)

Footnote 656: Ibid. (Back to Main Text)

Footnote 657: Philip to the English Ambassador, October 30: Ibid. (Back to Main Text)

Footnote 658: "Condigna animadversione plectendos." — Wilkins's *Concilia*, vol. iv. (Back to Main Text)

Footnote 659: Report of the Count de Feria: Tytler, vol. ii. p. 494. *Memorial of the Duchess of Feria , MS.*, quoted by Lingard. (Back to Main Text)

Footnote 660: *Cotton. MS. Vespasian.* F. 3. The letter is written in a shaking hand. The address is lost, and being dated the 14th of November, while Mary was still alive, it has been described as to her and not to her sister. But an endorsement "From the queen's majesty at Hatfield," leaves no doubt to whom it was written. (Back to Main Text)

Footnote 661: Among the apocryphal or vaguely attested anecdotes of the end of Mary, she is reported to have said, that if her body was opened, Calais would be found written on her heart. The story is not particularly characteristic, but having come somehow into existence, there is no reason why it should not continue to be believed. (Back to Main Text)

Footnote 662: Underhill's *Narrative*. (Back to Main Text)

Footnote 663: Burghley's *Execution of Justice*. (Back to Main Text)

Footnote 664: The number is variously computed at 270, 280, and 290. (Back to Main Text)